Workers in a Lean World

THE HAYMARKET SERIES

Editors: Mike Davis and Michael Sprinker

The Haymarket Series offers original studies in politics, history and culture, with a focus on North America. Representing views across the American left on a wide range of subjects, the series will be of interest to socialists both in the USA and throughout the world. A century after the first May Day, the American left remains in the shadow of those martyrs whom the Haymarket Series honors and commemorates. These studies testify to the living legacy of political activism and commitment for which they gave their lives.

Recent and forthcoming titles

Workers in a Lean World

Unions in the International Economy

KIM MOODY

VERSO

London · New York

First published by Verso 1997
© Kim Moody 1997
All rights reserved

Reprinted 1998, 1999, 2001

The right of Kim Moody to be identified as the author of this work
has been asserted by him in accordance with
the Copyright, Designs and Patents Act 1988

Verso
UK: 6 Meard Street, London W1F 0EG
USA: 180 Varick Street, New York NY 10014-4606

Verso is the imprint of New Left Books

ISBN 1–85984–867–2

ISBN 978-1-85984-104-4

British Library Cataloguing in Publication Data
A catalogue record for this book is available from the British Library

Library of Congress Cataloging-in-Publication Data
Moody, Kim.
  Workers in a lean world : unions in the international economy /
Kim Moody
    p.   cm.
  ISBN 1–85984–867–2 (cloth). — ISBN 1–85984–104– (pbk.)
  1. Trade-unions.   2. Working class.   3. Labor market.
4. Competition, International.   I. Title.
HD6483.M55   1997
331.88–dc21   97–28877
                                                         CIP

Typeset by SetSystems Ltd, Saffron Walden, Essex
Printed by Biddles Ltd, *www.biddles.co.uk*

Contents

Acknowledgements

Because I have learned from so many, it is hard to pick out those to thank. It was hard enough when I completed *An Injury To All* in 1988, which covered only one country. *Workers in a Lean World* covers many countries in a very different period and the debts I owe to people around the world are all the greater. Some, however, are obvious. In the realm of day-to-day work and my own development are: the past and present staff members of *Labor Notes*; the pioneers in analysing lean production and labor–management cooperation, Mike Parker and Jane Slaughter; Ken Paff and many other activists in the Teamsters for a Democratic Union; Jerry Tucker, Elly Leary, and so many in UAW New Directions; and countless other activists fighting for a more democratic, effective labor movement in the US.

Across the seas and borders my guides and mentors of recent years include: Heiner Kohnen and Jens Huhn at TIE-Bildungswerk/Germany; Francine Bavay and Christophe Aguiton at SUD; Michel Bousquet of the CGT; Ben Watanabe and Hideo Totsuka in Japan; Sheila Cohen in the United Kingdom; Hector de la Cueva of CILAS in Mexico; Carlos Vallejo and Robin White of the Comisiones Obreras in Catalonia; and though I have only met them a few times, Sam Gindin, David Robertson, and other leaders and activists in the Canadian Auto Workers.

This book could never have been written without the time I spent with workers and unionists from around the world, whether in their country or mine, whether in interviews or just hanging out and talking. There are too many to name, but they came from Canada, Mexico, Brazil, Taiwan, France, Germany, Spain, Japan, the United Kingdom, South Korea, and, of course, the United States. In addition to those mentioned above, there are also many researchers/activists who have shared observations and ideas that helped me piece together the evolving puzzle of lean production. In the realm of political economy I owe much to the work of Anwar Shaikh and Howard Botwinick.

I decided not to dedicate this book because there are too many candidates. But I would be remiss if I didn't acknowledge some of the groups that have inspired me in recent years, notably: the locked-out workers at A. E. Staley in Decatur, Illinois; the strikers at the Detroit News Agency papers; and all those Teamsters who have helped bring about the most far-reaching revolution in any union in the US. Out of these struggles, win or lose, come the kinds of working-class warriors this book is all about.

Introduction

This is not another globalization book. While there are three chapters that
discuss the dynamics and structure of the process called globalization, this
book will not tell you in great detail that the parts in cars and airplanes
come from different countries or that American music and clothing styles
(often produced elsewhere) can be purchased anywhere in the world by
those who have money. You probably knew that already. Nor will you be
told over and over that the world is full of sad-sack victims, though the
victims number in the billions and their plight will be recorded here. The
focus here is not on victims, but on resisters. Finally, this book will not
prescribe some policies to make the institutions of globalization more
representative or benign, though it will try to point to some ways to
change the intolerable behavior of these institutions.

The real topic of this book is the working class: its paralysis in the
face of global industrial restructuring; its difficulties in capturing or
even influencing its own organizations; its disorientation in the face of
changes in racial, ethnic and gender composition; its degradation in the
dog-eat-dog competition of the world market; and its rebellion against
these conditions. Amidst predictions of the end of trade unionism and
even of the working class, working people returned to center stage in the
mid-1990s. To be sure, they were always there in the wings, resisting
locally in the best ways possible while paralysed by the fear of job loss.
The working class never goes away; it is the vast majority; but it
frequently goes unnoticed by the media that frame our perception of
society.

The idea for this book came from my experience. As a member of the
staff of *Labor Notes* for almost twenty years, I have had the good fortune to
get to know hundreds of trade union activists the world around. The
majority of them, of course, are in the United States, but many of them
come from other lands near and far – from Canada to Japan, Mexico to
France, El Salvador to Germany, from Brazil to Britain, and more. While I
have had the patience to read much of the globalization literature, it is

these many union activists who have taught me what the deepening of international economic integration is really about.

When I started this project, in 1994, the rebellion was barely visible. While I was doing research in Europe, two events took place that gave me confidence in the project. The first was the general strike in Nigeria. I had done my Master's degree thesis on the Nigerian labor movement many years before and knew something of the risks these trade unionists were taking in the face of a ruthless military government. The incredible heroism of these union leaders and activists led me to look once again into that country. But before I got far, the movement was crushed by the same military that had crushed Nigerian labor over twenty-five years earlier. Support began to build among British trade unionists and American Black community activists, but it was all too little, too late. If I had had any doubts about the willingness of workers to fight when pushed to the wall, and the need for effective international solidarity, the Nigerian struggle put them to rest.

At the same time, while I was researching in London, I read in the *Financial Times* of a strike in October 1994 by an unnamed local union against General Motors (GM) in Flint, Michigan. Like the Nigerian strike, which brought the oil industry to a halt, it only made the international news because it disrupted a major transnational corporation (TNC). I knew who the GM strikers were and why they were striking. Their leaders were members of the dissident New Directions caucus in the United Auto Workers' union, just as the Nigerian strike leaders were political dissidents in their country. The proportion of heroism and risk was clearly different, but the motivation was not so different.

Reaction would vanquish them both for the moment. The military government of Nigeria would imprison strike leaders. GM, assisted by the national leaders of the auto workers' union and the mayor of Flint, would defeat the New Directions leaders in the next union election by telling the workers that there would be no new product for the plant and GM would leave Flint if the dissidents were re-elected. The "official" candidate won. The plant, however, was left with no new product, GM management headquarters left town, and other facilities were closed. It was one more reminder that these days most business decisions are made by transnational corporations in a world-wide context – giant businesses balancing resources between major markets. The pathetic attempts of union leaders and local politicians to "save jobs" by conforming to corporate priorities have little or no impact in the end. Whether this kind of protectionism is local, as in the Flint case, or national, as when unions support massive downsizing at corporations like GM or AT&T in the name of "competitiveness," it is a dead end for workers and their unions.

On the other hand, this approach fits well with the corporate shift toward lean-production methods in almost every industry, discussed in chapter 5. Most of these programs include labor–management cooperation structures and promote a company-minded "win–win" mentality. The problem, of course, is that there is no "win–win" solution to the age-old conflict between employer and employee. The adage that "our income (time, health, and safety) is their cost" remains as true as ever. Someone wins and someone loses something in this economic and social tug of war. That is the stuff of trade unionism.

This bonding of union leaders and employers takes on the grander ideological form of "social partnership" in Europe. In Japan it is known as enterprise unionism. Its academic name is often "human resources management." By whatever name it is known, a style of unionism that adapted to these management practices spread across the world in the 1980s. By now it is common among union leaders who populate both the national unions and labor federations and the institutions and meetings of the official international trade unionism dealt with in chapter 10.

This current of thinking now forms what one writer called "global business unionism," a post-Cold War version of old-style American "pure and simple" unionism.[1] It is ironic that none of the AFL–CIO's government-backed Cold War efforts to promote American-style business unionism was nearly as successful as the corporate offensive that put labor–management cooperation schemes on the industrial agenda in the past fifteen years. This is, to a large extent, a reflection of the fact that the lean-production methods that underlie this ideology are now almost universal across the industrial world. They have modified, though not eliminated, the mass-production techniques that preceded them. Like the mass-production techniques of earlier years, these lean mass-production methods have spread from manufacturing to almost every kind of work organized along modern lines.

"Global business unionism," like its American predecessor, essentially accepts the new order and settles for negotiating the price of labor. At the national level, mergers of unions are seen as a more efficient means of administering the wage bargain in this new lean era. Internationally, there is confusion about how to function in the post-Cold War epoch, strong nationalist practice dressed in the newer language of "partnership," and a debilitating protocol that inhibits effective action.

Books and essays stating that unions must go global to match employers are not hard to come by these days. What should be clear from what is said here, however, is that building a genuine, effective practice of international labor solidarity capable of halting or reversing the global race to the bottom will involve more than simply making international connections. Linking together weakened, bureaucratic, conservatized unions will not limit the power of TNCs.

So, this book does not offer some simple formula for creating a full-blown international labor movement. Instead, it looks at the roots and structures of globalization, their impact on the working classes of different parts of the world, and the most recent working-class responses to the lean regime in the workplace, the global jobs crisis, government-imposed austerity, and the general decline in working-class living standards around the world. If any picture of the globalization process necessarily involves some overwhelming "gloom and doom" analysis, it is the return of class confrontation in recent years that offers the hope.

The book also looks at the difficult problems associated with the increased differentiation within the working class that results from massive immigration, older racial conflicts cast in new economic molds, the rise of women as a proportion of the workforce, and the changing stratification of the workforce. Along with internationalization and union bureaucratism, this is, and in many places always has been, the greatest problem facing the working class and its organizations. "Global business unionism" typically addresses these problems by celebrating "diversity" without actually engaging in the more difficult fight for equality.

The old argument that a rising tide lifts all ships has never been convincing to those trapped in steerage. The rising tide must offer the opportunity to reduce and eliminate the old inequalities. As Jeremy Brecher and Tim Costello argued in *Global Village or Global Pillage*, the international strategy is one of "upward leveling" of incomes and conditions.[2] This must be true between different sectors of the class as well as between nations.

The perspective offered here is called "social movement unionism." The term is borrowed from the labor movements of South Africa, Brazil, and elsewhere in the Third World. The term itself may never catch on in the rest of the world, if only because it's a mouthful. But the conception is key to raising the forces necessary to confront international business and its allies. It goes beyond the "organizing model" of unionism used in the US in opposition to the older "service model" of American business unionism by asserting the centrality of union democracy as a source of power and broader social vision, and outreach as a means of enhancing that power.

Social movement unionism is one that is deeply democratic, as that is the best way to mobilize the strength of numbers in order to apply maximum economic leverage. It is militant in collective bargaining in the belief that retreat anywhere only leads to more retreats – an injury to one is an injury to all. It seeks to craft bargaining demands that create more jobs and aid the whole class. It fights for power and organization in the workplace or on the job in the realization that it is there that the greatest leverage exists, when properly applied. It is political by acting independently of the retreating parties of liberalism and social democracy, whatever the relations of the union with such parties. It multiplies its political and social power by reaching out to other sectors of the class, be they other unions, neighborhood-based organizations, or other social movements. It fights for all the oppressed and enhances its own power by doing so.

Perspective, Language and Limits

Ultimately, we are all creatures of where we are born and raised. So, while I have traveled in and read extensively about other countries, I necessarily (involuntarily) see the world from the viewpoint of someone raised in the United States. A life-long dissident, labor activist, socialist, internationalist, and anti-war activist, to be sure, but one who is rooted in that vague, almost undefinable, contradictory cultural storm that is the American experience. Indeed, when speaking of anything "American" it is usually helpful to qualify one's place in that oversized, oversegregated society, almost infinitely – a temptation I will, however, resist. Suffice it to say, the view of the world from Detroit is probably different from that from London, Lagos, or even Los Angeles.

One difference is language. Not just of English versus Spanish or South Korean, both widely spoken in the United States, but of terminology. Terms associated with politics and the lean-production regime differ over time and from place to place. For example, the term "neoliberal" is not widely used in the US outside of intellectual circles. In the US "conservative" embodies the policy cluster of deregulation, privatization, and austerity cut-backs in government social programs attributed to neoliberals in much of Latin America, Asia, Africa, and Europe. Because of its universal usage across the world, however, I have used "neoliberal" throughout the book with only this warning to American readers that it means conservative.

Even more bewildering, however, is the variety of terms used to described things like part-time and casual work: "contingent" in the US, "atypical" or "anti-social" in the UK, still other words in other languages. I use these terms sometimes together so that those reading in the "English-speaking" world get the idea. Thereafter, they are used interchangeably. Everywhere I try to be descriptive enough to make it clear that different terms, like "human resources management" or "management-by-stress," refer to essentially the same thing.

Although this book focuses on the international working class, it does not attempt to cover that class everywhere; that would be impossible in a single volume. The choices of which countries to write about are in part due to the limits of my own knowledge, but also relate to the way in which events have unfolded. The focus of the analysis here is on the developed industrial countries and those more industrial countries of the economic South or Third World. South Asia, the Middle East, much of sub-Saharan Africa, and the former and not so former Communist countries are not discussed in detail. There is no suggestion here that these parts of the world have no role to play in reversing the global race to the bottom imposed by the regime of globalization: they are too vast not to be important. Rather, there is the observation that the rebellion against this regime has begun in, and necessarily gains its initial strength in, those countries with a more developed organized working class. It is the potential of the labor movements in these two sectors of the world economy to join together in common action that holds out hope for all. So, I have focused on them.

Globalization and Globaloney

The view expressed in this book is that globalization is a long-term process, not a state of being. Transnational corporations operate world-wide, as do financial markets, but most things, including the production and consumption of most goods and services, still occur at the national level. This fact runs counter to much of our experience as consumers, at least in the United States, which suggests that a great many of things we buy are imported from low-wage countries, particularly more down-market clothing, sporting goods, and, increasingly, fruit. Although these lower-wage countries only produce about 15% of world output, they have been forced to become exporting nations by institutions such as the International Monetary Fund and the various multilateral trade agreements. Products like garments or sports shoes are likely to be among the first these countries produce for export. So we see a lot of them, despite the fact that most products in the world are not imported or exported by anyone.

The destructive competition of world markets reaches deeply into most corners of the world, to be sure. But the world market is by no means the seamless phenomenon of abstract theory. If it were, the transnational corporations and their neoliberal allies would not continue pushing so hard for the elimination of the many barriers they claim stand in the way of free commerce – including government welfare programs, legal rights of all kinds, and, of course, trade unions. The world remains a very uneven, fragmented, nationally divided one. In fact, the process of deepening international economic integration actually increases some aspects of fragmentation and inequality between nations.

When looking at the world economy, it is important to keep proportions in mind. Writings on globalization frequently dazzle the reader with huge figures. For example, a 1996 United Nations report on foreign investment says, "Investment inflows in 1995 increased by 40%, to an unprecedented $315 Billion." Impressive, but this is less than 5% of total world investment.[3] This proportion alone will tell you that even though overseas investment is big and growing, capital is not quite as foot-loose as is often suggested. Furthermore, an enormous amount of this overseas investment, about 75% in 1995, involves buying up existing businesses abroad through privatizations or mergers and acquisitions.[4] That is, it is not investment in some new facility. The idea, so prominent in popular globalization literature, that businesses pick up stakes and relocate offshore in the blink of an eye is largely "globaloney."

Of course, the world markets in currency and financial instruments, along with the increased relative mobility of capital, do have disciplining effects on governments, companies, and workers. What is more, both international and domestic investment decisions are made with an eye to global forces and markets. This means that the transnational corporations do reshape national economies through their international decisions. But these are tendencies, not "facts on the ground." Furthermore, much of the new market-driven world order is politically negotiated. The World Trade Organization (WTO), North American Free Trade Agreement (NAFTA), and the Maastricht Treaty in Europe, to mention a few, are negotiated by national governments. The regime these negotiations and policies are producing is not some one-world government, but a loosely structured network of multilateral agreements and institutions. This was made possible only by a political sea change that took place in the 1980s with the rise to power of neoliberalism across much of the world.

Many analysts see this neoliberal, multilateral regime as having irreversibly consolidated. Certainly, it still has a great deal of momentum. But the struggles of recent years in opposition to the effects and even the institutions of this regime show that political consolidations can be fleeting in historical perspective. Speaking of the mass strikes in Latin America in 1995, James Petras said:

> These large-scale social mobilizations explicitly rejecting part or all of the neoliberal agenda call into question the assumption of "consolidation." They open the perspective of the *decay* of neoliberalism and the construction of a political alternative based on a different socioeconomic model.[5]

That is the point of departure and the conclusion of this book. Neoliberalism, conservatism, still rules, but the decay of its regime is apparent in the resistance to it and in the failure of its promises of prosperity to be fulfilled for more than a handful of humanity. Its strategies for salvation (lean production, the unfettered market, and multilateralism) are at war with one another and with the vast majority of the world's population. While the alternative "model" may not be clear as yet, the human alternative is evident in the working classes of the world that have turned to rebellion. The day they unite, as the old slogan has it, is the day the alternative will become clear.

1

World-Class Working Class

As union membership and annual strike statistics fell in unison across much of the industrial world through the 1980s and into the 1990s, the experts proclaimed the working class a thing of the past. The diagnosis read: paralysis due to globalization, fragmentation, flexibilization. A deteriorative disease was said to have rendered this once combative social class too weak to survive the dog-eat-dog world of lean and mean transnational corporations and trimmed-down states. Its trade unions, like so many dinosaurs stuck in the ooze, were thought to have been by-passed by a high-tech age of non-stop world-wide business mobility. The most optimistic prognosis was that, unable to fight on, the organized working class had fallen into a coma of cooperation with its former foes.

Like Mark Twain's proverbial death notice, the diagnosis proved premature. By the mid-1990s the streets of continental Europe, Latin America, and parts of Asia were filled with hundreds of thousands of angry working people, long, bitter strikes had erupted in the United States, Canada's industrial heartland was swept by a series of one-day general strikes, and Britain experienced a new wave of strikes among postal, transport, and dock workers. In the Third World a new unionism had established firm ground in South Africa, Brazil, South Korea, and Taiwan and was on the rise in other countries of East Asia and Latin America. This new unionism demonstrated its power as 1996 turned into 1997 and South Korean workers paralysed that country, confronting its conservative government with a month of general strikes. Even before the South Korean strikes subsided, mass political strikes broke out in Greece, Belgium, and Ecuador. The new year also saw the first world-wide longshore workers' action in history as dock workers in over 100 ports took action in solidarity with the victims of dock privatization in Liverpool, England.[1]

The nature of these various struggles spoke to the times. The mass political strikes that hit Nigeria, Indonesia, Taiwan, France, South Korea, Italy, Belgium, Canada, South Africa, Brazil, Argentina, Paraguay, Panama, Bolivia, Greece, Spain, Venezuela, Haiti, Colombia, Ecuador, and elsewhere from 1994 on into 1997 were not called by political parties, as they often had been in past decades. Rather they were meant to fill a political vacuum created by the retreats of the old parties of the left. It was the working class itself, led or at least accompanied by its unions, that was taking on the right-wing/neoliberal (conservative) agenda that had come to dominate the politics of most nations. Unions across the world shunned party domination, but took on politics directly, albeit in a defensive mode.

These political strikes were based mainly in the public sector. While rail, transport, or other industrial workers frequently provided the shock troops, they were rapidly joined by workers from telecommunications, health care, banks, civil services, and the teaching professions. To put this another way, male workers in blue collars and jackets were joined in the streets by male and female workers in dresses, coats and ties, and uniforms of various colors. Across the world their numbers swelled into the millions as they contested austerity, privatization, and the slashing of their nation's most basic services. Everywhere, they were supported by the vast majority of the population.

Bitter strikes in North America, Britain, Germany, and elsewhere were waged around issues associated with new methods of work organization: working time and work schedules, contracting and subcontracting, casualization, work intensification and stress, declining health and safety conditions. In some cases, as at Britain's Royal Mail, where workplace organization remained strong, workers struck to defend it against "team working" and won at least for the time being. Fired Liverpool longshore workers sparked actions in ports around the world.

In North America, after years of apparent paralysis, workers discovered the weak points of just-in-time production. Strikes at individual GM plants in the US, for example, had rapidly closed down other facilities. A national strike against GM in Canada in 1996 had quickly closed down plants in the US. Here too the workers won much of what they demanded. Innovations in strike tactics became common. At the same time, a new militancy erupted among immigrant workers in the United States. Militancy and tactical innovation did not always guarantee success, but a new sense of combativeness and solidarity had replaced the concessions and surrenders of the previous decade for more and more workers.

The working class that launched these renewed struggles was in many ways different from the class that had begun its transformation, retreat, and organizational decline twenty years before. In much of the world, women now played a larger role in the workforce and the labor movement. Immigrant workers from the Third World brought greater ethnic, racial, and linguistic diversity to the working classes of North America and Europe. The organization of work itself had changed with "contingent" or "atypical" jobs forming a larger part of the workforce, particularly in the growing "service" sectors. Production systems were increasingly broken up through subcontracting and outsourcing, some of it overseas. The organization of production on which most old unions were based had changed irreversibly.

A whole new workplace vocabulary had helped to confuse experienced trade unionists and obscure once well-known facts of life on the job. "Competitiveness" and "globalization" were said to require a new spirit of cooperation between labor and capital. "Quality" required fewer workers to work harder and longer. "Participation" and "empowerment" demanded giving up old forms of protection for the hope of a job. Many union leaders seemed to buy into business' new vision of an infinitely flexible workplace and labor market in the belief that some jobs would be left at home.

Perhaps most disorienting for trade unionists in the industrial nations of the West was the shift in world economic activity and subsequent industrial restructuring that had occurred during the previous two decades. The rise of Japan as a major economic power had shifted a significant proportion of the world's production to Asia. In the West, this often reinforced a nationalist response, seen at its more extreme in the "Buy American" bumper stickers that decorated the cars of many union members in the United States.

At the same time, enough production had shifted to select parts of the Third World to raise the specter of massive job loss in the Western industrial countries. This shift took place in the context of an increase in international economic integration that further changed the rules under which unions bargained for their members. Often called "globalization", this process was, in fact, producing an increasingly fragmented world in which poverty and unemployment were on the rise.

Stitching this new world-wide economic order together across borders were internationalized systems of ownership and production dominated by the transnational corporations. Workers in production systems once contained within their own nation, now found part of that production located abroad. Not only did this mean job loss at home, it also meant that once neatly contained systems of national bargaining now came under pressure from lower-cost overseas units. In the new location, particularly in the Third World, this often meant "production enclaves" that had few links to the rest of the economy of the "host" nation and little real impact on employment. On the one hand, huge wage gaps put these workers in the different nations into competition; on the other, common employment in a shared production system laid the basis for solidarity if the national unions could make the international leap. Official labor internationalism was typically unable to make such a leap except on rare occasions or in specific campaigns – many of which were more symbolic than real. The challenge of creating a new grassroots internationalism was one of the most daunting of the period.

All of this was compounded by the neoliberal, that is, conservative, regime of free trade and business deregulation that placed the market, often the world market, at the center of all decisions. Economic integration, whether in Europe, North America, East Asia, or the Third World, was not simply integration or a bigger market: it was a new set of rules designed to favor capital over labor. Clothed in obscure theoretical terms, the shape of this new world economy was difficult to see for a long time.

Changes in the composition of the workforce in many industrial nations, along with the fear of job loss produced by international economic integration, also brought on a new wave of active racism and racist organization in Europe and North America. That working-class people were swept up in this threatening tide should come as no surprise. While racism and anti-immigrant sentiment are not new, nor unique to the working class, increased competition for jobs, housing, or income always lends racism a helping hand. As with so many other issues, the unions ignored this, or even played along, for years and were not prepared to resist racism actively. When, or if, they finally did it was often too little, too late.

Beneath all the confusing changes and new threats, however, something very basic remained the same. For all the talk of "empowerment" or "cooperation," the employer still ruled the workplace, determined who had a job, and pushed for more production in the name of profit. The employer–employee relationship had received several coats of brightly colored paint, but power and wealth remained where they had always been. In fact, wealth had shifted up the social scale and everywhere the capitalist class had improved its lot while labor had lost economic ground. Power, too, increased for capital as job loss and fear of job loss fueled the retreat of many unions.

Capitalism was still capitalism. Production for profit was still the order of the day and was, in fact, the motivation behind many of the changes themselves. Labor still produced these profits and, as always, was expected to produce still more. No one put it better than the American auto worker who wrote to his union saying, "Believe me, we know how hard it is to make a profit – we spend 50 to 60 hours a week at the company, working to make a profit for our employers."[2] Capital still fought to hold down or even reduce wages, benefits, and conditions. Labor's income was still capital's cost. Whether this was fought out on the plain of wages, conditions or benefits, or in the political arena, the old conflict was still at the heart of the matter. No overlay of teams, circles, participation schemes, or grand "social partnerships" had changed this one bit.

In fact, this old conflict had gotten worse. Driven by its own intensified international competition, capital was demanding and winning more. Working-class incomes were slumping almost everywhere. Life on the job was more dangerous and unhealthy than it had been for decades. Holding a job was more precarious. This last fact underlay the apparent passivity of the workers and their unions in most of the developed industrial nations that set in around the late 1970s or early 1980s. Capital skillfully used this new fear to wage what one American labor leader called a "one-sided class war."[3] Capital could fool the experts and those labor leaders far removed from the workplace with the language of quality and cooperation, and scare the workforce with the threat of job loss, but could not conceal the daily reality experienced by workers or the bigger social crisis the working class as a whole experienced over the years. Sooner or later what was old in the system would drive more and more working-class people to act against what was new.

As 1997 opened, South Korea's new unions demonstrated this proposition when they launched the second week of a national general strike. The scene of thousands of workers battling riot police became common as the new unions of the Korean Confederation of Trade Unions (KCTU) closed down many of South Korea's major industries and even hospitals and broadcast facilities. By mid-January the unions claimed that 630,000 workers had hit the streets in opposition to a government move to change the nation's labor law in such a way as to weaken the unions and open the door for massive lay-offs. Union leaders defied court summons and arrest warrants, and the confrontation continued.[4]

South Korea was supposed to be the world-class model of development – the ultimate Third World miracle, the proof of neoliberal effectiveness. In 1996, it was admitted to the Organization for Economic Cooperation and Development (OECD), the club of prosperous industrial nations. But by the mid-1990s, the glory days of the miracle were waning. This export dynamo was running a $23 billion trade and investment deficit by 1996. Several of its industries had been wiped out as new, lower-cost countries joined the global fray. Capital wanted to restructure to become competitive with these upstart Asian rivals. Industry pressed the ruling New Korea Party for action. The action took the form of a six in the morning legislative session that lasted seven minutes and passed eleven laws in the absence of the opposition parties. One of these laws amended the old labor law to allow massive lay-offs at any time and scab replacements during strikes. The new unions of the KCTU would remain illegal.[5]

That same day, the KCTU called a general strike and over 100,000 workers responded immediately. By December 31, about 400,000 were on strike, including some workers represented by the more conservative government-recognized Federation of Korean Trade Unions (FKTU). The strike was suspended over the new year's holiday, but resumed on January 3. On January 14 and 15, the FKTU again joined the movement, bringing it to its 630,000-person crescendo.[6] The strike movement was the creation of the new unions, and resulted from South Korea's entrance into the crisis that had already affected so much of the industrial world. Korean capital wanted wage restraint and workforce reductions to solve its problems. The old and the new combined and collided. The revolt of the South Korean workers was not a drama from the past played out in the Third World's most industrial country; it was a drama already being played out across all the economic lines that divided the "globalizing" world. Within weeks, this dramatic movement forced the government to retreat from its legislative intransigence and to release the few strike leaders it had dared arrest.[7]

Just before and during the stirring events in South Korea, mass general strikes were held in Greece, Italy, Spain, Belgium, and Ecuador. Once again, these were confrontations over government austerity plans. But in these cases it was governments elected by the working class who faced the wrath of the mainly public-sector workers and their unions. Social democratic governments in Greece, Italy, and Belgium, and a populist president in Ecuador, had appealed to the traditional grievances of workers and farmers to gain election, only to deliver austerity and privatization programs indistinguishable from those of the conservatives of South Korea, France, or anywhere else.[8]

The return of working-class action that became visible around the world by the mid-1990s had deep roots in the previous period and was shaped by it. The changes within the working class had been disorienting, but had also made new developments possible. Changes within the unions that led to action usually came from below – not always from the bottom ranks, but almost always from some layer beneath the top union leadership. The unions took on new roles: as champions of the interests of the working class as a whole, not just as representatives of their members, and as political surrogates for failed parties of the left. They did not always do all of these things at once or even well, but it was becoming clear that the active workers who brought with them the revival of unionism that surfaced in the mid-1990s had a broader agenda than the older leaders they either replaced or goaded to action. What was emerging was not just a revived labor movement, but in many ways a new one.

A Tale of Two Cities: Paris and London (Ontario)

No one called a mass strike wave of public-sector workers in France in November–December 1995. The three major labor federations, the CGT (Confédération Générale du Travail – General Confederation of Workers), the CFDT (Confédération Française Démocratique du Travail – French Democratic Confederation of Workers), and FO (Force Ouvrière – Workers' Force), had called a Day of Action on October 10 to protest public-sector wage freezes, but no one expected a month of on-going and recurring strikes that would sweep through the public sector. According to the experts, it was not supposed to happen at all. Fashionable French intellectual Alain Touraine had written in 1987 that although "the role of trade unionism is not over . . . the history of the workers' movement is." For others, even the existence of the unions was in question. France's union membership had dropped to 10% of the workforce, the unions having lost over half their membership in the previous 20 years.[9]

As in many countries, strike levels in the 1980s had dropped dramatically. Public-sector workers had been more willing to strike, probably because they had greater job security as civil servants. In the late 1980s there were some large public-sector strikes among nurses and rail workers. In 1993, and again in 1994 and 1995, Air France workers made world news as they blocked runways in opposition to a proposed privatization plan. Workers at France Télécom also struck against privatization. Private-sector workers, however, had experienced heavy downsizing in the late 1980s and, as a result, had been quiescent for some time.

Furthermore, France's three major labor federations continued to squabble about many things – the European Union, new work organization, which political party to support, and even the government's plan to drastically cut public services and reduce public-sector employees' health care and pension funds. Despite all these problems, it happened and it was more a "workers' movement" than a simple trade-union dispute.

The strike began on November 24 among workers at the national railroad (SNCF, Société Nationale des Chemins de Fer Français – National Society of French Railroads), followed by those in the Paris Metro (subway) on November 28. Although these workers were divided among the three labor federations (CGT, CFDT, and FO), they struck together and met each morning in their workplaces to discuss and vote on the day's actions. These remained the most consistent strikers until the movement finally ended on December 20. Between November 24 and December 20 other groups of public-sector workers came out sporadically; out one day, back the next, then out again for another day.[10] The movement was also characterized by massive demonstrations, which in most cities were larger than those of the general strike of 1968, particularly in the provincial towns and cities: 100,000 in Marseille, 80,000 in Toulouse, 60,000 in Rouen, and 50,000 in Bordeaux. Public support for the strikers was overwhelming despite the inconvenience caused by the rail and transit strikes.[11]

The issue in the strike wave was an austerity plan, called the Plan Juppé after the prime minister, that would have drastically reduced national rail services, increased taxes on the working class, lengthened the number of years required for a pension for public employees, and put health-care and pension benefits under control of parliament rather than under the old social fund that had existed since the end of World War Two. The Plan Juppé would have affected most of the working class and even the middle classes. The Socialist and Communist Parties, the traditional parties of the French working class, made no attempt to stop the plan. It was the rail and metro workers who took the lead, with the CGT and FO following suit and the CFDT leadership never actually supporting the strike. The push for united action came from the activist ranks of all three federations plus a number of independent unions and federations.

The movement soon extended well beyond the strikers. It became an expression of the frustration of the entire working class, who showed up in huge numbers at the demonstrations. As one French writer put it:

> The popular eruption was fuelled by deep exasperation. People had endured a lot while awaiting a promised tomorrow that, like the horizon, remained forever out of reach. They had wanted to believe in automatic and irreversible progress, but had suddenly discovered, for the first time in fifty years, that the next generation would probably have a harder time than its predecessors. Behind the December movement's specific and sectoral demands, its driving force lay in this massive rejection of a future which is no longer a future. It quickly became apparent that the strikers were fighting on everyone's behalf and that their aspirations placed a choice by society on the immediate agenda. They were struggling to resuscitate hope.[12]

The unionized workers had filled a void left by the retreating parties of the left. More importantly, they had drawn into the movement hundreds of thousands of other working-class people. In southern cities like Marseille this included many workers who had voted for the racist National Front. The strikers' demands covered both their own immediate issues, pensions and health care, and the broader issues facing the class, higher taxation on the working class, declining public services, and a right-wing government that would certainly not stop at the Plan Juppé if left to its own devices.

The strike not only forced the government to agree to renegotiate the whole deal – withdrawing some parts and modifying others – it also accelerated changes within the unions that had already been in the making. Rank-and-file pressure for unity before and during the strikes forced the leadership of the three federations to act in a more unified manner. It also sparked further debate within the unions about the future. The CGT's 45th Congress, that coincidentally took place in the midst of the strike wave, saw increased debate and dissatisfaction with the cautious approach of the leadership – with some militants calling on the CGT to call a full-scale general strike. Perhaps most important in terms of internal union matters, the movement encouraged a large opposition within the CFDT, whose leader, Nicole Notat, had supported the Plan Juppé.[13]

The strikes increased the strength of the new union SUD (Solidarité Unitaire Democratie), which had originated at France Télécom and the post office. SUD led strikes against privatization in 1993 and 1994, helping to postpone the plunge of the telecom workers into the marketplace. SUD stood at the head of a loose alliance of eighteen independent unions called the "Group of 10." In the wake of the strike, about, 3,000 rail workers who had been in the CFDT formed SUD-Rail. The independent teachers' union, the FSU (Fédération Syndicale Unitaire), also played a big part in the strike and in pushing a more aggressive style of unionism than the National Education Federation (FEN, Fédération de l'Éducation Nationale) from which it had split a couple of years earlier.[14]

What seemed clear was that out of the struggles leading up to the events of 1995 as well as in the heat of that movement, more and more workers were demanding a more democratic, aggressive, and unified type of trade unionism. Although the movement had lacked the revolutionary *élan* of the upheaval and general strike of 1968, the workers clearly expected their unions to take on important political issues directly. While the new unionism implied in these debates and new developments carries a deep and deserved suspicion of the old parties of the left, the Socialist and Communist Parties, it has also sparked debate within those parties. For example, at a spring conference held by the Socialist Party on "Globalization, Europe, France," a resolution rejecting the European Monetary Union (EMU) convergence budget-balancing criteria passed over opposition from the leadership. The Communist Party, for its part, has attempted to shake off its undemocratic image and to engage in open dialogue with other forces on the left.[15]

The movement of 1995 had some other political spin-offs as well. In an important departure from its practice of not endorsing events it didn't control, the CGT endorsed and participated in a November 25 women's rights demonstration of 40,000 in Paris. Union participation helped make this the largest women's rights demonstration in French history. In the summer of 1996, when the government sent the police to remove a number of African immigrants from a church in Paris in order to expel them from France, the CGT and other unions called on their members to support a protest march called by immigrants' rights groups – many did.[16] Issues that had long been ignored or only given lip service by the unions became part of the broader agenda.

The mass strikes of 1995 were a product of the new international economy. The Plan Juppé was part of France's effort to conform to the budgetary requirements of EMU. The Maastricht Treaty of European Union and the EMU, with its draconian budget-balancing requirements, reflected the most advanced form of regional international integration. Such regionalization of economic activity was apparent in North America even before the signing of the North American Free Trade Agreement (NAFTA). It was also evident in East Asia, where trade and investment ties between Japan and the other nations of the region had grown dense. Other "free trade" pacts, such as ASEAN in Southeast Asia or the Andean Pact and MERCOSUR in South America, represented regionalization subordinate to the major economic powers like the US and Japan. In each of these economic regions the price paid by the working class for integration on the terms of market regulation and transnational corporation domination was rising.

The problems of the French working class or those of French women and immigrant workers in France were not solved by the movement of 1995. Nor did the movement put forth the sort of revolutionary ideas of a broader social transformation as did the movement of 1968. But steps were taken toward a new kind of movement unionism that could not have been taken without it. In November 1996, some 50,000 truckers drew a lesson from 1995. Their strike became a unique workplace occupation – for their workplaces were the highways and harbors of France, which they effectively blockaded. Just as the rail strike of 1995 had crippled much of the country's commerce and, in fact, a certain amount of Europe's cross-border, just-in-time production, so did the 250 barricades the striking truckers set up. The British *Guardian* described it well:

> If the French lorry drivers' blockade has demonstrated one thing, it is how much Europe has become a single organism. Pricked in France it bleeds in Portugal, England, and Andalucia. A few days of confrontation on the autoroutes, and frozen chips languish in Holland, harvesting of Norwegian farmed salmon is delayed, oranges and lettuces rot in the Pyrenasian passes,

Christmas trees wilt in lay-bys, and car parts factories in Ireland and Spain face short-time working.[17]

Like the 1995 strikers, the truckers had the sympathy of the majority. In the end they won the retirement with 70% of full pension at age 55 they had demanded, a measure that would open more jobs. This was important because it was the first such mass strike of private-sector workers in recent years. The French truckers' strike also increased the power and prestige of the transport sector of the CFDT and intensified contacts between the rail and trucking sides of that union. Perhaps even more significant for the future was the international strike in Spring 1997 against a major Renault plant closure in Belgium by workers in France, Spain, and Belgium. The spirit of 1995 had spilled into the private sector and even across borders.[18]

The public-sector workers, however, will face more attempts to cut their jobs and conditions. The new EMU agreement reached in Dublin in December 1996 provides for strict budgetary limits. The terms of this agreement were called "tough" by a European Union official, who went on to state that countries that tried to stay outside the new currency due in 1999 would suffer even worse punishment, owing to "the displeasure of the financial markets." Yet, in the wake of the strikes of 1995–97, the EMU faced another setback in 1997 with the election of a socialist government pledged to oppose the draconian demands of EMU and to give a greater role to the state in national economic affairs.[19]

Across the Atlantic in the Canadian province of Ontario, another kind of political intervention took place at the same time as the 1995 French events and on into 1996 and 1997. In this, the industrial center of Canada, workers and their unions had seen a social democratic New Democratic Party (NDP) government turn on them, institute drastic cutbacks in the public sector, and then collapse in disgrace as the Conservatives took office to carry the neoliberal revolution even farther. The program implemented by the new "Tory" government cut deep into legislation won over the years by the unions and their erstwhile NDP allies and even deeper into public services and employment. In particular, the $1.5 billion cuts in Medicare, Canada's national health service, would affect everyone. This attack on public services followed years of massive private-sector job loss in Ontario associated with the US–Canada Free Trade Agreement of 1989 and NAFTA since 1994. The loss of so many jobs and businesses to lower-wage areas in the US, Mexico, or the Caribbean had contributed to the province's financial troubles, as Ontario's once prosperous industrial economy entered a deepening crisis – another consequence of international economic integration.[20]

Unlike the events in France or many other countries in the mid-1990s, the response of the Canadian workers came from the leadership of some of the most militant unions. The Canadian Auto Workers (CAW), the Canadian Union of Public Employees, and the Ontario Public Service Employees Union convinced the rest of the unions in Ontario that these moves had to be opposed. Everyone knew, whether they chose to admit it or not, that the NDP would be no help. It was up to the unions. Unlike in France, the Days of Action called by the Ontario Federation of Labor (OFL) were highly planned. The idea was to set off a series of one-day general strikes followed by mass demonstrations on the weekend, one city at a time across the province, until the government retreated.

The first Day of Action was held in London, an industrial city in the southeastern part of the province. Called on December 11, the response was massive. The Canadian Auto Workers, for example, report that thirty CAW-organized plants in the area came out on strike. City transit was stopped and the local post offices closed, as were many other unionized workplaces and most public-sector locations. Thousands of working people streamed into the streets of London joined by activists from other social movements. It was an event that many had doubted could be so successful. And while the atmosphere was one of joy at the accomplishment, it was also an expression of the anger felt by so many Canadian workers.[21]

The London general strike was only the first of several such Days of Action. The second was organized in Hamilton, an industrial city near Toronto. Here over 100,000 demonstrated the day after the general strike. Further one-day strikes, followed by mass demonstrations, took place in Kitchener-Waterloo and then in Toronto, Ontario's provincial capital and largest city. In Toronto it was estimated that close to 200,000 people demonstrated.[22]

The Days of Action had shown that when organized labor leads on issues of direct interest to all working-class people, the response is massive. The CAW and some of the public-sector unions had long been trying to push labor as a whole and its allied party, the NDP, in a more aggressive direction. Bob White, the former president of the CAW and a well-known militant, had moved up to become president of the Canadian Labor Congress. But resistance from more conservative union leaders, often those in the "international unions" based in the US, was stubborn and the NDP leadership unmoved. The Days of Action, however, posed the question in a very concrete way that appealed to the rank-and-file activists of most unions. As in France, the spirit of unity in the streets was strong medicine.

The Days of Action did not force the Tory government of Ontario to back down – at least not by early 1997. Perhaps it was the limitation of one-day strikes – a difficult enough venture to organize, but temporary enough for the government to ignore. The rail and transit strikes in France, after all, had lasted almost a month and crippled much of the nation. Those in South Korea had gone on for three weeks. The Days of Action were impressive, but their disruption was very localized and brief. Ontario's Tories also demonstrated a kind of stubbornness born of free-market ideology more akin to that of Reagan or Thatcher than to the statist (*dirigiste*) traditions of the Gaullist conservatives governing France in 1995.[23]

The unique political role played by the workers and their unions in France and Canada in 1995 and beyond has been played elsewhere in a growing number of countries as political parties and structures move to dismantle what protection or social provision they might once have surrendered to the working class in an earlier period of struggle. General or mass political strikes in Nigeria (1994), Indonesia (1994), Paraguay (1994), Taiwan (1994), Bolivia (1995), South Africa (1996), Brazil (1996), Greece (1996, 1997), Spain (1994, 1996), Argentina (twice in 1996), Venezuela (1996), Italy (1996), South Korea (1996–97), Canada (1995–97), Haiti (1997), Colombia (1997), Ecuador (1997), and Belgium (1997), all attempted to confront neoliberal policies.[24] In many cases, they had filled a vacuum created by the retreat of the traditional working-class parties or parties of the left with which these labor movements had been associated.

Two trends were emerging in many countries by the mid-1990s. The first was the growing separation or independence of the unions from political parties they had been dominated by (usually Communist or nationalist) or dependent upon (social democratic) but whose leaders and professional politicians had moved closer to the neoliberal, pro-market policies of the parties of capital. While the unions might continue to support the parties of the left electorally, they would now shape their own political agenda. This was partly the case for many unions in Canada, and even more so for those in Europe formerly associated with Communist parties, as in France, Spain, and Italy, and for labor federations across Asia, Latin America, and Africa.

Other cases were more problematic. In South Africa, the new unions of COSATU (Congress of South African Trade Unions) remained formally part of the triple alliance with the African National Congress (ANC) and the South African Communist Party. With the ANC in government and imposing a number of neoliberal austerity programs, however, the tensions between the COSATU unions and the government were visible by 1996. In effect, COSATU tried to stake out an independent role without breaking with the ANC government of Nelson Mandela. They waged strikes and protests, both over collective-bargaining matters and in an effort to make the government keep promises made in the Reconstruction and Development Programme.[25] It seemed likely that any real move toward independence would not come until after the 1999 elections and the retirement of Nelson Mandela.

Britain also appeared to be an exception to this trend. "Labourism" remained strong and the idea of any break from the British Labour Party unthinkable, despite Labour's shift to the center. Perhaps because of seventeen years of Conservative rule, the trade-union leaders were prepared to do anything to see the Labour Party return to government, on the one hand, and tenaciously held on to what little influence they actually had in the party, on the other. The new Labour Party leadership of Tony Blair seemed determined to diminish the influence and official role of the unions in the party's structure. Blair was one of a new generation of social-democratic "modernizers" prepared to surrender to the markets and "The City," London's financial district.

For most British trade unionists politics meant the Labour Party. The last general strike had been in 1926 and had ended in a failure that left deep scars. Yet, there had been moments in the 1970s and early 1980s when the unions had come close to playing the sort of role unions were now playing across the Channel and the Atlantic. John Monks, the new leader of the Trades Union Congress, Britain's sole labor federation, however, was committed to "social partnership" and the "human resources management" agenda of British industry. He was not the kind of person to find Tony Blair's pragmatism disturbing. Perhaps it will require a recent experience like Canada's, when Labour attempts to implement its version of neoliberalism with a heart following elections in 1997.

There were, however, signs of political dissatisfaction in the activist layer of Britain's unions. In 1995, Arthur Scargill, leader of the National Union of Mineworkers, took his union out of the Labour Party and formed the Socialist Labour Party (SLP). The SLP was to be socialist, at least in the sense of favoring public ownership of key industries and services. Indeed, Scargill and others often cited the Labour Party's 1994 repeal of Clause IV of its constitution, which called for "common ownership" of industry, as proof of the need for a new, genuinely socialist party. In fact, the Labour Party's leaders had long ago abandoned nationalization as a tool for achieving its increasingly modest reform goals.

The new SLP's radicalism appealed to trade-union militants who had seen so much of Britain's welfare state dismantled and their unions driven to the wall. But the SLP is very much a top-down affair, the personal project of Scargill. Almost from the beginning, "dissidents" were expelled and only a small leadership group allowed to speak for the party. Not surprisingly, given the priority many union activists saw in getting the Tories out of office, the SLP's candidates did poorly where they ran. While the SLP expressed the radicalism of many trade-union activists, its top-down structure and cliquish style of leadership went against the grain of most. By 1997, it seemed most likely that the SLP had been a false start.[26]

Across much of the world, however, the moves toward greater union autonomy and the tensions between party politicians and union leaders were accompanied by an increased role in politics. As party leaders adapted more and more to market-oriented policies that punished working-class people and made collective bargaining an increasingly defensive affair, the unions had little choice but to put forth their own demands and mobilize their forces to confront neoliberal government policies. In doing so, either consciously or not, the unions put themselves at the head of a broader movement of the working class – one that might include dozens of organizations created in the struggles of the last decade or more by one or another group, mostly located within the broader working class.

For workers, it was not just a matter of national economic policy, whether imposed gleefully by right wingers, hesitatingly by social democrats, or externally by the multilateral agencies. It was also the behavior of employers, who were now mostly transnational corporations operating in several countries and even world-wide, or their suppliers and contractors. This, too, had changed the balance of power against the working class from the workplace to the national bargaining table. No where was this more apparent than in the US.

America's War Zones

Although transnational corporations (TNCs) have been around for decades, their number and reach increased dramatically in the decades after World War Two. TNCs grew not only by building new facilities but by taking over other companies or acquiring some of their operations. By the 1980s they had reached deep into industries and geographic areas of the US once dominated by family firms or larger, but still national or regional, corporations. This brought both a new balance of forces and new work and production methods to many parts of the United States unaccustomed to being a direct part of the world economy. Along with the replacement of the family farm by corporate agriculture throughout the 1970s and 1980s, this created a deep social crisis across the United States, but perhaps most sharply in the Midwestern part of the country. This area was often called the "Rust Belt" because of its large older industrial centers. But it was also a region of vast grain fields, dotted with small industrial cities producing from and for American agriculture.

This occurred in the context of a broader crisis facing American labor. Deep economic restructuring in one industry after another, along with increasingly deep recessions in the mid-1970s and early 1980s put US unions on the defensive. Beginning with the concessions made by the United Auto Workers as part of the 1979–80 Chrysler bailout plan, an era of concessionary bargaining opened that has yet to end. The concessions came first in the most heavily unionized industries. Highly visible concessionary agreements in the strongly unionized auto and steel industries led employers across the economy to demand cuts in wages, benefits, and finally in working conditions. The firing of 11,000 striking air-traffic controllers by Ronald Reagan in 1981 put the government seal of approval on strike-breaking and a new era of industrial relations opened.[27]

In much of the Midwest of the United States things changed rapidly as global producers replaced formerly regional firms in many industries. By the 1990s, exports from this region of the US were growing at twice the rate of those from the country as a whole, and it was estimated that one out of six manufacturing jobs in the Midwest was export-related.[28] The entry of global grain-marketing firms like Cargill and Conagra into the US meatpacking industry in the 1980s and the rise of aggressive new companies like Iowa Beef Packers, for example, drove older unionized regional meatpackers like Swift, Cudahay, and Armour to the margins. The industry wage and benefits pattern created over decades by a once strong and militant union, the United Packinghouse Workers of America (UPWA), was also marginalized and rapidly fell apart.[29]

The more conservative United Food and Commercial Workers (UFCW), which had absorbed the UPWA in a 1979 merger, agreed to deep wage cuts across the industry in the hope of saving union jobs and preserving some sort of pattern, albeit a negative one. Militants at UFCW Local P-9 at Hormel's new state-of-the-art Austin, Minnesota, plant tried to draw the line in a two-year strike that became a *cause célèbre* in the mid-1980s. But their own international union turned on them and, despite broad support and a national solidarity campaign, they were defeated. This was the real pattern contributed by the leaders of the UFCW.[30]

Well into the mid-1980s, everything in the small industrial city of Decatur, Illinois, right in the middle of farm country, seemed local and as American as apple pie. Even the multinationals like Caterpillar or Firestone Tire were names known across the Midwest farm belt for generations. The A. E. Staley corn-processing plant in Decatur had been a family-owned business for nearly a century. Of course, Staley, like Caterpillar or Firestone, now had plants in many other locations. In 1988, however, the Decatur Staley plant was pulled irretrievably into the world economy when the British-owned sugar marketer and processor Tate & Lyle bought A. E. Staley. Many of the Staley workers attributed the changes that soon took place at work to the fact that the new owners were foreigners not familiar with or sympathetic to the way things had been done in Decatur. In fact, it was not the nationality of the new owners that motivated them, but the new trends in work organization sweeping the world in the 1980s.

By the late 1980s a new dimension would be added to industries that were being internationalized: lean production. The TNCs not only expanded and refocused their "bottom line" calculations to a world-wide measure, but as international and domestic competition became hotter they turned to what each thought was the global "best practice" in production methods. Discussed in greater detail later, lean production brought with it a number of changes in mass-production systems that almost inevitably meant more effort and longer hours for most workers – and shorter hours and lower wages for others. Unions frequently agreed to many of these changes in the name of job security – a way to hold on to well-paid jobs in a world where they were being threatened more and more every day. In the early days of these new ways of working, there was also the promise that workers would have some say on the job and conditions might actually be better.

In Decatur, such illusions had dried up by the early 1990s. The new ten- or twelve-hour day, four-day week turned into a sixty-hour week at the A. E. Staley, Caterpillar, and Firestone plants. Labor–management cooperation to improve "competitiveness" became the excuse for speed-up, and slack health and safety enforcement. Already dangerous by most standards, the work in these plants, above all at Staley, became more unhealthy and unsafe as hours lengthened and speed-up exhausted more workers. When labor-contract negotiations opened at these three major Decatur employers in the early 1990s, the companies wanted still more in the way of "flexibility." The cooperation ethos initiated a few years earlier at each company gave way to an aggressive stance toward the unions and workers.[31]

Central Illinois was labeled the "War Zone," as workers at the three companies and a local electrical utility were pushed to fight back. What became obvious was that all the talk about cooperation and competitiveness had been a prelude to even more demands for concessions as well as the means to disarm the unions. The balance of power had changed as big transnational corporations bought their way into these industries that drew from and supplied much of American agriculture. Not only was Staley now a TNC subsidiary, but Firestone had been bought by the Japanese tire-maker Bridgestone and was now known as Bridgestone/Firestone. Decatur, Illinois, had been transnationalized and transformed.

Caterpillar, already a transnational in its own right, represented a different, but also wide-spread, model of growth from Staley or Firestone. It didn't get bought up or even buy up others. Rather, it used the period

of cooperation to downsize many existing unionized plants and simultaneously build thirty-one new nonunion facilities, many of them suppliers
to the remaining union plants. By the early 1990s it had significantly
reduced its proportion of union workers to about 25% of its US workforce,
and created a network of operations that would allow it to keep supplies
rolling even during a strike at the unionized plants – should the company
decide to use scabs in the union facilities. In 1992, secure in its reinforced
position, Caterpillar refused to sign a national pattern agreement with the
United Auto Workers (UAW) that would follow that set earlier at John
Deere, as it had for decades. It needed more "flexibility" to compete
globally, its management insisted. The UAW struck in 1992, but called the
strike off when the company threatened to bring in replacement scabs. In
its place the UAW attempted to organize slow-downs, work to rules, and
other forms of in-plant action. The UAW would resume the strike in 1994,
even though Caterpillar was in a stronger position than before with many
months of inventories and a constant flow of nonunion parts.[32]

Local 837 of the Allied Industrial Workers at the Decatur Staley plant
decided they would not rush into a strike. Indeed, they contacted Ray
Rogers, who had helped run the aggressive "corporate campaign" for
UFCW Local P-9 a decade before. A little later they brought in Jerry
Tucker, a leader of the oppositional New Directions Movement in the
UAW, but also the pioneer in "running the plant backward," as he called
his approach to in-plant strategy. Tucker's "inside strategy," as it was also
called, galvanized a previously conservative, largely passive membership
into a highly synchronized fighting force within the plant. For several
months they brought production down again and again through coordinated actions designed and run by the workers with Tucker's help. Tucker
insisted you couldn't run a successful inside strategy by "remote control,"
from the outside, as the UAW had tried at Caterpillar. The Staley workers
ran the plant backward so well that, in August 1994, the company locked
them out.[33]

With the help of Tucker, the local union moved to reinforce their efforts
in Decatur with a plan to pressure Staley's major customers to switch to
other producers. The corporate campaign organized by Ray Rogers against
State Farm Insurance, a major stockholder of Staley's, did not seem to be
going anywhere, so the emphasis shifted to Tucker's plan for pressuring
first Miller Beer and then Pepsi-Cola into dropping Staley as a supplier.
Miller, with a high-profile "blue-collar" product, did not renew its supplier
contract with Staley, a sign that the strategy was viable.

The pressure campaign was carried out and supplemented by a massive
national solidarity effort that brought money and resources for the locked-
out workers and support for the Miller and Pepsi campaign. The local

union's best activists traveled the country as "road warriors," spreading the news and building support. Mass rallies were held in Decatur that brought union workers from all over the Midwest. They also took the struggle to Tate & Lyle's doorstep in Britain with some assistance from trade unionists there. As in so many efforts, however, the international solidarity was largely symbolic and ineffective.

The Staley workers faced two problems they could not resolve themselves. First, they were one plant of many producing the same product (corn sweetener) which were either owned by Tate & Lyle or acted as its suppliers, like Archer Daniels Midland. Each of these plants was a self-sufficient lean producer, so there was no just-in-time chain to bring down other plants, although there were high-profile customers like Miller and Pepsi. Second, in the midst of their struggle the Allied Industrial Workers (AIW) merged into the United Paperworkers' International Union (UPIU), a southern-based union with a conservative leadership and a bad track record of defeated strikes. A sign of the times, the strikers at Bridgestone/Firestone not only saw their employer bought up, but their own union, the United Rubber Workers, was absorbed by the larger United Steelworkers of America (USWA) during their strike. The USWA launched a pressure campaign against Bridgestone/Firestone, but in the end signed an agreement that incorporated many of the concessions in earlier offers.

The first problem made it very difficult for Local 837 to inflict significant economic damage on Tate & Lyle. The idea of soliciting help from other unions to pressure companies like Miller and Pepsi could have inflicted some financial damage if Pepsi had followed Miller's example. The second problem, however, asserted itself when the UPIU's leadership pulled the plug on the struggle and the Pepsi campaign in December 1995 before Pepsi was due to renew, or, it was hoped, not renew, its contract with Staley. Whether or not the Pepsi campaign would have succeeded will never be known. What was clear was that the strike had not only lost because of the weak position of the workers at this single plant, but because the UPIU leadership had been willing to accept defeat.

During the simultaneous struggles at Staley, Caterpillar, and Bridgestone/Firestone, who together employed a third of the Decatur workforce, the three local unions created an active alliance. They helped organize the mass demonstrations together and were drawn into city politics when the local government tried to deny them a site for one of their demonstrations and allowed its police to pepper-gas demonstrators. The three unions put together the Friends of Labor, which ran candidates for the city elections in 1995. Many of the leaders of these struggles had joined Labor Party Advocates, a union-based effort to create a labor party in the US, and generally adopted a class view of politics. The idea of independent political action by labor, plus the repression by the incumbent city regime, led to the effort to take over city government. The local union leaders, however, were new to electoral politics and lost in the elections – although the mayoral candidate they endorsed won. On a local scale, though, the attempt to intervene in local politics reflected the increased willingness of trade unionists to by-pass existing parties for direct intervention.

The end of the Staley lock-out was a complete defeat for the union. A worthless agreement was shoved down the workers' throats by the UPIU top leadership, a new local leadership was elected by a demoralized union membership, and only a few of the locked-out workers would return to the plant. The scabs would remain the majority of the workforce. Yet, the core of the "road warriors" had been deeply radicalized by the experience. They now saw things in class terms and from an international perspective that would have been difficult to grasp in the old, pre-transnational, pre-War Zone Decatur.

By comparison, the fate of the Caterpillar workers was not as bad. They too were defeated by the combination of increased corporate expansion and top-level union caution. But the Caterpillar workers rejected the surrender agreement the company offered them and returned to the plants to organize the union from the ground up, despite a management reign of terror and a lack of strategic guidance from the leadership of the UAW.

By the mid-1990s the "War Zone" had spread to many other parts of America. In the summer of 1995, members of six unions at the Detroit Newspaper Agency (DNA), the joint operator of the *Detroit News* and *Detroit Press*, surprised the experts once again when they engaged in pitched battles with police week after week. At its height thousands of union members from the UAW, the Electrical Workers, Steelworkers, and many other unions joined striking Teamsters and Communications Workers in these battles. When the court issued an injunction against mass picketing at the DNA's major printing plant in Sterling Heights, Michigan, the strikers and their active supporters took their mass pickets to the papers' distribution centers. The official union strategy was to hit the circulation of the two papers, which was in fact reduced by 37%, and to pressure local businesses not to advertise in the scab papers. The unions also published their own weekly paper, the *Sunday Journal*, which managed to achieve a circulation of about 165,000 by 1997.[34]

But the Detroit strikers faced two massive national newspaper chains: Gannet and Knight Ridder. These were not transnationals, but they were huge corporations with deep pockets who had already broken unions in other cities. As at Staley and Caterpillar, the DNA had convinced the union to cooperate in modernization. Then they turned on the union, putting forth a long list of lean-production-style changes: contracting out, downsizing, increased workloads, and new work schedules. Once the strike started on July 13, 1995, *Detroit News* publisher Robert Giles said "We're going to hire a whole new workforce and go on without unions, or they can surrender unconditionally and salvage what they can."[35]

The unions did not surrender, and some strikers and supporters, organized for a time within the union as the Unity-Victory Caucus and later independently as Friends of Labor, conducted unofficial guerrilla warfare against company facilities. A broader coalition, Action Coalition of Strikers and Supporters (ACOSS), pressured the union leaders to call on the AFL–CIO to organize a national march on Detroit, to "shut down Motown."[36] In fact, the leaders of the six unions endorsed the call, but the AFL–CIO dragged its feet. Lacking active support in the streets from the rest of labor, after the local union leaders discouraged direct-action tactics, the strike dragged on into 1997 with no clear resolution in sight. In February, the unions announced that the members would return to work without a contract. The unions would attempt to get the National Labor Relations Board to declare the strike an unfair labor-practice strike, which would require the company to dismiss the scabs and take back the strikers – except those fired for illegal conduct during the strike. Only after this retreat did the AFL–CIO agree to call the march on Detroit for June 1997.[37]

Not all such outbursts of class militancy were stymied. In Warren, Ohio, strikers at WCI, a locally owned company carved out of the wreckage of LTV plants in the 1980s, locked-out workers also rallied local working-class support. After a picketer was hit and injured by a scab truck, USWA Local 1375 called on workers in the area to come to their aid. Thousands of workers from steel, auto and other plants in the area answered the call. Some 7,000 workers marched on the steel complex to stop all in- and out-going materials. Rail workers agreed not to deliver anything for the duration of the strike. According to one official of Local 1375, the entire town sympathized with the strikers, understanding that they were fighting to save well-paid jobs that kept the town healthy.[38]

The 32,000 Boeing workers who struck for sixty-nine days in 1995 also managed to squeeze a partial victory, when they overwhelmingly rejected a contract approved by their own national leaders. The major issues in this strike were an attempt to impose a less comprehensive "managed health-care plan" and job loss from outsourcing. Boeing had shed thousands of workers in recent years by outsourcing about 40% of the work done in the US to overseas plants, many of them in Asia. The leadership of the International Association of Machinists, which represented the Boeing workers, came to the membership with a contract that had virtually no protection against further outsourcing. Members of a union reform group, called Unionists for Democratic Change, organized a rejection drive and forced the leaders back to the bargaining table. The new language was far from perfect, but the reformers felt they had achieved a partial victory.[39]

One of the most important confrontations of the mid-1990s was the series of local-level strikes that swept GM from 1994 through 1997. The demands of most of these strikes centered on lean issues, such as staffing levels, subcontracting, and health and safety. The universal demand to deal with these was that the company hire a specified number of additional workers. This demand, of course, came in the wake of GM's drastic 1987–96 downsizing. Corporate downsizing was a highly visible issue, made even more so by the demagogic condemnation of right-wing, politician Pat Buchanan during his failed campaign to be Republican presidential candidate in 1996. In much of the industrial Midwest, where most of them took place, these ten strikes (plus two others over other issues) were viewed sympathetically by other working people because they were about jobs. These strikes also revealed the weaknesses of lean production's just-in-time parts-delivery system.

The October–November 1994 strike at GM's Buick City assembly plant in Flint, Michigan, was well prepared in more than one way. For months the UAW Local 599's weekly newspaper carried educational articles about lean production and related issues to prepare the union's 11,000 members. Under the leadership of Local 599's president, Dave Yettaw, members were encouraged to file grievances over health and safety and other issues that could be the basis for calling a strike under the terms of their contract. The local union was deeply divided between Yettaw and the New Directions-affiliated Reuther Slate, who were critical of the UAW's top leadership and their direction, and the members of the Administration Caucus who uncritically supported them. But Yettaw was able to draw the membership to the idea of a strike over issues they saw as crucial: job loss and workload. Yettaw also went to various organizations and the press in Flint to convince them this strike would save jobs in the area. This was not easy, because the mayor of Flint worked closely with GM management. But many in Flint and throughout the Midwest understood the importance of fighting for jobs in a concrete way. In the end they won the 779 new jobs they had demanded.[40]

The Flint strike lasted only four days, but it shut down more and more plants each day. Workers from those that ceased work in the area around Flint joined Local 599's picket lines to show their approval. Indeed, the GM strikes were well received by many industrial workers and even more broadly by union activists, who could see the broader social significance for the towns and cities that had lost so many jobs during the down-sizing tidal wave of the early 1990s. The last of these strikes prior to national UAW–GM negotiations in 1996 took place at two plants producing brakes in Dayton, Ohio. Like Local 599, UAW Local 696 were demanding additional workers, but they also tried to stop GM from outsourcing production to a nonunion plant in North Carolina owned by the German brake producer Robert Bosch. This occurred just as Pat Buchanan denounced corporations like GM for cutting jobs through downsizing and outsourcing.[41]

The Dayton strike lasted seventeen days and closed down all but one of GM's assembly plants in the US, Canada, and Mexico. But outsourcing was a matter of principle to GM management and they refused to budge, even though the company had been closed down.[42] This was the moment for a bigger response from the UAW and labor as a whole. Both the UAW and the AFL–CIO had new leaders who claimed they were going to take on "corporate greed." The UAW didn't have to call a strike because its members were already out of the plants. It could have organized these tens of thousands of idle workers to demonstrate and call on other unions to join.

The mood across much of the country was such that many from other unions would have joined mass demonstrations, even if they were not ready to strike. It would have been a major political confrontation with "corporate America." Most likely it would also have embarrassed Bill Clinton, who faced an election in November 1996. So, for whatever reasons, the UAW leaders passed up this opportunity to provide broader leadership and publicly announced that the Dayton strike was simply a local plant issue. The Dayton strike won additional workers, as did all the GM strikes, but lost on outsourcing and returned to work. The Dayton strike was not the last such strike, however. Early in 1997, the UAW Local at GM's plant at Janesville, Wisconsin, also struck for and won new jobs. Indeed, a sort of mini-wave of strikes hit both major auto assemblers and supplier firms in early 1997.[43]

The willingness to strike, however, was by no means limited to big industrial situations. Public-sector strikes and actions also saw an increase, as state and local government workers took much of the brunt of government cut-backs. Indeed, globalization deepened these attacks on the provision of public services as local and state treasuries were drained to give tax breaks and subsidies to corporations willing to locate in their area, a form of competition that explained much of the fiscal crisis of government across the world by the 1990s.[44] Major public-workers' strikes occurred in 1996 in California and Oregon, where a week-long general strike of all state workers took on the movement character of those in Ontario and France.[45]

The willingness to strike, even against the odds, had returned to many groups of workers in the US. The Teamsters, under the new more militant leadership of Ron Carey, had led important strikes against Ryder's carhauling subsidary, the major freight employers, and United Parcel Service from 1993 through 1995. In these cases Carey and the new leadership succeeded in beating back most concessions demanded by these aggressive employers and winning some important gains at a time when many unions were still making concessions. Workers at Yale University struck in 1996 to resist attempts to contract out their work. In southern California immigrant Latino carpenters and drywallers struck by the thousands to demand wage increases and union recognition. Indeed, immigrant workers were playing a major role in the new militancy.

The new AFL–CIO leaders were not inclined toward French- or even Canadian-style direct action in the field of politics. But within the activist layer, and even among some of the top leaders of national unions, there was a growing commitment to political action outside, though not necessarily opposed to, the traditional dependence on the Democratic Party. Most of this activity was local in nature. In several US cities, for example, unions joined with other organizations to launch "Living Wage" campaigns that sought to establish a minimum wage above the national minimum for workers in the local labor market. What was new about these types of pressure campaigns was that they were meant to put unions in the leadership, along with others, in fighting for issues that would benefit all workers, particularly low-wage ones. It was a sort of localized social-movement unionism.

After five years of campaigning for the idea of an independent labor-based party, Labor Party Advocates, led by Tony Mazzochi of the Oil, Chemical, and Atomic Workers, decided to take the plunge and found such a party – really more a proto-party. Over 1,300 delegates from five national unions, several regional union bodies, and scores of local unions met in Cleveland, Ohio, in June 1996 to form the Labor Party, as it would be known. The delegates were mostly rank-and-file or local-level unionists and very blue-collar in the majority, although important delegations from service-sector and more heavily female unions such as the California Nurses' Association and a number of locals from the Service Employees' International Union and the Communications Workers of America played a significant part in the convention. After three days of vigorous debate and much caucusing, the new party carved out a radical program.[46]

One of the most hotly debated issues was whether or not to field candidates in the near future. Few delegates thought the new party strong enough to run for office at any level in 1996, but there was a difference of opinion over how long to put such engagement off or perhaps even whether to run candidates at all. It was agreed the new Labor Party would not attempt to run candidates for its first two years. The issue would be discussed again at its second convention some time in 1998. The convention voted to spend the next two years recruiting and participating in various local action campaigns, such as the "Living Wage" efforts.

The Labor Party was one of a number of independent political formations that received backing from one or another sector of organized labor. The other major national organization was the New Party, a national organization that focused on local politics. In Milwaukee, Baltimore, and elsewhere, the New Party participated in the Living Wage campaigns, but also ran candidates for very low-level offices where they were more likely to win. By 1996, the New Party had achieved a significant presence in the state of Wisconsin. Unlike most other third-party efforts, the New Party promoted a "fusion" strategy whereby Democrats would appear on the New Party ballot-line as well on that of the Democratic Party. It also ran independent candidates where that seemed realistic. There was a considerable overlap in the membership of union activists of the New Party and Labor Party in some parts of the country.[47]

Both parties made serious efforts to reflect the racial and gender diversity of the country in their leadership bodies and programs. The New Party appeared to have a greater number of African-American activists where they had local strength, particularly in Milwaukee. The Labor Party's new leadership committee, however, was to be balanced by race and gender. The programs of both parties were clear on social issues important to women and people of color, though the Labor Party convention had rejected the use of the word "abortion" in its reproductive-rights statement. The Labor Party also took strong stands on controversial issues such as opposition to US military intervention to protect anti-worker regimes and support for immigrants' rights.

What was clear was that on social issues, the environment, and other issues usually viewed as difficult for US unions to handle, the Labor Party program and leadership reflected much of the new reality of the working class in the era since the huge social movements of the 1960s and 1970s. The idea of a "pocketbook party" that would steer clear of controversial social issues in favor of simple economic demands was roundly rejected.

The unionists who formed the Labor Party, or participated in the New Party or other state or local independent political activities, reflected the best of the activist layer of the unions in the US. Much of what many of the white male activists had come to accept about the social issues once viewed as exotic or in some way threatening, they had learned from the necessity of reaching out to broader layers of the class and to the other social movements. Such transformations and growth in consciousness among the activists had been seen from the UFCW P-9 struggle in the mid-

1980s up through the fights at Caterpillar and Staley in the mid-1990s. The new leaders of the AFL–CIO encouraged this embrace of racial and gender diversity by the emphasis they put on these – at least at the level of leadership composition and rhetoric.

The qualification on all of this, of course, was that this sector of the activist layer of the unions was still a tiny minority of the total members of the unions, not to mention of the entire working class. Except for specific moments during these struggles, most members played little role in the on-going affairs of the union, and held on to old conservative ideas about society, including one or another degree of racism and sexism. While the active racist minority of working-class people attracted to explicitly racist organizations like the Ku Klux Klan was tiny, the heavy weight of socially conservative ideas, fueled by fears of job loss, was at least as much a barrier to bigger class developments in the US as the caution and "partnership" ideology of the labor bureaucracy.

The hope was that two-sided class war would continue to awaken a broader and deeper activist layer to the class and social realities of their own precarious existence. What was perhaps most hopeful was that there was now a somewhat organized wing of the activist layer of the unions fighting for a progressive, class-struggle agenda – something that had been largely missing during the last period of militancy in the US, from 1967 through 1973.

Class Perception

The evidence of a renewed, if still very basic and often contradictory, class view within the working class was abundant in the mass actions in Europe and North America. Running even deeper, however, across most of the industrial world was a growing sense of anger among working-class people at the attack on virtually all the social and working conditions they had won over the decades. Above all, there was the perception that there was no future for the next generation beyond low-paying part-time or casualized jobs. Better-paid secure jobs were being replaced by lower-paid, less secure jobs or, for many young people, no real job at all. All the things the last two generations of working-class people had fought for and come to take for granted were disappearing before their eyes. And no one, it seemed, was prepared to come to their aid.

In the US, *Newsweek* published an angry statement from just the sort of white male worker that the left had dismissed as hopelessly conservative. This blue-collar pipefitter told *Newsweek*'s readers:

I'm not asking for understanding or sensitivity here. I'm delivering a warning. In similar periods in our history, when the quality of life for working stiffs was diminished to please unfettered business interests, we've had strikes, demonstrations and boycotts. These actions were necessary to support our interests, but they were disruptive to our social fabric. Must we repeat this depressing process every 40 years or so?[48]

The same sort of consciousness could be seen among many of the recent strikers and those fighting to make their unions more democratic and responsive to the issues that now dominated both the workplace and society. *The Unionite*, an unofficial paper published by the Solidarity Action Team of UAW Local 974 at Caterpillar's giant Peoria, Illinois, complex reflected this concern with broad class issues as well as the immediate problems of the strike. Articles on tax policy, income distribution, and other strikes accompanied reports on their own struggle.

In a few cases it went much farther. For some of the veterans of the bitter struggle at A. E. Staley, the conclusion was, "We can see capitalism doesn't work." Dave Watts, the former president of what is now UPIU Local 7837, told one reporter:

Personally, I'm a socialist now. Don't get me wrong, I was brought up Catholic, a capitalist, and like anybody else I want to be comfortable. But capitalism just leaves too many people out.[49]

Strikes and struggles from Staley to the Detroit News Agency, from Yale to the casualized or contract jobs in Los Angeles' construction, building service, and waterfront trucking industries had made all America a war zone by the mid-1990s in the minds of millions of working-class people, whose lives and futures seemed more and more impossible. While few have traveled as politically far as some of the Staley activists, words like "working class" and "class war" were back in the American vocabulary by the mid-1990s.

In Britain, where the type of mass strikes seen on the European continent or in Canada were almost as unlikely as in the US, this type of "us versus them" class consciousness was even more in evidence. A Gallup poll showed that, in 1995, 81% of those polled answered "yes" to the question, "Is there a class struggle?" The figures were slightly lower in 1996 at 76%. Of Labour Party voters, however, 81% answered "yes." Interestingly, the "yes" answers to this annual poll in the 1990s were far above those of the 1960s and 1970s, at 48% to 60%, when unions were seen as a more powerful force and strike levels were much higher. A commentator reporting these figures wrote:

The powerful sense of "us" and "them" conveyed in such attitudes is not a niggling matter of income gradation, but of division across the board.[50]

It was easy to point out that this sort of class consciousness was still criss-crossed with older, socially conservative and, among whites, racist ideas, and that it lacked as yet enough positive political content to pose as an alternative to the neoliberalism and workplace regime it was rebelling against. Yet, in many countries this consciousness was producing a level of action and confrontation with capital from the workplace to the government that no other force in society had been able to rally for some time. For all the changes that had taken place in the past twenty years, the potential power of this sleeping giant, the working class, remained the central strategic force around which "the opposition" could rally if a future was to be found. It was being driven to play this role by circumstances that would not go away.

International Dilemma

By the 1990s, it was enough to utter the word "globalization" to obtain the submission of many workers, unions, or even nations to the needs of capital. In reality, the actual forces of internationalization were contradictory. On the one hand, the fear and insecurity they created tended to paralyse workers and their unions. On the other, their effects pushed workers to action – or at least those workers in the best position to act. Deepening internationalization pulled workers apart as production systems stretched across borders and introduced a new level of competition among workers. At the same time, it bound these workers together in common international production systems, often under a single employer. Global shifts in production destroyed many union jobs in the developed industrial countries, but proletarianized millions of new workers in both developed and developing nations. The world economy led to a political route by most of the traditional working class parties, but also called forth direct political intervention by workers and their unions at one or another level in a growing number of countries.

This political response, however, was still necessarily a national one, while international forces appeared to play a growing role in limiting options. Governments of all stripes were looking over their shoulders at the world-wide bond and currency markets that strongly affected their ability to act in the economic sphere. These markets were among the "governments" of the 200,000 computer terminals in the world's financial markets who conduct "a kind of global plebiscite on the monetary and fiscal policies of the governments issuing currency," that Walter Wriston, former Citibank president, talked of.[51] Added to these private market influences were the multilateral agencies whose job was to facilitate these markets: the World Bank, the International Monetary Fund, and the newly created World Trade Organization. Particularly for Third World nations, these agencies acted as austerity cops, imposing "structural adjustment plans" that invariably lengthened the poverty rolls and weighed heavily on the working class and most of the rural population. This, in turn, brought both retreat by the national political leaders into neoliberalism and revolt among the urban and rural poor who form the working classes of these countries.

"Globalization" could be seen behind both. But "globalization" was typically an amorphous, all-encompassing analytical device that frequently concealed more than it explained. "Globalization" itself needs an explanation and dissection if organized labor is to craft strategies that work. Is the world simply Wriston's 200,000 computers driving infinitely mobile finance capital around the world at the speed of light? What about the production of goods and services? The next three chapters of this book will deal with the processes of economic internationalization.

There is, however, one more contradiction that needs to be mentioned from the start. Crafting a strategy to deal with the changing economic world cannot be reduced to linking together today's existing labor movements in some formal sense. Linking together the walking wounded seldom wins a battle. While there is a revival of working-class and trade-union action across much of the world, the labor movements of most nations are still weakened from the ravages of the past twenty or more years of international restructuring, downsizing, and lean production. Furthermore, most of the leadership of these national unions and labor federations have themselves retreated down one or another path to "partnership" with the very foe they are simultaneously forced to fight from time to time. These leaders, thus, are one of labor's internal contradictions.

Today, as in the past, the top leaders form a bureaucratic layer at the pinnacle of organized labor that by nature is cautious. By training and profession, this layer is composed more of negotiators than fighters, although they will at times fight. By virtue of their position in relation to management, they straddle ground that lies somewhere between the capital they confront and the rank and file they represent. In this removed social place it is hard to take the day-to-day issues of work as seriously as the workplace activists or the ranks do. It is easier for these leaders to negotiate across-the-board wages and benefits than to tread on management's toes in the workplace – or even support those below who would do so. As in most things in real life, there are exceptions, but this picture of a cautious, in some cases retreating, leadership is a fact to be dealt with if labor is to become strong again.

The activist layer below them acts as a pressure that sometimes drives the top leaders to action, often helps create or deepen differences within the bureaucratic layer, and sometimes replaces them altogether. But this activist layer is affected by the fears and demands of the majority of the rank and file. At times, the demand for action comes from below and the activists, in turn, take action or pressure the top leaders to act. The ranks look for leadership as well and are more likely to find it among the activists. But fear of job loss has been a strong force for years and will not simply disappear, so that many within the rank and file will continue to act as a conservative force much of the time.

As any number of the struggles described throughout this book show, the rank and file is capable of great acts and of transforming itself through these actions. Insofar as these kinds of confrontational acts become more or less a feature of the growing resistance to the effects of globalization and neoliberalism, the opportunity for a greater transformation of consciousness and, hence, of what seems possible is inherent in the period unfolding before us. While romanticizing the rank and file will not help, it is, nonetheless, in the working class that hope for the future lies.

Unions today are contradictory organizations in which different groups play different roles at different times. Just as the working class is not some undifferentiated mass, so the unions and other working-class organizations are complex organisms. What seems clear, too, is that deep changes in these organizations are required to make them strong enough to rise to the difficult tasks of the day, particularly that of a new labor internationalism. To involve the millions, today's unions need to be more democratic. Any notion of "partnership" with capital needs to be discarded. As one American auto worker put it, "We need a partnership with the poor, not management."[52] This implies a more positive approach to other social-movement organizations that reflects the diversity of the class. In most cases, positive change in the unions and other working-class organizations will come from below – from some combination of actions by the activist layer and the rank and file. The goal of these changes is a social-movement unionism that is internationalist in outlook and practice. This is the perspective that informs this book.

Part I
Capital's Offensive

2

A Certain Kind of Globalization

Beginning in the 1980s and persisting into the 1990s, the world experienced a crisis in employment. By 1996, the International Labor Office estimated that nearly a billion people were either unemployed or underemployed across the world. In the developed industrial world as a whole at least 34 million were out of work, with unemployment rates hovering chronically above 10% in many of these countries. Disguising deeper employment problems, particularly in the United States and Britain, where official rates were lower, was the rise of part-time and temporary employment in place of "steady work." In eastern Europe and the former Soviet Union, where governments were abandoning centralized planning for market-based economies and isolation from the world market for rapid integration, economic activity actually dropped, while unemployment climbed from almost zero a few years previously to above 10% across the region.[1]

By the 1990s in the Third World, some 75 million people a year were being driven from their country of birth in the world's less prosperous nations in search of asylum and/or employment elsewhere. For those left behind in the less developed countries, high unemployment was compounded (some would say mitigated) by the growth of the informal sector, where millions eked out a living in their homes or in the streets of exploding urban conglomerations.[2] Only a handful of small countries in Southeast Asia seemed to defy the trends, and even these faced the beginnings of recession and industrial restructuring by the mid-1990s.[3]

Despite the promises and predictions of neoclassical economists and neoliberal politicians that deeper world economic integration and regulation by market forces would (eventually) bring prosperity as the world's resources were more efficiently allocated, the employment crisis grew as the process of globalization proceeded. The coming of recovery following the recession of the early 1990s did not bring relief to most countries, and it became clearer to millions that the so-called "efficiency" of the market or the competitiveness of business ran counter to the economic well-being of the vast majority. Partly a consequence of policy, partly of countless business decisions, partly of technology, and partly of the opaque forces of the market, this crisis in the provision of the means by which a majority of the world's people make a living deepened as international economic integration deepened.

The problem was that the world was not simply becoming more economically integrated, it was becoming more capitalist. As trade and investment barriers fell, government ownership and planning shrank, and private corporations became the major organizers of the world's economic activity, competition and its effects (such as workforce reduction) became more volatile. In terms of geographic reach, market penetration and regulation, and private ownership, the world has become more thoroughly subjected to the reign of a system in which the unending accumulation of capital is the object and profit the sole measure of success.

Globalization is a process, not a fact of life. The deepening of economic integration under capitalist terms is a reality, but its effects are very different in different parts of the world. Although deeply affected by this process, most world economic activity occurred within, not between, nations. The world remained a patchwork of national economies and economic regions tied together by those forces associated with the idea of globalization. The notion of a single seamless world economy was still far from a reality in the mid-1990s. What was real, however, was the universalizing of capitalism: operating both nationally in more places and internationally at various levels, always with profound results.

One result was the global jobs crisis, another was the following obscene fact reported by the United Nations:

> Today, the net worth of the 358 richest people, the dollar billionaires, is equal to the combined income of the poorest 45% of the world's population – 2.3 billion people.[4]

This system has now become world-wide. At the most obvious geo-political level, the collapse of the Communist regimes of eastern Europe and the Soviet Union at the end of the 1980s opened vast new territories to capitalist social relations and market functioning where only marginal trade with and borrowing from Western capitalism had existed for decades. This unprecedented transition had brought over 400 million people and some $1.5 trillion in gross domestic product into the world capitalist economy by 1994. If China and Vietnam are included, another

1.3 billion people and \$538 billion have come more or less directly under the regime of capital and its world market.[5] While few would mourn the passing of the dictatorships that dared to call themselves "socialist", the applause for the new market regimes has faded fast.

Somewhat less dramatic, but of at least equal significance, was the rise, from the late 1970s onward, of neoliberalism: the policy of dismantling much of the national regulation of economic life throughout the already existing capitalist world in favor of market governance, a process euphemistically referred to as "reform" or "liberalization." A sign of this was the fact that of the 373 national legislative changes governing foreign investment during 1991–94 in countries surveyed by the United Nations, only 5 "were *not* in the direction of greater liberalization."[6] Equally important was the accelerating elimination of publicly owned industry and services. Between 1988 and 1992, the world-wide sales of state-owned enterprises amounted to \$185 billion, not including the \$25 billion in privatizations in the former East Germany or an additional \$106 billion in commitments to purchase state-owned assets.[7] Then, of course, there were the multilateral trade agreements of the early 1990s that further opened the world market and restricted national regulation of trade and investment: the Maastricht Treaty, North American Free Trade Agreement, and the World Trade Organization, which supersedes and broadens the General Agreement on Tariffs and Trade.

"All that is Solid Melts into Air"

Taken together, these changes in geographic scale, regulatory regime, and ownership patterns are unprecedented in the rapidity, scope, and depth to which the world has been subjected to the forces of capitalist accumulation and market regulation. Even before the collapse of Communism, economic geographers Michael Storper and Richard Walker styled the new economic world as "a mosaic of unevenness in a continuous state of flux." Peter Dicken, whose *Global Shift* is the virtual textbook on globalization, calls today "an era of *turbulence* and *volatility*."[8]

So rapid and disruptive has been this combined process on the transition of the countries of eastern Europe and the former Soviet Union from centrally (and bureaucratically) planned and regulated economies to the new market-based capitalism that the World Bank chose to quote Karl Marx in the introduction to its 1996 *World Development Report*, which focuses on the transformation of the former Communist countries.[9]

The quote, which comes from the *Communist Manifesto*, is worth noting because of what it says about the way in which the economic system the

World Bank holds so dear actually spreads and the class that commands the system acts. In somewhat fuller form it reads:

> The bourgeoisie cannot exist without constantly revolutionizing the instruments of production, and thereby the relations of production and with them the whole relations of society.... Constant revolutionizing of production, uninterrupted disturbance of all social conditions, everlasting uncertainty and agitation distinguish the bourgeois epoch from the earlier ones. All fixed, fast-frozen relations, with their train of ancient and venerable prejudices and opinions, are swept away, all new-formed ones become antiquated before they can ossify. All that is solid melts into air, all that is holy is profaned, and man is at last compelled to face with sober senses his real conditions of life and his relations with his kind.
>
> The need of a constantly expanding market for its products chases the bourgeoisie over the whole surface of the globe. It must nestle everywhere, settle everywhere, establish connections everywhere.[10]

Though the language may seem old fashioned, the concepts are surprisingly up-to-the-moment in three important ways. First is the constant changing of the way goods and services are produced – the revolutionizing of the instruments of production. Certainly the alteration and adaption of mass production, Taylorism, and automation to lean production, team and "quality"-based work systems, and robotization and information-based technologies represents such a revolutionizing of the instruments of production – one that often seems to have no end itself.

Second is the disruption of social life. Here Marx was referring primarily to pre-capitalist societies, but it is evident that changes in production (downsizing, plant closings, contingent jobs, etc.) have reshaped the towns and cities we live in, the jobs we hold or lose, and the ways we relate to one another within and between nations. The unemployed and under-employed, the migrants and the homeless all stand as the symbols of the chain of social dislocation wrought by the race for profit and accumulation.

Finally, there is the concept of globalization itself. Writing in the middle of the nineteenth century, Marx saw the international spread of capitalism as inherent in the system and already well under way. Unlike much of the formal or academic discussion of globalization today, however, Marx did not see this as a process removed from human activity. The spread and constant renewal of capitalism has a human agent, the "bourgeoisie" or capitalist class. Increasingly organized today at its commanding heights in giant, transnational corporations, this class itself faces the dilemma of having the power to reshape the face of the earth through its thousands of daily decisions; while, at the same time, being subjected to the laws and tendencies of the political economy from which it so richly benefits.

Indeed, much of what appears as irrational (short-sighted profit-taking, disregard for its traditional national consumer base, defiance of environmental limitations, etc.), is rooted in this contradiction.

The capitalist system is driven, as its neoliberal policy-makers and apologists never tire of telling us, by competition. But it is not the orderly and largely passive "perfect" competition envisioned in their theories – a competition always tending toward a peaceful equilibrium and an optimal allocation of resources. Rather, as economist Anwar Shaikh put it, "It is war, in which the big devour the small, and the strong happily crush the weak. The laws which competition executes in turn frequently execute many competitors. And the principal weapon of this warfare is the reduction of production costs . . ."[11] It should be underlined that the object of this warfare is the highest rate of return on investment possible.

Indeed, the competition itself is rooted in the increase of the size of the capital (usually organized as a corporation or company) through the realization of a profit. This accumulation process is unending. As economist Howard Botwinick puts it concisely:

> the relentless drive to expand capital value is necessarily accompanied by a growing struggle over market share. These two dynamics, accumulation and rivalry, are inextricably bound up with one another.[12]

This relentless competition, in turn, means that far from quietly tending toward some equilibrium, capitalism is regulated by constant crises, some deep and long-lasting (like the Great Depression or the persistent crisis of profitability since World War Two), others brief but repetitive (as with business-cycle recessions like 1981–83 or 1990–93). Competition fuels crisis, among other ways, by driving firms to invest more and more to improve efficiency and reduce costs. Under these circumstances, the stock of capital (and the production materials it requires) tends to increase faster than the size of the profits generated by labor, even when, as recently, those profits grow quite dramatically. Thus, the ratio of profits to capital, the rate of return (profit) on this mounting investment, tends to fall.

The irony is that the amount of profits can grow and the size of the capitals (companies or corporations) become massive and the capitalists still face a falling rate of return. There is no crisis in the wealth amassed by those who command and own these businesses. Indeed, throughout the world the rich have been getting richer the more the rest of us are subjected to the socially disastrous results of their decisions – as the UN report on the world's billionaires reminds us.

As we shall see, in the US and increasingly elsewhere, an enormous intensification of work associated with downsizing and lean production has produced higher productivity in many industries, increasing the amount of profit produced by labor. But it is the rate of profit, not just the amount of it, that matters in the world of business competition. It is as though a rising surf of profits is overwhelmed and buried beneath a tidal wave of accumulated capital.[13]

Thus, the twin motors of competition (as in warfare) and crisis (particularly in the rate of profit) drive capital abroad in search of lower production costs that, it is hoped, will improve returns on investment. This is not simply a matter of optimal business choices in the search for what is best for the business, but also of what capital is fleeing (below-average rates of return on investment, high taxes, other businesses that have achieved lower costs or higher efficiency), on the one hand, and the real alternatives, on the other. The flight abroad, then, where costs are presumed to be lower, is one in search of above-average rates of profit, even where the gains are marginal. This is the age-old secret behind the global imperative of capitalism. Real capitalist competition is the root of both its crisis and its drive to globalization.

Crisis and Integration: A Long View

The road to world-wide integration of economic activity under capitalism has been long and turbulent. In 1820, for example, trade accounted for only about 1% of world economic output. By 1913, however, it had grown to 8.7%. This growth had been marked by a series of crises and financial panics in the 1870s and 1890s, and in the early years of the new century. What was even newer about the period from 1870 through 1913, according to an OECD study, "was a massive flow of foreign capital, particularly from the UK, which directed about half its savings abroad." Much of this went into railroads, which helped intensify international integration.[14] It was this export of capital that both the British liberal J. A. Hobson and the Russian revolutionary V. I. Lenin saw as underlying the scramble for colonies that eventually pushed the European powers toward war in 1914.[15]

Yet, by today's standards, the level of global integration was low. While some countries like Britain or Germany had high ratios of exports to domestic output (17.7% and 15.6% respectively in 1913) the US had only 3.7%, Russia 2.9%, and Japan 2.4%.[16] By 1994, in comparison, exports accounted for about 17% of world output, almost twice the rate of 1913. For the US it was about 8%, while for (the new capitalist) Russia it was 14%, and for Japan it was 8.7%. Britain was up to 20%, while Germany sent 21% of its output abroad in 1994.[17] Clearly, in trade terms the world is far more integrated today than when Lenin wrote *Imperialism*, with what now seems the ironic subtitle: *The Highest Stage of Capitalism*. Even the flow of capital abroad that impressed Hobson, Lenin, and others at that time was small compared with today's. The stock of capital (foreign direct investment – FDI) invested abroad in 1914 was $143 billion (roughly, in 1990 dollars) compared with $2,135 billion in 1993. By this definition, direct overseas investment (in the form of ownership) grew by fifteen times compared with a tenfold growth of world output in these eight decades, indicating that it was accumulation rather than trade that led the process.[18]

This growth in integration, however, has been far from linear. The growing integration of the world economy from the early nineteenth through the early twentieth century was shattered by three decades of war and crisis from 1914 through 1945. Economic competition turned into military confrontation in 1914 and again in 1939. The Russian Revolution pulled the vast collection of nations that composed the Tsarist (and later Stalinist) empire out of the world market after 1917. The world market itself fragmented as the major powers (Britain, France, US, Japan) formed rival currency and trading blocs. Faced with wild accumulation in the US and stagnation in Europe, the world careered toward the Great Depression, fascism, and another world war. Probably at no time has capitalism had less support around the world than in the years between and just following the two world wars. At no time had the system plunged so many people into economic deprivation, political repression, and total warfare.[19]

As Europe and Asia recovered from World War Two, the process of world economic integration resumed. World exports grew by ten times from 1950 to 1992 in real terms, doubling as a proportion of world output from 7% to almost 14%.[20] The accumulated stock of FDI, the most important kind of overseas investment, increased by five times in real terms from 1960 through 1993, reaching a total value of $2.1 trillion.[21] Never before had so much cross-border economic activity occurred.

The content of international economic activity also changed. Whereas prior to World War One most trade and foreign investment had been in primary agricultural and mining products or in improvements in transportation and communications, the driving force of the globalization process that began around 1950 was manufacturing. The proportion of manufactured products in total merchandise trade rose from 52% in 1952 to 73% in 1988. As a 1989 GATT (General Agreement on Tariffs and Trade) report noted, "manufacturers have played the dominant role in increasing the share of world production traded internationally."[22] Globalization was anything but a "post-industrial" process.

In the late 1980s, services began to surpass goods in total trade, but, as Peter Dicken points out in *Global Shift*, the largest portion of the growth in services came from business services such as telecommunications and financial and technical services related to industrial production and the distribution of its products. The pattern in foreign investment was predictably similar, since it was largely this investment by TNCs that created the trade in both goods and services. In other words, the alleged drive toward a post-industrial world was still pushed by industry itself.[23]

The agent of economic integration has also changed in form. In the era up to 1914 most overseas investment was "portfolio" investment, where the investor owned less than 10% of the overseas operation and the investment was frequently speculative in nature, while direct investment was mainly in railroads and extractive primary industries like agriculture or mining. Prior to 1914, there were at most a few hundred genuine transnational corporations. Today there are about 40,000, and they invest in every conceivable type of goods and service production. Their assets in 1992 were $3.4 trillion, of which $1.3 trillion was outside their "home" country. The sales of their overseas affiliates alone amounted to $5.4 trillion by 1992, which exceeded world exports of goods and services of $4.9 trillion.[24]

Indeed, the transnational corporations (TNCs) changed the shape and content of international integration. By the 1990s the TNCs dominated world trade and the "arm's length" trade between small nationally based producers envisioned in classical and neoclassic economic theory had all but disappeared. Trade was less and less between nations and more and more between or within capitalist corporations. The United Nations estimates that TNCs accounted for two-thirds of the value of all exports by 1993. Half of this, or one-third of total world trade, was intra-firm trade; that is, cross-border transactions between affiliates of the same corporation. Intra-firm trade for US TNCs was 42.4% of the parent firms' exports and 63.8% of their foreign affiliates' exports trading within the channels of the same TNC. The overall proportion of intra-firm trade for Japanese corporations was about 50%, while that for British firms was as much as 80%.[25]

Much of this "trade" is the basis of internationalized production, the newest and one of the most important aspects of today's globalization process. Indeed, the UN estimates that if all international transactions of TNCs are taken into account, including the huge overseas sales of foreign affiliates, by the early 1990s "only about one third of international transactions are not associated with international production."[26]

What is clear is that today's world economic integration is both deeper than and different from either of the two major epochs (1870–1914 and 1914–45) that preceded it. Trade and foreign investment compose a greater part of the world's economic activity. TNCs sit astride both of these aspects of integration and themselves form the major active force for integration.

As massive as these TNCs are, however, they are not monopolists in the classic sense. For one thing, even as they grow in size and consume one another through mergers and buyouts they proliferate in numbers. By the early 1990s, there were some 37,000 TNCs with 170,000 foreign affiliates. By 1994, only a couple of years later, there were 40,000 TNCs with 250,000 overseas affiliates.[27] Even by the conventional definition they are not monopolies in the context of the world market. In any case, this conventional "quantity" theory of competition misses the deeper point that the process of capitalist accumulation is what drives competition, regardless of the number of players. Far from being incompatible with competition, the growth in the size of businesses, their accumulation of capital, pushes them toward greater clashes with one another. Indeed, it is the constant clash of the TNCs, driven by their need to accumulate, that gives rise to the crisis that has driven globalization, in fits and starts, itself.

Crisis and Expansion since 1950

The deepening of international economic integration since the end of World War Two has not been a smooth or linear process as is often suggested in mainstream accounts. Prior to the 1990s, most conventional (neoclassical) analyses saw the rise of the TNC as a consequence of the continuous growth of trade. The argument went that increased world trade created a larger market, which was in turn an incentive for businesses to seek economies of scale through growth. The organization of production across borders, in this theory, is explained largely by the savings in international transaction costs (of doing business between different firms) to be had from bringing production under one corporate roof. While more up-to-date neoclassical analyses admit that in recent years, on the contrary, it is the growth of TNCs and their foreign investment that has spurred the growth in trade, their theoretical framework remains untouched.[28]

What is argued here is that the process of international integration has been led by overseas investment (accumulation), much of it in internationalized production systems. This has created more and larger TNCs, which, in turn, have promoted increased trade. A huge portion of the value of this trade, as high as 80% by one estimate, is in the capital and intermediate goods consumed by businesses in the production process.[29] In other words, it is the accumulation process that has expanded the world market and deepened the globalization process. With the beginning of the crisis of accumulation, however, trade slows down, along with growth in general, but, in reaction to the falling rate of profit, foreign direct investment speeds up as capital seeks higher profits.

After a period of recovery from the devastation of the war in Europe and Asia the rate at which trade grew accelerated. In the years from 1950 through 1973, world trade grew by an average of 7% a year. With the coming of recessions in 1974, the early 1980s and again in the early 1990s, trade slowed by almost half, to an annual average of 3.7% from 1973 through 1992.[30] The world stock of FDI, on the other hand, doubled from 1960 through 1973, and then from 1973 through 1993 grew by ten times. This race of foreign investment ahead of trade and national economic growth became spectacular in the second half of the 1980s (between the recessions of 1981–83 and 1990–93), when FDI grew at twice the rate of trade and four times that of world-wide gross national product.[31] With the coming of economic recovery after the recession of the early 1990s, FDI again leaped forward, growing by 9% in 1994 and 40% in 1995. In comparison, in 1995, world exports grew by 18%, while world domestic investment grew at 5.3% and output by only 2.4%.[32]

It is in the years since the 1950s that the phenomenon of intra-firm trade became significant as a result of the internationalization of production. While national accumulation slowed down, international accumulation accelerated and the so-called "global factory" was born. Capital was attempting to solve its accumulation (profit-rate) problem by expanding abroad in search of even marginal increases in the rate of return. The process of globalization accelerated and deepened – and with it the crisis in employment.

3

North–South Divide: Uneven Development

The internationalization of economic activity and the globalization of capitalism have altered the economic geography of the world in many ways in the past two decades. Not only have vast areas of the world been pulled into capitalism's world market, but enormous changes have taken place in the relative positions of the major capitalist actors and, hence, the location of much of the world's economic activity. The explosive rise of Japan as a pre-eminent economic power, the successful industrialization of the smaller Asian "Tigers" (Hong Kong, South Korea, Taiwan, and Singapore), and the entrance of China as a potential power-house have all shifted world economic activity toward East Asia and the Pacific Rim. The once near-hegemonic position of the US in the world economy has given way to a more equal status for the European Union and Japan. For example, where the US had provided almost half the world FDI in 1960, it provided little more than a third by 1985. Japan and Germany, which together provided less than 2% in 1960, were responsible for 20% by 1985.[1]

The structure of the world that has emerged, however, is even more fundamentally defined by two structural (more or less geographic) fissures or fault lines: one old, one new. The new geographic fissure in the world is the emergence in the last fifteen years or so of three major economic regions composed of the countries of North America and the Caribbean, East Asia, and Europe. These regions are clustered around one or another of the three giants of the world economy that the United Nations calls the "Triad": the United States, Japan, and the European Union. These three geographic regions form the territorial basis of most internationalized production systems. This dimension of economic geography has important implications for the strategy of worker organizations, particularly unions, and will be discussed in the next chapter.

The old fault line is the division of the world into wealthy and poor countries: the economic North, with about 15% of the world's population and around 80% of its economic output, and the South, with 85% of the world's population and 20% of its output. Most of the former (or liberalizing) Communist countries fit into the economic South regardless of their actual location, if only because their economies have collapsed to that level. They will be regarded as part of the economic South in this book, even though many were not part of the Third World as that used to be thought of. There are also a handful of Third World countries which have reached the threshold of Northern status by some conventional measures, notably the city-states of Hong Kong and Singapore, but most industrializing Asian Third World countries remain very poor by Northern standards.

The significance of the North–South division of the world for trade unions and workers everywhere is simply that the persistent and enormous gap between wages and incomes of workers on opposite sides of this fault line is the basis of the competition among these workers – a competition that did not exist outside of a few light manufacturing industries only a couple of decades ago. The straddling of this fault line by cross-border (TNC-owned) production systems producing primarily for consumption in the North has changed the nature of entire labor markets and the terms under which workers of both North and South confront their employers. The North–South wage and income gap is, of course, the major reason that corporations based in the North invest in production facilities in the South in the first place.

Neoclassical economic theory predicts that market regulation and internationalization will equalize wages and bring the benefits of industrialization to all – that income convergence, not divergence, should be the course of development. What is clear, however, is that the uneven development of the world economy that began about 200 years ago with the accelerated growth and spread of capitalism, and was carved into the structure of the world through conquest and colonialism, has only increased. So far as wages go, it is now clear that under today's capitalist market regime only a downward trend in the wages of workers in the North could begin to forge an equality, based on mutual poverty. In any case, outside of a handful of small Asian countries, there is no significant trend toward equality, despite the decline of real wages in many developed industrial countries. So far as most of the economic South, including the former Eastern Bloc nations, goes, the persistence of uneven development combined with the intersection of economic regionalization spells disaster. For some parts of the world, notably sub-Saharan Africa and parts of Asia and Latin America, it means exclusion from industrialization and modernization altogether.

North and South: Uneven Development

Despite the massive increases in overseas investment and the considerable industrialization of parts of the South, the distribution of economic activity between the economic North of the twenty-five or so wealthiest (OECD-affiliated) nations and the economic South has not changed much over the years. This fact runs counter to the impression of many union activists in the United States, Canada, and Europe that investment and, hence, jobs are flowing into Third World countries in vast quantities. Nevertheless, while there is definitely an increase in production in a number of Third World nations, the wealthiest countries of the North, where most of the TNCs are based, continue to produce the lion's share of world production and to absorb most of the investment, trade, and profit that flow from it.

There is, of course, some job shift within the major TNCs as a result of their overseas investment. The World Bank, for example, reports that, "60 percent of worldwide growth in the payrolls of multinational corporations occurred in these countries [of the economic South] between 1985 and 1992."[2] Yet, much of the loss in jobs and income among workers in the North is not the direct result of the export of capital or jobs, *per se*, but of a combination of neoliberal policies and cost-cutting efforts within the North itself. In addition, there is real or implied competition between workers in different countries, owing to the enormous gap in labor costs. It is this latter form of competition among workers, particularly through internationalized production, that makes even the relatively small (in global terms) shift of production toward the Third World and former Communist countries so important.

At the same time, the ability of capital to pit workers in lower-wage countries of the South against higher-paid workers in the North and vice versa rests precisely on the maintenance of the enormous income and wage gap between North and South that is the historical result of the uneven development of capitalism on a world scale. Genuine industrial development throughout the Third World or in the now devastated regions of the former Communist world would, over time (and free of severe repression), deprive the TNCs, and capital generally, of this enormous income and wage gap that is the very basis for internationalized competition among workers and the attraction of capital to the economic South in the first place.

The most visible enforcers of this income gap today are institutions such as the World Bank and the International Monetary Fund. As the United Nations' (UN) *Human Development Report 1996* argues, these multilateral agencies at first imposed "stabilization" programs that "involved cutting public spending, reducing wages, and raising interest rates." They have more recently imposed draconian structural adjustment programs that "involved reducing the role of the state, removing subsidies, liberalizing prices and opening economies to flows of international trade and finance."[3] In return for loans, often directed at nothing more than repaying past debt to the leading financial centers of the North, poorer nations are forced to accept austerity programs, plunging the majority of their people into a race to the bottom in which only the TNCs win.

A clear, dramatic symbol of uneven world economic development is the fact that the gap between average income levels in the different regions and nations of the world has widened with the development of capitalism itself. In a study for the OECD, economic historian Angus Maddison divided the world into seven regions with western Europe and its "Western Offshoots" (US, Canada, Australia, and New Zealand) at the top, and Asia and Africa at the bottom. He then calculated that the gap in per-capita income between the richest and poorest regions grew from three-to-one in 1820, to nine-to-one in 1913, to sixteen-to-one in 1992. In other words, the gap grew by more than five times as the world became more capitalist, more industrial, and more integrated. Even the World Bank is forced to admit that in terms of incomes, "Overall, divergence, not convergence, has been the rule."[4]

Looking only at the post-World War Two period, the same gap grew from eleven-to-one in 1950 to twelve-to-one in 1973, and then to sixteen-to-one in 1992. What this indicates is that the income gap, at its extremes, actually grew faster after the 1973 recession and the acceleration of globalization. The gap in average income between the developed industrial economies and the developing world as a whole (not just its extremes), also widened in the past thirty years. In 1960, average income per capita in the Third World was 18% of that in the developed countries; by 1990, it had fallen to 17%.[5]

In terms of global income distribution among individuals, uneven development is reflected in the startling fact that, as the UN reported:

Between 1960 and 1991 the share of the richest 20 percent rose from 70 percent of global income to 85 percent – while that of the poorest declined from 2.3 percent to 1.4 percent."[6]

Despite decades of "development" and the growth of a number of industrial Third World countries in Asia and Latin America, the shift in production from the North to the South has been relatively small. In 1970, the OECD nations of the North accounted for 85.4% of the world's manufacturing output – excluding the Communist countries. By 1987, these same nations accounted for 81.6% of this output. This represented a shift of about four percentage points, significant, but hardly earth-shaking, given all the foreign investment. Using a somewhat broader measure that includes the former Eastern Bloc countries, the UN estimates that the share of developing Third World countries in manufacturing output grew from 11.7% in 1975 to 15.4% in 1993, while that of the former European Communist countries fell from about 8% to 7% over the same period.[7]

Some regions of the Third World did much better than others. For example, East and Southeast Asia's share grew from 4% to 5.4% of world manufacturing output, while that of Latin America fell slightly to 4.5%, and sub-Saharan Africa's remained stagnant and small at 0.3%. Furthermore, throughout the Third World and even in East and Southeast Asia those industries in which these regions had significant shares (excepting oil refining) were mainly in lower value-added producing industries like clothing and footwear. China, often mentioned as a super-producer of the future with a fifth of the world's population, accounted for 2.2% of world manufacturing output in 1993.[8]

The enduring reason for the inequality between North and South is that the wealthy families, businesses, banks, and corporations based in the countries of the North own and control most of the world's capital – whether as money or as plant and equipment. These same businesses in the North exported 94–98% of all FDI and received about 80% of it through the 1980s; that is, most of the time, only about 20% of overseas investment from the North flows South.[9]

The developing nations do better during recessions in terms of inward-flowing investment. The proportion of FDI flowing into the developing countries grew from 18% in 1987–91 to a high of 39% in 1994 and then fell to 32% in 1995 – while that going to the former Communist countries in eastern Europe grew from almost nothing to 3.8% in the same period. Even though total FDI flows shrank during these years, the amounts as well as the proportion going to the South grew. A significant portion of this investment, however, was in privatizations rather than new production facilities. From 1988 through 1992, 14% of the FDI going to Latin America and 67% of that going to eastern Europe was for the purchase of former state enterprises. Even accounting for this, however, the inflows of FDI to the developing countries more than doubled during the 1990s.[10]

Despite the increase of investment by Northern TNCs in the South in this period of rapid internationalization, from 1980 through 1994 the portion of the world's total economic output (GDP – Gross Domestic Product) produced in the North (OECD nations) rose from 71% to 80%. No matter how much these nations shifted investment abroad even as the rate of investment within the North slowed down during these years, wealth continued to accrue to corporations and entrepreneurs in the same handful of countries that controlled the bulk of capital in the world in 1914.[11]

Part of the reason that the economic South remains so far behind the North is simply that FDI flows compose only about 5% of the world's gross fixed capital formation in any year. Furthermore, 80% or more of this FDI went into the North itself through the end of the 1980s. Even when the proportion of FDI going to the South rose, in the first half of the 1990s, an average of almost 70% still went into the North.[12] In fact, the only period in which the gap between North and South was reduced at all was during the period of import-substitution industrialization (1945–70), when many of the economies of the South were highly protected from the world market.[13] Clearly, the bulk of capital formation remains in the economic North. It does so, what is more, for reasons inherent in the system itself.

Uneven development between nations and regions is rooted in the same drive toward accumulation and competition that produces internationalization. It is simply the other side of the coin of this competition – that which takes place within and between firms in the already developed nations. The most basic way in which capitalist businesses seek to become and remain competitive is through investment to improve efficiency in existing facilities. In today's world this tendency is evident among firms that seek to imitate the existing "best practice" of the most profitable companies. In manufacturing, the rush to imitate Toyota's superior version of lean production, first by auto producers, then by firms producing all manner of products, is a clear example. The introduction of world-wide telecommunications networks within major corporations, first by banks in the 1980s and now by every kind of business, is another.

This form of imitation is more than flattery, it is the essence of the accumulation of fixed capital. From 1950 through 1992, the value of non-residential structures per person employed grew by 70% in real terms in the United States. Countries that saw much of their physical plant destroyed during the war experienced even faster growth in the same period: Britain by four-and-a-half times, Germany by nearly four times, France over three times, and Japan by a spectacular fifteen times.[14]

Even more characteristic of modern capitalist competition than the building of new business structures, however, is investment in labor-saving and cost-reducing equipment and technology. In today's lean world, this usually means robotics, advanced automation, and information-based technology. From 1950 through 1992, the stock of machinery and equipment per employed person in the US grew by 160%, or more than one-and-a-half times, in real terms. In Japan, it grew by eleven-and-a-half times. In Germany during those years the real value of machinery and equipment increased by seven times, while that of France grew by fourteen times – twice the rate of Germany. In absolute terms the US and Japan each had about $40,000 in accumulated machinery and equipment per worker, while France and Germany each had just over $30,000, and Britain $23,000 by 1992.[15]

Another way of measuring the impact of investment by Northern-based businesses seeking efficiency advantages over competitors is to look at which nations consume the world's production of machine tools. In 1987, the developed economies of the North consumed 62% of the value of that year's sales of machine tools, eastern Europe and the former Soviet Union 22.5%, and the developing nations 14.5%. By 1992, the industrial North was consuming 70%, the former Eastern Bloc countries a mere 6.9%, and the developing world 18.3%. The entire increase in the Third World was in Asia and almost all of that was accounted for by China, South Korea, and Taiwan. The share of the Northern nations would certainly have been larger if 1992 had not been a recession year. In terms of numerically controlled machines, reflecting more closely the "best practice" of industry in the 1990s, four industrial nations (Japan, Germany, United States, and France) consumed 78% of the total value of the world sales of these machines in 1987, and 80% in 1991.[16]

As businesses within the industrialized world compete through investment in technology and/or increased capacity, they grow within the country of origin. This is the simplest form of capital accumulation: the concentration of capital at the national level. Since about 95% of all fixed capital formation is national, as opposed to overseas, and over 70% of such investment occurs within the twenty-five industrial nations of the North, it is clear that competition reinforces the concentration of capital within the North, despite increased flows of that small part of investment devoted to FDI to the South.[17]

It is as the resting place of this capital investment that the nations of the North retain their dominant position in the world economy. As dazzling as the figures for the flows of international finances may be, they are not the true measure of national wealth. As *Business Week* wrote in mid-1997:

What makes a country rich? Not the amount of money in its bank accounts and stock markets. Rather, the true nature of a nation's wealth is its accumulation of the tools of production, such as computers, machinery, and vehicles, combined with the skills and education of its population.[18]

Paradoxically, the rise of internationalized production, in particular, reinforces this concentration of capital within the developed nations as a result of the increased overall capital requirements of this type of production. As Saskia Sassen has shown, the rise of internationally decentralized production associated with lean production has *increased* the central control required by the TNCs. Ironically, the complex infrastructure of control over decentralized production, product flows, and finances becomes more important as the level of technology rises and internationalized systems of production develop. Sassen shows that both the decentralization of production and the rise of world-wide financial markets have increased the need for telecommunications and information technologies in particular.[19]

Speaking of the role of these technologies, she writes:

> These technologies, which make possible long distance management and servicing and instantaneous money transfers, require complex physical facilities, which are highly immobile. Such facilities demand major investments in fixed capital and continuous incorporation of innovations. There are, then, huge entry costs at this point for any locality seeking to develop advanced facilities. Established telecommunications centers have what amounts to an almost absolute advantage.[20]

The increased dependence on infrastructure and producer-service industries is also the basis for the reassertion of select "global cities," located in major nations of the North, as the major power centers in the generation of world-wide accumulation. At the other end of the FDI trajectory in the Third World, this same cumulative requirement for infrastructure and producer–service industries in modern accumulation becomes one more barrier to genuine industrialization.

The importance of telecommunications to the international production systems and financial markets obviously creates the need for telecommunications networks and facilities in the Third World that are compatible with and up to the standards of those now evolving in the OECD nations – digital switching, fiber optics, satellites, wireless services, etc. This implies considerable modernization and investment on an almost global scale. Most of the traffic and basic infrastructure, however, remains within the industrialized nations. It is worth noting that the distribution of revenues from telecommunications services will also become more unequal as privatization and deregulation force the international rates of former national telephone monopolies in the South down to the declining levels of the major operators in the North.

It is indicative of the centralizing tendency of the new systems that the big burst of FDI in telecommunications services from 1985 through 1990 involved acquisitions of telephone companies (many of them recently privatized) around the world by a handful of the largest telecommunications service providers, mostly based in the US, France, Japan, and Germany. US FDI in telecommunications grew eightfold from 1989 through 1991, almost all of it in acquisitions.[21]

Indeed, telecommunications led the phenomenal growth of both FDI and trade in services during the 1980s and accounted for 70% of all foreign infrastructural investment in the developing world in the period 1988 through 1995.[22] But, as Sassen writes:

> Again, a handful of countries account for 70% of global activity in services. There is, then, a reconcentration of international transactions in the highly developed countries and a particularly high concentration of all activity accounted for by the United States, the United Kingdom, and Japan.[23]

Uneven development is also encouraged by the type of investment TNCs make in Third World and former Communist countries in their quest to reduce costs. Investment in another industrial country might well involve major production facilities, like Japanese auto "transplants" in the US or Europe. In the less-developed nations, however, it is more likely that only a portion of production is outsourced or subcontracted for re-export (as in the *maquila* plants of Mexico or the export-processing zones of Asia and the Caribbean) as components for use in the larger facilities of the "home" country.

Although located in the Third World, these export-oriented plants are linked to those in the older centers of production and there are few linkages to the host economy and hence little industrial spin-off. In the case of the Mexican *maquilas*, for example, less than 2% of the inputs were from Mexican sources during the rapid expansion of the 1980s.[24] Technology transfer is limited by the increasingly stringent patent and copyright laws demanded by the TNCs and now encoded in the "intellectual property rights" sections of NAFTA and in the new WTO. As one study points out:

> Studies of investment in developing countries such as Lim and Pang ... have shown that export platforms have fewer links with the local economy than investment oriented to the local market. Too often, countries lure foreign MNE's [TNCs] as a way of compensating for their own inability to stimulate indigenous enterprise. Whatever one hopes to gain from inward investment, whether capital, employment, technology, or exports, studies have repeatedly demonstrated that it can only serve to complement domestic initiatives in the same area.[25]

Another aspect of this division of labor in international production between "export platforms" and the core industrial facilities based in the North is the degree to which they produce different proportions of value added. The more capital-intensive industry of the North, whether in goods production or in capital-intensive services like telecommunications, typically produce more of the total value added than the labor-intensive facilities located in the Third World. There are, to be sure, exceptions and it is likely that the rate at which each worker produces value added may be higher in the South owing to low wages. But the proportion of value added in the final product generated in the "core" operations based in the "home" country or some other country of the North is much greater.[26] Thus, the bulk of value added produced by the overall international production system will remain in the North. Those Third World countries that are the exceptions and have significant capital-intensive "core" facilities, like South Korea, Taiwan, or Brazil, are those that form the upper layer of the South.

FDI as well as portfolio investment in the South also tends to reinforce the position of the Northern TNCs because they are the destination of the profits from their overseas investment, and the interest and principal on Third World debt. Certainly, a significant proportion of the profits from investment in the Third World and former Communist countries returns through the various circuits of capital to the centers of accumulation embodied in semi-finished industrial goods, transfer prices, repatriated profits, interest on the loans that financed investment, or even as flight capital to the North, which alone amounted to about $300 billion in the 1970s and 1980s. The growth in speculative portfolio investments and privatizing auctions in Latin America since 1989, for example, has increased the flow of rewards Northward.[27]

Virtually all the debt accrued by the elites of Third World and former Communist nations is owed to money-center banks or international financial institutions in the industrial nations, particularly the US, Britain, and Japan, or is speculated on as bonds. This debt doubled from 1980 through 1994 to almost $2 trillion. As a proportion of the GNP (Gross National Product) of all these nations it rose from 26.5% to 37.6% in the same period. The annual service on this debt consumed almost 17% of the South's exports by 1994, up from 13% in 1980. Statements from governments and banks in the North that the Third World debt crisis was resolved by the early 1990s meant only that the nations of the South were meeting their payments regularly and default was not likely. That is, enormous amounts of capital in money form were flowing both into the South and back into the North.[28] Hence, no crisis.

The debt, whether initially borrowed in the 1970s by Third World elites and governments or the 1980s by crisis-ridden Communist regimes, is also the excuse for the punitive structural adjustment/export-oriented policies imposed by the IMF and World Bank. This too contributes to the stagnant or declining position of many nations of the South in the globalization process. Formerly protected industries are destroyed, government employment and services are reduced, local businesses are replaced by international retailers, and non-traditional agro-business exports replace domestic food production. Indeed, the overall orientation of the economy is altered to suit the conditions of the world market. Increasingly, these countries are dragged deeper into a world market (global GDP) that is growing at half the rate of trade. Clearly, not everyone can win in such a situation.

Not even the expansion of trade expected from the liberalizing impact of the World Trade Organization (WTO), however, holds out much hope for the economic South. Even the official figures from the World Bank and OECD published at the time of the signing of the WTO pointed toward little growth and continued unevenness. The often-mentioned World Bank estimate of $213 billion or the 1992 World Bank–OECD estimate of $274 billion in increased world GDP by 2002 represents less than a 1% gain (above "normal" growth) by the end of that period, with less in earlier years. But as the OECD also points out, two-thirds of this gain will accrue to the OECD nations – with the European Union countries getting the lion's share ($80 billion by 2002). The shift in trade from 30% to 33% for the "rest of the world" is explained almost entirely by China's recent entry into the world market. The "unequivocal losers," according to the OECD, are Africa, the Caribbean, and Indonesia, with the rest of the Third World unaffected.[29]

In fact, the uneven structure of the world economy means that matters will be far worse than the OECD and World Bank studies make out. Marx noted that while historically commerce begets industry, "industrial supremacy implies commercial supremacy."[30] The old unequal exchange relations have already been growing in importance and are certain to get a new lease on life under the tutelage of the WTO. In terms of trade, over half the exports of the Third World are still in low-priced primary goods, while 82% of the OECD's exports are in higher-priced manufactured goods.[31] Furthermore, the historic direction of primary goods' prices is downward in a pattern characterized by fluctuations; while, in contrast, the direction of the prices of manufactured products is more or less consistently upward.[32] This is a function of "industrial supremacy" of high value-added goods over those with low value added. Its consequence is a long-term deterioration in the terms of trade for Third World countries dependent on primary goods exports, another fact that perpetuates unevenness.

"Industrial supremacy," in Marx's sense, also places the nations of the South at a disadvantage in world trade in an even deeper way. As discussed above, both the international division of labor between high-productivity (capital-intensive) facilities in the North and relatively low-productivity (labor-intensive) ones created by TNC investment in both enclave/branch plant or export-platform operations abroad, on the one hand, and the generally low productivity that prevails in the "host" nation as a result, on the other, mean that the nations of the South face a disadvantage as independent trading powers because of low overall productivity. Only low wages and the general backwardness they are based on sustain their position in the world trading system.

Looking at the factors and dynamics that make nations successful under conditions of free trade, Anwar Shaikh concludes:

> It is only by raising both the level and the growth rate of productivity that a country can, in the long run, prosper in international trade. This may be done through internal means, through (directed) foreign investment, or with the help of other nations. But it will not happen by itself, through the magic of free trade. On the contrary, precisely because free trade reflects the uneven development of nations, by itself it tends to reproduce and even deepen the very inequality on which it was founded. It follows that success in the free market requires extensive and intensive social, political, and infrastructural support. While this may seem like heresy to the free marke-teers of the world, it is nothing new to those familiar with the actual history and practices of successful capitalist nations.[33]

None of this means there is no industrialization within the economic South. Looked at in relative terms, in many of the countries of East Asia and some in Latin America the proportion of industry in total economic output runs at 30–37%, which is comparable with that of most industrial countries of the North. Many of these countries achieved the boost into more industrial status through import substitution industrialization prior to incorporation into the world market as export producers. This state-driven internal import substitution industrialization strategy provided a head start for the export orientation that began in the 1960s or 1970s for countries like South Korea and Taiwan, as well as export late-comers like Brazil and Mexico. These countries tended to have significant heavy industries and development more like that of a Northern country – though they all remain poorer.[34]

However, simply scoring well in terms of the industrial proportion of the economy guarantees neither high incomes for the majority nor perma-nent status as a global player. As Gary Gereffi argues, using the concept of core for the economic North:

Second, while industrialization may be a necessary condition for core status in the world economy, it is no longer sufficient. Mobility within the world economy should not be defined simply in terms of a country's degree of industrialization, but rather by a nation's success in upgrading its mix of economic activity toward technology – and skill-intensive products and techniques with higher levels of local value added. Continued innovations by the advanced industrial countries tend to make core status an ever-receding frontier. Third World nations have to run faster just to stay in place.[35]

The dynamics of uneven development don't simply leave the countries of the South a slightly more industrialized version of their former selves. For the majority, the consequences of globalization and unevenness are contradictory. On the one hand, such industrialization as has occurred has brought countless Third World women into wage-earning employment for the first time. While this doesn't free them from the double duty of home work and wage labor that is the lot of working women the world around, it does weaken the patriarchal domination that has characterized most village life. Although the pay is very low, the hours very long, and the conditions poor, where this employment allows some independence, women express a strong preference for this urban-based employment over village life.[36]

On the other hand, the vast flow of humanity from the countryside to the cities that has accompanied the destruction of domestic agriculture and its replacement with industrialized agro-production has engendered a huge and growing informal sector of self-employed, semi-employed, and underemployed workers throughout the Third World. The consequences of this for workers everywhere are severe. As one recent study of Latin America put it:

> the absorption of rural migrants and unemployed workers into the growing informal sector (comprising self-employed street vendors, hired hands, workers in small workshops, day laborers, repairmen, prostitutes, domestic servants, and the like) and the spreading shanty-towns has contributed to the restructuring of contemporary capitalism. This large informal sector depresses wages and reduces the costs of reproducing the urban labor force for both local business and TNCs.[37]

This dynamic, spurred by globalization, uneven development, and structural adjustment plans, is at the root of persistent poverty. As the International Labour Organisation (ILO) noted in 1995:

> In many developing countries the majority of the labor force are still employed in the low-productivity rural and urban informal sectors of the

economy. Underemployment is endemic and most of the poverty in these countries is in fact concentrated in these sectors.[38]

This vast impoverished workforce not only depresses wages in the South, but is the source of the competition that affects workers in the North as well. The next chapter will look at the major way in which this competition works, but it should be obvious that the perpetuation of such poverty is not in the interests of workers anywhere – North or South.

Not even the top layer of industrial Third World countries are totally immune to the forces behind uneven development as more and more low-wage nations engage in export trade. Recently, the deepening of world-wide competition and the greater openness of their markets have thrown many of even the most advanced industrializing countries of East Asia into crises that imperil at least some of their industries.[39] For all the progress made by these more industrial countries of the South, it should also be borne in mind that the number of countries with less than 10% of their output derived from manufacturing grew from 24 in 1971 to 42 in 1989.[40]

The expansion and deepening of capitalist market regulation and competition holds out no promise for lessening the enormous income and wealth gap that is the basis for internationalized production and the competition between workers in different countries. This will take major efforts by unions and workers' organizations the world around. In the long run, it will require a change in the entire system of how wealth in its various forms is allocated around the world and within nations: it will take a journey beyond capitalism itself. That journey begins in today's struggles and tomorrow's strategies for cross-border actions that cross the North–South divide.

Limits to Globalization I

Much of what is written about globalization needs to be taken with a pinch of salt (and perhaps a shot of tequila as well). For one thing, as the analysis above shows, the uneven nature of the way in which capitalism spreads its tentacles around the world creates a self-limitation to that spread and to the degree to which genuine industrialization or development takes place. For another, capitalism is a crisis-ridden as well as crisis-driven system. While trade and foreign investment have grown significantly, the basic process of accumulation has slowed down with the falling rate of profit. The total drop in the rate of return on capital from the end of World War Two to the end of the 1980s was estimated to be 25% for the US by Shaikh and Tonac in *Measuring the Wealth of Nations*.[41]

Obviously, such a decline would lead to a slowdown in growth. Indeed, for the OECD nations as a whole, gross fixed capital formation fell from an average of 22.2% of GDP in 1960–73 to 21.3% in 1980–89 to 20.4% in 1990–93. As would be expected, real GDP also grew more slowly for these industrial nations: 4.9% in 1960–73, 2.6% in 1979–89, and 1.7% in 1989–93.[42] Slower growth in turn implies less ability to expand or globalize unless or until the system resolves its profitability crisis.

Higher growth rates in a few East Asian Third World countries, which are already slowing down, do not really offset this problem because they account for such a small proportion of the world's output. Furthermore, the intermediate status that most of these countries have simply creates more unevenness. At the other end of the economic South is sub-Saharan Africa, which has fallen further down the economic ladder. Similarly, within Latin America a certain polarization in economic circumstances has left some nations, like Bolivia, Haiti, Honduras, and Nicaragua, far behind. Far from some sort of global homogenization, the spread of capitalism has created even more economic fragmentation. The increasing openness of markets does not remedy this, it compounds it.

Clearly, the combined forces of the crisis of accumulation and uneven development are a barrier to anything like total globalization as its advocates usually envision it. Capital attempts to reinforce its centers in the heat of competition at the same time as it seeks extra profits abroad. This is limited to a handful of nations whose export strategies tie them to a small number of more prosperous countries – and, to a lesser extent, to the low-income nations in their region as well. Integration between these few countries is deepened, but it is hardly global. Entire regions of the world are left out of development, even as they are subjected to world market forces.

There is a good deal of truth in what the author of one textbook said when he wrote, "the traditional *international* economy of *traders* is giving way to a *world* economy of *international producers*."[43] Yet, there remains a difference even in the ways in which the process of globalization and the wealth of nations are measured. As the *Business Week* quote cited on page 57 argued, the true wealth of nations is the measure of its capital stock.[44]

Globalization, on the other hand, is almost always calculated in terms of flows of trade, investment, and, most recently, burgeoning financial markets – basically in terms of the circulation of money. Adding up the "tools" of the world tells you nothing about international integration or economic power since they are so unevenly distributed. Capital, the heart of wealth and power, is still measured by firms (ownership) and nations, the degree of globalization by cross-border transactions. This, in itself, speaks volumes about the limitations of globalization as a useful analytical concept in unraveling the power relations of today's capitalist world. While there are powerful international market forces, world-wide corporate operators, and production systems that stretch across borders, there is no seamless global market, no corporation operating with the same weight everywhere, no production system that spans the entire world. What is global is capitalism as an economic system. Just how it organizes production systems across borders is extremely important in figuring out labor strategy and will be discussed in the next chapter.

4

Corporate Power and International Production

The second, more recent, structural division of the world is that between the three major economic regions clustered around the three economic superpowers that the United Nations calls the "Triad": the US, the European Union, and Japan. Each of these regions is characterized by intense trade and investment among the countries in the region, with corporations based in the major power playing the dominant role. In the case of the US and European Union formal multilateral agreements on trade and investment (NAFTA, Single European Market, and Maastricht) give the major part of these regions a juridical basis, whereas in the case of Japan the regionalization is informal or limited to bilateral agreements.

What is most important from the point of view of union and worker strategy, however, is that what ties each of these regions together is the growth of regionalized international production systems owned and/or controlled by TNCs operating out of the "home" country (or countries) in the North. More often than not these cross-border production systems reach across the North–South divide. This fact simultaneously unites workers across borders in the same production systems, dominated by the same TNCs, who are often the common employer, and, given the enormous wage differences, creates the basis of competition among them. This same force of internationalized production pulls workers apart through competition and pushes them together in common employment and production.

Internationalization proceeds from the growth of large nationally based capitalist corporations through investment, acquisitions, and accumulation abroad. Prior to World War One only a few hundred companies were truly transnational in that they produced goods or services in more than one country. Today, tens of thousands of corporations engage in production in scores of countries. But the shape of this internationalization, its geographic specificity, is determined by how actual production is created and located.

Much attention has been given to the world's volatile, 24-hour financial markets in the literature on globalization. They have their real functions in the circuits of capital and their speculative side in the markets for "derivatives," commodities, and currencies, as well as stocks and bonds.[1] Some of them have a strong disciplining effect on national economic policy – in the North, the currency and bond markets; in the South, commodity markets. But for activists from workers' organizations (and, for that matter, grounded economic analysis) it is the actual production of goods and services that matters most.

Economic geographer Neil Smith put it well when he wrote:

> It is all very well that $500 million can be whizzed around the world at the push of a button, but it must come from somewhere and be en route to somewhere. This somewhere is the production process, where in order to produce surplus value it is necessary that vast quantities of productive capital be spatially immobilized for relatively long periods in the form of factories, machinery, transport routes, warehouses, and a host of other facilities.[2]

It is in these real spaces, not in financial cyberspace, that human beings perform work and earn a living, whether they are employed by a bank in New York, London, or Tokyo, or a garment sweatshop in Los Angeles, Toronto, or Hong Kong. It is also, of course, in the real spaces of production that workers produce the world's wealth – including that portion of it that is "whizzed around the world at the push of a button" – and confront their employers, be they large or small, global or local.

Production Chains

Today very few final goods or services are produced in a single facility in a single location. Even very specialized producers usually depend on others for inputs. On the other hand, the concept of total, vertically integrated production, in the supposed manner of Henry Ford's River Rouge complex, where virtually everything needed to make a car was produced, was always a myth. Ford assembly plants in the "golden age" typically had at least 2,000 first-line supplier plants, despite Ford's attempts to integrate some component production down the "backward linkages" of the production chain. Then, as today, it was not Ford, but GM, whose production was most vertically integrated.[3]

Production of complex goods or services has almost always required a production chain: a series of production phases which are often separated in space and time. The introduction of cost-saving technology in the heat of capitalist competition tends to increase the complexity of both the product and the production process. The production of components, producer services, or other inputs becomes more specialized and the overall production process more extended in both time and space. Production becomes more round about.[4] Even in state-of-the-art lean production, a component cannot arrive "just-in-time" if it has not been made somewhere else at some prior time.

Marx described the dilemma imposed by the increase in capital's spatial expansion in the following terms:

> The more developed the capital, therefore, the more extensive the market over which it circulates, which forms the spatial orbit of its circulation, the more does it strive simultaneously for an ever greater extension of the market and for the greater annihilation of space by time.[5]

The struggle to annihilate space by time has been largely conducted by development of the means of transportation and communication. First, roads and canals; then railroads, steam boats, the telegraph, and the phone; and now multi-tiered containerized freighters and gigantic tankers, interstate highways and autobahns, airplanes, telecommunications, etc., have been the means of reducing the time between spaces of production and/or sales. Indeed, even as the speed and volume of transportation and communications have vastly increased in the twentieth century, their costs have fallen dramatically. Ocean-freight costs, for example, are a quarter of what they were in 1920, while air-transport costs are less than a fifth of what they were in the mid-1930s, and trans-Atlantic phone calls perhaps 1% of their cost in the 1940s, according to World Bank estimates.[6]

Thus, technology enables the greater separation of production locations, making cross-border production chains viable as never before. Given the advance in communications technology, today's ever-so-global major financial institutions can, for example, serve business customers in New York or London, while processing the data used in these transactions in the Caribbean or Ireland. Using efficient transport systems, GM can use Mexican-produced parts in cars assembled in Michigan and sold throughout the US or Canada, or Spanish-made body stampings and/or Czech-made engines in a car produced in eastern Germany and sold in western Europe.

The first and oldest type of international production chain is where production is located in one or another foreign nation for the purpose of producing for that nation's (or adjacent) markets. While the company is operating in several countries, its major final production facilities are located separately in those countries. Production, in this case, is only international to the extent that the parts for production in the "host" country come from the "home" country of the corporation. In general, this was the way in which US auto companies like Ford and GM became international operators in the 1920s and 1930s. In those years they invested in Britain, Germany, Argentina, and Mexico in order to produce for those markets, which were highly protected at that time. For the most part, components came either from the US or were produced in the "host" country. In this case, the production chain ended in the "host" country where the final product was sold. Such corporations may be "global" in reach, but their production is focused on a specific "host" nation.

This kind of overseas investment and production did not have much impact on auto workers or unions in the "home" economies, because these GM or Ford products were not imported into the "home" market to substitute for domestic production. In fact, it was during an expansion of this simple type of international production that industrial unions in the auto industry were born in the United States. While many examples of this sort of "globalization" still exist, a second type has become far more common in the last twenty years.

The second type of overseas production chain is internationalized or cross-border production for export back to the "home"-country market. This is where production for the "home" market (and possibly others as well) is decentralized, with the production chain extending across borders into one or more "host" countries, but the bulk of output being sold in the "home" country. A clear example of this and of the change from the old multinational type is the North American auto industry today. Prior to World War Two production for the US auto market was mostly based in the US, while overseas production was of the multi-country type. Big Three (GM, Ford, and Chrysler) auto production stretched into Canada, but Canadian workers were unionized, with labor contracts and wages comparable with those in the US, and little direct competition occurred. Production in Mexican plants was solely for the Mexican market until the late 1970s.

Things changed significantly after 1978 when the Big Three began investing in Mexico for export to the US This production accelerated rapidly during the 1980s as the Big Three built dozens of parts plants, a number of engine facilities, and even a few high-tech assembly plants in Mexico all of which exported the majority of their production to the US.[7]

Exports to the US and Canada of cars produced in Mexico rose from a mere 20,500 in 1986 to 778,000 in 1995. Following the passage of NAFTA, the top 25 parts suppliers, including Ford and GM, increased the number of plants from 192 to 210 by 1995, with output increasing in value from $6.4 billion to $9.5 billion in 1995.[8]

This new cross-border system meant that workers in Mexico making about $3.50 an hour in 1982 were working in the same production system, often for the same employer, as US and Canadian workers making around $14 an hour. Even the independent parts suppliers that located operations in Mexico during the 1970s or 1980s tended to be US-owned companies with shops in the US, so that auto-parts workers also tended to have common US-based employers. As Mexican wages plunged under the austerity imposed by the administration of Carlos Salinas de Gortari, the IMF's structural adjustment plan, and the 1994 collapse of the peso they caused, the hourly wage gap grew to $1.50 to $17.00 an hour, or in the auto industry slightly less at $3.87 to $24.82.[9] These workers were employed by the same company, contributing to the same product, and working under similar (or worse) conditions, but receiving totally different wages. In effect, by locating (or contracting) even a relatively small proportion of the total value of their production for the US market across the border in Mexico, the Big Three auto makers had created their own internal labor markets and a whole new basis for creating competition among their employees.

Japanese auto makers followed a similar pattern in East Asia, outsourcing more and more component production to South Korea and Taiwan and later to lower-wage locations in Indonesia, Malaysia, and the Philippines. Investment by Japanese auto makers in the US followed a similar pattern. At first, Japanese-owned assembly plants (tagged "transplants" by critics), using parts mainly imported from Japan, were built in the 1980s. Eventually, however, they followed the sourcing patterns of US auto makers, setting up parts plants both in the US and in Mexico for re-export into the US. This was partly due to the rise in the value of the yen, which made importing parts from Japan too costly. This also led Honda to export US-made cars to Japan.[10]

With the opening of eastern Europe, European Union-based auto companies have followed suit by locating or purchasing facilities in the Czech Republic, Hungry, and Poland, where wages are similar to those in South Korea or Mexico. Most of this production is for export (as parts or even cars) into the European Union. Germany, in particular, was binding these countries to its economy. This region was buying 30% of its imports from Germany by 1996, and, as *Business Week* put it, "supplies German industry with cheap factories and labor."[11]

Locational factors and regionalized outsourcing apply within the subordinate free-trade areas as well. The Brazilian auto industry, which shipped 60% of its exports to Europe and North America in 1990, now emphasizes production and sales within the MERCOSUR region of Brazil, Argentina, Uruguay, and Paraguay. Sixty-nine percent of Brazil's auto exports now go to Argentina alone. The industry uses extensive outsourcing, but gets the majority of its parts within the region.[12]

Along with lower wages and costs and a certain pre-existing level of skill, location has become a key factor in the competitive investment calculations of the world's auto makers and other producers of durable goods. Indeed, for industries producing heavy or bulky products or components, the proximity of low-wage, Third World or former Communist nations was central in the drive toward regional, cross-border production systems. It has become a central feature of contemporary lean production as well, as modified forms of just-in-time parts delivery became more important.

Major business-oriented service industries, such as finances, travel, and telecommunications, develop cross-border production chains as they follow industry. Major banks and insurance companies based in the big financial centers of the North, like New York, London, and Tokyo, open offices to finance investments, including mergers and buyouts, in important centers of production in the South. Travel and telecommunications companies follow suit to service both manufacturing and finance, and so on. Deregulation and privatization in all these areas are necessary for the North-based firms to take control or enter the market. Most of this is now underway or has already been accomplished in major Third World countries.

Production chains are established in services mainly by buying up overseas operations. Telecommunications provides a good example. Indeed, major telecommunications companies such as AT&T, British Telecom, most of the US Bell operating companies, France Télécom, Telefónica in Spain, and others have been on a Third World buying spree for several years now. They have also been developing global networks through joint ventures and alliances.[13] The interconnections already exist and only require some reconfiguration and upgrading. Operations in the Third World inevitably require drastic modernization. But the growth of international telecommunications traffic and the proliferation of information-based services also means an enormous investment in the Northern centers of world finance and business. Rapid change, re-engineering, and downsizing occur at both ends of the intensified production chain, creating a crisis for workers and their unions throughout the chain.

The concentration of telecommunications centers in or around cities like

New York, Tokyo, London, and many smaller corporate and financial centers of the North and a few in the South, means that the major telecommunications enterprises in the region tend to dominate the new configurations of ownership and business-oriented service provisions of the region, even as they extend their global reach through alliances much like the auto companies. Unlike auto, however, neither time nor space are barriers to service delivery of telecommunications services anymore. So, for example, British Telecom can conduct the international traffic for the Republic of Georgia's phone service from London. Nevertheless, European operators like British Telecom or France Télécom tend to dominate that region as the national companies are privatized and or deregulated and open competition becomes a requirement under the European Directive on Telecommunications.[14]

Production chains are also value chains in both goods and producer-service industries. The amount of value added created by labor at each phase of production (beyond labor costs) determines the total amount available for profit at the end of the chain. Lowering costs at various phases of production has become a more important part of business strategy as "best-practice" technology has become more wide-spread among competitors. As cost advantages from technology shrink because everyone has the same technology (regardless of how they got it), locational cost advantages become increasingly tempting – and, these days, possible. In practice, corporations will use both technology and location at the same time in hope of achieving some advantage.

Regionalization of Production

If proximity is an important factor in the regionalization of cross-border production, it should be clear that the focus, the end point, of these production chains is where the money is. They are focused on the wealthier markets of the Triad, where 80% of world domestic sales take place and 75% of exports end up.[15] For one thing, the largest producers are necessarily the greatest consumers, since much of what is consumed within a nation is consumed by businesses along the production chain. For example, about 60% of the value of manufacturing production is purchased by companies as intermediate goods.[16] Capital purchases account for another 9–10% of national output.[17] Business and producer services compose another portion of national output consumed by business. Even the average consumer increasingly appears as part of the corporate hierarchy as income distribution shifts upward within most countries of the North.

Owing largely to uneven development, as well as neoliberal austerity the world around, the majority of the world's population is more or less outside the global marketplace altogether. As Richard J. Barnet and John Cavanaugh put it in *Global Dreams*:

> Of the 5.4 billion people on earth, almost 3.6 billion have neither cash nor credit to buy much of anything. A majority of people on the planet are at most window shoppers.[18]

Most of these "window shoppers" live in the economic South. Thus, whether the TNCs are selling their goods and services to themselves, to other firms, or to affluent consumers, the action is where the money is – the Triad of the North.

A TNC creates an international production chain focused on its "home" market or another market within the Triad through investment or purchases of facilities abroad (FDI). This, in turn, creates trade between facilities or contractors of the TNC in the parts or services required to produce the final product (intra- and inter-firm trade). The United Nations Conference on Trade and Development (UNCTAD) has tracked this process in its studies of international integrated production systems. They have shown that the intensities of two-way trade and FDI are significantly greater within each Triad region than world-wide. The intensity of FDI within the regions is somewhat less than that of trade. But this is largely because the big increase in FDI in services and mergers and buyouts between the Triad countries themselves – which statistically reduces the proportion of intra-regional FDI compared with FDI between regions.[19]

This doesn't mean that trade and investment between countries in the different regions aren't important or that there are no truly global production systems. Even within clearly regionalized production systems like those in auto, some sourcing is done outside the region. Furthermore, a few industries like electronics or aerospace have both strong regional and global or interregional production chains. The growth of regionalized international production chains will also tend to increase all international trade generally.[20]

Indeed, today's Triad of major economic regions differs from the battling trade and currency blocs of the 1930s not only in the relative porousness of the markets of the three regions, but in the intensity of investment, trade, and corporate ties that run between them. The regions of the Triad are launching pads for the competitive positioning of the TNCs in the markets of the Triad and, to a lesser extent, the elite markets of the South. The governments of the Triad are dragged into this competition as they compete for TNC investment or as they seek trade advantages for their

TNC "homies." But the Triad nations are inextricably linked by the dense web of corporate interactions that gives globalization its reality as a process.

Nevertheless, the regionalization of production in many important industries, particularly those with a unionized base in both North and South, has strong implications for trade-union strategy at the end of the twentieth century. It is along these regionalized production chains that workers can begin to make contact, to exchange information on corporate strategies, to organize mutual support, and to make common decisions about future actions. It is, after all, one thing to find and sustain contact with one's counterpart across a vast ocean, and quite another merely across an adjacent border. The very measure designed to put one worker in competition with another worker on the other side of the border is also the channel for communication and collaboration among workers across borders. It is a starting point for internationalizing the labor movement itself.

The Hierarchy of Corporate Control

The growth of decentralized production inherent in internationalized production chains and the fact that many of the newer and older production sites are smaller in terms of employment, and possibly physical size, has led to a number of theories about the decentralization of business power. Some postulate the rise of small-business entrepreneurs in industries like electronics as evidence of the growing importance of small business. Others, notably Michael Piore and Charles Sabel, have written about the proliferation of small firms, frequently clustered in industrial districts, as a new era of "flexible specialization" in which both mass production and the corporate giants that once organized it play a decreasing role.[21] These views, however, miss the actual place of such small producers and businesses in the production chains that have evolved in the last ten to twenty years.

Hierarchical business control of the world's production, and particularly that production linked to the world market, is far greater today than at any time in the past. At the top of the production hierarchy sit the top 100 TNCs, all of which are based in developed nations of the North. Not including banks or financial firms, by 1993 these top 100 TNCs owned $3.7 trillion in world-wide assets, of which $1.3 trillion were outside the "home" country. This was a third of all outward accumulated stock of FDI in the world.

TNCs directly employ about 73 million workers, 51 million in the countries of the North and about 12 million in the developing countries. It is estimated that these numbers double or even triple when indirect employment through contractors and other arrangements are included. While even the expanded estimate represents only a small percentage of the world's 2.5 billion-person workforce, it is that part of the workforce that is most transnationalized and most at the center of global accumulation.[22]

The breadth of corporate control, as well as the size of the top TNCs, has grown, in part, through an enormous upsurge in mergers and acquisitions both within and between nations in the 1980s and 1990s – all part of the "war" that is capitalist competition. The dollar value of all cross-border mergers and acquisitions doubled between 1988 and 1995, when it reached $229 billion.[23] This type of activity is referred to as the centralization of capital, the pulling together of existing capitals, or the conquest of some by others, even though it does not necessarily produce fewer firms. It is another, often cheaper, way of extending the market and capital of a company in addition to the concentration of capital achieved by investment in new facilities or equipment. We have seen that a significant amount of FDI flows into the South was in terms of privatization purchases. FDI flows directed at mergers, buyouts, or equity stakes between TNCs in developed nations of the North are even more spectacular.

Between 1990 and 1993, cross-border mergers, acquisitions, or equity stakes composed an average of 70% of the flow of FDI among the developed OECD nations.[24] While the phenomenon of mergers and buyouts is newer in Europe, the advance of economic integration has spurred aggressive cross-border buyouts. Between 1984 and 1991, for example, over 900 mergers and acquisitions took place among manufacturing firms, 141 among financial institutions, and 51 among distribution companies in the European Union. French companies have been the most aggressive buyers, while British firms were the most sought after purchases. In the same period, 85% of inward FDI into the US was in mergers or buyouts.[25] The rate of mergers and acquisitions within the major nations of the North has also been high since the mid-1980s. Only in Japan, among the Triad, were such mergers rare. This was largely because of Japan's already highly centralized system of *keiretsu*, or giant interlocking corporate networks of banks, service, supplier, and assembly firms.[26]

As these corporations position themselves in the major markets through acquisitions, they also extend their production and control abroad. The expanding webs of control that criss-cross the world today can be seen in the rapid proliferation of overseas affiliates from about 174,900 in 1990 to over 251,450 by the mid-1990s. Following the pattern of increased FDI toward the South, the proportion of the affiliates in the Third World and former Communist countries rose from 53% in 1990 to 63% in the mid-1990s.[27]

Few industries have seen as dramatic an overseas expansion and shift in ownership patterns as telecommunications. Until only a few years ago, telecommunications operators were nationally bound in scope, usually a monopoly, and typically state-owned – except in the US and part of Canada. Privatization and deregulation are well underway in both North and South, and yesterday's national company is today's global operator. The change in ownership, however, is all in one direction. The major operators of the North have been buying or constructing facilities in both North and South, creating, as we noted, both global and regional networks or production chains.

The competition for the global and regional business of the major TNCs is increasingly intense. It is more than likely that a half dozen or so of today's biggest companies will dominate world telecommunications services some time in the early part of the twenty-first century. The move toward buyouts has already been joined by mergers among the US Bell companies; formerly seven, they numbered only five by late 1996. In telecommunications centralization is certain to produce fewer North-based major players, who, in turn, control most of the profitable operations of the South. By 1996, even before the ink was dry on the new deregulating Telecommunications Act, the major regional phone companies created by the break-up of AT&T in the 1980s were themselves merging. Southwestern Bell, already part owner of TELMEX along with France Télécom and the Grupo Carso in Mexico, merged with Pacific Tel. Bell Atlantic, with extensive overseas investments, acquired the adjacent giant NYNEX, a major operator in Europe. AT&T, MCI, and Sprint all made alliances or mergers with overseas telecommunications operators in order to compete for the growing global business network market. Europe's national telecom operators moved rapidly to become similar global players. In 1996, British Telecom intensified the global competition when it extended its 20% stake in MCI by completing a merger of the two companies.[28]

To this direct increase in TNC overseas presence must be added the hundreds of thousands of subcontracting relationships. As mentioned earlier, corporate control over these international networks of production has increased, among other reasons, because the high costs of the financial requirements and communications technology needed to operate internationally make the TNCs less willing to take risks. The emphasis on world-wide quality control and standardization characteristic of the current phase of lean production is also a source of increased TNC control over both affiliates and contractors.

As Bennett Harrison argues in his study of corporate control in the global economy, *Lean and Mean*:

> In other words, in many cases the legally independent small firms from which the big companies purchase parts, components, and services may not be all that independent, after all, but should rather be treated as de facto branch plants belonging to the big firms. *Production* may be decentralized into a wider and more geographically far-flung number of work sites, but *power*, *finance*, and *control* remain concentrated in the hands of the managers of the largest companies in the global economy.[29]

The UNCTAD also estimates that there are thousands of "strategic alliances" and joint ventures between TNCs or with local, nationally based firms. Because the relationship here is more complex than that to a supplier, and may or may not involve equity stakes, these types of alliances are often cited as evidence of the decentralization of power. But, as Harrison argues, these too must be seen in the context of international production networks or chains with all of the engineering, financial, and quality controls that implies. Whether we are speaking of a complex alliance such as Europe's Airbus Industrie, or that between British Telecom and MCI to create a global network, or a simpler joint venture like the GM–Toyota NUMMI auto-assembly plant in California, the production systems themselves follow the hierarchical pattern of all capitalist production, while the governing role of the large corporations or governments involved is clear.

As Harrison concludes, concerning the systems of international production that have taken shape in the last ten to twenty years:

> The empirical evidence seems overwhelming that the evolving global system of joint ventures, supply chains, and strategic alliances in no sense constitutes a reversal – let alone a negation – of the 200-year-old tendency toward concentrated *control* within industrial capitalism, even if actual *production* activity is increasingly being decentralized and dispersed.[30]

What emerges, then, is not some disorganized fragmentation of capital into tiny units or isolated production sites. Rather, a clear hierarchy of control dominated by a small number of corporate giants becomes visible. Today's hierarchical production chains are commanded from corporate headquarters mostly in a dozen or so of the major industrial powers of the North, and run down the production chain, sometimes through lower-wage areas of the North, on to the economic South.

In industries like clothing or semiconductors, the production chains often run very deeply into the informal economies of the Third World – all the way down to homework. These are the production chains, populated mostly by women workers, recently made famous by the revelations of child and near-slave labor, and in the early 1980s as one end of the "new international division of labor." Employment patterns and the reach of the TNCs at the very bottom of such chains can be unstable and difficult to trace. Notorious middlemen and jobbers often have more control over working conditions and pay than the small contractors and micro-capitalists that employ many of these women – not only in the Third World but right in the heart of the Triad as well. Even in these cases patterns do emerge, organizations do take shape, and important pressure points do become evident.

The implication of international production chains for labor strategy is that millions of workers across borders and across the North–South divide are linked in common systems of production, which are to a large extent regionalized. The hierarchy of corporate control means that they also share common employers. Thus, if the implied or real competition between workers in the internal labor markets of the TNCs is the problematic side of this coin, the implied or real leverage these workers have over the production chains they work in, and hence over their common employer, is the side on which to base a strategy to counter the competition through common action.

Capital Mobility and Patterns of Regionalization

While regionalization is the rule and the domination of production chains by TNCs generally the case, it is evident that the exact patterns of control or regionalization will differ across industries. Furthermore, as investment patterns change, so will production and ownership patterns, so that the mobility of capital becomes an important issue in any international labor strategy. Much of the popular literature and some more serious theoretical accounts focusing on "deindustrialization" or the "new international division of labor" in the 1970s and early 1980s implied a level and speed of capital mobility that was almost the mirror image of neoclassical trade theory's proposition of immobile capital. In fact, capital is neither infinitely mobile nor absolutely immobile. While physical capital can be transported across borders in some form, TNCs do not usually "move" plants as we often say. They build or buy new facilities and close old ones – or, more frequently, departments or sections of old ones.

For the most part, the mobility of capital, like capital replacement generally, operates through a circuit in which money capital is turned into physical capital, which, in turn, produces an enhanced (by profit) money capital.[31] In general, capital is only mobile because it can be turned into or borrowed as money with which to buy new plant and equipment or to purchase them from someone else through mergers or buyouts. Both the letting-go of older operations and the purchasing or constructing and equipping of new ones are a costly matter and not done lightly. Typically, such business decisions involve long-term planning rather than snap judgements – as the rapid mobility theories some times imply. In practice, as we have seen, the actual shift in manufacturing production of about 4% of the world total from North to South since 1970, while significant, hardly confirmed the deindustrialization thesis of super mobility.

Furthermore, some of the measures of capital mobility are considerably lower in practice than one would expect in the era of multi-trillion-dollar over-the-counter markets in bonds and "derivatives." One indicator of the degree to which some of these more-or-less globalized financial markets actually penetrate nations to produce real capital mobility, as opposed to simple speculation, is the proportion of foreign equities and assets held by major international fund managers in leading developed nations. In 1991, in terms of value, it was 5% for the US, 23% for Japan, 27% for Germany, 3.7% for France, 34.2% for Britain – the US–Europe average being 11.4%. While the fund managers in some countries are obviously more adventurous, the average is fairly low when you consider that most of these foreign assets are those based in other countries of the North. Another such indicator is that the divergence between national savings and investment rates one would expect under conditions of high capital mobility have not emerged. One reason for relatively less capital mobility between nations lies in the global financial regime itself – the uncertainty of currency exchange rates, which can reduce or even wipe out the value of overseas assets.[32] More important than the vagaries of the world financial markets, however, are some of the characteristics of contemporary production and the capital it uses.

The image often put forward by popularizers of the instant mobility of capital thesis is that of a garment sweatshop operator packing up his sewing machines to move abroad when his women workers rebel and demand a wage increase. While such micro-capitalists frequently close and move under such circumstances, it is more likely that these contractors will move across the street than overseas, for they are little more than poor people themselves with scarcely more mobility than their employees. The greater problem in this and similar labor-intensive industries is not one of capital mobility at all, but of the ability of middlemen, jobbers, final producers, or major retailers to change contractors at will. The flexibility of this industry consists in the multiplicity of contractors to choose from in all the major sites of clothing production, North and South.

For most manufacturing industries and heavily invested or "sunk" service industries, genuine capital mobility remains limited by past investment and location. Although much of the computer-based capital of today is much lighter and smaller than in the past, it remains embedded in large facilities such as factories, mills, assembly plants, telecommunications facilities, office buildings, research complexes, and postal or package-delivery systems. Concepts like "the virtual corporation" or "agile manufacturing" rest not so much on capital mobility as on the proliferation of other facilities, much like the bottom of the clothing industry's production chain. Unlike the tiny garment loft, most of the suppliers and contractors in such industries as diverse as food production and refrigerators are themselves relatively immobile for periods of time.

Using the idea of the production chain and the concept of "core" (North) and "periphery" (South) production locations, Roberto Korzeniewicz and William Martin examined the changes in distribution of production of the world automobile industry and two of its major suppliers, tire and steel production, from 1970 through 1987. What they discovered is that for vehicle production itself, there was very little shift from North (core) to South (periphery and semi-periphery) in spite of the rise of the South Korean industry. In the case of tires the shift was somewhat larger, although absolute output still grew in the North, as it also did for vehicles. Only steel saw a shift to the South as the North American and European steel industries downsized drastically in the 1980s and world steel production declined – as did steel as an input into automobiles. Despite the growth of South Korea, Brazil, and Mexico as producers and exporters of vehicles, over 90% of final production remains in the US, Canada, Europe, or Japan.[33]

The strong tendency for major production facilities to stay in the North reflects what was said earlier about the impact of competition on investment and the concentration of capital in the "home" country, as well as the primacy of the Triad markets. All the major firms in an industry like auto must compete with the best practice set by the *regulating capital*; that is, the capital that achieves the lowest cost structure, primarily through the most advanced technology.[34] This explains both the tendency of capital-intensive "core" facilities to stay in the North and much of the enormous job loss in the North itself.

Contrary to much popular thought, it is not primarily investment or location abroad that has been behind the job loss in the auto industry in the US or Europe. Dicken writes:

> Hardly any of these job loses can be attributed to a relative shift of automobile production to Third World countries for, as we have seen, such geographical relocation has been very limited.

Rather, Dicken locates the job loss in new technology, and international sourcing by the big assemblers.[35] The introduction of new technology occurs mainly within the "home" country of the producer as a consequence of competition. While it helps keep production in the North, it costs jobs there as well. He might have added the enormous downsizing and labor intensification associated with lean production as a major contributor to job loss.

Aside from new technology, the work intensification due to downsizing, and the lengthening of work time, the major source of national job loss in the Triad countries of the North in auto and other capital-intensive industries comes from cross-border outsourcing. While the globally sourced "world car" projected by Ford in the 1970s never really happened, the regionally sourced cars of all major players have become the norm. Yet, in the case of the US, much of this outsourced production was still performed within the country – more and more of it in nonunion, lower-wage locations. This is less a problem of international union strategy than of national union policy. Sourcing networks in Europe show the same pattern, with extensive sourcing in countries like Spain and Portugal. Just as US producers in North America have shifted some parts production to Mexico, so European-based producers are shifting some to adjacent former Communist countries in eastern Europe. But the bulk of production and facilities remains in the "core" countries.

As mentioned above, auto production in Japan has followed a similar pattern. At first supplier firms were clustered around the major assembly plants of producers such as Toyota or Nissan. But rising costs, a more competitive atmosphere internationally, and, after 1985, the rising yen led these "reluctant multinationals" to become genuine TNC producers as they outsourced more parts production to South Korea and Taiwan and, more recently, to Malaysia, Indonesia, and Thailand. Simultaneously, however, the Japanese auto makers embarked on a cost-cutting strategy at home, involving massive investments in new technology in their "home" operations, which they hoped would offset the impact of the yen on their prices.[36]

In a service industry like telecommunications the massive sunk investment required in the major centers of the North to produce global networks actually reinforces Northern dominance. The loss of jobs is not due to some transfer of jobs South but occurs everywhere, owing to re-engineering in the North and modernization in the South. Outsourcing, subcontracting, and upstart firms in specific services are also big problems for unions in this and other service industries because the contracting firms tend to be nonunion or small. But, as with domestic outsourcing in auto, this is more a problem of national-level union strategy and policy than of internationalization *per se*.

The point here is that the shifting of production to the South by capital-intensive industries based in the major Triad markets has been and will be limited by reasons of capital costs and the need for proximity to the assemblers and major markets, as well as potential currency and political problems abroad. Furthermore, when major shifts are made, they tend to be stable for a significant period of time. At the same time, the enormous restructuring of auto and other manufacturing production within each Triad nation along lean-production lines paradoxically provides somewhat of an alternative to a major shift to the South, even though this new system emphasizes outsourcing to lower-cost producers. Increased in-house productivity along with the just-in-time emphasis on parts delivery create strong disincentives for long-distance outsourcing of all but the lightest parts.

Limits to Globalization II

The previous chapter looked at the limits to globalization in terms of the limits on investment and particularly those on investment in the Third World. While capitalism as a system has become global, its own dynamics create a very uneven world, which puts strict limits on the creation of anything like a homogeneous world economy. Instead, it creates a fragmented world economy in which wealth, and hence markets, as well as production are not evenly distributed. There is no "level playing field", as is constantly promised by the advocates of globalization and free markets.

In addition, the distribution of trade and investment is highly structured within and between regions, rather than randomly around the earth. Given the growth of economic regions based on geographically specific and limited regional production systems, the world economy has not been globalized so much as regionalized. In terms of both trade and FDI, economic flows are primarily between the three Triad nations, and also between each Triad nation and those clustered around it regionally. Very little of the world's major economic flows runs between Third World or former Communist countries within each Triad region.

This point is not a small one for the workers and their unions within these production systems. For workers in capital-intensive industries dominated by the top TNCs, clear lines of ownership or control, common production chains, fairly large production units, some geographic stability, and frequently high levels of unionization North and South provide advantages for making cross-border contacts, exchanging information, and developing common strategies that would be far more difficult in a truly globalized production. Furthermore, changes are taking place in the way work and production are organized that affect all the industrial nations of the North and many of the more industrialized countries of the South. The coming of lean production has provided a common experience that is disorienting in many ways, but that also increases the pressures of work and the degree of exploitation wherever it exists. It is a way of working with its own limits and its own incentives to rebellion.

5

The Rise and Limits of
Lean Production

Lean production was born in Japan and developed to cope with a capital shortage caused by the devastation of World War Two. It was made possible by the repression of organized labor that occurred in the early 1950s.[1] Japan had been an industrial power since the turn of the (last) century. Defeated and destroyed during World War Two, however, the recovery of its industry and the welfare of its large corporations first got a boost into the world economy during the Korean War. The shortage of capital required its corporations to improve competitiveness and cut its costs through intensified work, longer hours, and a multi-tiered production chain with progressively lower wages. The defeat of the unions in the early 1950s provided the opportunity. As Taiichi Ohno, the creator of *kaizen* (constant improvement), himself put it, "Had I faced the (militant) Japan National Railways Union or an American union, I might have been murdered."[2]

Ohno, and others who followed his example to get competitive, modified the classic system of mass production first developed by Henry Ford. While the term "lean production" is frequently used in counterposition to mass production, as in the MIT International Motor Vehicles Program (IMVP) group's *The Machine that Changed the World*, it is in fact streamlined mass production that draws more consistently on the knowledge of the workers to do the streamlining. Practitioners of lean production tend to view it this way. Peter Enderle, Manufacturing Director of Adam Opel AG (GM) in Germany, put it like this in a company brochure about the "Opel Production System" at the new Eisenach assembly plant in eastern Germany:

> Lean Production – this calls for a combination of the specific features of manual skill and the benefits of mass production. Manual skill ensures a high level of flexibility and high employee capabilities whereas mass production on the assembly line ensures benefits such as rapid throughput times and low unit costs.[3]

Lean production produces high-volume output through the standardization of product and process beyond Henry Ford's wildest dreams. It attempts to capitalize on economies of scale (output per unit of capital) as much as the more fashionable economies of scope (ability to produce different products with the same unit of capital) associated with flexibilization. Real flexibility in lean production lies primarily in the combination of information-age technology and worker experience with archaic forms of work organization such as contracting-out, casualization, old-fashioned speed-up, and the lengthening of working time.

Nor is there anything particularly "post-Fordist" about lean production other than the tendency to decentralize the production chain. The term itself, which refers to mass assembly-line production, was first used by the Italian Marxist Antonio Gramsci in his famous *Prison Notebooks*. One of his keener insights was that Ford's policy of paying above industry-standard wages of $5 a day in the 1920s was primarily a way to end the high levels of labor turnover produced by the inhuman rigors of his assembly line.[4] In that sense, of industry paying relatively high wages for highly intense, routine work, most industries that ever qualified are still "Fordist." While wage restraint is typical these days, wages are seldom the major target of cost-cutting. In any case, lean methods are directed at producing for mass markets whether they are producing cars, refrigerators, telecommunications services, or semiconductors. In this sense, they remain "Fordist," as that term is most commonly used.

Indeed, to a much greater extent today than at the height of "Fordism" in the 1950s, lean facilities are producing for world markets. It is also worth bearing in mind that most of the techniques associated with "Fordism," notably the labor-intensive assembly line, along with the "scientific management" design of jobs through time-and-motion measurement, remain in practice today from Toyota City to Eisenach, Germany. Indeed, the world's only genuinely "post-Fordist," team-assembled auto-production facility, Volvo's Uddevalla, Sweden, plant, was deemed uncompetitive and closed in 1993 after only four years in operation.[5]

While lean production has brought some near-qualitative innovations, such as the enormous reduction in die-changing time in the auto industry, most new efficiencies involved in *kaizen* are quantitative or even marginal. Most aspects of lean production, such as extensive outsourcing and the just-in-time parts-delivery system that ties suppliers to assemblers, are quantitative cost-cutting measures in the context of value maximization. Even with competition driving more and more firms to adopt lean methods, it is doubtful that anything they achieved in the past twenty years can match the 8 to 1 reduction in labor hours per car wrought by Henry Ford with the introduction of the moving assembly line.[6] Indeed, according to one study, the number of hours per car in Japan fell by less than a 2 to 1 ratio from 1970 through 1988.[7]

Management-by-Stress

There is a lot of hype about lean production. Nowhere more than in the MIT IMVP group's *Machine that Changed The World*, where they claimed that Toyota's Japan plants produce "with half the amount" of labor and materials of North American or European plants.[8] Other researchers have criticized the MIT group's methods and figures, but the promoters of lean production everywhere continue to praise the system's efficiency.[9]

Few dispute that, on average, Japanese auto (and possibly other, less studied) plants were more efficient in the late 1980s than most of those in Europe or North America – though, as the methods spread, this may no longer be the case. The question is, however, what made them more efficient? Part of the answer lies in what can be seen at Toyota's Tahara, Japan, assembly plant 4 – it is more automated than most North American or European plants, although they too are moving in this direction.[10] More automation, fewer labor hours – it's simple arithmetic. But automation is not necessarily cost-cutting, since it is itself a substantial cost. Nor was automation a stranger to classical mass production – although some types, such as robotization, are fairly new.

What is different about lean methods is the continuous search for marginal improvements in costs by constantly stressing and readjusting the production system and, above all, the labor process. Lean production is run by a system of "management-by-stress," a term coined by Mike Parker and Jane Slaughter of *Labor Notes*. *Kaizen*, just-in-time, multiskilling, job rotation, teams, quality management, numerical and functional flexibility, extensive outsourcing, and all the well-known features of lean production are the means to reduce the resources, including labor, needed to produce a given product or service. This is done by a constant process of stretching one phase of production to the "breaking point" by reducing the number of workers and/or the mass of materials available, and then recalibrating the other phases of the production process.[11]

Efficiency and improvement are defined as cost reduction – as they always have been. A training manual from the GM–Suzuki joint venture CAMI assembly plant in Ingersoll, Ontario, Canada, put it succinctly: "Kaizen must always be tied to concrete cost reductions."[12] While minimizing materials through just-in-time (JIT) delivery or design-for-manufacturing is important, in practice, cost reduction most frequently applies to labor. In particular, getting lean means eliminating as much non-value-added labor time as possible. The Canadian Auto Workers (CAW) describe this as follows:

> All costs associated with non-value added functions are waste and are to be eliminated, whether it is buffers between operations, slack time, waiting time, walking space at work stations or more generally indirect labor such as the skilled trades.[13]

While most of the popular literature emphasizes the role of teams and workers' empowerment, the basic methods of reducing time are those of classical Taylorism or "scientific management," whether in Japan, North America, or Europe.[14] The notion that Toyota or anyone else abandoned what is essential in Taylorism is simply mistaken. In fact, jobs are timed and retimed, designed and redesigned using the same time-and-motion tools. The reduction of labor time it takes to make a product applies not only to eliminating non-value-added jobs, but to eliminating rest times by workers performing value-added work. Breaks are reduced to the absolute minimum and the "pores" of working time are filled in. Whereas an assembly-line worker at GM's old mass-production plants worked (was in motion) 45 seconds of each minute, today's NUMMI workers in California work the standard Toyota 57-second minute.[15]

Nor is the fact that workers participate in this process by sharing their knowledge of the job something different than Taylorism. Taylor himself said that "scientific management" required:

> the deliberate gathering in on the part of management's side of all the great mass of traditional knowledge, which in the past has been in heads of workmen, and in the physical skill and knack of the workmen, which they have acquired through the years.[16]

What is different is that in the early years of the Toyota system workers had been required to make this knowledge and skill known to management on a regular basis. In general, teams are one way in which this transfer of knowledge takes place, but the outcome is not worker empowerment or autonomy: it is highly standardized work timed down to the last breath. Tayloristic job-cycle times, for example, are essential to the Japanese versions of lean production and the authority to make the changes remains in management's hands.[17]

The quality "movement," as some call it, has increased the emphasis on standardization of tasks in lean production and, hence, on management control of the labor process. As used by its theorists and practitioners alike, "quality" does not mean excellence or durability, or any particular characteristic of the final product – except that it conforms to the specifications laid down by management. Indeed, the concept of "conformance to requirements" is central to this version of quality and applies to the production process. Like lean production generally, it means cutting costs, in this case by eliminating mistakes in production – zero defects. While this might sound benign, it means that work must conform to requirements, standards, etc.[18] Conformity, not creativity, is the goal. Under these circumstances, not even theoretically autonomous work groups have anything like real autonomy.

Writers of the Human Resources Management (HRM) school tend to emphasize the "empowerment" and participatory side of lean production. This academic field, however, differs from industrial relations, sociology, or economics, in that it has no particular methodology other than the survey, while its studies "tend towards prescription rather than description."[19] It tends to be vague, propagandistic, and biased against independent trade unionism. As another industrial relations scholar put it:

> HRM is best seen as a cultural construction facilitating the management of meaning. As a virtual reality, the projected identity of HRM has much in common with a hologram: as we move around the image different facets of its contoured and contradictory nature becomes visible. This helps to explain why, conceptually, it appears to be an evolving moving target, and why, empirically, it has no fixed (or fixable) form. As argued elsewhere, this "brilliant ambiguity" is necessary to its socio-cultural objective: to undermine, if not destroy, the institutional basis of collectivism and legitimate the transition to an individualized unitary concept of the employment relationship.[20]

The ideology of HRM actually runs up against the real imperatives of lean production. HRM propagandists seem to believe the hype about worker autonomy and empowerment. Their emphasis is on how teams, broad job definitions, rotation, pay for knowledge, etc., transcend Taylorism. One Canadian HRM study, for example, uses a 1991 Ernst & Young survey showing the proportion of companies using "cycle time analysis" and "process simplification" (deskilling), both "associated with traditional or 'Taylorist' approaches to work organization," as evidence that changes to new ways of working are "not widespread."[21] The survey shows that 74%

of firms questioned in Japan use cycle-time analysis and 82% process simplification. The comparable figures for the US are 60% and 47% respectively, while in Germany, where lean production had barely a foothold in 1991, they were 47% and 34%.[22] What the HRM specialists have failed to understand is that Tayloristic methods actually increase with lean production.

What is becoming clearer is that the teams are no longer regarded as necessary once the dynamics of management-by-stress are at work. Much of the cluster of programs that defines the HRM "model," in particular, is simply a means to cost reduction, discarded when the workers have disclosed what they know and a better method is found. This was made clear at Toyota's Tahara plant by the personnel director, who confirmed that management, not teams, directed job design, workflow, and everything else at Toyota. When sweeping changes were made at Tahara in 1992, the teams were not even consulted. In fact, the teams no longer functioned at all by 1994.[23]

Far from finding genuine participatory management, even where teams existed, a 1990 survey of manufacturing firms in the US Midwest concluded, in fact, that:

> The results suggest that there are diverse ways for participative programs to relate to these new techniques. Perhaps more important, there are a significant number of cases where neither workers nor their unions were involved in the implementation of these programs. Further, when unions are involved in implementing these techniques, this involvement tends to be over traditional matters such as wages and job classifications and through the traditional process of collective bargaining. All of these results cast serious doubt on the extent to which management is in fact becoming more participative and labor relations more cooperative.[24]

Things are not so different in Germany, where lean methods are more recent. At the Mannheim Mercedes Bus plant there are no teams, but, as one worker put it, there is "clandestine kaizen." That is, jobs are constantly recycled, tightened up, loaded up. Between 1992 and 1996 the workforce at the Mannheim plant was reduced from 15,000 to 10,000.[25]

As a study of the GM–Suzuki "greenfield" joint venture, CAMI (in Ontario, Canada) points out, in an auto-assembly plant teams don't really have much impact on the way cars are produced. The writers argue:

> At CAMI, vehicles are still put together in the traditional way pioneered by Henry Ford – all major assembly tasks follow the logic and pace of the drag line. Even sub-assemblies, such as those for the instrument panels, are built on moving lines. Hence, work at CAMI is not, for the most part, a team-

based production system, but a system of teams superimposed on a traditional assembly line operation in which output arises from the efforts of individual workers carrying out standardized tasks.[26]

David Robertson, research director of the CAW, made the point that teams no longer seem to be necessary to lean production in an address to German auto workers in 1994. He said:

Even if you resist teams, or quality circles, or other managerial initiatives or jointness in general it doesn't mean you have stopped lean production.[27]

Increasingly, management is using "competitive benchmarking" to change and eliminate jobs. As Robertson puts it:

Benchmarking studies try to find where it is that management does its best – the quickest, the cheapest, the fastest techniques and production practices.[28]

Benchmarking is an old practice and is, in fact, a basic piece of capitalist competition with a basis in political economy. As economist Howard Botwinick has argued, firms within a given industry must seek the best-practice levels of the industry's "regulating capital," the company with the lowest cost structure.[29] For years, Japanese producers have been the global regulating capitals in many industries and the source of emulation for other firms. But the actual conditions that make a company the regulating capital can change. Internationally, such non-production factors as exchange rates impact on costs and profit rates, placing a former regulating capital at a disadvantage in other markets, at least for a time.[30] This is precisely what happened to Japanese auto producers in the late 1980s into the 1990s. To rectify this, the former regulating capital must find new ways to cut costs, which was why management at the Toyota's Tahara plant 4 retooled and reconfigured the facility in 1992.[31]

Benchmarking is also the method by which lean "best practices" are diffused across borders *within* the TNCs. As with competition between firms, nationally and internationally, this internal benchmarking tends to produce a convergence of work and production practices even where the national industrial-relations systems and trade-union culture are very different. A United Nations report describes the process:

The diffusion of best practice manufacturing and management methods under integrated international production ... could result in a cross-border convergence of work organization and conditions and quality of employ-ment within integrated TNCs. If production is tightly co-ordinated across affiliates in different countries, each one of them would be under pressure not to diverge from global (or regional) best practice.[32]

This effect is well documented in the automobile industry. As two British industrial-relations scholars note, however, it is common in most companies with strong central-management structures. They cite a European food multinational and ABB, a European producer of power transformers and auto parts. They give the following description:

> ABB's power transformer business, for example, is introducing a "comprehensive set of benchmark metrics, measuring quality performance, on-time delivery, customer satisfaction, productivity, inventory, manufacturing through-put time, as well as total through-put time."[33]

Whether through benchmarking, teams, or clandestine *kaizen*, the outcome of management-by-stress is job reduction, on the one hand, and speed-up and job-loading, on the other. Interviews with auto workers from Renault in France (1994, 1996), Peugeot in France (1996) and the UK (1996), GM at Bochum (1994, 1996) and Eisenach (1996) in Germany and Ellesmere Port in the UK (1994), at Nissan (1994, 1996) and Volkswagen (1994, 1996) in Spain, Rover/BMW in Oxford, UK (1994); testimony at TIE auto-worker conferences in Germany and North America; as well as conversations with workers from dozens of plants in the US, Canada, and Mexico over the past several years, all reveal an identical tale of what happened when lean methods were introduced: substantial job elimination, with or without new technology; faster and harder work pace; and increased difficulty in handling grievances related to production or working conditions.[34]

Teams and quality circles do, of course, have a function that cannot be performed through benchmarking. They are a method of by-passing (or avoiding in the first place) the union and undoing the structures and rules created by "job-control" unionism – a misnomer that refers to the work rules, job descriptions, and other contractual limits on management's authority in workplace collective agreements. They also have an ideological function, which is to tie the workers and the union to the goals and objectives of the corporation – to inculcate the ideology of partnership in competitiveness. The widespread practice of "job-control" unionism in the US is one reason why teams are universal there. In Britain, the old traditions of workplace organization through shop stewards, coupled with extensive informal agreements and job demarcations, also encouraged management to use teamworking to undo what is left of these traditions. The series of strikes by British postal workers, one of the last groups with strong workplace organization, against the introduction of teams through the autumn of 1996 were based on a clear understanding by the workers of the function of teams.[35]

Another method of dismantling workplace union rules or "restrictive " (for management) workplace practices involves the active embrace of the union and its integration into aspects of the company structure. Ironically, this sometimes begins when the union demands representation or consultation up the hierarchy of the company. In the auto industry in the US this became known as "jointness." Elly Leary and Marybeth Menaker, in *Jointness at GM: Company Unionism in the 21st Century*, show how the structure of joint company–union committees replicates the company structure and binds more and more of the union's own structure to the company. This corrodes union democracy, as more and more decisions about union policy and practice are made in high-level joint committees. More generally, it brings the union's independence from management into question.[36]

An almost as elaborate version of jointness exists between AT&T and the Communications Workers of America (CWA). Begun in 1993, the Workplace of the Future program featured joint boards and councils at every level of the company. The union was to be consulted about all major investment plans, cut-backs, downsizing, or other business changes. Its purpose was, as AT&T Vice President Bill Ketchum said, "to secure the future – the future for the company, but also the future for the employees and the unions."[37] In fact, this scheme was put in place in 1993, only 5 months before AT&T announced it 4,000-person workforce reduction, a year before a proposed additional cut of 15,000 workers, and 3 years prior to the AT&T grand-slam, 40,000-job-reduction announcement. Each time, the union complained that the company had not consulted them.[38]

Another aspect of management-by-stress is the break up, the "vertical disintegration," of production processes previously performed within the same firm and often within a single complex. More and more of the work previously performed "in-house" is outsourced to other facilities, either belonging to the company or more commonly to allegedly independent contractors. Again, the CAW (Canadian Auto Workers) study put it well:

> The differences between lean companies and other companies *are not found* in developments such as teams, suggestion programs, small group improvement activities, multiskilling or the like. The biggest differences are found in practices such as the massive outsourcing (contracting out) of parts and final assembly. The outsourcing is done with low wages, insecure employment and fully using production capacity.[39]

Extensive outsourcing was part of the original Toyota system. Production consisted of a pyramidal chain of facilities, with Toyota's "life-time" employees composing as little as 25% of the workforce. Down the supplier chain there was no life-time job, and wages and conditions fell. At the bottom, women, almost totally absent from Toyota's "core" facilities, work in low-tech, labor-intensive plants.[40] As labor costs rose across the board in the 1970s and 1980s, however, Toyota and other Japanese producers in many industries began "moving" a good deal of the work down the production chain, first to the four Asian Tigers, then to even lower-wage sites in the ASEAN countries, and now to China.[41] This pattern has been repeated in North America, with Mexico as a major site of outsourcing, and is now unfolding in the European Union, with North Africa and eastern Europe as outsourcing locations.[42] This is one of the ways in which the tendency toward international regionalization takes shape.

The measure of outsourcing is usually the amount of "content" in a product done "in-house." In the US auto industry much was made of the differences in the level of in-house content around 1990 between Chrysler (35%), Ford (45%), and GM (70%). More recent estimates, however, put GM's current in-house content closer to 49%, since its downsizing in the early 1990s. Ford had gone down to 39%, while Chrysler had slightly reversed its proportion of in-house work to 36%[43] Toyota's in-house content was measured at 27% by the IMVP group.[44]

Outsourcing and the threat of outsourcing are the basis of introducing competition between workers in different plants both inside and outside of the company. In the US the union contracts in the auto industry allow local unions to join with local managers to "bid" on work against workers in another plant – a practice called "whipsawing." One GM worker described it like this:

> Given an opportunity to "bid" against outside suppliers to keep work, many members spent countless hours analyzing the work process to develop innovative proposals to reduce cost and improve quality and service.[45]

In this particular case, GM outsourced the product anyway. In the process, however, the union members themselves had revealed to management how to speed up and load up their work.

The contracting out of work is not limited to manufacturing. Here's how one US truck driver and Teamster member described the process at his employer:

> The trucking company where I'm employed frequently gives away my work. The freight goes to a fly-by-night local firm whose underpaid drivers are forced to lease their trucks from their boss and buy their own health insurance. And a day later, I'm laid off for lack of work.[46]

In manufacturing, lean outsourcing also involves a rationalization and reduction of the number of first-line suppliers. The IMVP group notes that during the 1980s US auto companies followed the Japanese example by reducing the number of direct suppliers from "a range of 2,000 to 2,500 at the beginning of the decade to between 1,000 and 1,500 at the end." They note that by that time the number of suppliers per assembly plant in the US was down to 509 in the US, and 442 in Europe, compared with 170 in Japan.[47] What this neat count of the supposed rationalization of the supply chain overlooks is that it is accomplished by the lead suppliers, in turn, outsourcing more production to even lower-paying suppliers, some of them in other countries.[48]

Flexibility is a major buzz word in lean production. While some writers emphasize the flexibility inherent in the new technology, it is the functional (deployment), numerical (staffing level), and time (scheduling) flexibility of the workforce that provides much of the cost reduction in the "core" of production.

Functional flexibility is achieved by the reduction or elimination of job descriptions or demarcations, whether inherited from Taylorism or embodied in the union agreements. This, of course, is one of the major differences between classical mass production and its lean variant – one of the few real, though only partial, departures from Taylorism. Functional flexibility also involves job rotation and the ability to work a number of different jobs. Usually labeled "multiskilling," this practice is more accurately called multitasking, since the actual jobs are simple standardized tasks that are really part of deskilling in the classical Taylorist manner.[49] In Britain, Canada, and the US, this has required an intense offensive by management against traditional forms of "job control", whereas in continental Europe weaker traditions of workplace organization and bargaining, along with the cooperative ethos of works councils in some countries, have made it easier.[50]

Time or scheduling flexibility is meant to allow round-the-clock operations in order to utilize fully the firms capital assets with as few workers as possible. It is also a buffer for market fluctuations. Time flexibility is found in new forms of shift scheduling and rotation and in the massive use of overtime, sometimes without overtime pay.[51] The lengthening of the work day through overtime is another of lean production's archaic forms of increasing exploitation. But, as part of the management-by-stress set-up, it has another use as well.

As the CAW argues, "Overtime is the buffer in lean production."[52] It has been used this way in Japan since the early days of lean production. Rather than hiring new workers, more overtime is scheduled. In the US, overtime and downsizing have gone hand-in-hand in the 1990s. When business is slack, overtime is reduced. In Europe, where average working hours tend to be shorter than in the US, the trend is toward "annualized hours" or "time corridors" that allow management to work shifts of thirty hours for part of the year and forty or more in other parts of the year. Premium pay for weekends and overtime are often eliminated under these systems.[53]

Overtime frequently accompanies and eases the way for downsizing through re-engineering. This is particularly the case in telecommunications. At NYNEX's Switching Control Center in New York City, for example, the workforce went from sixty-five technicians and three clerks in 1989 to twenty-seven technicians and one clerk in 1994. This occurred during the transition to digital switching, which actually created more work. While this was going on workers reported working as many as twelve to sixteen hours a day, and on weekends.[54]

Lean production's most recent innovation, one that did not originate in Japan, is the imposition of new shift systems designed to keep a facility in operation on a 24-hour basis. An OECD study on new scheduling patterns describes the economic motivation as follows:

> In recent years, plant utilization time has been considerably extended in most industrialized countries. The reasons for this increase in operating hours are primarily increasing capital intensity and the accelerating pace of technical change. As capital intensity increases, firms can considerably reduce capital unit costs by extending operating hours. Furthermore, the capital employed is amortized more rapidly, with a consequent reduction in the risks associated with large-scale investments.[55]

The OECD report goes on to show that firms are solving this utilization problem by using "a range of new instruments, including working through breaks, staggered operating hours on expensive machines, a combination of full-time and part-time shifts, variations of annual shut-down times, and multiple job holder systems."[56] While some continuous-process production systems have had rotating shift work since their birth, the new kinds of shifts being introduced in North America and Europe find a home in any kind of manufacturing setting.

Until recently, for example, virtually all auto-assembly plants in the world worked on a straight two-shift, five-day-week basis. Now, new shift patterns and other scheduling changes are being introduced across the industry. In North America, they tend to be known as "alternative work schedules" and involve three rotating crews working ten- or twelve-hour days, four days a week – plus a great deal of overtime, which extends the week to five or six days.[57]

Numerical flexibility is found in both contracting out and the extensive use of casual labor – usually part-timers and temporary workers, or "fixed-term" or "zero-hour" contract workers as they are usually called in Europe. In the US temporary workers have long been thought of as extra office help. But, by the mid-1990s, Manpower, Inc. had replaced GM as the nation's largest employer, and the total number of temporary workers employed by personnel supply services had reached over two-and-a-half million by 1996.[58] Similarly, part-time jobs were associated with retail work or the growing service sector. By 1993, over 30% of part-time workers labored in manufacturing, construction, transportation, or utilities. While the vast majority of part-time workers are still women, women from 22 to 64 years of age have slightly decreased the rate at which they work part-time (45.2% to 44.6%), while the proportion of men in the same age group has doubled (3.7% to 8.1%).[59]

The chain of numerical flexibility stretches all the way to homework. While it is probably most prevalent in clothing production, it can be found at the end of the production chain even in the automobile industry. Most of all, it has become global, existing in the North, where it was thought to have disappeared years ago, as well as in the South. Sheila Rowbotham attributes its rise in the South to two major causes. She writes:

> The growth of homeworking in the Third World has been partly because of industrial restructuring in which work not only for the local market but also for international export has moved to the cheapest sources. Homework has also grown because rising prices in Latin America and Africa have made it impossible to gain a livelihood for families even where the men are in formal employment.[60]

In fact, the same causes have brought the return of homework to the North. Rowbotham documents homework, and organizations of homeworkers, in the US, Canada, Britain, and Italy.[61]

Contracting, casualization, and homework are archaic forms of labor organization common in the nineteenth century. At that time they were virtually synonymous with "sweated labor." A British Royal Commission said in 1888 that sweating existed "very largely wherever the system of subcontracting prevails." At the turn of the century the Illinois Bureau of Labor Statistics further equated the two, saying, "sweating consists of farming out by competing manufacturers to competing contractors of the material, which in turn is distributed among competing men and women to be made up."[62] This is a reasonably accurate description of how lean production organizes its contractors and casual workers.

Of course, there are some differences. Temporary workers today are more likely to wait at a phone or visit a temp agency than line up at the factory gate. Part-time workers may have permanent jobs and some may even prefer part-time employment, but it has been involuntary part-time employment driving the growth of part-time work since 1979.[63] Contract workers brought into the "core" operations are likely to be employed regularly by a contracting firm. And the chain of contractors and suppliers is likely to be electronically linked and even coordinated in a way sweatshops a hundred years ago never could be. As the shop stewards' convener at Peugeot's Ryton, UK, plant put it, "We're all wired up these days. If someone coughs in the office here, they hear it in Paris."[64]

Another example is AT&T in the US which runs a nonunion subsidiary called Transtech, which in turn contracts with Accustaff, a temp agency, to bring in 3,000 workers in its telemarketing operations. AT&T also contracted with Bell Atlantic for telephone-operator services, but then switched its contracts to a nonunion holding company called CFW. Both of these set-ups allow AT&T to exploit thousands of workers who are beyond union coverage, since they are not AT&T employees, and receive none of the health-care or retirement benefits of regular employees.[65]

The extent of part-time and temporary employment in Europe differs from country to country because of legislation limiting these practices in some and not in others. But the trend toward the increased use of "fixed-term" or "zero-hours" contracts and other forms of temporary work, as well as of part-time workers, is unmistakable. In the UK, the proportion of workers in part-time work rose from 16.4% in 1979 to 24.1% in 1995; for men it rose from 1.9% in 1979 to 7.7% in 1995; for women, who compose the majority of part-time workers everywhere, it went from 39% to 44.3%. In France the incidence of part-time work in the same period rose from 8.1% to 15.6%, in Germany from 11.4% to 16.3%, and in Canada from 13.8% to 18.6%.[66]

Italy and Spain present a different pattern. Part-time and temporary work was illegal in those countries until recently. In Spain, the explosion of temporary jobs after 1986, when the law was changed, filled much of the demand for workers in "contingent" or "atypical" jobs. Such temporary workers are everywhere in Spain. For example, at the Nissan assembly plant in Barcelona's Zona Franca there are 500 temporary workers on top of the 3,600 regular employees. Similarly, Telefónica, the partly privatized national phone company, is using increased numbers of temporary contract workers in the process of "commercialization" required by a European Commission Directive.[67] Indeed, Telefónica workers in Barcelona told the story of the "missing floor," a floor in the old telephone central office long thought to have been sealed off, where the union (Comisiones Obreras) discovered hundreds of temporary contract telemarketing employees that management had tried to conceal.[68] In Italy, neither temporary nor part-time jobs have become as common as elsewhere, though part-time work has been on the rise, particularly among large retailers, where as much as 50% of the workforce is now part-time. Italy also has a large "informal" sector, which can provide some of the same flexibility associated with "legal" casualized work.[69]

Part-time work remains women's work. Although the rate at which men work part-time is rising at a faster rate almost everywhere, women still compose 70–90% of the part-time workforce across the developed industrial nations.[70] A large part of this employment is in traditional service and retail-sector jobs long populated by women. Many of these industries have grown, increasing the number of part-time women workers. What is more, retailing has dramatically changed across the industrialized world as late and weekend opening times become normal and giant retailing operations replace local small businesses.[71] But contracting and casualization in traditionally full-time types of work have also increased in manufacturing down the production chain, health care, telecommunications, graphic arts, and publishing.

The gendered distribution of much of this "atypical" or casualized work has often been described as offering flexibility for women. One British study, however, puts the question of whose flexibility is at stake in context. It argues:

> Clearly atypical work does give some options to women with caring responsibilities unable to take typical work but that does not mean that it is meeting equally the flexibility needs of both employers and atypical workers. Indeed in some ways the flexibility which employers gain through atypical working serves to impose rigidities on workers: the homeworker constantly waiting for work and having to fit in with suppliers' delivery and collection schedules; the "On-call" part-timer not knowing when work will be available and afraid to refuse work when offered; the part-time worker required to vary hours at short or no notice, and the arrangement of hours which are less than ideal for many women trying to wrestle with paid work and domestic commitments.[72]

Not all contract workers are part-time or temporary. Industries as diverse as oil refining and telecommunications bring in contract workers who are regularly employed by a contract firm. Like outsourcing, this is a form of numerical flexibility. This type of contract worker is appearing in manufacturing plants, as well as service industries, around the world. For example, independent contracting firms do all the internal transport and inventory management at Rover–BMW in Britain and at SEAT–VW in Matorell, Spain.[73] At GM's Zaragoza assembly plant in Spain, an independent company makes seats inside the GM plant.[74]

This kind of inside subcontracting is increasingly a characteristic of "greenfield" lean plants. At GM's Opel assembly plant in Eisenach, Germany, for example, 700 workers, a third of the workforce, are employed by 28 outside contractors. Since these workers are not GM employees they are not represented on the works council or by the plant union. In-bound permanent contract workers will also be a feature of Volkswagen's new plant in Argentina where workers from twenty-four different firms will work side-by-side in the same facility, producing the same cars. This is the work of J. Ignacio López de Arriortua, the outsourcing wizard, who jumped from VW to GM and back to VW, spreading the doctrine of maximum outsourcing and contracting, but also of forcing contractors to adopt lean methods leading to "reductions in investment, direct labor, floor space and set-up time."[75]

Numerical or staffing flexibility and time or scheduling flexibility work together as an essential part of any genuinely lean production system. An OECD study described it well in a discussion of new trends in Germany that would apply almost anywhere:

> "Flexible staffing" in the quasi-outsider segment of the company labor market, and "flexible scheduling" among the insiders seem to increasingly represent the standard method of absorbing fluctuations in the volume of work. If such fluctuations occur, first, temporary employees are usually withdrawn and fixed-term contracts allowed to run out; second, if necessary, the labor input in the firm or in certain departments is further reduced by phasing out overtime, introducing short-time work or lengthening holiday periods; and third, natural attrition is no longer offset by replacements.[76]

The only qualification needed here is that short-timing or lengthening of holidays would be unlikely in North America.

If this flexibility is combined with functional flexibility, speed-up and job loading, which is itself constantly increased through management-by-stress, it is evident that a firm's employment will shrink not only with cyclical market declines, but more or less continuously over time even if the market holds up or expands. More precisely, the "core," once-upon-a-time beneficiaries of "life-time employment," will shrink in numbers, while insecure part-time, temporary, and contract employment will, as a result, grow throughout society.

Finally, lean-production methods, like mass production when it first spread, will be imitated and partially implemented in all kinds of employment settings. Subcontracting to lower-wage firms can even be a cheap substitute for genuine lean methods and certainly for technological innovation. The decentralization of the labor process and diffusion of casualized jobs, involuntary part-time employment, and "sweated" subcontracting, which are the cheapest forms of "lean" cost-reducing, particularly in labor-intensive manufacturing or service industries, has clearly increased. Indeed, industries like clothing and semiconductors are based on this sort extended chain of low-wage, mostly female, labor.[77] Whether it is implemented fully or partially, given different names, or modified by workers' resistance (as it frequently is), the basic features of lean production as developed in the automobile industry in Japan have become perceived as the global best practices in one industry after another and have spread across the world.

The Spread of Lean Production

There is not much doubt that competition is the driving force behind the spread of lean production globally and some version of benchmarking a common method of emulation. Nevertheless, since lean production is not identical from company to company even in Japan, there are a number of versions to be emulated. Furthermore, different kinds of production systems (service delivery, continuous-process manufacturing, etc.) call for different mixes of lean techniques. Worker and/or union resistance is also an important factor in modifying lean systems. For example, the unions at the greenfield SEAT–VW plant in Matorell, Spain, struck eighteen times to prevent teamworking, and management surrendered. Yet, in most other respects the Matorell plant is a lean facility.[78] Finally, as will be discussed below, lean production has its own built-in limits. Japanese firms have abandoned or modified some earlier practices. Not surprisingly, a 1993 British study found that British or North American firms in the UK tended to use more lean practices than Japanese-owned enterprises there.[79]

Measuring the extent of lean-production practices in any country is further complicated by the fact that much of this work is done by people working in the HRM field. HRM advocates measure the extent of change by the proportion of firms using some or all of the participation programs, broad job definitions and rotation, performance-related pay schemes, and sometimes functional flexibility that are part of most versions of the HRM "model." Merely scanning industry for these forms of work organization often overlooks the reality of lean production in the standardization of work, the force of just-in-time linking of jobs and facilities in driving work, or the undermining of conditions through extensive contracting out. With this warning in mind, however, some of the HRM studies provide an idea of the extent of lean practices.

Using extensive survey material (i.e., asking management what they do), Paul Osterman of MIT shows that in 1994 over half of all US firms surveyed used teams, while about 40% used quality circles (QC), and a third had TQM (total quality management) programs. Asked more vaguely about employee involvement, over 80% who answered a 1991 Harris poll said they had "significant" or "some," but this would probably include those with old-fashioned suggestion programs. About one-third of firms reported having two or more new practices such as employee participation, quality (QC or TQM), or job rotation.[80] Larger companies are more likely to have one or another participation program than small ones. A survey of Fortune 1,000 companies showed that the proportion of them having one or more employee participation programs grew from 70% in 1987 to 85% in 1990.[81]

A deeper measure is found in a 1990 survey of eighty-five manufacturing firms in the US Midwest. The survey measured the use of just-in-time (JIT), statistical process control (SPC), total quality (TQ), cell manufacturing, work teams, and employee involvement – a cluster of programs much closer to full lean production. Management answers indicated that the following percentage of firms used these techniques: employee involvement 79.6%, JIT 52.1%, SPC 79.2%, TQ 56.3%, cell manufacturing 31.9%, and work teams 31.3%.[82] The low occurrence of work teams is probably explained by the high incidence of "employee involvement," which is the name often used to cover *kaizen* activities. This is the case, for example, in steel. On this evidence, there seems to be a significant proportion of firms in the US attempting to implement programs associated with lean production.

In Canada, HRM-style measures show much less implementation of programs associated with lean production, with only 24% of firms having some kind of participation program in 1993.[83] There is not much doubt that this is due to the persistence of "job-control" unionism, resulting from greater opposition and resistance on the part of unions, and to the greater union density in Canada than in the US – 35% compared with 15%. Whereas in the US most union leaders have been willing to circumvent or even give up much of this contractual language, in Canada unions have been more resistant to any sort of concessions.[84] Nevertheless, testimony by workers and union officials in both auto and telecommunications in Canada indicate that, with or without employee participation or union approval, lean-production methods like JIT, SPC, TQ, re-engineering, and cell manufacturing are widespread in Canada, as are workforce reductions[85]

In 1995, GM CEO (Chief Executive Officer) John Smith told the *New York Times*, "There's a real focus on getting lean in Europe among all the auto makers." While GM's North American operations were regarded as less than lean, Smith had been president of GM's Saturn operation and then led the outsourcing trend in GM's European operations until 1988. Smith was allies in company politics with outsourcing guru 'Inaki' López in Europe. In 1992, GM-Europe took another big step toward leanness when the state-of-the-art Eisenach assembly plant opened. Some estimates of the cuts in GM's European component operations' workforce go as high as 70%.[86] By the mid-1990s, GM had moved to trim drastically the workforce at many older assembly operations.

Britain was the beachhead of lean production in Europe, with the process accelerating after Nissan opened its Sunderland assembly plant in 1986, much as Japanese transplants and the NUMMI and CAMI (Canada) joint ventures had accelerated the process in North America. Even before the plant was up and running, Nissan was able to get a deal from the conservative Amalgamated Engineers' and Electricians' Union that gave management complete control.[87] The plant was state-of-the art and a model of competitive lean production – a best practice to be imitated. A 1991 survey of British manufacturing firms showed that, of those who replied, 72% used continuous improvement, 68% JIT, 59% SPC, 68% quality circles and 56% total-quality controls.[88] This could reflect the low cost of British labor compared with Japanese or the fact that manufacturers in Japan were beginning to modify or eliminate some features of lean production, as will be discussed later.

Under fire from the Thatcher government and restricted in action by new labor laws, resistance was difficult. While it was extensive in areas of traditional strength like auto, the general practice of British unions has been to move from "opposition to grudging acceptance."[89] By 1994 the Trades Union Congress had adopted a position favorable to HRM. The Transport and General Workers' Union, the major union in the car industry, had embraced HRM by 1996. A notable exception to this acceptance is seen in the 1996 strike of workers at the Royal Mail against the introduction of teams and other lean practices.[90]

In Europe, aside from Britain, traditions of workplace bargaining are weak. It was not until the 1970s that workplace organization and bargaining became general. Much of this was a result of actions by the state in the aftermath of the increased militancy of the late 1960s and early 1970s. By the 1980s, works councils and other consultative structures had become common on the continent. These were not *kaizen* teams or quality circles, but, as consultative bodies in the context of weak shopfloor bargaining traditions, they sometimes helped open the door to lean production in the 1990s.

In Germany, for example, one study describes the process by which quality circles and teams came to German industry as follows:

Some unions and works councils at first rejected such participation initiatives, especially quality circles, but in most cases they have now accepted them, and some representatives of the unions and works councils regard them as a first step towards "codetermination in the workplace."[91]

Not all German union and works council representatives hold such a positive view, however. Militant stewards and works councilors at GM's Bochum plant argued that the acceptance of teams and other lean measures, particularly massive job loss, was a matter of the national union's (IG Metall) policy, not theirs. They also pointed out that the works council is forbidden to strike or negatively affect the interests of the enterprise.[92] Its theoretical ability to veto major changes is, as Ulrich Jurgens points out, limited to: "(a) the selection of personnel in the case of layoffs, (b) the scheduling of overtime, and (c) changes in the system and determinants of wages and salaries."[93] While the works councils can and do attempt to bargain informally over other issues, they have no actual authority in areas such as work organization, workforce reduction (other than who goes and who doesn't, seniority not being a factor in Germany), or technology. Nevertheless, following the policy of the IG Metall they have signed agreements clearing the way for team work.[94]

The rapid introduction of lean-production methods into Germany is particularly significant because Germany was thought to have the high-tech, high-skills alternative – the "virtuous circle" of high-end markets, skilled labor, and codetermination. But the crisis of accumulation that finally hit Germany, along with the entrance of the Japanese into the European market (via the UK and Spain), changed all this. The recession of the early 1990s provided the crisis needed to make drastic changes.[95] The opening of the "greenfield" GM Opel assembly plant in Eisenach in eastern Germany provided the new benchmark. This is a model lean facility, with all the paraphernalia and, according to one shop steward, incredible "pressure on the workers."[96]

Despite the rapidity with which lean methods are being introduced throughout Germany's auto industry and elsewhere, the coming of lean production follows the pattern set in existing "brownfield" plants in the US and Britain in the 1980s and into the 1990s (following the standards set at "greenfield" transplants and various joint ventures such as Mazda and NUMMI). Lean production is often introduced piecemeal, though in fairly rapid succession, in older facilities. Frequently, major changes are introduced first in one department, or even one work station, at a time to minimize resistance.[97] Workforce reductions don't necessarily come as giant lay-offs, but through accelerated attrition aided by buyout and early retirement packages. This piecemeal, but rapid, means of going lean – the pattern in auto and telecommunications industries in the US – makes resistance more difficult and union control over the process all but impossible.

The same pattern and problems were experienced in the UK after Nissan set the benchmark at its Sunderland plant in 1986. Speaking of the rapidity of change, British shop stewards at Ford's Dagenham plant wrote:

> Within all this the unions have to some extent been overwhelmed. For example, stewards are supposed to be present at all problem-solving groups, but we don't have enough stewards to cover them.[98]

In France lean practices, including downsizing and outsourcing, spread rapidly. The unions, with weak workplace organization, did not mount opposition and the works councils set up under the 1982 Auroux Laws lacked the power to regulate the process. Furthermore, the unions were divided on the new work organization. The CFDT generally supported the changes, while the CGT was more suspicious, but not absolutely opposed.[99] By the early 1990s, it was estimated that there were 30,000 quality circles functioning throughout French industry – the largest number in Europe.[100] At both Renault and Peugeot, participation programs and productivity pay have helped pave the way for massive workforce reductions in recent years. In a startling move toward leanness, Renault's blue-collar workforce fell from 110,000 in the mid-1980s to 65,000 in 1996. This involved closing the old Boulogne-Billancourt assembly complex, which had once employed 35,000 workers, and replacing it with a "greenfield" lean plant at Cléon that employs 5,567 workers, while much of the parts production was moved to its other plants in Europe.[101] At Peugeot, which employs lean methods similar to Renault, the giant plant at Socheaux went from 32,000 in the 1980s to 19,500 in 1996, while that at Poissy went from 20,000 to 9,000.[102]

In Italy, the unions, particularly the CGIL (Confederazione Generale Italiana del Lavoro), have embraced the new work methods and not resisted "downsizing." The course of introducing more lean and flexible work and production organization was, however, somewhat different because of the existence of joint labor–management works councils set up under successive legislative efforts. This included the 1984 Protocol of the IRI, Italy's industrial state-holding company, which employs about 300,000 workers and tends to set standards for all industry. Workplace-level bargaining only started in earnest in the 1980s, following the disastrous defeat of the 1980 Fiat strike, and in the context of a drastic restructuring and modernization of Italian industry. The unions cooperated in this effort, creating a "de facto cooperation" that lent itself to the introduction of workforce (numerical, functional, and time) flexibility and reductions, total quality management, and so on.[103]

Wherever one looks in the developed industrial capitalist world, and in most of the more industrialized countries of the South, lean-production methods are either the norm or rapidly spreading. While their implementation may be partial, haphazard or slipshod, and is almost certain to be modified once complete, the problems and pressures of this extension of mass production are being felt by the working class across the world. From being a "new way of working" that promised a more humane workplace, it has been revealed as a system of brutal work intensification and a means of by-passing or undermining unionism.

"Unbundling" and Vulnerability

The lean-production, management-by-stress system, taken as a whole, has a tight internal logic. Its various pieces (*kaizen*, flexibility, outsourcing, JIT, etc.) are held together in a constant state of tension and flux designed to reduce the workforce and the overall cost structure of production. The tightening up of a job cycle in one part of the system should lead to a recalibration of the whole system. Conversely, a breakdown at any point in the total system of production, from assembly or service delivery down the production chain, will rapidly impact the entire system.

At the same time, this system did not spring forth intact overnight: it has evolved over time, is frequently implemented piecemeal, and continues to be modified as a result of internal breakdowns, market pressures, or worker resistance. Furthermore, there are considerable differences in how companies structure and implement lean production, even between Japanese companies like Suzuki and Toyota, for example.[104] In addition, national differences in economy or labor-relations laws also shape the way in which lean methods come to various countries to some extent. Indeed, looked at from the idealized viewpoint presented by the MIT IMVP group, lean production is as varied as earlier versions of mass production.[105]

The fact that the reality of lean production is not always in accord with its internal logic and that it varies in practice from firm to firm, country to country, and industry to industry has led some analysts to speak of "unbundling" the system. Steve Babson puts it this way:

> Thus "unbundled," lean production can be taken as a variable mixture of discrete elements, selectively recombined on a case-by-case basis.[106]

The very fact that management is continually altering and modifying the system, not to mention constantly reorganizing itself, is testimony to the reality that the combinations that produce today's "best practice" are, to some extent, failures. Worker resistance of the everyday variety as well as the occasional visible struggle or dispute are a factor in these failures – as well as in potential successes.

In a discussion of lean methods in the European airline industry, Paul Blayton and Peter Turbull make the point this way:

> There can never be "one best way" to convert potential into concrete labor and thereby make a profit, only different routes to partial failure, if for no other reason than the simple fact that any management strategy which seeks to exploit labor power will be contested.[107]

While productivity increases in the "core" and cost-cutting down the production chain are certain to remain a central goal of capital, there is nothing in the forces of global competition that dictates the 57-second minute versus the 45- or 50-second minute, 50- and 60-hour work weeks, or any particular speed of work where the workers and/or the union have the power to resist. Although the management-by-stress logic of lean production appears essential, even such central features as teams and just-in-time delivery have been modified.

Ironically, the very internal logic of lean production also makes it highly vulnerable to disruption, as its own practitioners and theoreticians recognize. Indeed, the MIT IMVP group argues that lean production must be a humane system precisely because it is "fragile." They say, "to make a lean system with no slack – no safety net – work at all, it is essential that every worker try very hard."[108] The cooperation/competitiveness ethos of management-by-stress is, of course, meant to motivate such effort. But when, as inevitably happens for one or another group of workers, this ethos is shattered on the reality of work intensification, long hours, and health-threatening conditions, the fragility of the system becomes a weapon of resistance.

This vulnerability of the system's own logic has been demonstrated by the strikes at GM in the US that began in 1993. Each of these strikes began to close down other facilities across GM's tightly integrated production chain. The longer the strike, the more plants went down. The longest, the seventeen-day strike at two Dayton, Ohio, brake plants, closed all but one assembly plant across the US, Canada, and Mexico, along with scores of parts plants and independent supplier firms.[109]

It is not only the JIT link between plants that provides workers with a weapon of resistance. Even within a given plant, at least where a fairly tight management-by-stress set-up prevails, disruption in one sector should be felt elsewhere in short order. Of course, this vulnerability of the system is not always apparent to the workers in any one sector or plant. But practice makes perfect in resistance as in production, and the practice of "mapping the workplace" in order to locate points of vulnerability can be applied to lean production's logic with telling results.[110]

A brief look at the difference in the 1996 bargaining with GM in the US, on the one hand, and Canada, on the other, provides a clear insight into the difference the union's stance and actions can have on deepening or resisting aspects of lean production. In the US, the United Auto Workers' leaders not only agreed to continue its "jointness" program with GM, to renew its "living agreement" approach, whereby top management and the pinnacle of the union hierarchy can change local working conditions (flexibility) at will, and to permit unbounded overtime and outsourcing, they also agreed to introduce a new element of wage flexibility granted earlier to Ford, allowing the pay of workers in its parts plants to fall behind those in assembly over time. Indeed, the new contract language virtually takes wages in parts plants out of the collective-bargaining sphere by granting GM the right to pay at the local "prevailing wage" of the top one-fifth of UAW members in a given area or of the top one-fifth of companies in that area. This formula breaks the sixty-year-old practice of a single union standard within the Big Three auto companies.[111]

The Canadian Auto Workers (CAW), bargaining with GM at the same time, made no such concessions and, in fact, won some gains on reduced annual work time. Whereas the UAW granted GM (and Ford and Chrysler) the right to cut their workforce by 5%, the CAW put a stop to outsourcing or any workforce reductions during the life of the contract. The UAW, of course, settled without a strike, while the Canadians struck for three weeks during which workers at GM-Canada's Oshawa, Ontario, fabrication plant seized the facilities for a day. Naturally, the strike in Canada closed plants down the JIT chain in the US as time went on.[112] The lesson here is that resistance matters, particularly when the union leadership is willing to stick to its guns, and that elements of lean production or competitiveness the company sees as essential can be stopped or modified. Struggle can begin to "unbundle" lean production.

Limits to Lean I: Space–Time Tension

The MIT IMVP group sees lean production as universal salvation, at least for the world's automobile industry. What is increasingly clear, however, is that this streamlined mass production embodies many of the same limitations as classical mass production, or, for that matter, any form of capitalist production, as well as some of its own. Aside from the resistance it inevitably engenders, these limits are of two kinds: a time–space tension in the organization of the production chain; and the reproduction of the accumulation crisis that induced the spread of lean methods in the first place.

Some of the difficulties of lean production lie in the organization and dynamics of the system itself. As Erica Schoenberger suggests, time is closely related to flexibility in the system, in that getting new products to market first has become one of the more important tactics in competition. She argues that the most important aspect is the reduction of product-development time. But this must be coordinated with actual production if the firm is to beat the competition to market. Just-in-time production facilitates this, but also introduces new spatial constraints.

In Schoenberger's view, this "first-to-market" strategy strongly implies two spatial characteristics of lean production: that final production be near the market in question; and that both the product-development and the production systems be within a workable geographic distance. Noting, after the works of David Harvey, that the advances in transportation and communications had been adequate to solve time–space problems for simple mass production, with its just-in-case delivery system, Schoen-berger argues that the new emphasis on time as a competitive factor changes things.[113] She writes:

> a new round of "time–space compression" has had, in my view, the unusual effect of reproposing the problem of space for the system. In other words, the once-solved problem of distance has become unsolved again, and this despite the fact that the techniques and costs of transportation and communication have steadily improved. The old time–space strategy has become invalid, and a new one is being worked out in its place.[114]

The original solution to this problem in Japan was proximity – hence the construction of Toyota City, as well as a generally concentrated industrial belt across southern Japan. But, since then, both cost and market consider-ations have led the Japanese, with others following suit, to expand production chains geographically, on the one hand, and to locate new assembly facilities in the major markets of North America and Europe, on the other. This has involved a significant change from Japanese industry's export orientation, but also a new risk factor, considering the cost of sunk capital investments involved.

While Schoenberger sees a general tendency for production to return to the major countries of the economic North in order to be strategically placed in each major Triad market and to reduce spatial separation within the production chain, there actually appear to be two contradictory sides to locational questions, at least in manufacturing. Cost and spatial considerations seem to be contradictory forces of attraction on firms engaged in extended lean production. Cost has a tendency to win out in the production chain, with component production moving toward lower-wage and -cost areas or even abroad; while the need to be inside each major market has drawn more and more final assembly, and, in its trail, supplier operations, to major centers of the Triad.

What this tension produces are successive waves of investment and outsourcing accompanied by the writing off or sale of older, less efficient, facilities. Both the restructuring of the 1980s and the downsizing of the 1990s included this sort of change. This kind of flux in the production system is very disorienting for workers and their unions and gives the impression of the infinite mobility of capital discussed earlier. It is also, undoubtedly, a source of the constant management shake-ups that characterize this era, as well as the parade of "new" management fads (like buying a corporate "culture") and quality schemes. As the one-time effects on profits of early market entry or newly developed products or features wear off, management looks to place blame and develop yet another round of "innovative" marketing and production strategies. Whereas simple mass production was characterized by long-range planning, lean mass production necessarily produces a tendency toward short-sightedness and "short-termism."

In fact, this space–time contradiction helps reproduce capital's classic crisis of accumulation as new, often duplicate production systems are placed in the major economic regions. Ironically, the extensive outsourcing, often at considerable geographic distances, both reintroduces transport costs into the JIT chain, even as it reduces labor costs, and transfers to the supplier company a portion of the value added from which profits are extracted, compounding the crisis of accumulation.

Limits to Lean II: The Crisis of Accumulation Compounded

The most fundamental limitation to lean production, however, lies in its own dynamics as a system of capitalist production. Indications that lean production did not mean the transcendence of capitalist crisis began to appear in its land of birth in the 1990s. With the world-wide recession of the early 1990s, lean production in Japan entered a period of crisis similar to that experienced by simple mass production in the West in the 1970s and 1980s. In 1993–94 many Japanese TNCs announced massive workforce reductions, while Nissan announced it would close its new high-tech Zama plant.[115] Life-time employment came to mean that redundant "core" workers moved down the supply chain to lower-wage jobs, while supplier employees were laid off.[116] To be sure, this was partly a result of the world-wide recession of the early 1990s, but it was the first time in over two decades that such a recession had had a significant impact on the Japanese economy.

Japan had, in effect, repeated the experience of the US auto industry of a decade and a half earlier. First, its legendary productivity gains hit the wall in the 1980s. Whereas the average build hours per vehicle had fallen from 254 in 1970 to 139 in 1980, they only fell to 133 in 1986 and stayed there for the rest of the decade. While these figures are still lower than those for North America or Europe, the British analysts who compiled and calculated them conclude that, "there is apparently an irreducible mini-mum of well over 100 motor sector labor hours in any car." These figures are particularly significant because they include labor hours in the compo-nent-supplier sector of the industry.[117]

To deal with this limitation and to move into the North American and European markets, Toyota and Nissan had invested heavily in new technology and expanded capacity in the 1980s – reversing the original capital-scarce strategy in order to remain competitive. Industry analyst Maryann Keller described Toyota's situation by the early 1990s:

> Japan's struggling economy was only part of the headache. Toyota had just completed a massive spending binge that had stretched its resources. New factories in Tahara, Kyushu, Great Britain, and Kentucky, along with heavy investments in new models had dangerously raised fixed costs.[118]

What this suggests is that, in line with what was said above about increased investment, not only did Japan's once "leanest" auto producers face overcapacity, they also faced a crisis in their rates of profit. That is, accumulated investment was outrunning the growth of profits. The more they invested to improve competitiveness, the more they compounded the problem. Indeed, this is what the Japan Auto Workers' Federation report argued when it said, "the companies make only little profit."[119] The floor on build hours suggests there is no easy way out for Japanese auto makers.

Ironically, this problem is further compounded for Japan's auto com-panies precisely because of all the outsourcing of production that helped make them the low-cost "regulating" capitals. Extensive outsourcing means that the ratio of value added to sales (a proxy for the company's potential profit margin – though not profit rate) is low for Japan's assembler companies. Between 1983 and 1991, Japanese auto-assembler firms averaged from 13% to 20% value added to sales ratios, compared with 28% to 38% for US auto companies.[120] This means that no matter how efficient or low-cost the Japanese *industry* is, the major assembler *firms*, Toyota, Nissan, Honda, etc., have a low pool of value added from which to glean profits. As they "share" work with other companies, they naturally must "share" the profits created by the labor that performs that work. In terms of the distribution of value added, material costs, and investment in new plant and equipment, very little has changed in the structure of the auto industry in the past twenty years.[121] What outsourcing and contracting have changed is the "ownership" pattern of the industry's production chain and, hence, of the value added from which profits accrue.

Furthermore, the assembly end of the industry is the most capital-intensive. For example, to use US figures for 1994, the assembly sector invested $21,728 per production worker in new plant and equipment, while the parts sector invested only $11,535 per production worker.[122] While there are fewer than ten major assembler firms in the US investing just over half of the annual total, there are literally thousands of independent auto-parts producers investing just under half the total, indicating that the difference in capital intensity between the assembly and parts firms is, in fact, enormous. As North American and European auto-assembler companies increase outsourcing to lower average production costs, they actually intensify the tendency of the rate of profit to fall. In effect, lean production's propensity to outsource and contract as much labor as possible is an unintended shot in the foot for the major producers of cars and trucks.

The Japanese industry's response through the mid-1990s has been mixed. Most of the TNCs were moving more and more production out of Japan, on the one hand, and putting cost-cutting pressures on their suppliers, on the other.[123] Toyota continued to expand capacity, while Nissan closed its greenfield Zama plant. Toyota, however, also began modifying some features of leanness. As mentioned, the teams went dormant at Tahara. Even more significantly, however, some buffers were built back into the assembly lines.[124] Indeed, it was reported in 1995 that Toyota was modifying its production system in a less than lean direction, allowing larger inventories, in order to deal with growing production problems.[125]

As the world market has recovered, Japan's auto companies have, reportedly, decided to reduce the content (and price) of their cars by stripping luxuries and other up-market features in hopes of regaining lost market share at home and abroad.[126] Assuming these features are produced by contracting supplier firms, this would increase the proportion of value added produced in-house and perhaps improve profitability somewhat. The down-side is that lower selling prices will reduce the amount of value added per car unless these companies make some more productivity breakthroughs. It seems, however, that this has become more and more difficult at given levels of technology. This would imply a continued profitability crisis for lean production in its birthplace, soon to be replicated by imitators abroad.

The bad news, of course, is that the continued crisis of accumulation and the limits to further genuine innovation almost certainly mean even greater pressure on the workforce. One indication of this has been the return to the lengthening of work time in the US and elsewhere or various ways of chiseling on shorter work time in Europe as a way of increasing the value produced by the workers. Furthermore, the recipe for decentralizing production processes through the creation of extended production chains of progressively lower-paying work sites and casualized labor is contributing to a deepening social crisis of the working class that began over two decades ago and shows no sign of relenting.

Part II
Capital's Cops

6

Corporatism, Neoliberalism, Free Trade, and the State

In the past two decades the world has seen a major political transformation: a move by governments in almost all countries of the economic North, and most in the South as well, from the political center or left-of-center to the political right. In the late 1970s, twelve of western Europe's eighteen governments were held by social-democratic or labor-based parties. In the US, the Democrats dominated Washington; in Canada, the Liberals sat in Ottawa. Whether liberal or social democratic, basic economic policy was still based on "Keynesian" state-led economic regulation in combination with the welfare state, albeit, perhaps, a modified one.

A decade later, the majority of Western governments were conservative. Their economic policies were based on a combination of market regulation, drastic reductions in the welfare state, increased state regulation of trade-union activity, and usually an aggressive insertion into the international economy.[1] The history of this transition is beyond the scope of this book, but the reasons for and meaning of the transition are important to understanding the condition of organized labor and the possibilities for the future.

The first response of capital and its political allies to both their own crisis and the increased working-class militancy of the 1960s and 1970s, was not recourse to the market, but the assertion of the state, usually under a center-of-the-road liberal or slightly left-of-center social-democratic government. Wage freezes and guidelines swept the industrial world in the 1970s. This usually involved some top-level agreement between the government, the employers, and the trade-union leadership. In much of Europe, this sort of tripartite scheme became a regular, even institutionalized, way of managing the economy. Frequently called "corporatism," it was an attempt to "integrate trade unions with the state executive/bureaucracy and associations of business in the framing, legitimizing, and administering of public policy."[2] The public policy, of course, was directed at resolving the economic crisis through restraining labor costs and controlling trade-union behavior by incorporating the leaders into various government structures, usually some tripartite board of government, business and labor.

Corporatism was well within the Keynesian economic and social consensus arrived at across the industrial world in the post-war period. Under this consensus, trade unionism was more or less accepted or tolerated. Hal Draper put this sort of acceptance well when he wrote:

> It is the pattern of all countries that, as soon as the bourgeoisie reconciles itself to the fact that trade unionism is here to stay, it ceases to denounce the institution as a subversive evil that has to be rooted out with fire and sword in order to defend God, country and motherhood, and turns instead to the next line of defense: domesticating the unions, housebreaking them, and fitting them into the national family as one of the tame cats.[3]

While tripartism was evident in Britain and marginally even in the US and Canada, across continental Europe governments deepened their corporatist attempt to "domesticate" the unions and regulate workplace conflict by introducing new or extended workplace representation (works councils). Some of these reforms are still in evidence: the French Auroux Laws of 1982, joint consultative committees in Italy, enterprise committees in Spain, and the deepening of German codetermination. Largely cooptive in intent, these reforms were supposed to address the rebellion against inhuman working conditions and authoritarian management by providing an orderly institutional channel for discontent.[4] No doubt these representational schemes eased the way for overall restructuring then, as they have more recently with the introduction of lean methods.

Corporatism, however, was wrought with contradictions. As Leo Panitch writes:

> corporatist structures require of trade unions, as their contribution to the operation, not that they cut their ties with their base, but rather that they use those ties to legitimate state policy and elaborate their control over the members.[5]

This, in turn, calls for a greater centralization of the whole bargaining process, which enhanced union power for a time, something the employers began to chafe against by the 1980s.

An additional problem was that the role played by union leaders in restraining economic demands inevitably put a strain on their "ties with their base." This was particularly difficult during the 1970s because of the high rates of inflation across most of the developed economies. In fact, nominal wages rose rapidly through the 1970s and even the 1980s in Europe as workers attempted to keep pace with the rising cost of living. The centralized bargaining encouraged under corporatism aided the winning of wage and benefits increases. Strike levels remained fairly high across much of Europe and Canada through the 1970s.[6] Increasingly, capital saw no advantage to a set-up in which labor was not genuinely restrained and centralized bargaining favored an upward trend in labor costs.

In any event, the Keynesian economic underpinnings of corporatism were doomed as the crisis of accumulation deepened with the severe recessions of 1974–75 and 1981–83, the international monetary order encoded in the Bretton Woods set-up collapsed, the need for deep international economic restructuring became apparent, and increased international economic integration reduced the state's ability to control the national economy. By the early 1980s, the depth of the world-wide economic crisis was visible to all, as was the inability of the social-democratic or centrist governments to deal with it. Probably the most striking failure, because it was the most radical last gasp of social democracy, was that of the Socialist Party government of France elected in 1981 and led by François Mitterrand.

Mitterrand attempted to pump up the slumping French economy in the midst of a world recession by a combination of classically Keynesian expansionary spending and the nationalization of several banks and major industrial firms. The result was that the financial markets panicked, capital fled abroad, the franc plunged in value, imports flooded the country, and inflation increased. International capital and the world market took their revenge on radical social democracy and won. Mitterrand reversed these policies within twelve months. Instead of protecting the nation's industry and workers, he moved into the camp of drastic restructuring, privatization, and increased marketization.[7] The implications of this were unmistakable.

Neoliberalism: Insurgency and Infiltration

Global economic crisis had demonstrated the limits of the old Keynesian approach and opened the door for a new policy doctrine. This new policy approach was neoliberalism: a mixture of neoclassical economic fundamentalism, market regulation in place of state guidance, economic redistribution in favor of capital (known as "supply-side" economics), moral authoritarianism with an idealized family at its center, international free-trade principles (sometimes inconsistently applied), and a thorough intolerance of trade unionism. It differed from the old conservatism of the post-war years in that it dismissed the social solidarity dimension of much of European Christian Democracy. What distanced neoliberalism most from the older pragmatic conservatism was that it was highly ideological; that is, market-based policies were carried out because a very abstract, idealized economic doctrine said they should be. Neoliberal ideology attributes to the market almost mystical powers to cleanse a sick world economy. It does not hesitate to use the state to affect economic trends, but it does so in ways that free up market forces, rather than restrain them.

Given the depth of crisis by the early 1980s, international capital and a new, though not necessarily young, generation of aggressive right-wing politicians were ready to adopt and implement this ideology. Faced with high unemployment, restructuring, and crumbling real wages in the wake of failed social democracy and centrist liberalism, millions of regular people, including a lot of working-class people, voted to give the new policies a chance. As one writer put it:

> There was from the outset a clear correlation between the depth of the economic crisis in the individual states and the electoral success of New Conservatives. Where unemployment rose most rapidly to over 10 percent by 1982 – in Belgium, the Netherlands, Denmark and Britain – there also the New Conservatism was registered earliest and most forcefully.[8]

The spread of neoliberal and conservative doctrines has been breathtakingly rapid and global. ILO economist Guy Standing summarized it like this:

> The increasing difficulty of redistributing income within industrialized countries, and the inflationary pressures there, coincided with this shift of economic dynamism [to Asia], and precipitated the crunching halt to social progress and to the widespread adoption of "supply-side economics" that has swept the world, beginning in the late 1970s in the UK and USA, and being adopted by stages within Europe and exported to Latin America, Africa, and most recently South Asia in the name of "structural adjustment." Its biggest triumph was to come in the 1990s, when Russia and other parts of the former eastern bloc adopted the same prescription under the name of "shock therapy." The tide is still flowing in that direction. It is not to defend the previous era to note that the labor market and social consequences of this global experiment have been dire and tragic.[9]

In the 1990s, popular disillusionment with conservative governments brought new electoral victories for centrist and left-of-center parties. But by the time these parties, most of which rely on working-class votes, returned to government they had, themselves, adopted much of the neoliberal agenda. Privatization, "commercialization," market regulation, and a hostility to trade-union freedoms marked the public utterances and policies of the new brand of liberals and social democrats who sought or gained national office. The practice and policies of these left-of-center neoliberal emulators were not as sharp or radical as those of the conservatives they imitated. Furthermore, unlike their conservative opponents, they were likely to qualify their new allegiance to flexibility and markets with some talk of "basic minimum standards of fairness," as a 1996 British Labour Party document put it, but the change in direction for social-democratic policy was unmistakably neoliberal.[10]

This turn represents something like the third sea change in social democratic politics, not only in Europe, but around the world in this century. The first came in the years leading up to World War One, when social democracy transformed itself from a revolutionary to a reformist movement. Socialism, it was argued by Eduard Bernstein in Germany and the Fabians in Britain, could be achieved through gradual, peaceful reforms. This was classical reformist socialism. The second great sea change, or retreat, came in the 1950s, when most of the major social-democratic parties in the world repudiated the idea of state ownership as the basis of socialism. This represented a big change because the traditional reformists saw the state as the (gradual) organizer of socialism. This change was led by politicians such as Hugh Gaitskell in Britain and Willy Brandt in Germany. While many parties did not bother to note this change, it was dramatically underlined by the 1959 Bad Godesberg Program of the German Social Democratic Party, which eliminated the socialist goal altogether.[11]

The new social democrats of the post-World War Two era saw no such role for the state as organizer of social ownership of "the means of production." Rather, they saw the state as regulator of capitalism and "socialists" (for they still used the word) as the organizers of the alleviation of the excesses of capitalism; that is, as administrators of the welfare state.[12] Keynesianism became the economic ideology of social democracy. The role of the state still loomed large, but not as the "expropriator of the expropriators." No one summed up this new twist on "socialism" better than William Winpisinger, who was president of the Machinists' union in the US during the 1980s and one of the few high-ranking US labor leaders to call himself a socialist. With his well-known American-style candor he said, "I'm for the kind of socialism that makes capitalism work."[13]

The new social democrats of the 1990s have taken another step by essentially abandoning the regulation or guidance of the economy by the state in favor of neoliberal market regulation. Their economic policies might be described as surrendering to the market. For example, they seldom seek to undo the market-based "reforms" of the previous right-wing governments. Some, like Felipe González, went as far as many rightist neoliberal governments in freeing up market forces. A 1996 British Labour Party document, while not going as far as the Spanish Socialists, says, for example, "we must avoid rigidity in labour market regulation and promote the flexibility we require." It calls instead for American-style "basic minimum standards of fairness."[14] Indeed, much of the transformation of social democracy in Europe appears as an emulation of the US Democratic Party, which, of course, has been moving in a neoliberal direction for years.

Today's neoliberal social democrats act not so much as the radical dismantlers of previous state regulation, as do the right-of-center neoliberals, but as the leaders of a more gradual retreat from this older regulation. Rather than the organizers of state intervention, they are now the organizers of a more or less gradual disengagement. Whereas yesteryear's social democrats could be regarded as maximalist economic regulators, today's are minimalists. When Tony Blair's British Labour Party says it wants "minimum standards," you can believe the word "minimum." While Labour and the social democrats have not abandoned their role as administrators of the welfare state, they have tolerated or presided over its reduction; that is, its minimalization.

Thus, by the mid-1990s, neoliberalism was not simply the labor movement's political rival, it had infiltrated the mass political parties on which the majority of workers had come to depend for decades. One did not have to hold a brief for the last generation of social-democratic and liberal politicians to realize that the situation had deteriorated seriously. Labor's political line of defense was not simply retreating before a powerful enemy; it was in many ways defecting to that enemy.

Naturally, neoliberalism provided either endorsement of or a quietly opened door for the growing employer assault on union wages, conditions, centralized bargaining practices, and in some countries on union rights and freedoms. Beginning in the 1970s in the US, unions saw the judicial arm of government chip away at these rights. The early 1980s saw the President of the United States fire striking air-traffic controllers. The 1990s saw the massive use of replacement workers (scabs) to break strikes at companies with long bargaining relationships and cooperation programs like Caterpillar and A. E. Staley. In Canada in the 1980s, a series of federal and provincial laws restricted the right to strike for over a million public-sector workers. In Britain in the 1980s, the Thatcher government passed the (anti-) Trade Union Laws, severely restricting union actions. The use of replacement workers, as at Timex in 1993, has also become common.[15]

While continental Europe has so far been spared strike-breaking or union-busting, the employers' offensive has taken the form of an assault on centralized bargaining. Across western Europe employers pushed for and frequently won the devolution of collective bargaining from nationwide multi-firm agreements to individual company-level labor contracts. Even where multi-firm bargaining remains more or less intact, the weight of bargaining issues has shifted more and more to the company level as flexibility issues take up more of the bargaining agenda.[16]

The Retreat from "Social" Europe

The rise of neoliberalism is not simply an ideological change of mind or a function of the failure of the Keynesian economic policy options that underwrote North American liberalism and European social democracy. The twin processes of globalization and regionalization have changed both the rules of the game and the old balance of class forces. The process of European economic integration provides an example of this: one in which the odds were always against organized labor and the working class.

There is an important political distinction between the "social dimension" of European integration and the rise of neoliberalism, deregulation, and competition. In general, the concept of the "social dimension" came from the member states in the 1980s, where and when social democracy still had considerable influence. It was always resisted by business, particularly UNICE, the European employers' association. "Competition policy," on the other hand, originated from the start at the European Community level. The ideas of free trade and internal competition within each member state were embodied in the treaties on which the whole process of integration and unification is based, and expanded as the treaties became more comprehensive.[17] This, of course, is vigorously supported by UNICE and business in general. In other words, the deck is stacked in favor of increased market regulation and against the social dimension or state regulation.

Ironically, the Single European Act of 1987 accelerated both the process of "free trade" and market integration among the twelve member countries (now eighteen) and the process associated with the (primarily German) "social-market" concept of the corporatist era. This was first embodied in the 1989 Social Charter and then in the Protocol of the Maastricht Treaty (known as the "Social Chapter"), signed in 1991 and ratified in December 1993. The implementation of the Single European Act required the signing nations to pass into national law some 300 European Community directives, most of which dealt with business and commercial matters that would create the free flow of products, capital, and people.[18]

The Single Market set off or accelerated four processes that spelled trouble for European workers and their unions. The first was the simultaneous inward rush of US and Japanese capital from TNCs based in those countries fearing a protected "fortress Europe," and the equally dramatic outward flow of European capital to North America, Asia, and eastern Europe. This was the period of accelerated world-wide foreign direct-investment flows. The second, closely related, trend was the rush of mergers and acquisitions across Europe as companies sought to improve their market position in the new Single Market. The third was the predictable consequence of the intensified competition created by the anticipation of "free trade" and of the first two trends: the downward pressure on labor costs and the associated greater emphasis on enterprise-level, as opposed to industry-level, bargaining.[19] This latter process, in particular, was associated with the fourth trend, the rise of lean production in Europe, beginning in the mid-to-late-1980s.

Thus, European trade unions, still very nationally focused, faced a growing number of larger TNCs throughout Europe. These were mostly headquartered in the UK, France, Germany, the US, or Japan. Even as they grew more transnational in character, these TNCs demanded that bargaining be decentralized within each nation. Company-level as well as plant-level flexibility was demanded as lean-production methods increasingly became the best practice to emulate. The emerging imbalance was clear to all and the demand arose from the European Trade Union Confederation (ETUC), the voice of the national federations across Europe, for a counterbalance of some sort. This demand was backed by the French Socialist Party, in particular, and supported by the then European Commission President Jacques Delors. Its outcome was the 1989 Social Charter.[20]

The ideology behind the Social Charter was pure 1970s corporatism. This sort of ideology lingered on within the European Commission in part because its prestige and power rested on the sort of tripartite negotiations that characterized corporatism. Indeed, the negotiations over the Social Charter were a multinational example of the national schemes already under enormous pressure from organized big business and the TNCs. Big Euro-business and the TNCs weighed in on this debate as well, forcing the Commission to drop a number ETUC-supported provisions – most notably the "Vredeling Directive," which would have given unions very extensive access to company information and the right to consultation on many issues. Business viewed this as a foot in the door for EU-wide collective bargaining, something they would hardly support at a time when they were working to dismantle centralized bargaining within most countries. Notable for their opposition to all of this were the British government, on the one hand, and the American-based TNCs operating within the European Union, on the other.[21]

The result of this business backlash was that the Social Charter was not included in the text of the 1991 Maastricht Treaty of European Union, but appended as a Protocol known as the "Social Chapter." The right of "subsidiarity," under which nations could give their national laws precedent over EU directives, was expanded. The European Works Council Directive, long a goal of the ETUC, was severely watered down to exclude any hint of collective bargaining before it was passed in late 1994.[22] The "Action Programme" of the Social Charter was declared exhausted, while post-Maastricht statements from the European Commission concerning the social dimension, particularly in the 1993 White Paper, said there was "not a need for a wide-ranging programme of new legislative proposals in the coming period."[23] In short, the social dimension had lost what momentum it had once had.

More recently, the whole focus of the European unification process has switched from this social dimension to European Monetary Union (EMU). This has two implications. First, of course, it simply means that genuine negotiations toward any expansion or defense of the idea of "social" Europe, the so-called "social dialogues," are at best on the back burner for the foreseeable future. The second is that both the process of achieving EMU and, should it happen, its actual implementation provide more outside force bearing down on national bargaining and labor costs. Two British industrial-relations scholars described this well:

> with further moves towards EMU, existing systems of national pay bargaining founded mainly on multi-employer bargaining will encounter a new set of constraints. It is not simply that there will be considerable pressure to keep domestic inflation rates as low as possible, given that the ability of national governments to compensate by devaluation will be progressively reduced. Restructuring stemming from the single market, coupled with EU efforts to make qualifications more transferable across borders, will encourage pay comparisons; these will be much easier to make because a single currency will make pay settlements much more transparent.[24]

EMU is also designed to reduce the welfare state across Europe by strict budgetary limits that will make even today's remaining social provisions difficult to maintain. Speaking of this "strange monetary structure," Daniel Singer argues:

It is designed to reduce public expenditure on health, old-age pensions and other welfare services while encouraging private insurance. Its other task is to render the minimum wage meaningless and eliminate all the limitations introduced since World War II on the employer's freedom to hire and fire as he pleases. In short, it is to build Europe *à l'americaine.*[25]

It would be an exaggeration to say that all the institutions of corporatism or "social Europe" have been wiped out or will be imminently. The process of erosion, and even reversal, however, is clear and is deeply embedded in the whole top-down process of replacing state regulation with market regulation. A "social market," such as that practiced in Germany for the past twenty years, is, after all, a market that is hemmed in by a dense network of institutions designed to limit competition and ameliorate its impact on the working class. What is occurring across continental Europe, including eastern Europe, is the unraveling of such institutions and their replacement with pro-market institutions or forces.

For some time, labor leaders across the US and Canada have looked to Europe's social-market model in hope that this could be their future. What has happened instead in North America is the implementation of free trade, if not really a single market, between three nations with different institutional arrangements, none of which matches those of continental Europe. Unless Europe's working-class organizations can expand the massive opposition they have mounted in the last couple of years, it is far more likely that Europe's future will look more like that of North America than the other way around.

NAFTA and Neoliberalism in North America

The North American Free Trade Agreement (NAFTA), signed in 1993 by Presidents Clinton and Salinas and Prime Minister Mulroney, came into force on January 1, 1994. It was in many ways the culmination of a long process of unequal economic integration between Mexico and the US, on the one hand, and Canada and the US, on the other. In terms of both imports and exports, by 1994, US trade with both Canada and Mexico was larger than with any other country, except Japan. In terms of its investment position, its accumulated FDI abroad, US investment in Canada was exceeded only by that in Britain, while among Third World countries, investment in Mexico was surpassed only marginally by that in Brazil.[26] Direct integration between Canada and Mexico was and is minimal, the US economy being the core around which other economies are to cluster.

NAFTA differs from the European Union (EU) project in three important ways. First, it directly incorporates a major Third World nation, Mexico, creating wage and income differentials greater than any within the EU. By 1995, with the collapse of the peso, the differential between total wages and benefits in the US and Mexico was almost twelve to one.[27] Furthermore, the weight of Mexico is significant, as it includes a quarter of the total NAFTA-area population of 378 million people.[28] The only other nations that will be allowed to join the NAFTA region will be Third World nations with similarly low income levels.

Second, NAFTA, unlike Maastricht, does not provide for the free flow of labor across borders. This has two effects that are unfavorable for Mexican workers and lay the basis for increased competition with workers in the US and Canada. One is that it allows capital to keep Mexican wages artificially low by restricting migration and maintaining, despite advanced labor laws in Mexico, an authoritarian set-up that could not be reproduced in the US or Canada. Another is that although the border is porous, the illegal status of undocumented workers from Mexico or elsewhere allows them to be exploited to a degree that legal workers could not be. This tends to enforce low-wage status, as undocumented workers do not have recourse to the same rights or institutions in many cases as legal immigrant or citizens of the US or Canada. A clear example is the way in which differing legal status has divided migrant farmworkers in the US, often limiting their ability to organize and struggle for better wages and conditions.[29] This means that the pressures are very strong to keep Mexican workers (both in Mexico and the US) as the low-wage competition in many manufacturing and service jobs. One more downward pressure on wages.

Third, there is no proposed political union or structure to oversee the project and there is no real pretense of any social dimension; the labor and environmental "side agreements" are toothless afterthoughts. One analyst described the process leading up to the labor agreement:

> Responding to political pressure from organized labor in the US, President Clinton agreed to negotiate a side accord on labor, which would be added to the existing document. The history of that negotiation is a progressive weakening of language and enforcement mechanisms almost from the first moment an accord was promised. . . . Phrasing in the end would direct each country, "to establish its own domestic labor standards," thereby precluding any continental minimal standard.[30]

Unions can bring complaints to the National Administrative Office in each country, but the only mechanism for resolving complaints is negotiations between the governments involved. By default, the real power over how economic integration will proceed falls to the US-based TNCs and the US government. Because of the significance of the wage and income differentials between Mexico, on the one hand, and the US and Canada, on the other, in looking at the build-up to the impact of NAFTA the emphasis here will be on Mexico.

In its actual content, the NAFTA deals more with matters of investment, technology, and the production of goods and services than with traditional trade issues. In arguing for the agreement, the US International Trade Commission stated its most basic purpose. "By codifying liberal trade and investment policies in an international agreement ... a US–Mexico FTA would increase the confidence of investors in the Mexican economy."[31] The preamble of NAFTA reiterates its intention to "Ensure a predictable commercial environment for business planning and investment."[32] NAFTA, in short, offers American capital both the opportunity to increase its world share of foreign direct investment (FDI) through extensive investment in Mexico and the ability to extend lean production into a low-wage labor market that is also, as *Business Week* argues, "smart, motivated," and increasingly well trained.[33]

Investment in Mexico by US firms is not new. Major corporations such as GM, Ford, Chrysler, and General Electric, as well as many smaller firms, have operated in Mexico for decades. But this earlier investment was limited in many ways by the Mexican government's import substitution industrialization (ISI) strategy and its production was almost exclusively for Mexican consumption.[34] The initial turn toward export production came in 1982 with the debt crisis and the subsequent collapse of the domestic market. Auto companies such as GM, Ford, Chrysler, and Nissan, all of whom built new assembly facilities around the late 1970s, regeared their production toward exports to the US.[35] The investment in manufacturing plant that accelerated during the 1980s, particularly after 1985, was meant to produce almost entirely for export, mostly to the US. Furthermore, it was heavily "outsourced," with operations linked to production systems in the US, largely through "intra-firm" trade within the channels of the corporations themselves.[36]

American outsourcing in Mexico was initially based in a system of "in-bond" production governed by special trade laws that prefigured "free trade" in many ways. Known colloquially as the *maquiladora* program, it allowed US firms to by-pass Mexico's restrictions on foreign ownership and operate wholly owned plants along the winding 2,000-mile border, using US-originated materials and producing exclusively for re-export into the US. Although the *maquila* system was launched in 1965, it did not take off until the 1980s, when it grew from 620 plants employing 119,000 workers in 1980 to 2,069 plants and 508,505 workers in 1992.[37]

As investment grew and plants proliferated, the level of technology rose and the early labor-intensive plants, though still present, were eclipsed by those with a rising capital–labor ratio. Employment in auto-component *maquiladora* plants, for example, rose from 7,500 in 1980 to 93,278 in 1989, while garment and textile employment rose only from 17,570 to 41,517 in the same period.[38] Among these automotive *maquilas*, Jorge Carillo notes: "The growing number of high technology plants among IMA (automotive *maquilas*), traditionally thought of as intensive assembly plants with an unskilled labor force and low wages, represents a significant change."[39] Another indicator of the growing capital–labor ratio, according to *La Jornada*, was the 17% decline in the average number of workers per *maquila* plant from 1982 to 1990.[40] In addition, the US Big Three auto makers began to build capital-intensive assembly and engine plants outside the *maquila* system, though also located in the north and oriented mainly toward export to the US.[41]

The move up the ladder of technology also confirmed the incredible advantages of combining low wages with high technology well within a feasible geographic framework. The Ford/Mazda Hermosillo, Mexico, assembly plant provided the lean-production model. Launched in 1986, the Hermosillo plant embodied all of the latest lean wrinkles in plant layout, technology, and flexible workforce deployment. Its initial cost was $500 million, with construction savings of 33–50% below US costs. The workforce of 1,600, which proved to be as efficient as any in the US, cost about $2 an hour per worker in wages, benefits, and taxes, or about $7 million a year. A comparable workforce in a US Ford plant would have cost $30 an hour or nearly $100 million a year. The annual savings in wages were $93 million. Since the cars produced in Hermosillo sell at the same price as comparable American-made models, Ford would recoup its investment in a little over five years. This represents a rapid acceleration of turn-over time for its capital.[42]

While preliminary steps to include Mexico in a North American agreement began in the mid-1980s, US capital did not find the Mexican economic and political system suitable for a seamless market or expanded state-of-the-art investment. This had nothing to do with cultural differences, real or alleged. It was simply a matter of incompatible economic institutions and the traditional nationalist and corporatist politics of Mexico's governing party, the Institutional Revolutionary Party (PRI – Partido Revolucionario Institucional), that supported them. The transformation required to establish "free trade" with Mexico was profound. Dan La Botz summarizes it like this:

> Between 1982 and 1994, Miguel de la Madrid, Salinas, and their followers, transformed the state-party and its relations with Mexican society. Under

their leadership, the PRI abandoned its revolutionary nationalist ideology, revamped its old corporativist structure, and gave up its protectionist economic development model for the panacea of free trade. Some have argued that the counter-revolution of the 1980s was as important as the reorganization of Mexico under Cárdenas in the 1930s.[43]

Prior to the 1980s, Mexico stood out as one of the Third World "miracle" economies: a successful, though occasionally troubled, example of import substitution industrialization. It had achieved annual growth rates of over 6 percent a year from 1940 to 1980. Manufacturing grew by an annual average of 7.6 percent from 1960 to 1980, with heavy industries growing by more than 10%.[44] Real wages in manufacturing had risen for decades, surpassing those of the Asian "miracle" economies and reaching a third of those in the US by the early 1980s. This growth was led by the state sector, which comprised over 1,500 enterprises, including petroleum, steel, mining, railroads, airlines, and telecommunications. Domestic family farm agriculture, protected by the Mexican constitution in the *ejido* system, was subsidized with low-interest credit. The policies of successive governments were assertively nationalist and populist, though never anti-capitalist or particularly permissive toward genuine trade unions. American and other foreign capital was accorded a significant role in this industrialization process, but within terms laid down by Mexican law and the permanent governing party, the PRI. The production of most industries, whether Mexican or foreign owned, was for that nation's domestic market.[45]

By the late 1970s, however, the world economic climate had changed. Three decades of global free trade and competition, combined with a decade of falling profit rates throughout the OECD nations, meant that competition among major capitals within the markets of the OECD nations had rendered older accumulation strategies obsolete. Direct investment in low-capacity plants producing for limited Third World ISI-oriented markets like Mexico's was not going to increase the overall profit margins of most multinationals. Furthermore, the financial, communications and transportation systems so crucial to the new methods of production were state-dominated and outmoded by the standards of multinational capital. Finally, Mexico was a thicket of tariffs and other barriers to the movement of materials between production sites in different countries.[46]

The opportunity to change all of this arose in the early 1980s, when Mexico lost its ability to meet interest payments on its external debt. As in the rest of Latin America, the debt crisis ended the period of growth and import substitution. The great flaw in the import-substitution strategy had always been its reliance on imported capital goods and materials; this was the basis of the debt accumulated in the 1970s. It was exacerbated by the transfer of capital to the US and Europe through the circuits of international production and finance controlled by the multinational corporations. High interest rates and, in Mexico's case, fluctuations in oil prices, finally produced "La Crisis" and killed genuine growth for a decade.[47]

The transformation wrought under the administrations of Miguel de la Madrid (1982–88) and Carlos Salinas de Gortari (1988–94) amounted to a basic redesign of the Mexican economy and of the corporatist practice of PRI rule as well. In the eight years prior to the announcement of the NAFTA in 1990, prices of many necessities were raised, wages frozen, the reprivatization of the banks begun, wholesale privatization of productive enterprises carried out, the GATT signed in 1986, long-standing tariffs and investment restrictions lifted or drastically reduced, and some twenty-five industries deregulated in the American manner.[48] In 1990, the US International Trade Commission reported, with its usual ideological zeal, that "based on the premise that excessive and obsolete regulations were largely responsible for inefficiency in the use of Mexican resources, Mexico has implemented a far-reaching program of deregulation."[49]

At the heart of this neoliberal project was the privatization of Mexico's considerable state sector. From December 1982 through the end of 1992, 1,158 of the country's nearly 1,500 state enterprises and 18 nationalized banks were privatized or liquidated, bringing the government a grand total of $34.5 billion in income.[50] Included among the privatized enterprises were telecommunications, steel, mining, airlines, and banking. In that period, the state sector fell from 25% of the GDP to 17%. The cost in jobs was estimated by Mexico's National Institute of Statistics at 200,000 by 1991.[51]

Privatization brought Mexico's small but wealthy capitalist elite into the modernizing coalition crafted by Carlos Salinas de Gortari and the "técnicos" wing of the PRI. The cosmopolitan elite of this class are represented in the 37-member Mexican Businessmen's Council. These thirty-seven leading business personalities control the country's top seventy-one private companies, which account for 22% of the annual gross domestic product, and are represented in the five largest privatizations, which amounted to 80% of the value of all privatizations up to 1991. Many of the privatizations and a good deal of the new investment take the forms of joint ventures with US and other foreign capital. Thus, for Mexican capital, structural adjustment and NAFTA provide a boost into the growing transnational capitalist class.[52]

The object of the IMF (International Monetary Fund) structural-adjustment program and of the Salinas administration's own policy contributions was to restructure Mexico from its old state-led import-substitution strategy to a neo-liberal export-oriented model that could underwrite payment of the country's external debt. In its first phase, this was not accomplished by a dramatic increase in exports, but by a relative decline in imports. In fact, from 1980 through 1989 exports grew at only half the annual rate that they had from 1965 through 1980. Imports declined at an annual average rate of 4.7% from 1980 through 1989. Only the *maquila* sector provided growing exports, rising from 18% of total exports in 1980 to 55% in 1991.[53]

By 1990, Mexico resembled the sort of free-market Third World country US capital sought. Mexico possessed a literate, industrious workforce adaptable to high-tech labor with its wages disciplined by Confederation of Mexican Workers (CTM – Confederación de Trabajadores de México), itself dominated by the ruling Institutional Revolutionary Party, on the one hand, and a growing army of unemployed and underemployed, on the other. Its economy was largely privatized, deregulated, and structurally adjusted by the most rigorous IMF standards. Its financial, communications, and transportation systems were all modernizing rapidly, and there were few annoying restrictions on the movement of capital or goods. The groundwork was laid for a greater continental shift.

Mexico's neoliberal project, however, was not the success envisioned by de la Madrid, Salinas, Zedillo, the PRI's technocrats, or their US supporters. By 1993, even before NAFTA had gone into effect, the economy had ground to a halt, and in 1994 it went into recession, even though the neighboring US economy was in recovery. By the end of that year newly elected President Zedillo had to let the peso float on the world market, which led to a 40–50% devaluation. The expected massive inward flow of investment didn't materialize. About 70% of total investment was in stock purchases and short-term bonds, which paid incredibly high interest. Investment in manufacturing actually fell from $2.5 billion in 1994 to $1.5 billion in 1995.[54]

Of course, this did not mean that investment in Mexico stopped. US auto and auto-parts firms continued to shift some production to Mexico, although at a slower rate. About 18 new parts plants were built between 1992 and 1995, compared with 192 in the previous decade or so. In the northern state of Coahuila, a joint venture between US-owned Cone Mills and Mexican textile producer CIPSA began building a new denim complex that would employ 7,000 workers.[55] There was also large-scale investment in telecommunications, as major US and European firms jockeyed for position in Mexico's recently deregulated telephone industry.[56]

In fact, capital began to flee Mexico in amounts reminiscent of the 1982 crisis. It was not simply the recession and currency crisis that put a hold on Mexico's economic plans. On January 1, 1994, symbolically, the day NAFTA went into effect, the Zapatista peasant rebellion began in the state of Chiapas. The new president, in office less than a month, faced a brand-new political crisis on top of the economic crisis. Zedillo's response was a new austerity program and more wage restraint, on the one hand, and initial brutal repression of the Zapatista rebellion, on the other. When the latter brought 150,000 on to the streets of Mexico City, Zedillo turned to negotiations with the Zapatistas. While these have been inconclusive, the Zapatistas in effect launched a national movement for political reform that is still a potent force in shaping Mexico's future.

Neoliberalism and NAFTA did not solve Mexico's economic problems; rather, they compounded them as that country's state-led economic set-up was drastically altered and the nation left to flounder in the globalizing world economy. But they had, nevertheless, accomplished one of the major goals of neoliberal reform. They held down and even reduced wages and working-class incomes in Mexico. In 1995, manufacturing hourly labor costs stood right where they had been in 1975. Only in 1975 they were almost a quarter of US hourly labor costs, while in 1995, they were 9%.[57] Furthermore, the modernization and rationalization of Mexican industry had cost two million formal-sector jobs, as hundreds of state enterprises were privatized and thousands of smaller Mexican firms succumbed to competition from more efficient American, Japanese, or European TNCs.[58]

Growing competition between workers with a 12-to-1 or greater wage differential, persistently high unemployment rates in all three countries, and weakened unions in the US and Mexico spell disaster for working-class earnings throughout the continent. There is no doubt that this process will continue to produce greater inequality: in the US during the 1980s and 1990s three-quarters to four-fifths of families lost both real earnings and income share; at the same time the share of income to capital rose, while that of labor declined.[59]

Free Trade and Global Exploitation

The forces putting workers into competition with one another in North America, Europe, or Asia, with or without a formal multilateral trade agreement, are compounded by the more general imposition of market regulation through the new World Trade Organization (WTO). This organization and the global agreement on which it is founded supersedes the General Agreement on Tariffs and Trade (GATT), first negotiated in 1947 and renegotiated seven times since.[60] What is significant about the Uruguay Round negotiations that produced the WTO is that it was the first "round" that went beyond reducing tariffs on traded goods to include investment questions, trade in services, intellectual property rights (of businesses), and non-tariff barriers, such as local content laws, to trade in general. The WTO is by far the most sweeping international economic agreement to date. As such, it unleashes new market forces in crucial areas of investment and services.

While it is difficult to assess just how destructive the forces unleashed under the new WTO will be, the general direction of its impact, in combination with the regional agreements and national deregulation efforts, is clear. It will increase pressures to cut costs in order for businesses to stay competitive and, therefore, put still more downward pressures on labor costs and working-class incomes in particular. This is not just what was argued in chapter 3 about increasing the income gap between the economic North and South. It means a redistribution of income from the global working class to the global capitalist class.

In a 1993 dissenting report, two World Bank economists warned of exactly this type of redistribution as a consequence of the WTO:

> We are concerned that global economic integration via free trade will favor a privileged minority at the expense of the majority in both industrial and developing countries.

As workers' real wages fall around the world:

> Northern capitalists must get richer to consume ever more if the North is to provide markets for Southern products and raw materials.[61]

In fact, long before the World Bank economists issued their warning, this world-wide redistribution of income in favor of capital and the rich was well underway. Between 1960 and 1991, the proportion of world-wide income that went to the top 20% of the world's population doubled, from 30% to over 60%.[62] Income inequality has soared in the US, Britain, Canada, most of Latin America, and virtually all the former Communist countries in recent years. Increased global business competition in combination with neoliberal domestic policies is the basic reason.[63]

As in the case of Mexico above, export-oriented growth models of development are being imposed on developing countries through IMF/ World Bank structural-adjustment programs the world around. They must export to pay their debt and to afford more expensive manufactured or capital goods from the North. The WTO forces them to open their markets to Northern imports and investment. Northern capitalists, whether retailers like Nike or the GAP or manufacturers whose Southern-based facilities are part of an international production chain, or a service such as telecommunications, are the "consumers" in this global trade set-up.

Most international trade is within or between TNCs or other businesses. Thus, so far as international trade is concerned, capital has broken the link between mass consumption and working-class incomes implied in Keynesian theory. Northern capitalists and Southern capitalists are trading with one another and both need to get richer to make the set-up work. The surest way to do that is to increase the exploitation of workers everywhere by reducing real wages and incomes (including social benefits), increasing productivity, or doing both at the same time. Neoliberalism, lean production, and free trade are the ingredients for such a recipe.

The State and the New Multilateralism

What of the state or government in all of this? Is the world really reduced to governance by the 200,000 computer terminals facilitating the world's financial markets? Can't the national state still provide a measure of protection from the race to the bottom created by global trade and competition? Or, is the national state simply disappearing before the forces of globalization, as the futurists say? A quick look at your annual tax bill will probably tell you that the national state lingers on, with a high price tag at that. More than that, the persistence of high-tech armies defended by the political right, and semi-tech civil services' always being the butt of right-wing demagogy, should tell us that the day of the nation-state is far from over.

Most countries spend more of their gross national product on this supposedly disappearing institution today than they did in the era of Keynesian extravagance.[64] So, the state, like the nation itself, remains a part of the global mosaic. At the same time it seems clear that the direction of state policy has changed under the regime of neoliberalism. The question remains, however, of whether this is simply a matter of policy or whether there is something deeper going on that has altered the mission of the state.

The state is not disappearing, because capital needs it to function both domestically and internationally. Among the most basic tasks of the state in capitalist society are: laws protecting private property; the establishment of a currency; measurements; laws regulating business and financial transactions; the enforcement of these laws by the police and military; the provision of basic infrastructure too large for private business to finance; countless services, from the post office to the control of fisheries, education and other aspects of the reproduction of the various social classes beyond the scope of the family; the mediation of conflicting interests within the capitalist class through the courts and other tribunals; and the regulation of the struggle between capital and labor through labor laws, courts and tribunals; and police or military power when necessary.

The fact that the state has to mediate between and regulate different sectors of capital gives the modern state a certain autonomy. That is, no single group of capitalists controls the state permanently, and the capitalist class itself is too heterogeneous in its interests to control it directly as a class. Capital can and does act together on matters of basic interest, usually with the biggest actors leading the way. Capital certainly spends fortunes on influencing government decisions of all kinds. Much of the operation of the state, however, is delegated to professional politicians, high-ranking civil servants, military personnel, etc. As a result, the process of policy-making is contentious and complex, tending to conceal the class nature of the state.

The state has generally been forced to add to this list of tasks and services such things as welfare measures, women's rights, civil rights, pensions, or ecological standards as concessions (or pre-emptive measures) to the working class or other social movements over the last hundred years or so. Today, in the wake of a changing balance of class forces, the state is attempting to take many of these concessions back or reduce them. The basic function of protecting, regulating, and servicing private business property, however, remains at the core of the capitalist state. In many countries, laws and agencies limiting the actions of labor have increased, while police forces have grown in order to deal with the social effects of globalization and neoliberalism – poverty, crime, and class conflict.

The form of the state varies from country to country and era to era. Fascism, authoritarianism, and military rule in much of the twentieth century arose in response to the struggle of social classes (capital, rural oligarchy, labor, peasantry) and/or various economic crises. Despite increased international integration, more "normal" institutional, cultural, and historical differences between the governmental structures of countries persist, such as types of elections, forms of representation, power of the presidency, or the relative importance of the military. Beneath all these differences, however, the basic functions of protecting private business property, mediating internal conflicts between different capitalist interests, and regulating the struggle between capital and labor form the irreducible core of the modern capitalist state and the reason why it will not disappear.

In many ways, the growth of the international economy has expanded some of the functions of the state. The infrastructure of the world market, its ports, airports, roads, and railroads, are provided by national states or their contractors, not by any global authority. The countless bilateral and multilateral trade and commercial agreements that facilitate the world market are negotiated by national governments. These days, spy operations gather not only political and military information, but business intelligence as well. And when capital gets in trouble abroad, it is its "home" nation-state that comes to the rescue through negotiations, pressure, or military threat or intervention.

Since capitalism is an expansionary system, the state has played an international role from the earliest days of commercial capitalism. As historian Giovanni Arrighi argues in *The Long Twentieth Century*, the capitalist world market has always been organized by a leading dominant power or conflicting centers of power governing different geographic regions of the world. For most of the eighteenth and nineteenth centuries, the world market was organized by the British state through its colonial empire and dominance of the seas. In the twentieth century this system of regulation collapsed as the world fragmented into trade and currency blocs and the British Empire fell apart. Following World War Two, the United States became the dominant power, regulating the world market through the Bretton Woods system of currency control and, increasingly, open trade. This system, however, fell apart by the early 1970s as capital's world-wide crisis of accumulation grew.[65]

The vacuum of world market regulation was filled not by a new power, but by the giant TNCs that arose in the post-war period. Clearly, a multiplicity of competing TNCs cannot actually regulate a world-wide system of trade and investment. Nor do they want or have the ability to create a world state. They have opted instead for a system of multilateral agreements and institutions that they hope will provide coherence and order to the world market. Through their "home" governments, the TNCs have attempted to negotiate forms of regulation through the GATT, the new WTO, and the various regional and multilateral trade agreements. They have also transformed some of the old Bretton Woods institutions, notably the World Bank and IMF.

All these multilateral agreements and institutions have two things in common. They all attempt to limit the ability of national states to regulate the behavior of the TNCs, and all attempt to guarantee in various ways the sanctity of private business property. Most of the multilateral trade agreements, for example, rule nationalization and other forms of direct state economic regulation to be in violation of free trade. The European Union directive and the NAFTA provisions on telecommunications, for example, require signing nations to open their telecommunications markets to competition and their national telephone companies to operate as commercial ventures.

The multilateral trade agreements also attempt to protect private business property. They protect TNC technology ownership through so-called "TRIPs" – trade-related intellectual property rights clauses. Investments abroad are protected by "TRIMs" – trade-related investment measures.[66] Indeed, private business ownership is to be expanded under this multilateral regime. The World Bank and IMF impose "structural adjustment programs" that require countries that sign these agreements to privatize most of their state-owned enterprises and open their economies to the world market.

In effect, the TNCs and neoliberal politicians have attempted to include one of the major functions of the state (business-property protection) in agreements and institutions that limit the power of real (national) states. Market regulation replaces national state regulation not only internationally, but, increasingly, domestically as well. Actual regulation of markets is minimal in all the multilateral agreements, but the states that sign the various agreements and support the World Bank and IMF have agreed to world-wide property rights. This is a historically unique system of world-wide economic "regulation" with no one really in charge – except, as a last resort, major powers like the US. This new multilateralism was built out of the materials at hand and its architecture based on a body of economic theory that is highly abstract and ideological in nature. Most of this jerry-rigged structure is less than a decade old.

There has always been a "tendency toward autonomy" inherent in the capitalist state because of the need to regulate the conflicting interests of capital. This autonomy makes the state susceptible to pressure from the working class and other oppressed social groups from time to time. The increased importance of world market forces and of the multilateral agreements that limit state actions in many ways is a means of limiting this tendency toward autonomy from outside. On the one hand, the TNCs continue to need the national state and its laws to protect property and regulate the class struggle domestically, as well as to negotiate multilateral agreements that protect them internationally. On the other hand, to protect their property internationally, they need to strip these same national states of their traditional ability to regulate business behavior or to nationalize in whole or part business property. The national state is indispensable, but its ability to regulate the national economy had to be reduced and limited for the TNCs to operate freely on a world-wide level. Multilateralism has become the method of accomplishing this.

To put this another way, the state is to retain its ability to protect property from internal conflicts, crime, or working-class rebellion at home. This protection is increased, both at home and abroad, by externally (multilaterally) removing the ability of the state to nationalize or otherwise expropriate or limit the property of the TNCs should the government fall into the hands of a radical or revolutionary working-class or nationalist party or movement. The ideology to provide the cover story for this maneuver lay at hand in the form of neoclassical economics. Funding for this intellectual project was no problem. What is perhaps less understandable is the degree to which so many parties and leaders of the labor movement around the world have bought into the ideas and imperatives of this new function of the state as the local agent of the international system.

Part of the answer to that question lies in some of the objective consequences of the new world economy. The world market itself has always played somewhat of a limiting role on individual states. The freedoms or limits on a state depended on the economic and industrial power of the individual states – their place in the hierarchy of the world market. Capital markets, in particular, limited the possibilities of any given nation and its state once the hierarchy of international economic power was in place – as in uneven development. Today, with the multilateral institutions reshaped to play enforcer, particularly in the economic South, and the limitations on the individual states more clearly spelled out in the multilateral agreements, objective market forces have even more power to discipline nations. This includes, of course, the mobility of capital, which creates a major disciplinary force on governments as well as on the working class of any nation.

Just as democratic and nationalist ideologies form a major source of the legitimacy of the state, so the new market realities become internalized in the thinking of everyone from policy-makers fearing market retribution to workers in fear of losing their job. While Walter Wriston's 200,000 computer terminals cannot watch (nor do they care about) every marginal decision about wages or business location, the knowledge on the part of government officials, corporate managers, trade-union leaders, and rank-and-file workers that there are potential "global" consequences to such decisions becomes itself a governing factor. By and large, transnational capital and its intellectual and political allies have succeeded in setting the terms of debate to such an extent that it is often difficult to tell just which threats or consequences are real and which are not. As in the overused concept of "globalization" itself, there is a lot of hype and mystification concerning the limits of the state in the new world economy. The disciplining market forces are real, but each and every threatened consequence is not.

The notion that the national state is being dissolved in a seamless world market is mistaken. That there are potentially negative consequences for policies the "markets" and those who dominate them don't like is, however, real. The question becomes just what is really important to these markets or to the TNCs, and what can they do about it? Markets can deny capital to a nation, something devastating to Third World nations. But what of the nations that currently house the bulk of the assets of these markets? What happens if North America or Europe or Japan or some combination of those economic powers decides to take a different course? Could they change the course of the world economy over time?

For the working-class movement in any country, the answer to this highly speculative question lies not only in theory or analysis, but in the willingness to act – to test the new world economy as no one yet has. The traditional parties of the working class in the West have shrunk from such a risky proposition. They have internalized market ideology to the point of paralysis, and have no way of sorting out what is real and what is threat or hype, because they will not confront these forces or institutions in any substantial way. It will be argued later that there is a transitional politics for the working-class movement that seeks to test today's realities by defying the rules of the game. But there is also a trade-union side to this.

Trade unions have a regulating role in a capitalist economy. By taking labor out of competition in terms of wages, benefits, and major conditions, unions have again and again forced capital to seeks alternative means to the end of profitability. The best known of these is that the imposition of higher labor costs tends to force capital to invest in technology to improve productivity. In other cases, such as the trucking industry in the US, unionization and the imposition of high wages forced a rationalization of a very decentralized industry. To the neoclassical economist this represents a serious distortion of the market; to the trade unionist and the working class it represents a step forward.

The great challenge of the coming century for the organized working class everywhere is whether the working-class organizations across the world can move together in a similar direction and impose a measure of regulation on international capital and the TNCs. The attempts by unions in much of the industrial world, though not in the US, to shorten the work week suggest one line of international action that could counter the global jobs crisis.

Part III

Labor's Response

7

Pulled Apart, Pushed Together

The deepening of international economic integration, along with the rise of lean production in industry and neoliberalism in government, has brought about far-reaching changes in the structure of the workforce at both national and international levels. Drawing on this trend, a frequent theme these days is that all the currents, like lean production, outsourcing, casualized labor, workplaces with fewer workers, the feminization of the workforce, etc., are producing a working class that is or will be too fragmented to compose a labor movement in any real sense, much less take on the broader task of social change. The evidence of fragmentation is found not only in these trends, but in the general decline of union density, the simultaneous rise of decentralized bargaining, and the growth of racial, ethnic, and gender diversity within the workforce and the working class in many developed countries.

At its most pretentious, the theme of working-class fragmentation is presented as "postmodernism," an intellectual fashion that sees class as *passé* and the very fragmentation it describes as a positive development. While this sort of thinking on the political left goes back decades, it always imagines that its observations about divisions within the working class are something new. For example, in an article all too appropriately entitled "Power to the Person," a British theoretician of this "postmodernist" view, wrote in the late 1980s:

The economic structure of the 1980s has produced deep divisions within the working class. Established occupational, sexual and cultural identities, sources of solidarity and common identification are dissolving. Choices in consumption, lifestyle, sexuality, are more important as an assertion of identity.[1]

A similar view, without the individualist conclusions, was voiced more recently by US radical intellectual and activist Joel Rogers. Rogers works closely with union and working-class community activists on a number of projects, yet in an article calling for a new politics in America, he voiced a similar fragmentation theme. He argued that old "organic solidarities" of factory and neighborhood within the class were being destroyed and being replaced by more limited identities.[2]

Most of these arguments begin from one or another "golden age" thesis about a time when the working class was "organically" united and supposedly did not face significant divisions of occupation, race, ethnicity, or gender. Outside, perhaps, of the Scandinavian countries, it is hard to image where this "golden age" of "organic" solidarity ever actually existed.[3] In the US, for example, it is difficult to understand why one would see the exclusion of African-American or Latino workers from many jobs and unions through the 1960s, the "golden age" if there ever was one, as superior to the tensions that arise from racist reactions to their inclusion as a major force in many unions more recently. Equally mystifying is the implication that while women worked primarily in the home, there was no gender problem in the working class and that this division arises only as women enter the paid workforce. This view seems not only historically and analytically superficial, but quite insensitive to the realities of working-class life, yesterday or today.

A far more sensible and sensitive approach to the changes that are taking place and the problems they present has been proposed by Richard Hyman, who writes:

> A mythical belief in some previous golden age of proletarian unity and unproblematic trade union solidarity distorts our perception of current labour movement dynamics. A more sensitive historical understanding allows us to view the question of disaggregation in less cataclysmic terms. Conversely, from historical experience we can learn that there are no short-cuts to the identification and (re)definition of interests in solidaristic manner: it is always necessary to campaign and struggle for (relative) unity among workers and their organizations.[4]

Clearly, the shape of the workforce and therefore of the working class is changing throughout the industrialized world. It is important, however, to sort out what really represents increased fragmentation and what represents a different way in which workers are pushed together by capital. It is equally important to understand that the recomposition of the working class by industries, occupations, gender, ethnicity, and race is and always has been a recurrent feature of capitalism. And with recomposition comes internal conflict born of inequality. The state of the working class at any given moment is necessarily riddled with contradictions.

Marx made this observation in 1849:

> This organization of the proletarians into a class, and consequently into a political party, is continually being upset again by the competition between the workers themselves.[5]

A decade later he wrote, "the competition among the workers is only another form of the competition among capitals."[6] Ironically, it is on the basis of this competition (as an aspect of the capital–labor relationship) and the need to suppress it, that unions arose in the first place, to "take labor out of competition." Organization and action by the workers to impose standard or minimum wages and conditions on the employers across a given occupation, industry, or market were the means. Such standards were always difficult to maintain as business reorganizations, technological transformations, and the shifting winds of industrial change disorganized yesterday's standards and agreements.

But it is and always was organization that is the answer to this problem. As the above quote from Marx indicates, the working class forms itself truly as a class only through organization – in fact, a plurality of organizations cutting across the class as well as unifying it. It is not only competition in the labor market that is the problem, but the fact that in most countries the working class is formed and then reformed, to a much greater extent than the capitalist class, out of diverse human materials that do not necessarily share a common history at any given point.

Looking at the early history of the British working class, one historian put it this way:

> The crucial strategic problem confronting labor movements was how to mobilize the maximum solidarity from a socially defined constituency which has no essential unity in the sphere of consciousness, but on the contrary a series of particularistic loyalties and preferences and a widely differing experience in everyday life, a mosaic of individual histories. The analysis of working class politics begins with this dialectic – the contradictory and dynamic intersection of unifying and fragmenting tendencies within the class as a whole.[7]

While workers share a common relationship to capital and, hence, a strong common economic and social interest, their consciousness and "identity" are also shaped by many other experiences and forces, particularly where racial, national, or gender inequality underlies these differences. While the elements of class consciousness are always there beneath the surface, this consciousness, like organization, must be built. Speaking of more recent times, Leo Panitch makes this point in a slightly different way when he writes:

> Mass working class parties were rather the essential condition in the twentieth century for the reinforcement, recomposition and extension of class identity and community itself in the face of a capitalism which continually deconstructs and reconstructs industry, occupation and locale.[8]

Trade unions, though more limited in their goals, face the same dilemma: the need to reinforce, recompose, and extend a common working-class identity. Today, the "contradictory and dynamic intersection of unifying and fragmenting tendencies within the class" is more contradictory and dynamic than it was twenty or thirty years ago. Hence, the tasks of both union and working-class political organizers are more difficult than then, although probably no more difficult than a hundred years ago or sixty years ago. The lesson to be drawn from the social movements of the past thirty years or more is not to dissolve class as an active social identity, but to recognize that even class identification is inextricably interwoven with other identities, group interests, and particular oppressions that cannot be ignored or subordinated. Academics and futurists can write the working class off because it is diverse and changing along with the sweeping changes in work. Working-class people themselves have no such luxury, given the crises that have invaded their lives.

Hyman makes another important point by arguing that while today's changes in work may well be undermining old union structures and habits, they also present the opportunity to change working-class organization. He writes:

> From a different perspective, however, the restructuring of employment creates both a need and an opportunity to reconstitute collective relations within the working class: within individual trade unions, between different organizations, and between the unionized and the non-unionized. The growing importance of the female workforce, of part-time and other 'atypical' forms of employment, of non-industrial and non-manual occupations – and the combination of such trends – can be a powerful impetus toward a renewal of trade unionism and the development of new demands in collective bargaining, new methods of organization and action, and new forms of internal democracy.[9]

Competition, on the one hand, gives rise to unionism, but, on the other, new forms of competition and industry undermine the old forms of unionism. So, the history of unionism has moved, roughly, from craft unions to general unions to industrial unions and, now, to some hybrid of the last two. Mixed in with and intersecting these "models" were and are politically based unions, as in France, Spain, Italy, and parts of the Third World. In fact, across the industrialized world, unions are changing their shape and debating directions. Mergers among unions are one such form of change, but it is clear that much more is needed if organized labor is to mobilize the existing ranks and organize those now outside of unions: two of the most essential tasks in the era of globalization and crisis.

The answer lies in the concept of social-movement unionism: a unionism that both organizes all who can be brought into unions and reaches beyond unions to the working class as a whole; a unionism that is prepared to take a class stand in the workplace, in the neighborhoods, and in political life, as well as to reach across borders in all these efforts. The shape and practice of social-movement unionism will be found in that of the newer unions in Brazil, South Africa, South Korea, and other parts of the Third World, as well as in the newer forms of activity across North America and Europe. They have in common a grassroots democracy long dormant in many unions. Their vision is such that they naturally take up the banner of class-wide issues, even if their struggles originate in their own interests. To win in this broader endeavor, they reach out to other social groups to create a broad, but mostly working-class-based, movement.

Before discussing social-movement unionism in more detail, it is necessary to look more closely at the theories and realities of class fragmentation or reformation. Is the working class dissolving or changing and, if so, how?

Changing Division of Labor

Many of the changes in work and in the workforce we see across the industrial world are the consequences of an ever-changing division of labor, much of it associated with lean production and internationalization. Capitalism has always been characterized by an increasingly complex division of labor. In medieval times, most nonagricultural products were produced locally by craft workers and their helpers. While large structures, such as multi-story buildings or ships, along with metal products and armaments, have always required large numbers of workers divided by different skills and functions, and factories can be found in ancient or Renaissance times, the factory system as a general form of production is unique to capitalism.

The factory, and in imitation the modern office, medical, or other service complex, represents an articulated technical division of labor within a single facility. But soon production chains develop, as each factory (office, etc.) requires inputs it is cheaper to purchase than produce, given the particular focus of its operations. "Flexibility" in early capitalist production and often today consists of nothing more than the division of labor between different production facilities and firms.

Both the internal technical division of labor and that associated with production chains change continuously with technological and organizational innovations. Much of the rise of service industries, which is simultaneously associated with the decline of manufacturing, is, in fact, nothing more than the continued extension of the division of labor. For example, manufacturing firms that once employed maintenance, cleaning, research, clerical, or computer-programming workers, now import them from a "service" company that specializes in that type of labor. Indeed, even some production workers these days come from personnel agencies listed as "service" companies. New forms of capital costs, such as advanced telecommunications systems necessary for extended production coordination, are leased or rented from telecommunications "service" providers, rather than purchased as capital goods, and worked by direct employees.[10]

All that has been said about the changing structure of the workforce that results from the "vertical disintegration" of production (the rise of "atypical" or "contingent" jobs, the outsourcing or contracting of work, geographical dispersion, extended production chains, etc.) reflects a changing division of labor that is largely the result of business and organizational decisions. While they have a market or cost logic in the battle for competitiveness, neither this logic nor technology directly determines the new shape of the division of labor. Rather, competition forces a decision, while new technology enables such decisions, but it is capital or its management that provides the content of the decision.

One of the most obvious forms of "vertical disintegration" of production has been the geographic dispersion of production facilities. In the US following World War Two, for example, rather than adding to or recreating large integrated production complexes, capital began to locate facilities in different parts of the country. This trend began immediately after the war in the 1940s and was facilitated by the Interstate Highway system constructed in the 1950s. In large part, this was a conscious strategy to avoid strong centers of unionism associated with former urban locations. Much of this was accomplished, however, long before the era of crisis and prior to the impact of globalization.[11]

Labor historian Ronald Schatz described this process in the US electrical equipment industry, showing that "vertical disintegration" was, in its first and most geographically fragmenting form, as much or more a feature of the "golden age" as of today:

Starting in the mid-1940s, consequently, the corporations moved operations out of older, large factories and into newer, smaller facilities in the border [upper South of the US] states; the South; the Pacific Coast; rural sections of New England; Puerto Rico; and other countries . . . General Electric [GE] was one of the first major CIO-organized firms to carry out this strategy. In the 1920s all of GE's plants were located in the Northeast. In 1952, GE already had 117 plants spread out over 24 states. By 1961, it had 170 plants in 134 cities with much larger concentrations in the West and South than before.[12]

As a corporation, GE was growing larger and producing more. But its individual factories employed relatively fewer workers and were much more geographically dispersed than before the war. What took place was not shrinkage or "deindustrialization," but a conscious reorganization of the division of labor. All this was accomplished early in the "golden age" and long before deepening international integration took hold.

Andrew Sayer and Richard Walker, who have done a great deal to develop the concept of the division of labor in today's society, argue that the new business organizational forms and innovations may be more important than the break-up of production *per se*. They write:

So, while there is evidence of an increase in vertical disintegration, an increase in what might be termed "vertical organization" in both vertically integrated and vertically disintegrated cases could be of more significance.[13]

What this means is that, as production systems are broken up, "disintegrated," or outsourced, what is needed to coordinate this is more extensive organization. All this extended and geographically dispersed production, as Sayer and Walker put it, requires "planning, directing, and orchestrating immense divisions of human labor enmeshed in a thicket of social relations."[14]

In approaching the question of workforce fragmentation and its impact on unions, it is necessary to look more closely at just how capital is "planning, directing, and orchestrating" the changing division of labor. Is "vertical disintegration" of production systems simply producing smaller workplaces and companies, as is often stated these days? Or is the sort of ownership control described by Harrison in chapter 4 and the "vertical organization" suggested by Sayer and Walker at work?

Bigger or Smaller Production Systems?

Postmodernists, post-industrialists, and others who see the working class dissolving into unrelated or even antagonistic fragments usually point to the declining size of the manufacturing workforce, the decrease in the number of workers in factories or other traditional workplaces, and the decentralization of production as evidence of this fragmentation. These trends provided Rogers' evidence of decaying "organic solidarities," for example. Since all these trends are real, it is presumed that the fragmentation of the working class is a permanent and irreversible feature of society.

What these theories overlook, however, is what is most basic about capitalist society: the capital–labor (employer–employee) relationship, the "social relations of production." Trade unions in all their different forms arise from this relationship. American truck drivers from the 1930s through the 1950s organized the workers in a myriad of small companies into a single union as effectively as auto workers employed by giant corporations. Women garment workers employed in "sweated" networks of small contracting firms organized themselves in the early years of the twentieth century, as did casualized dock workers in the late nineteenth century. Truckers and auto workers had to tame regional or national markets, while more fragmented garment workers and longshore workers had to organize only a local labor market. All these groups of workers faced serious ethnic or racial divisions and had to find ways to overcome them in order to organize effectively. Garment workers and dock workers usually lived in concentrated neighborhoods, auto workers and truckers, regardless of their local living arrangements, lived all over the country. In other words, there is no simple formula for effective organization: unionism must follow the structure of capital and the organization of production.

As the previous chapter argued, the structure of capital (business organization) and production has changed in recent years and will continue to change in the future. What matters is the direction of this change and labor's ability to follow it. Is capital fragmenting into smaller units? Are production systems, in fact, smaller? What is argued here is that, properly understood, neither capital nor production occurs on a smaller scale today than in the past: rather, the opposite is the case.

You have only to look around you to see that the production of "stuff" is much greater and the number of services available in return for money is almost infinitely more diverse than forty years ago during capitalism's "golden age," not to mention a hundred years ago. The small manufacturing firms of mid-nineteenth-century England that resulted from the "Industrial Revolution" could not possibly have turned out the variety or quantity of goods we take for granted today. Neither could the banks nor the new telegraph companies of that era have produced anything like the variety and quantity of services provided by today's financial and telecommunications giants. In general, an increasingly complex division of labor and far more massive and elaborate business organization, as well as technological innovation, have made all of this possible.

The other side of this coin, of course, is that the very technology that enables much of this phenomenal production of goods and services, and which grows with competition, also reduces the amount of labor needed to produce them over time. Marx, who had much to say about the growth of the working class, also observed, when speaking of the two types of surplus value produced by labor:

> In the second form of surplus value, however, as relative surplus value, which appears as the development of the workers' productive power, as the reduction of the time relative to the working day, and as the reduction of the necessary laboring population relative to the population, in this form there directly appears the industrial and the distinguishing historical character of the mode of production founded on capital.[15]

So, the reduction of the labor force in any given facility at a given level of production is "the distinguishing historical characteristic" of capitalist accumulation. The fact that production facilities, large or small, will tend to employ fewer workers as the productivity of those workers increases is inherent in the system. In fact, measured by the number of workers, the average size of the factory in the US has been declining since around 1930.[16]

It does not follow from this, however, that either production systems or capitalist firms have gotten or will get smaller. In fact, the tendency is for capitalist firms to grow through accumulation, mergers, or acquisitions, while production systems are extended, as in the case of GE above, as the division of labor becomes more complex. The irony here is that production systems have grown so large and complex over time that the giant facility of yesterday is not large enough to enclose more than a fraction of the overall process. Pointing out that it is not simply a matter of new technology (miniaturization, communications, automation, etc.), but of "the division of labor and organizational capability," Sayer and Walker argue that, in fact, the problem is that production has outgrown the vertically integrated factory or production complex. They write:

> If large factories are less useful today, it may be that the division of labor has expanded so that the factory is insufficiently large to encompass entire production systems, so another way must be found.[17]

In the view of Sayer and Walker, the tendency toward "vertical disintegration," or the splitting up the production process into different units, is an organizational decision, enabled by technology but not necessarily determined by it. It changes the old division of labor, reducing employment in any one site and maybe even over the whole system. Often, this break-up of the production system is motivated by the desire to escape union wages and conditions, which are seen as rigid and costly. But, in the end, the production system as a whole is larger.

Such decisions, however, are not always in one direction. For example, US West, the Baby Bell phone company covering a huge geographic area in the western United States, a company that used all kinds of outsourcing and contracting arrangements, announced in 1993 that it would close 500 offices and concentrate its workforce, which would be cut by 9,000, into 18 "megacenters." This was the product of "process re-engineering" and would cost $3.8 billion. Telecommunications technology is such that location is scarcely a factor. But US West, reading the future of its market, apparently decided to abandon low-profit rural areas for major urban centers where the glitzy services of the future can better be afforded.[18]

In general, of course, the direction of the past fifty years has been toward decentralizing production systems. But does this mean smaller firms? For all the talk about job creation by smaller companies, the answer is "no." As Sayer and Walker also point out, some of those promoting the idea of smaller-scale firms as the wave of the future "are exceedingly cavalier about whether they are referring to firms or workplaces in their models."[19] Referring to what was quoted above, Sayer and Walker go on to write:

> The same principle applies to firms. Today, the buying and selling of entire firms, and the assembling and dismantling of giant conglomerates, is an everyday occurrence: capitalist empire builders are treating megacompanies in the same terms the latter have treated their subsidiaries.[20]

The speculation they end with is that perhaps the corporation as we have known it has become so massive as to be outgrown and replaced with business alliances "along a neural network of production and circulation." Others have called this "agile production," a step beyond lean, whereby companies produce specific products by temporarily clustering or allying with complementary firms. The analogy often used is that of hospital emergency-room teams, which will change in occupational structure according to the medical problem faced.[21]

While business alliances are definitely part of the contemporary picture, they tend not to be quite so promiscuous, for good business reasons. Most production systems, unlike doctors, nurses, and orderlies, are "sunk" in specific places and, despite flexible technology, are suited only to certain kinds of operations. Chasing one another around to glue together temporary production systems is not likely to be very economical or efficient.

What actually seems to be happening, still, is that, far from being outgrown, megacompanies and business empires continue to expand, often internationally.

In terms of the fragmentation of the workforce, a quick look at the US will tell us something about what has happened in recent years. As already noted, the level of merger and acquisition (M&A) activity remains very high in both the US and Europe. Unlike the M&As of the 1960s, however, today's megadeals tend toward the "back-to-basics" type; that is, those that merge operations in the same or closely related types of production. So, for example, as market regulation takes hold in the US, traditional phone companies are merging with one another and buying up cable-TV and/or cellular-phone companies.

Whether through mergers or simple growth, companies are getting bigger and the bigger ones are employing more of the workforce. While, for example, there were many more single-plant manufacturing firms (288,000) than multiplant firms (81,000) in 1987, the multiplant firms employed 72% of the production workers, the most recent figure available, compared with 63% in 1963. These multiplant firms produced 82% of the value added in 1987. Furthermore, the number of multiplant operations grew faster than single-plant operations. Another indicator that companies are getting bigger is that billion-dollar corporations of all kinds increased their share of total corporate assets from 49% in 1970 to 72% in 1990.[22] Overall, 70% of the manufacturing workforce is employed by the 1% of firms that employ 500 or more workers.[23]

For some reason, figures in the more recent 1992 US Census of Manufacturers were not aggregated. In the automobile industry, however, while there has been a decline in the workforce, large-scale facilities remain the norm. Thus, from 1987 through 1992, the proportion of those in assembly facilities with 2,500 or more production workers fell from 82% to 76%. Those working in assembly plants with 1,000 or more production workers fell even less, from 95% in 1987 to 94% in 1992. Even in the parts sector of the industry, where facilities are smaller, the change was hardly dramatic. The percentage of those working in auto parts and component facilities of 1,000 or more production workers fell from 48% to 43% in that same period.[24] Needless to say, the assembly end of the industry is dominated by a very small number of companies that also dominate the parts sector.

Looking at the question of small firms as generators of employment in the developed industrial countries, Bennett Harrison concluded this was largely a myth. Examining the major Triad powers, he wrote:

Over the past quarter century, there has been no upward trend whatsoever in the small firm share of employment in either Japan or West Germany –

the two most successful national economies in the world. In the United States, a (modestly) growing relative share of smaller units of production in recent years is discernible in the census data only for the manufacturing sector, and only among individual plants, not for entire firms.[25]

In other words, when the capitalist employer is understood as the firm, not just the individual facility or workplace, there is no trend toward small employers. The workplace often gets smaller in terms of the number of workers, as the employer squeezes more productivity out of the remaining workers, but most workers are still employed by large capitalist firms – whether these are final producers, suppliers, contractors, or even personnel agencies. Furthermore, most of these firms are getting larger in terms of production and assets, despite downsizing and outsourcing. Indeed, in real terms, the value of assets per employee in manufacturing grew from $9,300 in 1963 to $26,040 in 1987.[26]

Outsourcing, even when it goes to a nominally independent company, is increasingly organized by large TNCs on their terms. If the entire production chain, organized because the total production system has become, as Sayer and Walker argue, bigger, not smaller, is considered, it is almost certain that most production systems today incorporate a larger proportion of the total workforce than in the past.

In this respect, genuine fragmentation in the relationship between labor and capital has not really increased, it has simply changed in form along with the changing division of labor. Unions have been much slower on the organizational learning curve than capital, which has developed the "organizational capability" to make real changes over a period of time.[27] The major question today is whether organized labor in the industrial North can learn the organizational, political, and strategic lessons needed to organize successfully in this new situation.

Recomposition and Racism

Fragmentation of the old division of labor and the shaping of a new one necessarily involves both anxiety and conflict between different groups of workers as they are forced to compete for new and existing jobs. While the competition may actually affect only a minority of workers at any given time, the anxiety of workers in a labor market with large numbers of unemployed, underemployed, and new entrants (women, youths, immigrants) is likely to be felt throughout the working class. Pre-existing racial and gender attitudes and institutional discrimination (employment segregation, pay differentials, glass ceilings, etc.) will push this competition and conflict along racial and gender lines.

Active racism and anti-immigrant sentiment have become an increasingly common feature in more and more industrial nations. The rise of white-supremacist and/or neo-fascist groups in the US and across Europe appears as the tip of an actual or potential iceberg on which the organizations of the working class can be broken. The fact of massive, persistent unemployment and a growing proportion of lower-wage, casualized jobs intensify underlying racism even where actual competition between different racial groups is not direct. Immigration resulting from changes in the international division of labor adds an international dimension to this kind of intra-class conflict.

Modern white racism, the doctrine and practice of racial superiority, has its origins in European conquest, slavery, and colonialism – all of which created capitalism's initial accumulation in the hands of European investors, laying the basis for uneven development. This is a long history, which includes not only the conquest of the "new world" and its peoples, the institution of slavery in the Western Hemisphere, and the slave trade, in which millions perished, but the prolonged war between Christian Europe and the Islamic world that culminated in the expulsion of the Moors and Jews from Spain in 1492, an act that made western Europe not simply Christian, but virtually all white. Indeed, anti-Semitism, which began in medieval Europe, is certainly a precursor, as well as an active element, of modern white racism. The fact that the enslaved Africans in the US were neither white nor Christian also provided, as African-American historian John Hope Franklin pointed out, one of the first forms of the theme of racial inferiority that came to characterize modern racism.[28]

Though it is an old, unscientific way of viewing the differences among human beings, both ideologically and institutionally, racism played such a crucial role in the origins of capitalism and has been reproduced over these hundreds of years in many so different ways, it is virtually impossible to separate it from the geographic, economic, occupational, social, and ideological structures of modern capitalist society. The argument that capitalism, as a social and economic system, does not "need" racism to function is simply too abstract because the history of this social-economic system is too intertwined with the history of white-supremacist ideology and occupational segregation – first and foremost through slavery and colonialism, and later under conditions of rural peonage and wage labor.

Modern racism reached its most persistent form in the United States, which was the only country in which former slaves and a succession of conquered people of color (native peoples, Mexicans, and Puerto Ricans in particular) occupied the same geographic space and political structure as the dominant majority white population. In Europe, anti-Semitism provided the most explosive and tragic form of racism in the first half of the twentieth century. It has only been since World War Two, however, that former colonial (or other Third World) peoples of color have sought to live within the former colonizing powers of Europe in significant numbers.

Racism toward peoples of color in the US has long been a weak point for organized labor. Formal exclusion of African-American, Latino, and Asian workers from craft unions persisted into the middle of this century – and still persists in various informal ways in many places. When the AFL and the more progressive industrial unions of the CIO merged into a common federation in 1955, for example, the white leaders of both groups rejected an attempt by African-American labor leader A. Philip Randolph to ban the exclusion of Blacks from any union. This fight raged within organized labor into the 1960s as a part of the great upheaval of Black Americans in that period. While formal discrimination was finally banned, de facto discrimination by many unions in certain high-paid trades continued.[29]

For a moment in the 1930s and 1940s, the new industrial unions rose to the challenge, bringing Black and Latino workers into these unions on an equal basis. The leaders of the CIO realized that industries like steel, auto, and meatpacking could not be successfully organized without the active support of the Black workers. This did not mean an end to racism in the ranks, as the "race riots" in Detroit in 1943 revealed, but it did mean a commitment by the new unions to foster civil-rights legislation and work for more equal treatment of Blacks in industry. Black workers did play a central role in organizing new unions in many industries.[30] But, outside of steel and coal mining, the CIO had by and large failed to organize the former slave-states of the "Old South." Ironically, this was partly due to the resistance of the rural elite of the South, who were supported by labor's "friends" in the Democratic New Deal administration through a system of agricultural subsidies. Although there were numerous attempts to organize along with many strikes, including the massive textile strikes of 1934, industrial unionism was largely defeated in this region.

Following the war, the South became the Achilles heel of organized labor. Michael Goldfield described this it way:

> The failure to organize the South left both a political and economic bastion of reaction (represented by the control of the Senate and House committees [of the US Congress] by openly racist Southern Dixiecrats) and helped to stabilize a section of the country that represented both a source of cheap labor and an area of lower-than-union wages.[31]

By the end of the war, however, the South had been transformed by rapid industrial development and seemed riper for organization. In 1946, the CIO launched Operation Dixie to organize the South. CIO president Philip Murray called it the "most important drive of its kind ever undertaken by any labor organization in the history of the country."[32] While most of the South was still nonunion, the CIO had a few areas of interracial strength such as Birmingham, Alabama, to draw on. Historian Robin Kelley summarized this strength:

> In essence, the CIO in Birmingham was not just another federation of labor organizations. Unions such as SWOC (steel workers), Mine, Mill, and the UMWA (coal miners) evolved during their formative years as broad-based social movements, enriched by Southern cultural traditions and fortified by an unusually pronounced civil rights agenda.[33]

But the national CIO unions that emerged from the war and the 1946 collective-bargaining round were not the social-movement organizations they had once been, much less those of Birmingham. Their leaders were now concerned about stable bargaining relationships and their problem-ridden political alliance with the Democratic Party. The alliances built with African-American organizations during the organizing phase in places like Detroit were languishing, and by the 1950s inoperative.[34]

Instead of using Birmingham as an interracial launching pad for Operation Dixie, Murray waged war on the largely Black leadership of the Communist-led Mine, Mill and Smelter Workers. This would last until 1949 when Mine, Mill was expelled from the CIO along with other Communist-led unions. In this fight, white members of the United Steelworkers, Murray's union, were pitted against Black leaders and members of Mine, Mill in a bloody fight for political control of the local CIO.[35]

More generally, by this time, the CIO had put racial egalitarianism on the back burner. Blacks were excluded from the CIO executive board in Alabama and the CIO's political action committee in that state refused to register Blacks to vote, for fear of alienating whites. Hosea Hudson, a Black Communist and organizer for the Steelworkers, had this to say about the record of the Steelworkers in Alabama:

> The steelworkers' leadership wasn't lukewarm on fighting for the rights of the Negro people. It was worse than lukewarm.[36]

Operation Dixie collapsed almost before it got off the ground from fratricidal conflict with a strong racial dimension initiated by the CIO leadership. Then, in 1947, matters were made worse when Congress passed the Taft–Hartley amendments to the National Labor Relations (Wagner) Act prohibiting sympathy or secondary strikes, which could have aided organizing efforts, and allowing states to ban the union shop and require every worker in a unionized workplace to pay dues voluntarily. The former slave-states were among the first to pass such laws and to become so-called "right-to-work" states. Along with the failure of Operation Dixie, this created, in effect, a union-free region in the nation.[37]

As the proportion of Black workers in the North grew, however, they became a major part of the unionized workforce outside the South. The entrance of large numbers of urban Blacks into industry in the wake of the civil-rights movement, along with the organization of public-sector workers, where people of color had a better chance at employment, brought large numbers of African-American workers into unions. In fact, Black workers are more likely to be union members than whites. By 1983, 27% of African-American workers were union members compared with 19% for whites. As many of these urban jobs were wiped out in the restructuring of the 1980s, the proportion of African-American workers in unions fell to about 20% by 1994, but was still above the 15% of white workers who belonged to unions. While Blacks composed 11.3% of the employed workforce in 1994, they were 15% of union membership. But in the mid-1990s over half the African-American population still lived in the South, where unionism remained weak.[38]

In effect, at first, many unions participated in America's original two-tier wage system where Blacks in comparable jobs earned less than whites, and Blacks were much more likely to hold different lower-paying jobs. As African-American workers entered unionized jobs in large numbers, however, this wage differential fell dramatically in regions of union strength. This reflected the fact that union members, on average, make almost 20% more than nonunion workers, although even here the union premium among Blacks is lower than average at 18%. In states with high levels of unionization, the wage gap had virtually disappeared by the 1970s. With the return of economic crisis and restructuring, however, the Black–white wage gap widened again. In 1979, an African-American worker was likely to earn 10.9% less than a white in a similar job, but by 1989 that differential had grown to 16.4%. While this gap grew from about 14% to 17% in the South, in the industrial and more union-dense Midwest and northeast the wage gap actually grew from less than 1% in 1979 to 14% and 19% respectively in 1989.[39] Workforce restructuring and declining unionism were unquestionably central to this enormous increase in the racial two-tier system.

Recently, organizations in the South, notably Black Workers For Justice (BWFJ), have raised the cry of "organize the South" once again. It had become obvious that a good deal of the "outsourced" work of industry had moved to the South over the years. Manufacturing employment in the

South grew from 30% of the national total in 1982 to 33% in 1992.[40] The city of Rocky Mount, North Carolina, where BWFJ has its base, is a perfect example. It is ringed by "branch plants" of major automotive parts, pharmaceutical, and other manufacturing corporations. While in the city itself there are smaller garment shops, these "branch plants" tend to be large factories with over 1,000 workers. Although BWFJ has helped build some in-plant organizations that include both Black and white workers, these plants remain nonunion and without labor contracts. Racism and the failure of the unions to deal with it was a major factor in the failure of a number of recent organizing drives in this area.[41]

Racism also shaped the place of the various Latino or Spanish-speaking peoples in the workforce of the United States. Conquest brought a huge portion of Mexico and all of Puerto Rico under US rule in the nineteenth century. Since that time immigration has brought millions more Spanish-speaking people from Latin America and the Caribbean to the US – often as a result of the impact of expanding US capitalism or military intervention in the region. The current Latino population resident in the US is thought to be about 25 million people. Once concentrated in the Southwest and on the island of Puerto Rico, Latinos now make up large proportions of the populations of many major cities across the US.[42]

The history of Latino workers in the US economy in the twentieth century, like that of African Americans, is in large part that of movement from agrarian employment of one kind or another to industrial or service-sector employment – except that this history recently draws on areas outside the US as well as inside. Latino workers also played a disproportionately significant role in the organization of some CIO unions in the 1930s. For example, in 1936 at US Steel's South Works in Chicago, where Mexican workers were only 5% of the workforce, they composed 11% of the union's membership. They also played a big role in the bloody 1937 strike against the so-called "Little Steel" companies. By the 1940s, Chicano or Mexican workers held leadership positions in CIO unions in southern California, and even AFL unions were competing for Latino members. Latino workers played the leading role in organizing copper and other mines in the southwest, and cross-border solidarity with the new CTM unions in Mexico was not unusual. Discrimination, however, generally kept the majority of Latino workers in low-wage jobs, then as now.[43]

This history is complicated by the different ethnicities and legal status that cuts across the Latino workforce: Chicanos, Puerto Ricans, Mexicans, Dominicans, and Cubans; citizens, documented immigrants, those covered by "amnesty," and undocumented workers.[44] Terms like "Latino" or "Hispanic" are themselves contested terrain. For example, in Miami, reports one study, virtually no one uses the term "Latino."[45] The fact of a common language among the various Latino groups and discrimination and hostility by the dominant white society, as well as conscious recruitment policies by many employers, however, combine to create multiethnic Spanish-speaking enclaves in many US cities. What is perhaps most important is that, despite the hostility of the dominant society and the poverty of so many Latinos, the growing urban communities of Spanish-speaking people have an increased sense of power and expectation that is making them part of the revitalization of the labor movement in the US.

As Zaragosa Vargas points out in a recent study, the location of Latino workers within the US labor force is determined by a combination of racial and ethnic discrimination, on the one hand, and the dynamics of capitalist restructuring, on the other. Vargas writes:

> The restructuring of the US economy is characterized by the following: the rapid growth and expansion of subcontracting, sweatshops, and industrial homework; the downgrading of job skills; the rise of high technology industries that employ low-wage production workers; and the rapid growth of the service sector. The majority of Latino workers have been incorporated into the low-wage industrial manufacturing and service sector and into farm labor where they form the main workforce. Recently arrived Latino immigrant workers are concentrated in hotel and restaurant work, retail food stores, and food processing factories.[46]

Footholds established years ago in unionized industries like steel and auto in southern California and the Chicago/Gary area, and mining in New Mexico and Arizona, and garment in a number of areas were largely wiped out in the restructuring of the 1970s and 1980s. Often these Latino workers refused to "go gentle into that good night" of low-wage work. The militant, though ultimately defeated, strike by the mostly Chicano membership of the United Steelworkers at Phelps Dodge's Arizona mines in 1983–84 was one of the trend-setting struggles of that decade. The long struggle to keep GM's Van Nuys, California, assembly plant open led by UAW Local 645 and its president, Pete Beltran, pulled together another pioneering coalition with the Latino communities of Los Angeles.[47]

The new sectors in which Latino workers are forming a major part of the workforce are in some cases important pieces in internationalized production systems or in the world economy more generally. Their importance often rests on the fact that they provide the margin of competitiveness – whether they are the bottom end of a manufacturing process or the services on which so much international business activity depends these days. Furthermore, some areas of high Latino population concentrations in the US, like Miami, Los Angeles, or New York, are strategically inserted in the international/regional economy.

Today, by official count, there are over 10 million employed Latino wage and salary workers. But Latinos are the fastest growing group in the US and it is expected they will make up a much larger proportion by early in the next century. It is almost certain, furthermore, that the official figures underestimate the number of Latinos working in the US because of the large number of "concealed" undocumented workers. As of 1994, Latinos composed about 9% of union membership, about the same as their official proportion of the workforce. Since most newly arrived immigrants (about a million a year or more) are unlikely to be union members, this means the proportion among the older Latino population, including immigrants who have been in the US for a while, is actually higher. Looked at from another angle, the proportion of Latino workers who belong to unions is just over 14%, about the same as for white workers.[48]

Some unions like the Clothing Workers, now called UNITE (Union of Needletrades, Industrial, and Textile Employees), have put serious resources into the South. The newly elected leadership of the AFL–CIO has stated that the organization of the South and of industries employing large proportions of Black, Latino, and immigrant workers are its major objectives. But, as BWFJ has pointed out repeatedly, the issue of race cannot be swept under the rug. This fact is underlined by another aspect of racism that has arisen not only in the US, but across Europe and even in Japan: the growing hostility toward immigrant workers from the Third World.

Immigrants and Unions in America

Immigration from the Third World is another aspect of capitalist crisis, globalization, persistent uneven development, and the changing division of labor, as well as of decades of US military intervention abroad. In its early post-World War Two phases it was also often a matter of policy, as capital in the developed nations sought new sources of low-wage labor in the growing service sector, the bottom end of production chains still located in the "home" market, or even on the assembly lines of mass-production industry. The "guest worker" program in Germany and the "Bracero" program in the US, discontinued in 1965, are examples of such policies that began before the economic crisis was widely felt. The US Immigration Control and Reform Act of 1986 (ICRA) specified the level of documented workers, created "amnesty" for immigrants in the country since 1982, and imposed fines on employers who hired undocumented workers. In effect, ICRA provided employers with what they wanted: an increased legal immigrant workforce, on the one hand, and a semi-porous border that still made many workers "illegal," in effect dividing the immigrant workforce by legal status, on the other.[49]

Capitalist crisis affects not only the developed industrial nations that are usually the object of Third World labor emigration, but the Third World itself. For Africa, Latin America, the Caribbean, and large parts of Asia, the 1980s were an economic disaster, sometimes accompanied by the kinds of wars and military interventions that are the heritage of colonialism and neo-imperialism. The growth of transnational agro-business, furthermore, sent millions of peasants from the land, usually to urban centers in their own country, but sometimes north to the US or Europe in search of work. One author summed up the unstoppable pressures of global labor migration as follows:

> In the next 20 years, 732 million workers will enter the labor force in developing countries, a number exceeding the 686 million in the labor force of the developed world and far exceeding the number of jobs which will be created in the developing world.[50]

The world's estimated foreign-born population grew from about 76 million people in 1965 to 106 million in 1985, and then to 125 million as of 1995. While immigration between nations of the economic South occurs regularly and, in Africa and South Asia, massively, the major flow of immigration is from poorer to wealthier, from agrarian to industrial regions. The US, Canada, Australia, western Europe, and the Middle East oil kingdoms are the major "host" areas.[51]

Increasingly, continued immigration into and growing immigrant populations within the North coincided with economic crisis, industrial restructuring, rising unemployment, and the beginning of erosion of the welfare state throughout most of the North. Pre-existing racism was directed at immigrant workers, even though many of them had resided in the country for years or even decades. Immigrants were blamed for job loss by fearful citizens, unemployed youths, and manipulative politicians. In Germany, the US, France, and Britain anti-immigrant sentiment was a major recruitment theme for extreme-right, neo-fascist groups.

The focus here will be on the United States, because, among other reasons, "the United States is the No. 1 recipient of immigrants, receiving as many as the rest of the world combined."[52] Mexico is by far the biggest source of immigrant labor in the US, with a reported 13.5 million Mexicans living there as of 1993.[53] More recently, significant flows have come from Asia, Central America, and the Caribbean. Most of this is "economic" migration, but a good deal of it originates in the chaos created by the US military interventions of the last four decades in Southeast Asia and Central America.[54]

The US–Mexico border has become a virtual war zone in which the US Border Patrol and the Immigration and Naturalization Service (INS), known to Mexican and Central American migrants as "La Migra," have waged a murderous battle against undocumented immigrants. In the early 1990s over a million immigrants a year were apprehended by the INS and sent back across the border – mostly to try again to enter "el norte," where wages were ten to twenty times what they were across Mexico and Central America. Physical abuse and even murder are frequent tools used by the INS.[55] The INS also wages constant war on the smaller number of immigrants from the Caribbean, particularly Haiti. Racism is a big factor in both the anti-immigrant legislation of the past ten years and the brutality with which it is enforced.

Organized labor in the United States has a long and sorry record on questions of both race and immigration going back to the exclusion of African Americans from both the earliest trade unions and the craft unions of the American Federation of Labor and the almost universal trade-union support, including the more egalitarian Knights of Labor, for the Chinese Exclusion Act of 1882.[56] Aside from overt racism, the usual arguments against open immigration focus on the competition that large numbers of immigrants would bring to the labor market, which is already full of unemployed workers, and the alleged docility of immigrants, particularly those without legal documents. Both of these arguments have been challenged from inside and outside organized labor in recent years.

At a reception held by the Farm Labor Organizing Committee at the 1996 founding convention of the Labor Party a staffer for the Teamsters' Union and an organizer for the reform group Teamsters for a Democratic Union (TDU) had (more or less) the following exchange. The Teamster staffer said that while he had always believed in open immigration in the past, he was under a lot of pressure from union members, who saw the flow of immigrants as a threat to their job security, to take limits on immigration seriously. The TDU organizer replied, "How many immigrants hold high-paying Teamster jobs? Just about zero. Right? Or take a look at Detroit. Almost no immigrants, yet it's an economic basket case. Los Angeles or Miami, full of immigrants, are boom towns compared to Detroit." The Teamster staffer conceded the point.

The entry points of immigrant labor in the last couple of decades have been closely tied to the nature of the reorganization of the economy and the changing division of labor discussed above. These entry points are not random, but are based on the recruitment needs and policies of employers in limited sectors of the economy, on the one hand, and discrimination, on the other. In particular, immigrant workers are concentrated in low-wage manufacturing generally, electronics assembly, garment sweatshops, meat-packing, some construction jobs in areas of high immigrant concentration like Los Angeles and Miami, local service industries based on low-wage labor, and agricultural labor. Employers in industries like garment, electronics assembly, meatpacking, and hotels and resorts actively recruit certain immigrant groups.[57]

In the past twenty years or so, this recruitment process has been closely tied to the restructuring or formation of these industries. While the recruitment of farm labor for US agriculture goes back many decades, agro-business engaged in newer types of crops, such as chilies grown in Texas and New Mexico, actively seek out Mexican migrant workers – preferring those without documents in the (mistaken) belief they will prove more docile than local Chicano or documented immigrant workers. In the garment industry former large employers have tended to abandon their large factories and outsource more and more pieces of production to small contractors. In the southwest United States, for example, big companies like Levi Strauss, Lee, and Farrah closed large, unionized plants and subcontracted or relocated much of their work around the region or in Mexico or Central America. More generally, fashion houses and brand-name producers returned to the sweating system of a century earlier and even reintroduced homework, in spite of the fact that it is illegal in the US.[58]

In meatpacking, particularly beefpacking, the old unionized firms were largely driven out or bought up by new aggressive competitors like IBP, Conagra, and Cargill, the latter two beginning as global grain traders that have since moved up the food-chain market. These companies altered the product and technology of the industry, making its "disassembly lines" even more mass-production in character and its product (boxed beef) more standardized. As they opened new plants they brought in workers from closed slaughterhouses in the region and, increasingly, from Southeast Asia and Mexico. For the first time, they introduced significant numbers of women into the slaughterhouses.[59]

What this means is that there is very little direct labor-market competition between immigrant workers and the better-paid white males who appear most hysterical about immigrant workers. There is, however, competition among immigrant workers themselves and, in cities like Los Angeles, Chicago, and Miami, with African Americans, Chicanos, Puerto Ricans, and some women workers (of all races) seeking employment in lower-wage service or manufacturing jobs. This, along with some competition over housing and urban services, does give rise to conflict between different communities of color in cities like Los Angeles and Miami. In other words, this sort of competition is largely segregated among low-wage groups of workers in industries that depend on low-cost, labor-intensive production methods.

What does not seem to be the case, however, is that this competition has any particular impact on the overall wage structure of the US, perhaps because these wages hover around the minimum wage anyway. That is, it is not primarily this labor-market competition that is holding down or bringing down wage levels, but the interrelated changes in the division of labor, intensifying international competition among businesses, and the conscious effort to cut costs through lean production and related outsourcing and contracting. Of course, over the long run, a growing population of lower-paid workers will impact the overall wage levels of society as employers reorganize production to reduce high-paid labor inputs. This, however, would be true regardless of who the low-wage workers were. The real question here is, can these low-wage workers be organized? Or, to put it another way, can US unions make the necessary changes to create a hospitable "home" for immigrant workers as well as native-born workers of color?

Throughout the history of the US trade-union movement, immigrant workers, along with other racial minorities and women, have often been viewed as unorganizable. Much of this is simply racism, but some of it stems from the fact that it is often these groups that fill the most casualized or fragmented types of work. Los Angeles and other centers of immigrant population are sites of street corner "shape-ups" where day laborers are hired for all kinds of work. Electronics, garment, and other light manufacturing with high proportions of immigrants (or women, or people of color) tend to be characterized by large numbers of small shops, while service workers tend to be spread out across any urban area. Most of these kinds of jobs have high turnover rates compared with society's better-paying jobs.

Yet, as will be discussed in more detail, the evidence is that not only can many of these workers be organized, they often take the initiative in organizing themselves. The history of unionism among immigrant workers in the US is a very long one. But, whereas most of the immigrant groups prior to World War Two were white Europeans, post-war immigration has increasingly been composed of people of color from Latin America, the Caribbean, and Asia so that racial hostility on the part of the dominant white population is intertwined with economic anxiety even where direct labor market competition does not occur. Until recently, help has not always been forthcoming from US unions, whose leaders and members have often viewed the new immigrants as either "unorganizable" or simply undesirable.

In his study of a successful Los Angeles organizing drive among undocumented immigrant workers, mostly from Mexico, Hector Delgado demolishes many of the arguments about the unorganizability of these workers. He points out that family networks, dense community ties and support, and the general lack of a consistent presence of "La Migra" in large urban areas like Los Angeles play a part in making even undocumented workers quite organizable. He also points out that the determination of the union involved is important. He writes:

> Another important mitigating factor was the union's determination to organize these workers. This is in part, but not solely, a question of resources; innovative strategies and the determination of unions to organize these workers are important variables as well.[60]

Some important examples of organizing among immigrant workers and workers of color will be given below, including groups of casualized workers, but first it is necessary to look at the other major dividing line within the working class that has been affected by the changing division of labor and is often cited as another source of fragmentation: gender.

Women and the International Division of Labor

Two trends often associated with theories of class fragmentation are the growth of women as a proportion of the workforce generally, particularly in part-time and other "atypical" work, and the employment of Third World women at the lowest-wage end of internationalized production systems. In both ways, women play a disproportionate role as low-wage workers in the changing division of labor – in both the shift to "service" jobs and the "vertical disintegration" or restructuring of manufacturing. To put it another way, the changing division of labor, both domestically across the developed industrial world, and internationally has a strong gender dimension.

In general, women's labor-force participation rates have been rising for several decades and in most industrial nations have reached at least 60%, while male participation rates have dropped somewhat. Across the industrial world as a whole, women had gone from about a third of the workforce in 1960 to 42% by 1993, while in the most industrialized nations the proportion was even higher. A good deal of this increase was accounted for by the rise of part-time work; women compose from 66% to 90% of this part of the workforce.[61]

This gender dimension is a reflection, of course, of a much more ancient hierarchical and unequal relationship between men and women in capital-ist society. A well-known traditional aspect of this inequality is that women were expected to stay home, while men earned a "family wage" big enough to support the entire family. The family wage eroded over the years and women entered the workforce to help support their families. But the women who did enter the labor force took on the "two shift system," one of paid labor on the job, the other of unpaid labor at home. Another is that historically, women are paid less than men, no matter what the job. Although no longer a reality, the concept of the male "family wage" lingers on as one of many excuses for unequal pay.

Sexism and institutional gender stereotyping play a big role in shunting women into labor-intensive service and light-manufacturing jobs that would be poorly paid no matter who held them. The enormous growth of retail, clerical, and white-collar jobs since World War Two has provided the bulk of women's employment growth. But the prejudice that guides women into low-paying jobs and helps keep female wages low also aids companies willing to overcome stereotypes when it is profitable. As mentioned above, when the new, more aggressive, meatpacking companies reorganized production methods in the 1980s in the US they actively sought women, as well as male immigrant, workers even though this work does not conform to the stereotype of "women's work." Similarly, the reorganization and geographic relocation of the poultry industry during the 1980s created new "disassembly" plants employing thousands of women in similarly bloody and dangerous, if slightly lighter, jobs. Women clerical and manufacturing workers share more than low pay and sexual harassment on the job; they share repetitive stress injuries.[62]

By and large, as one study of women workers in Europe put it:

> Women and men are segregated in the labor market. The gender boundaries to the types of jobs the sexes usually do mean that in effect women and men are in different labor forces, and are not readily substitutable. Economic restructuring therefore has a different impact on women and men, and the simple hypothesis that women act as a buffer or cushion for male employ-ment must be rejected.[63]

At the same time, it is clear that women workers are the source of much of the flexibility provided by part-time and temporary workers. They also fill many of the jobs at the low-wage end of extended production chains, which means that although inequality prevails, men and women perform-ing different jobs within the division of labor of an industry are nonetheless linked by a common production system and, perhaps, a common employer.

Though women workers do share a specific and unequal role in restructuring and the changing division of labor in most industrial countries, this does not, in itself, create greater fragmentation of the class than the previous situation where women stayed at home. In fact, it makes more sense to view the growing presence of women in the workforce as a source of potentially increased unity within the class. That is, women and men now share in the labor–capital relationship more directly than at any time in history. Furthermore, they are sometimes linked in the same extended production chain. In addition, of course, employment tends to create greater independence and self-confidence, even where the "second shift" at home remains, and this can contribute to efforts to organize.

As with workers of color or immigrant workers, the major question for organized labor and the working class more broadly is whether or not the majority of women who are outside trade unions can be brought inside, and the gender wage gap reduced. A positive answer to this question depends on unions dealing with sexist attitudes and practices, as well as with issues related to the unequal position of women in society and the workforce. Affirmative action, pay equity, child care, and reproductive issues must become more a part of labor's agenda.

In the 1970s and 1980s, the role of women workers in the emerging international systems of production was analysed in the "new international division of labor" (NIDL) theory. A central theme of this theory was that the changing global division of labor was quite gender and geographically specific. Capital moved more and more production out of the industrial nations of the North, investing heavily in labor-intensive Third World production facilities. The more capital-intensive jobs that stayed in the North would be dominated by men, while the new overseas labor-intensive jobs would be filled by women. The "global factory," associated with the NIDL theory, was, thus, a gender-segregated one.

While women working in *maquiladora* plants in Mexico or Central America or in export zones in Asia or the Caribbean certainly fit this description, the actual course of globalization turned out to be more complex. The rise of women in the labor force in the Third World was not only a result of increased foreign direct investment and the decline of traditional industry in the North, as important as that has been. Another feature of the restructuring of the 1980s *within* much of the economic South was the decline of large-scale industry originally created during the import-substitution period that had provided stable male employment. As these industries were dismantled, downsized, or privatized across the Third World, male jobs and incomes declined or dried up, and more women entered the workforce in search of incomes. This created a labor pool on which the export-oriented "structural-adjustment" plans and export zones of the 1980s could be based. In other words, in much of the Third World, women's increased labor-force participation was matched by significant decreases in male participation rates in the formal economy, accompanied by the growth of the informal economy, which absorbed both men and women.[64]

Another trend that departs from the predictions of most NIDL analyses was that some of those industries expected to relocate in the Third World didn't. Thus, a majority of world employment in the garment industry remains in the North – albeit largely because of the protection offered by the Multi-Fiber Agreement trade agreement.[65] The European clothing industry has remained surprisingly intact, owing largely to a focus on upscale products and markets and the protection provided by the Multi-Fiber Agreement (MFA), which allows high protective tariffs. Italy was second only to Hong Kong as an exporter of clothing through the 1980s.[66]

In addition, some of the industries with well-known gender segregation, such as electronics, retained significant proportions of employment in the developed nations owing to technology and the rise of customized production. The other side of this coin is that entire industries in the US and elsewhere were restructured or built around the employment of low-paid, often immigrant, labor *within* the industrial North.[67] In effect, the Third World came to the industries rather than the other way around. In garment or electronics, these workers would tend to be women, but men also played a large role in new low-wage manufacturing and service industries in the North. For example, the contract cleaning workers organized by the Service Employees International Union in Los Angeles through the "Justice for Janitors" campaign in 1991, were both men and women. For another, the "global factory," while gender-segregated, turned out to be more typically regional, based around one or another Triad country, than randomly global.

Newly organizing phases of internationalized industries based primarily on female labor tend to be geographically clustered around urban concentrations, whether Bangkok or Los Angeles, Ciudad Juárez or New York City. This fact, by itself, creates both a more supportive collective setting and greater interaction among workers than, say, the newer auto parts, meatpacking, or poultry plants located in small-town America. In his remarkable book, *In the Cities of the South*, Jeremy Seabrook describes again and again how both neighborhood and employment solidarities arise among women in new Third World industrial centers like Jakarta, Bangkok, and Dhaka. In these situations gender, class, and sometimes ethnic identities intermingle to unify rather than fragment. Sometimes these produce successful attempts to organize or recruit to unions.[68]

The garment industry provides a clear example of both the geographic concentration of production sites and the regional nature of production more generally. The garment industry in the US is divided into a number of distinct product sectors: sportswear, high fashion, Men's and Boy's, Women's and Misses. New York City and adjacent areas in New Jersey form the center of the high-fashion industry, while most sportswear is produced in either New York or Los Angeles. Contractors can be located farther away, but are typically either within the US or in adjacent areas in Mexico or the Caribbean. Workers in both the "core" and the contracting phases of the production chain tend to be women immigrants. Both high fashion and sportswear are very time-sensitive in terms of changing tastes and markets, which is the primary reason they remain inside or very near the US. Men's and Boy's wear is a more capital-intensive, mass-production industry with a much more straightforward production chain, running from textile plant to mass-production clothing plant. These tend to be located near the textile industry in the southeast US, with a large proportion of women and African-American workers.[69]

As in the Third World, geographic, gender, and ethnic concentrations within industries where women compose a high proportion of the work-force cut across generally fragmented or extended production systems. Here again the simple "global factory" thesis proves inadequate and closer analysis shows that even in highly competitive, import-sensitive industries like garment, there are other potential avenues of organization than the traditional shop-by-shop style of American unions. These can be found in both gender and ethnic solidarities as well as a strong tendency toward geographic concentration. What is involved is the recognition of the dialectic between such potential gender or ethnic solidarities, on the one hand, and equally potentially debilitating divisions within the working class, on the other. In today's world diversity can be a powerful weapon when those who would organize the working class also take on the struggles for greater equality and for issues that affect the interests of women, immigrants, or specific racial or ethnic groups. In any event, diversity of one or another sort has always been the condition of the working class to a greater extent than any other class in history. The key to advancing its interests has always been in the ability to organize as a class from the "particularistic loyalties" and "mosaic of individual histories" that is the dormant state of the working class.

Recomposition and Organizing the Unorganizable

One of the theses of fragmentation not mentioned above, which is drawn largely on the sociology of the 1970s and 1980s, is that old working-class neighborhoods have dissolved throughout much of the industrialized world, adding another dimension to the dispersal of the working class of the "golden age." What this thesis overlooks is that new working-class neighborhoods have taken shape, while many old ones remain. Some of these newer neighborhoods are drawn primarily from the population of the same country, such as the high-rise working-class areas outside Barcelona, the working-class "estates" around London, or the working-class suburbs that surround many American cities. Others are primarily populated by immigrants, as in much of the US.

Whether one looks at the new immigrant neighborhoods in cities as different as Los Angeles and Paris, what one sees is that immigrant workers form neighborhoods that are in many ways like those new working-class neighborhoods forming in the newly industrializing countries. They may not be shanty towns, as in much of the Third World, but these new bustling urban areas are thick with working-class humanity and provide a solid base from which to organize.

Delgado, in the study cited above, argues that the successful organizing drive he analyses depended not only on the efforts of the union, but also on family and community ties that strengthened over time even for undocumented workers.[70] Vast immigrant communities like those in Los Angeles, Miami, Chicago, and New York provide fertile ground for organizing, as efforts like the Los Angeles "Justice for Janitors" campaign in 1991, the mass strikes of Mexican immigrant drywallers in 1992, framers (carpenters) in 1993, and water-front truckers in 1995 showed. Even smaller rural areas have proved havens for unionization among farm workers as the migrant groups that form the workforce settle down. Baldemar Velasquez, president of the Farm Labor Organizing Committee (FLOC), which organized workers in the tomato and cucumber fields of Ohio and Michigan and forced food-processing giant Campbell's to the bargaining table, attributed part of FLOC's success to the tendency for farm-worker neighborhoods to take shape in the region.[71]

At the other end of the process of recomposition are new working-class suburbs like Sterling Heights, Michigan, just north of Detroit. This oft-studied and, despite its name, entirely flat area, dates back only to the 1970s. It has long been viewed as the quintessential white-flight American working-class suburb in which privatized, individualized lives are lived in isolation. It is the "home town" of the Reagan Democrat. Detroit African Americans often refer to its residents as the "sterling whites." Like many of the other towns around it, it is blue-collar white Middle America.[72]

It is, however, not a "Leave it to Beaver" suburb of ranch-style homes and sprawling lawns. Rather, it is a "city" of low-rise apartment complexes surrounded by parking lots. There is more green on average in the center strips of its main thoroughfares than around its housing developments. Its avenues are lined with auto plants, union halls, family-style (not just fast food) restaurants, and bars, where working-class people congregate to talk, watch sports on giant TVs, or dance. A large plurality of its male residents work in the auto-assembly and parts plants around metropolitan Detroit, while most of the women work in low-paying clerical or service jobs. At the same time as it often gives the Republican presidential candidate a majority of its votes, it also consistently re-elects one of the country's most liberal Congressional representatives.[73]

For all its contradictory and conservative consciousness, Sterling Heights became the scene of one of those class explosions that have come to characterize the lean-production era. In July 1995 striking Detroit Newspaper Agency (DNA) workers belonging to the Teamsters' Union and Communications Workers of America made national news when many of them, along with a few hundred sympathizers from other unions, like the United Auto Workers and the International Brotherhood of Electrical Workers, fought the police to a standstill in front of the DNA's major printing plant, right in the middle of Sterling Heights. This level of struggle continued for several weeks and culminated in late September with a mass picketline of 3,000 or more workers, many of them auto workers, that once again engaged the police assaults in spite of heavy pepper gas.

The mass picketing was eventually outlawed by the business-friendly courts of the land, but the fight spilled over into the politics of Sterling Heights. That fall, strikers and supporters from other unions invaded a city council meeting to demand that the city manager who had called out the police again and again be fired. He was. But the reaction came soon, with the company and the mainstream politicians organizing the counter-revolution and putting the city manager back into office after defeating most of the pro-union council candidates. The unions had been completely unprepared for such a political confrontation. Nevertheless, the city council continued to be the scene of confrontation as strikers and supporters invaded time after time.

What all this revealed, and what became clear before long, is that these alleged "Reagan Democrats" did not share the mainstream view of class relations or the prevailing ideology of competitiveness – a word pronounced only with venom on the picketlines. Indeed, the language and slogans of the strike were the stuff of class antagonism already invading much of Middle American life as the future gets bleaker and bleaker for American workers of all kinds. Strike actions spread across the metropolitan area into the inner city and to other working-class suburbs much like Sterling Heights. Organizations from metro Detroit's various white, African-American, and Latino communities expressed support for the strikers in sentiment and action. In effect, the Detroit Newspaper strike became an embryo of social-movement unionism in one city.

The Detroit Newspaper strike was, like Staley or Caterpillar or GM or Boeing, a classical-lean production strike over outsourcing, contracting, and new work schedules. To workers across Detroit's labor movement, the DNA's far-reaching proposals for work reorganization symbolized one more loss of good, union jobs in the area and a place to draw the line. So, well into the second year of the strike workers from other unions joined strikers in guerrilla warfare against the DNA and the local state, while tens of thousands ceased to buy the daily papers they had read all of their lives. A few went farther along the line of rising class consciousness. A couple of dozen strikers joined the Detroit metro chapter of the newly formed Labor Party and one ran for State Representative as an independent in the white working-class suburb of Shelby Township. His program called for a $10-an-hour minimum wage and job creation through a 32-hour work week.[74]

The racial segregation of neighborhoods, such as that which character-ized Sterling Heights, on the one hand, and Detroit's inner-city ghetto, on the other, is nothing new for any social class in the United States. Concentration and separation within an urban area has been imposed on Blacks, Latinos, or immigrants from the Third World and actively sought or accepted by whites during the entire history of the United States. There was never a racial "golden age" in which Black and white or Latino and Anglo workers mixed freely. Similar concentrations of newer immigrant peoples have arisen in Europe in the last three decades or so. While they have not experienced the same degree of segregation as people of color in the US, racial and cultural hostility among the white population is strong.

In the US, only employment and unionism brought these workers together in an uneasy, but durable alliance – and then only a minority of them. One of the objects of social-movement unionism must be to overcome the spatial separation of different racial groups within the working class through active forms of common struggle, but also by taking to heart the specific needs and demands of the communities of color, whether they are "native" or immigrant. What is involved here is neither some liberal notion of racial harmony and integration that must precede class unity, nor some postmodernist or corporate romanticization of diversity which leaves inequality for the vast majority intact, but a more dialectical notion of a fight for equality linked to a fight for class advancement. The movement must learn to draw on all its strengths, of which ethnic concentrations are often one, albeit a contradictory one. A few examples are offered below.

Few jobs are traditionally more casualized, seasonal, and geographically dispersed than agricultural labor. In the US since World War Two, these jobs have been filled primarily by immigrant workers, mostly from Mexico and more recently from the Philippines, Haiti, and other parts of the Caribbean basin. Even when they become citizens or are drawn from native-born groups (Chicanos or Puerto Ricans) all are workers of color in a nation with enduring racist institutions, and most speak another language than English. To make matters worse, agricultural labor was excluded from the National Labor Relations Act, so that there is no clear legal framework for establishing collective bargaining.

It is hard to imagine a group of workers with more disadvantages than farm workers. Yet, since the 1960s, when Cesar Chavez's United Farm Workers (UFW) caught the nation's attention and organized California's agro-business-dominated fields, farm workers across the country have organized unions and won labor contracts. They have drawn on a common ethnicity, but have needed and frequently received support in their organizing efforts, though at first not always from the AFL–CIO or other unions. They have organized themselves rather than being organized by an existing US union, and they have drawn on deep family and community ties as well as much broader solidarity efforts to win. They have, in short, adopted models of social-movement unionism, albeit without using the term, and won.

One of the most remarkable stories in the history of farm worker organizing is that of the FLOC, based mainly in the tomato and cucumber fields of Ohio and Michigan. FLOC succeeded in organizing the workers in Ohio and Michigan, many of whom were still seasonal migrants in the 1970s, but strikes against the growers failed as the major buyers shifted their contracts to other growers and the growers brought in scabs. Like the UFW, FLOC relied on a massive national boycott to win collective bargaining. But FLOC's boycott was not directed against the growers, who, unlike in California, tended to be fairly small family farmers. The boycott was directed against Campbell's, the giant US soup and condiment producer that was the major customer of the Midwest growers. FLOC leader Baldemar Velasquez reasoned that the real power in the fields was that of Campbell's, who set the prices that limited wages. It was also clear that Campbell's made a highly visible target for a broader movement in support of FLOC.[75]

FLOC's seven-year campaign ended in victory in 1986, when Campbell's and the growers agreed to enter into an unprecedented three-way agreement. FLOC had forced Campbell's and the growers to recognize an independent body with no legal standing to oversee representation elections and contract negotiations. Velasquez acknowledges that the tendency for migrant farm workers to settle in the areas where they do most of their work, in this case Ohio and Michigan, allowed the union to become a more stable organization.[76] While FLOC did not receive the same kind of backing from the AFL–CIO that the UFW had in the 1960s, it was supported by many unions across the country.

Anyone who drives to the border crossing at El Paso, Texas, at about three in the morning will see hundreds of Mexican men sleeping in the streets. They are agricultural laborers who have crossed the border to work in the chili fields of Texas and New Mexico and they are waiting for the trucks that will take them to work.[77] This ragged army of day laborers encamped in the streets along the border may seem like the furthest thing from a stable union base, but most of them are, in fact, dedicated union members. They belong to the Unión de Trabajadores Agrícolas Fronterizos (Union of Border Agricultural Workers – UTAF).

The UTAF is unique even among farm worker organizations in that it directly recruits in both the US and Mexico. Most of its members were undocumented immigrant workers, whom the growers preferred to more secure documented or local Chicano workers. Employer hostility and anti-immigrant sentiment among the local population made the odds against the UTAF enormous. Working with organizations in both Mexico and the US, however, the UTAF sought and won "amnesty" status for all workers in the Texas and New Mexico chili fields under the ICRA, which meant that they became legally documented immigrant workers.

To gain "amnesty" status each worker had to apply to the US government under the terms of the IRCA. The union helped to sign up some 3,000 workers, who became the core of the union and who, in turn, signed up others. In the late 1980s the "amnesty" campaign became a union organizing drive. As UTAF leader Carlos Marentes acknowledged:

> The amnesty program gave us a big boost and suddenly all these people lost their fear of being deported. They joined the union.[78]

But recognition by the growers was far from automatic. Like FLOC, UTAF faced the fact that there is no legal framework for union recognition of farm labor. In 1990, UTAF led a successful strike at harvest time. The union struck again in 1992. UTAF received some help from FLOC and an El Paso organization, discussed below, known as "La Mujer Obrera," as well as other unions in the area. Basically, however, these workers organized themselves and pulled together what amounted to a massive political campaign to change their legal status.[79]

Elements of social-movement unionism have also been used to organize urban-based immigrant workers. The best known of these campaigns was the 1991 "Justice for Janitors" campaign in Los Angeles, which involved mass actions and community support and brought thousands of Mexican and Central American immigrants into the union. The strategy adopted by the Service Employees International Union (SEIU) Local 399, which directed the campaign, was that used for over a hundred years to organize casualized contract workers. The idea being that you must first organize a significant majority of the contractor firms in the relevant local labor market, while links through the immigrant communities provide the key recruitment mechanism. The SEIU had targeted ISS, a Danish-owned international contractor of janitorial labor, as the largest contractor in Los Angeles. From there they were able to move on fairly rapidly to organize the other contractors. More recently a variant of this "whole-market" strategy was used to organize 1,000 contract workers in New York City's "demolition" industry, 90% of whom were Ecuadorian immigrants.[80]

Unions, however, are not the only workers' organizations active among casualized or low-wage workers in various immigrant, Latino, and African-American communities across the US. Since the early 1980s a new type of organization, usually called a workers' center, has arisen in many areas of new employment. The oldest of these are found in the border town of El Paso, Texas, where women garment workers created an organization called "La Mujer Obrera" (The Woman Worker), New York City's Chinatown, where local service workers belong to the Chinese Staff and Workers' Association, and in the "runaway" branch plants clustered around the small industrial city of Rocky Mount, North Carolina, where Black Workers For Justice (BWFJ) have organized both factory committees and community-based campaigns.[81]

These organizations differ in their view of unions. Some, like La Mujer Obrera and the Chinese Staff and Workers' Association, have had bad experiences with union officials and are highly suspicious or view unions as too narrow, or even racist. Others, like BWFJ and the newer Latino Workers' Center on New York's Lower East Side, want to bring workers into unions whenever possible. What these organizations have in common is their relationship to groups of workers in jobs and places usually regarded as difficult to organize. Their approach is to educate and train a worker leadership in the communities in which they are based who can organize and lead a variety of actions in both workplace and neighborhood. Like the communities in which they are based, these organizations have much in common with the working-class neighborhood or gender-based social-movement organizations across much of the Third World.

In Los Angeles, the Los Angeles Manufacturing Action Project (LAMAP) set out in 1995 to combine a number of these different approaches, building on ethnic identities and community organizations and a multi-union alliance to organize some 15,000 mostly immigrant workers employed along the Alameda Corridor – a 21-mile strip of small and medium-sized manufacturing firms. From the start LAMAP worked with community organizations and the California Immigrant Workers' Association, a union-backed project that acts as a workers' center for immigrants. The project invested time in community educational programs to expand its base before even attempting union drives.

LAMAP draws on the strengths of the Latino and immigrant communities of Los Angeles. The attacks on immigrants, including Proposition 187, which denies immigrants access to many health and social services, have galvanized the Latino community. Joel Ochoa, community organizer for LAMAP, says, "Now we have a social movement in the making and labor needs to make itself available to that movement and labor needs to join it." Ochoa goes on to explain how the dynamics among Latinos, both citizens and immigrants, are an opportunity for labor. He says:

> I have been saying for some time now that Latino workers are targeting the labor movement. Look at the Drywallers, the workers at American Racing Equipment, and the activity in the apparel industry. What you find is that workers are developing campaigns before they even talk to a union organizer. They are organizing themselves and then choosing a union they want to represent them. Imagine what we could accomplish if we created an organizing environment where multi-union actions are taking place throughout the Alameda Corridor.[82]

LAMAP won one of its first victories when it supported a strike by 170 delivery drivers for Mission-Guerrero Tortillas. Represented by Teamsters Local 63, the seven-week strike received support from the Latino communities where LAMAP had been organizing and from the Los Angeles labor movement.[83] Whether LAMAP's plan to organize the Alameda Corridor would work or not remained to be seen, but it was clear that they were drawing on the strengths of workers who had been largely ignored by unions for a long time.

The new money, $30 million for 1997, and encouragement coming from the new leaders of the AFL–CIO also helped to put the organizing of America's growing nonunion workforce back on the agenda. Many of these organizing drives would certainly be crippled by the traditional, bureaucratic approach of much of the US labor movement. But new strategies and tactics were being debated and tried across the country. While racial and gender divisions within the workforce remained barriers to unity, they also provided opportunities when white workers and union leaders transcended or dealt with the deeply rooted racist and sexist practices of so many unions.

For all their problems, the unions remained the most diverse, least segregated organizations in the United States. While it would be naive to believe that racism had been purged from the unions, the evidence was that a union context tended to bring out the best in workers' attitudes and practice. The re-election of Ron Carey and the reform forces in the Teamsters in December 1996 provided an example. Ken Paff, national organizer of the Teamsters for a Democratic Union put it this way:

> The idea that white workers won't elect Latino or Black leaders is simply wrong. The Teamsters are overwhelmingly white. But they elected the most diverse leadership ever to run the Teamsters union. Whatever these white workers might think about race in some other context, in the union they understand the need for unity and representation. Not just in the national elections. We see this all around the country. The smart white activists don't just tolerate this diversity, they seek it out. The union context brings out the best in people.[84]

Skeptics point out that while multi-racial slates in union elections at the local level are already common, seldom is the candidate for top office an African-American, Latino, or Asian. In other words, racism has not simply disappeared and the white majority still seeks ultimate control. True enough, but at the same time the cultural change involved in the acceptance of a multi-racial union leadership should not be dismissed or underestimated. Only a few decades ago, this practice was unthinkable in all but a few unions. People and their long-held attitudes can be changed in the course of struggle and in the context of class organization.

A class or union "identity" speaks to a real material need that draws people together. If the institutional bases of racism and sexism are not addressed this unity can collapse far more rapidly than it took shape. But the opportunity to forge unity is there in the reality and organizations of the class. As organizing proceeds, yesterday's insurmountable fragmentation sometimes becomes today's innovative path to organizing. And organization at many levels, coupled with consciousness, is the only thing that transforms this often dormant class into an agent of social change.

Conclusion

The shape of the working class in all corners of the world has changed as capitalism itself has altered its geographic, organizational, and technological contours. As old structures of the working class are altered, however, new ones arise. Yet, far from dispersing workers in some random fashion, capital has brought more workers into more extensive production systems, themselves controlled by the largest units of capital. As in the past, the working class seeks out ways to overcome new divisions of labor, as well as new cultural divisions within its ranks.

The paralysis of much of the working class in the developed nations is not simply a function of these changes, as important as they are. Like the changes themselves, the apparent passivity of the organized working class for so long is also linked to enormous transformations in the industries and economies in which people work. These are not permanent states of being, but constant transitions. These trends are part of the inherent instability of the system and its constant need to change and degrade work and society in ways that subordinate the majority to the will of that tiny minority that controls global capital. The great irony of this constant need to change things in favor of capital's insatiable needs is that it brings not only barriers to working-class action, but forces that make the class confront those barriers and seek new channels of resistance and rebellion.

8

Crisis of the Working Class

The working class throughout most of the developed capitalist North, except Japan, has been through a prolonged and deepening social crisis since the 1970s. This crisis has three major elements, all of which are rooted in capital's response to the general crisis of accumulation. The first began in the 1970s and can be characterized as a world-wide restructuring directed at eliminating "excess capacity" in many basic industries. The second element is the growth of casualized and contract work of all kinds brought on in part by the outsourcing and contracting associated with lean production.

The third and most recent element of the crisis is the downsizing spree of the 1990s. This last type of restructuring is not directed so much at overall capacity reduction in any given industry, but results from re-engineering, on the one hand, and attempts by major corporations to return to "core competencies," on the other. All these have in common a tendency to reduce the workforce of the industries and firms they hit hardest, though to different degrees and in different ways. They can all be regarded as forms of restructuring, but will be treated distinctly. Together, they have thrown most of the Western working class into social and organizational disarray.

From Militancy to Paralysis

Capital's post-war "golden age" brought with it rising expectations across much of the industrialized world. By the late 1960s, student rebellions were evident across the world, the women's movement and feminism arose on a larger scale than ever before, mass movements of African

Americans and Latinos challenged white supremacy in the US, and in some countries gays and lesbians organized and demonstrated for their rights. Opposition to the US war in Vietnam galvanized a generation of radical activists across the globe. Third World liberation movements, following the Cuban example, tried to organize the peasantry into a revolutionary force. The 1960s through the early 1970s seemed to be one of those historic moments pregnant with possibilities. And at the very height of this period, the industrial working class reasserted itself.

A new industrial militancy swept North America and much of Europe (including Poland and Czechoslovakia) from the late 1960s through the 1970s in many countries. In the US this period saw increased militancy in the form of high strike-incidence rates and numerous wildcat strikes, including national or multi-state wildcats by postal workers, coal miners, and truck drivers in 1970. Official strike statistics surpassed those of the 1930s and came close to the all-time record of 1946 with 66 million days lost in 1970.[1] In Canada, the strike wave lasted longer, peaking in 1976 when one and a half million workers struck, costing the employers over 11 millions days lost.[2] In much of Europe, strike levels remained high throughout the 1970s, though the peak by most measures was the period 1970–74, when 578 days per thousand workers were lost in 11 major western European countries.[3]

Unions in the US, Canada, and many western European countries grew in the wake of high levels of militancy well into the 1970s. In the US, although union density continued to slip, the number of union members hit its highest level in 1980, with just over 20 million members. Of particular importance in the US in the 1960s and 1970s was the growth of public-sector unionism and the consequent rise in the proportions and numbers of women and people of color in the unions – a transformation that remains key today.[4] In European countries that had seen high levels of militancy, union density actually grew. In Britain, it went from 40% in the 1960s to 50% in the second half of the 1970s. In Italy, in the same period, it grew from 29% to 49%. In Germany, it was a more modest 34% to 37%, and in France from 20% to 22% in the early 1970s.[5]

This period of militancy and growth was above all a rebellion against the accelerated speed-up that was capital's response to the early phase of its accumulation crisis. It was particularly strong among the younger workers who had entered the factories of the industrial North in the 1960s. In western Europe more titanic and political confrontations, such as France in 1968, the "Hot Autumn" of 1969 in Italy, the central role played by workers and unions in the overthrow of fascism in Spain and Portugal, and the 1973–74 miners' strike in Britain, brought down governments and put the question of how to deal with the organized working class back on

the political as well as the industrial agenda of most countries of the North.
Yet this wave of militancy came to an abrupt end in the second half of the
1970s throughout the developed capitalist countries.

International Industrial Restructuring

Even as working-class militancy took companies, governments, and most
of the left by surprise in the late 1960s through much of the 1970s, the
world was changing rapidly. The simultaneous rise of new economic
powers in the East, notably Japan, the return of a crisis of accumulation,
the deepening of international economic integration, and the collapse of
the Bretton Woods system that had governed the world currency system
brought on new recessions and the gigantic industrial restructuring that
swept North America and western Europe from the mid-1970s through the
1980s. The growth of capital's post-war "golden age" along with the
entrance of new players led to overcapacity in many basic industries. In
the West, industries like steel faced the new Asian competition with
obsolete facilities. For example, steel production in the OECD countries of
the economic North dropped from its 1973 peak of 430 million tons to an
average of about 370 million tons in the 1980s. Both the European
Community countries and the US saw significant declines in steel production in that period, while Japan's production rose by about 25%, and that
in the developing nations more than doubled in the 1980s.[6]

The perception of overcapacity is a function of the falling rate of profit,
not simply insufficient demand. As corporations experience a drop in
returns on investment at the margins of a certain level of production, they
will tend to cut back production to a more profitable level. What was
distinct about this period of restructuring was that it involved large-scale
reductions in the ability to produce – not just a reduction of labor with the
same or greater output, as in the downsizing of the 1990s.

Millions of industrial jobs, many of them higher-paid union jobs,
evaporated as industries like steel, shipbuilding, machinery, and automobiles closed facilities and reduced production capacity across the West.
In the first phase of restructuring between 1974 and 1983 North America
saw 8% of its manufacturing jobs disappear while Europe took an astound-
ing 20% drop.[7] British historian Eric Hobsbawm summarized it like this:

> Britain lost 25 per cent of its manufacturing industry in 1980–84. Between
> 1973 and the late 1980s the total number of employed in manufacturing in
> the six old-industrial countries of Europe fell by seven millions, or about a
> quarter, about half of which were lost between 1979 and 1983. By the late

1980s, as the working class in the old industrial countries eroded and the new ones rose, the workforce employed in manufacturing settled down at about a quarter of all civilian employment in all western developed regions, except the USA, where by that time it was well below 20 per cent.[8]

It was obvious that the industrial working class that emerged by the mid-1980s was not only smaller but in a state of shock from the catastrophe that had swept most of its communities and workplaces. There would be some more episodes of militancy such as the Spanish and Portuguese working classes' central role in the overthrow of fascism from the mid- to late 1970s, Britain's public-sector workers' "Winter of Discontent," or the American coal miners' strike of 1978–79. But the industrial struggle that had marked the period from 1966–74 ended, and a drastic slide in union membership and density began in all but a few Western industrial nations.

The number of union members in the US actually grew until 1980, even though union density had fallen in the US from 34% in the mid-1950s to about 25% in 1980, owing largely to service-sector growth.[9] As industrial restructuring caught up, however, union density in the US slipped more or less continuously, until it hit 15.8% in 1993 and then 14.5% in 1996. In the private sector, it fell even farther, to 10.2 % by 1996. This decline was accompanied by significant concessions in wages, benefits, and working conditions that, of course, could not have any real impact on job loss, owing to international restructuring. In Canada, organized labor proved more resilient, falling from about 37% in the 1970s to 35% in the late 1980s.[10]

Union density also declined across much of western Europe after the growth of the 1970s. In the UK it plunged from 50% in the 1970s to 41% in the 1990s. In the same period in Italy, union density dropped from 49% to 38%. France and Spain suffered the most drastic declines, falling respectively from 21% to 10% and from 50% to 10%. Germany held steady at 34%, while union density actually increased in the Scandinavian countries. It should be borne in mind that these measures of union strength do not have the same social meaning in much of Europe as in the US. While union membership is very low in Spain and France, union coverage (the percentage of workers covered by union-negotiated agreements) is very high, owing to legislation that calls for the extension of union agreements to nonunion firms in the same industry or region: 68% in Spain, 91% in France. Germany has similar provisions and a coverage rate of 81%. Overall, higher institutional support for unionism and collective bargaining in most of continental Europe has left union density rates above their pre-1968 levels except in Spain and France. In these two countries, however, as recent events have shown, the unions retain the ability to mobilize on a class basis far beyond their membership.[11]

In most of western Europe as well as in the United States, the impact of restructuring receded as the process slowed down to rates more "normal" for the average "creative destruction" of capitalism. By most estimates the period of drastic restructuring in western Europe lasted from the mid-1970s through the mid-1980s.[12] For the US it probably lasted somewhat longer, while in Canada the impact of the US–Canada Free Trade Pact of 1989 and NAFTA have prolonged the process.[13] A somewhat different process of restructuring is now unfolding among the four Asian "Tigers" (Hong Kong, Taiwan, South Korea, and Singapore).[14]

Restructuring to remove excess capacity, however, was only one side of the impact of intensified international and domestic competition. Another aspect was the enormous business reorganization that took place from the mid-1980s through the mid-1990s. As Dunning argues, TNCs as organizations tend to be in a "continual state of metamorphosis."[15] International functioning and intense competition produce constant reorganizations and shifting business alliances.

Probably the most significant trend in business reorganization in the last decade-and-a-half was the enormous wave of mergers and acquisitions (M&As) in North America and western Europe. In the US, the number of M&As doubled between 1985 and the mid-1990s, while their value rose from $150 billion in 1985 to a peak of $317 billion in 1989, then dropped significantly until it rose again to $359 billion in 1994 and almost $450 billion in 1995. The resurgence of mergers and acquisitions in the US in the mid-1990s indicates that the centralization of capital, the attempt to capture market by swallowing the competition, would continue. It may also reveal that alliances and other non-equity joint ventures were not about to replace the "war" of the marketplace.[16]

The number of overseas acquisitions by US firms rose steadily from 91 in 1985 to 455 in 1992. The trend in value was similar to that of domestic M&As, rising from $3.7 billion in 1985 to a peak of $27 billion in 1989, then falling to about $14 billion through the early 1990s and rising slightly to $17 billion in 1994. Acquisitions in the US by foreign firms were higher, following a similar pattern: $28 billion in 1985 rising to $69 billion in 1989, then falling until rising slightly to $38 billion in 1994.[17]

What these trends suggest, aside from the obvious rise of business interpenetration, is first that M&As are a "cheap" way of expanding and defending market share at home and abroad.[18] Second, however, is that the more rapid decline in the value of M&As than in their numbers from 1990 through 1993 indicates that the merger or acquisition of smaller firms is most likely related to lean production's tendency to reorganize supplier chains, forcing mergers of formerly smaller suppliers. In the European Community, where M&As were a relatively new phenomenon, their frequency rose dramatically in the second half of the 1980s, as in the US. M&As by the top 1,000 EU corporations rose from 208 in 1984–85 to 492 in 1988–89. The proportion of cross-border M&As rose from 40% to 55% of the total in the same period as firms raced to position themselves across the continent after the Single European Act of 1989.[19]

What these mergers mean, particularly in North America and Britain, is that unions that once represented a firm's eligible workforce now find themselves part of a multi-facility company with different or no unions in its other facilities – a drastic change in the balance of forces. The impact of this on European trade unions is even more complex than in the US because different national labor movements are involved. The implementation of the European Works Council Directive (September 1994), which requires firms with operations in two or more countries to set up EU-wide works councils, will provide a point of contact for union officials from different countries, but these cross-border councils are only consultative and have no bargaining power.[20]

Another problem, and one of the reasons for declining union membership and density, is that mergers and acquisitions inevitably involve shrinking parts of the merged firm as less profitable facilities are stripped. Changes in ownership are also, of course, frequently the occasion for changes in work practices and organization associated with lean production. This was certainly the case in Britain at Rover, when first Honda and then BMW bought the facility from its British owners, and at Chrysler, when it was bought by Peugeot; at SEAT in Spain, when Volkswagen bought that formerly state-owned company, at GM's Fremont, California, plant, when GM and Toyota jointly reopened it as NUMMI; and at A. E. Staley, when Tate & Lyle bought that firm.[21]

A Changing Working Class, Not a Disappearing One

As a dynamic and destructive system, capitalism is always reshaping the nature of work and the workforce that performs it. Eric Hobsbawm described the greatest such transformation of our time:

> The most dramatic and far-reaching social change of the second half of this century, and one that cuts us off forever from the world of the past, is the death of the peasantry. For since the neolithic era most human beings had lived off the land and its livestock or harvested the sea as fishers.[22]

Note that he is talking about the "second half of this century" and is referring to the industrial nations at that. While the peasantry has not quite "died" in the world's South, the proportion of people working in agriculture in the world dropped from 53% in 1980 to 49% in 1990.[23] It is also sobering to bear in mind that by the end of this century half or more of humanity will live in cities. These new urbanites will enter the race to sell the one "commodity" they possess – their ability to work. This is simply another way of saying that the world's population is becoming more working-class.

This idea runs against the grain of much of the fashionable literature coming from the political left and right alike. While predicting the demise of the working class is a long-standing practice, it is now common to predict the "end of work" altogether.[24] The world is or will soon be "post-industrial," it is said. Speaking specifically of the industrial working class, post-industrial guru Peter Drucker wrote:

> No class in history has ever risen faster than the Blue Collar worker. And no class in history has ever fallen faster.[25]

Actually, even considered in the narrow sense of industrial blue-collar workers, the "fall" has been less than complete. It would probably surprise many people to know that the number of production workers employed in US manufacturing has not changed much since 1950. In most years, the number of manufacturing production workers hovered between just under 12 million and just above 13 million. There were only five years in the entire post-war period when more than 14 million were employed, all in the 1960s and 1970s.[26] In the industrial (OECD) nations of the North as a whole there were 115 million people employed in "industry" in 1994 compared with 112 million in 1973. In each of those years, about two-thirds of the employees were hourly paid, nonsupervisory, blue-collar workers. In the economic South as a whole, including the former Communist Bloc countries, the number of industrial workers rose from 285 million in 1980 to 407 million by 1994.[27] So, if we are looking at the world, it is clear that industrial work has not only not ended, it has grown.

The statistical "fall" of the industrial working class is more a function of the rise of service work than of its own demise. It is, nevertheless, inevitable that industrial employment will shrink in relation to output, as discussed in chapter 7. The surprisingly static number of manufacturing workers who turn out the goods of the industrial nations have become progressively more productive. By 1995, more or less the same number of production workers in US manufacturing produced five times what they could in 1950.[28]

No one would deny that service employment is outrunning industrial employment. As a proportion of total employment in the industrial (OECD) nations, service employment grew from 52% in 1973 to 64% in 1994. Although this is a very long-range trend, there is a tendency to exaggerate its pace and extent. For one thing, the hours worked in industry are typically longer than those in retail and service jobs. In the US in 1995, the average work week in manufacturing was 41.6 hours, compared with 28.8 in retail and 32.4 in services. In Europe the differences are not as great because the industrial work week is shorter, but manufacturing average weekly hours were 39, compared with 35 for retail and services.[29]

The difference in hours is explained by the incidence of part-time work, which is much greater in the service sector. In the US, in wholesale and retail about 30% of the workforce is part-time, while in the catch-all service category it is 24% compared with 7% in the goods-producing industrial sector.[30] One reason why there are so many service-sector workers is that they work fewer hours. Another is that in the US five-and-a-half million multiple-job holders (73% of the total) work in the service-producing sector. This means there were actually millions fewer service *workers* than the number of *jobs* the official statistics show.[31]

The industrial workforce also includes millions of workers in transportation, and telecommunications, who show up in the service-sector columns of the official statistics. Many of the "services" provided by these workers, however, have become part of the production process itself as industry has altered technologically, decentralized, and internationalized. If these workers were recorded as employed in industry, this would place another seven-and-a-half million workers in the EU in the industrial sector, and over six million in the United States.[32]

Lower Pay, Worse Jobs

More important in the lives and conditions of the working class in the industrial world than the shift from goods-producing employment to service-sector jobs has been that from well-paid jobs to poorly paid, increasingly casualized jobs. This is occurring within the industrial sector as well as between industrial and service jobs. That is, it is not just a matter of losing a high-paid, probably unionized industrial job with good benefits to a lower-paid service job with few or no benefits. Jobs within each sector are getting worse, and all jobs are paid less as lean methods and neoliberal policies spread and deepen.

A good example of how this works can be found in the US automobile industry, once one of the most highly unionized and highly paid places to work in the country. A recent commentator writes:

> During the late 1970s, when most components manufacturers were wholly owned subsidiaries of the Big Three, two-thirds of the hourly workforce in the industry belonged to the UAW. But today, with outsourcing, only one quarter of the components workforce are union members. This growth of the non-union workforce has also had a devastating effect on the earnings of workers throughout the auto industry. Between 1975 and 1990 the percentage of low-wage employees in its total workforce grew by 142 percent, from 17 percent to 40 percent – proof, if nothing else, of the claim that lean production lowers the number of high-wage employees needed to produce cars.[33]

The 80% of the total workforce in the US that hold working-class jobs saw their real average weekly earnings slip by 18% from 1973 through 1995. Real hourly earnings in that period fell by 12%, indicating that the growth of part-time work had reduced the average weekly income of US workers by another 6 percentage points.[34] Indeed, part-time jobs grew from 15.6% of the total workforce to 18.6% in that same period.[35] Of course, the concentration of part-time jobs is higher among this 80% of the workforce than among the middle, managerial, and capitalist classes who compose the upper 20%.

The degradation of work down the production chain through outsourcing and contracting doesn't end with part-time or temporary work. Homeworking of the most primitive kind has found its way back into the economies of the North; it is now common in the garment industries of such countries as Britain, Canada, and the US, and has even been found in the automobile industry.[36] A local reporter discovered families on the west side of Cleveland, Ohio, assembling metal screws and plastic washers by hand in their homes and making less than $1 an hour. These unusual assembly "teams" included children as young as 8. The UAW says, "Once assembled, the screws would end up at a company listed as a supplier to Big 3 automakers" (GM, Ford, and Chrysler). The union also points out that most of the adults would have worked in small or medium-size parts plants a dozen years ago.[37]

In Japan, the leader in all these trends, part-time and temporary work grew from about 16% in the early 1980s to about 31% by 1993 and remained at this level through 1995. Given that Japan has been the trendsetter, this might be the expected level of "non-regular" or "atypical" employment in other industrial countries. However, in Europe this is difficult to determine, since some countries, like Spain, Portugal, and Britain, have much higher levels of "non-regular" work and lower levels of wages. It appears that some regions of the EU will carry a disproportionate burden of irregular employment and low wages, much as some regions in the US do. What seems clear, however, is that most nations of the economic North have a way to go before they reach Japanese levels. Since most of these jobs are lower-paid, this means continued downward pressure on wages generally throughout the OECD countries.

Reflecting this pressure, as well as international competition with very low wages in the South, poverty grew across the industrial nations. The decline in US wages spread to full-time workers, with the incidence of low (poverty-level) wages rising from 10.5% in 1979 to 17% in 1990. For women the rate is about double.[38] In terms of income, poverty in Europe rose to the US level of 17%, or 57 million people, by 1997, according to a European Union study cited by *Business Week*. Free-market Britain matched Greece, with a poverty rate of 22%. Of course, Europe's more generous, if also declining, welfare provisions soften the impact of this increased poverty to a degree that America's do not. The trend, however, is unmistakable.[39]

Across the industrial North, the pace of nominal (not adjusted for inflation) wage growth in manufacturing has dropped to half or less of what it was in the 1970s everywhere. The United States, Sweden, New Zealand, and Greece were the only industrial nations to show an actual decline in real (adjusted for inflation) hourly wages, but throughout the OECD countries the rate of growth has slowed to a near standstill despite low inflation rates. For European OECD countries, annual real hourly wage increases slowed from 3.3% in 1973–79 to 1.3% in 1979 through 1989, and 1.4% in 1989–93. In this final period, real hourly wages grew by less than 1% across the OECD nations as a whole – minus the US.[40]

The downsizing of the first half of the 1990s represents something different from traditional industrial restructuring. It was a major step toward leanness for many corporations that cut across many industries. Unlike most of the North American and European restructuring of the 1970s and 1980s, the downsizing of the early 1990s was not meant to reduce the long-term capacity or final output of the industry in most cases. In both North America and the EU, it typically involved businesses returning to their "core competency" by divesting some assets. AT&T's 1995 divestiture of its manufacturing and computer divisions was a prime example.[41] Most of all, however, downsizing was a cost-cutting (labor-reducing) measure in the context of the fight for larger market share. It was not the company that was downsized in most cases, but the workforce. Whether it is implemented through high-tech process re-engineering (as in telecommunications) or simple speed-up and job-loading (as mostly in auto), its object is to get more work out of a smaller workforce – a traditional capitalist objective. It is one of the latest wrinkles in lean production, pure management-by-stress.[42]

While re-engineering is certain to become another more or less permanent feature of lean production, particularly in service-producing industries, drastic downsizing on the scale of the early 1990s is limited by market-share considerations and the pressure it puts on the workforce. Indeed, by the mid-1990s, many firms and market analysts were questioning the wisdom of too much downsizing.[43] It is a tempting shortcut because it works up to a point; even in the 1990–93 recession productivity grew in manufacturing and some service industries. Furthermore, corporate managers feel satisfied by it. In a 1991 survey of business executives conducted for the Conference Board by Harris (which covered restructuring as well as pure downsizing) almost half of those who responded said they were "very satisfied" with the results, while another 41% said they were "somewhat satisfied." A mere 0.9% expressed dissatisfaction.[44]

The public-sector equivalent of both outsourcing and downsizing is privatization. This has been at the heart of neoliberal policy everywhere – many of the big strikes and labor demonstrations in Canada and western Europe have been in opposition to privatizations or drastic reductions in public services. As of 1992, 58% of the value of privatization sales occurred within the developed industrial countries. In western Europe, the UK accounted for three-quarters of the value of such sales.[45] But much of the privatization occurring in the industrialized countries doesn't take the form of sales. Rather it is, as in private industry, a matter of gradually contracting out all sorts of services once performed by public employees. So, for example, in the US the Privatization Council estimated that government payments to contractors rose from $27 billion in 1975 to $100 billion in 1992. By 1995, it was up to $114 billion.[46] As with all contracting out, it is likely that the contract workers who replace public employees make less money and have less job security.

In addition to privatization, neoliberal governments along with the European Commission have introduced various forms of "commercialization" of publicly owned enterprises or services. The European Commission Directive on Telecommunications, for example, requires that all telecommunications enterprises, including state-owned ones, function as competitive businesses by 1998. This includes opening their basic network to competing private firms.[47] In Britain competitive norms have been introduced into local (council) public-sector work through "compulsory competitive tendering," whereby the various agencies or departments must bid for the work against some real or even hypothetical private agency.[48]

By whatever name it goes, the neoliberal competitiveness agenda is creating a job crisis throughout the developed industrial world. Altogether almost a billion people were unemployed or underemployed by 1996. European Union unemployment rates are above 11%.[49] In the US unemployment is hidden in underemployment. Between January 1993 and June 1996, 27% of all the net-wage and salary jobs created were part-time or temporary.[50] This job crisis, in turn, is lowering the wage levels of labor markets across the industrial world. All this, of course, is driven by the intensified competition associated with deepening international integration. The final focus of this pressure is inevitably the workplace.

Crisis on the Job

Wall Street insider Stephen Roach brought the impact of lean production and downsizing on the workplace to public attention when he told the world, "the so-called productivity resurgence of recent years has been on the back of slash-and-burn restructuring strategies that have put extraordinary pressures on the workforce."[51] Roach warned of a "worker backlash." Indeed, his revelation came only a couple of months after the strike by workers at two GM parts plants in Dayton, Ohio, had closed down GM's entire North American assembly capacity. These and many other workers who had struck from 1994 through 1997 against the conditions imposed by lean production were echoing what Japanese auto workers had already said.

In 1992, the federation of Japan's enterprise unions in the auto industry issued an unprecedented report on the condition of the Japanese industry and its workers. "The employees are exhausted," the report said.[52] While the report stopped short of criticizing lean production *per se*, it was clearly critical of the pace of work and length of working time. On a tour of the Tahara plant assembly line, Canadian Auto Workers' research director David Robertson, who had visited auto plants all over the world, commented that he had never seen workers perform at such a pace.[53]

While studies of the impact of lean production on actual working conditions (as opposed to institutional arrangements) are few and far between, there is little doubt that there is a transformation of the workplace going on that is having a disastrous impact on the health, safety, and lives of workers and their families. In auto-assembly plants in the US, for example, the average incidence of illness and injuries in 1990–92 ran at five times the average level of the early and mid-1980s.[54] This is particularly significant, since these rates usually drop during a recession like that of the early 1990s. In fact, in the US, injury and illness rates rose dramatically in most major industry groups from the mid-1980s through 1990–94.[55]

Probably the word most associated with rising work-related health problems is "stress." A 1993 European study argues:

> Excessive stress can effectively destroy the quality of life for the individual, his or her family and for society as a whole. It has become as dangerous as pollution to modern society.[56]

While the ILO calls stress "one of the most serious health problems of the twentieth century," there are few studies of the impact of work-related stress over time. It is acknowledged, however, that it is extremely widespread. For example, 75% of Americans say their jobs are stressful. In Canada, the figure is 60%.[57] Mostly, the evidence is anecdotal, but it is nonetheless convincing.

For example, it is common for auto workers in the US to say that it is very unlikely that anyone starting in an auto plant today could make the 30 or 40 years needed to reach full pension. Telecommunications workers report a massive and rising incidence of RSI (Repetitive Stress Injury) since more people work longer hours with computers. People are taking the early retirement associated with downsizing in this industry because they know they cannot work much longer. In industry after industry, the combination of intensified work, longer hours, rotating shift work, and job insecurity is taking an unrecorded toll on the health and safety of workers subject to lean methods.[58]

Even business representatives will argue that stress is expensive. The ILO says that stress-related diseases cost "industry" $200 billion a year in the US and 10% of GNP (Gross National Product) in the UK.[59] In fact, individual corporations do not bear most of the extra costs. In some countries they are covered by national health-care systems funded through general taxes, where business seldom fares worse than the working class. Health-insurance premiums, for those lucky enough to have them, are regarded as part of the labor costs unions won years ago – not as some new cost for stress-related illnesses. Workers who don't have health insurance are simply in trouble, because companies do not take on the responsibility for their medical costs. Absenteeism, lateness, and even illness stemming from stress (or anything else) are increasingly handled by policies "so draconian that workers risk losing their jobs with only the most minor infringements of a total attendance pattern."[60] Most of the real costs of stress and other work-related health problems fall on the public, through taxes, or on the workers and their families.

The HRM posture that a company's workforce is its most important asset is simply that – a posture. The reality is, as the London Hazards Centre put it:

Unfortunately, the evidence from hazards centres and occupational health projects around the country is that, far from valuing their workforce, the majority of employers see them as an expendable commodity, to be exploited for maximum productivity, then discarded when ill-health threatens to incapacitate them.[61]

The reason for this was well stated in 1989 by Sir John Cullen, then Chair of the Health and Safety Commission of the UK:

The enterprise culture, the opening up of markets, and the need to survive competition place business under unprecedented pressure which means that increasing numbers of people – the public as well as employees – are potentially at risk.[62]

The focus of all this pressure is the workplace. The options available to workers facing these problems can be described as "fight or flight." The "flight" alternative is seldom an option any more because of high unemployment levels and the growing proportion of poor jobs, which are likely to be as or more stressful. In Japan, where unemployment is still very low and the "flight" option still viable, labor turnover among new hires in the auto industry was 25%, while half the new hires in recent years left in less than five years.[63] In the West, the "flight" these days, as the ILO points out, is likely to be into drugs or alcohol. Management's response is not to eliminate or reduce the source of stress, but to sponsor "personal stress management" and substance-abuse counselling.[64]

From Paralysis to Resistance

By the mid-1990s, the pressures on almost every aspect of working-class life had become increasingly intolerable. Anger and frustration over an eroding present and a hopeless future had become a general state of mind among working-class people across the industrial world. Lean production, neoliberalism, European Monetary Union, NAFTA, structural adjustment in Latin America and South Africa, and, now, restructuring in East Asia, all pushed more and more workers and their unions to act.

Despite the many problems of the "fight" option in today's labor markets, with companies in many countries now willing to deploy "replacement" workers, workers have turned in this direction once again. In the US, in 1996, strike statistics, while still very low, rose for the first time in years, with the number of strikes by 1,000 or more workers going from 195 in 1995 to 237 in 1996.[65] What is more, the workers who have taken the fight option have discovered and shown others that lean production, because of its very tightness, is highly vulnerable to disruption at almost any point in the production chain. Extensive outsourcing in combination with JIT delivery of parts makes strikes in either supplier or assembly plants an effective way to close down much or all of the system. This was the highly visible impact of the 1996 strike at two GM parts plants in Dayton, Ohio, which closed down all but one of GM's assembly plants in the US, Canada, and Mexico.[66]

Strike action also returned to other industries in the US that did not benefit from JIT leverage. In the steel industry, where restructuring had been drastic, important strikes at WCI, an independent company carved out of the wreckage of LTV, and Wheeling Pittsburgh set a new tone in that industry. Thirty-two thousand members of the Machinists' union struck at Boeing in 1995. From 1995, the year in which official strike statistics hit an all-time low, strikes broke out at universities, newspapers, hotels, public agencies, hospitals, and other service settings, as well in factories and transportation.[67]

A similar turn toward industrial militancy could be seen alongside the mass political strikes in Europe in both public- and private-sector jobs. Important strikes in Britain's Royal Mail and London Underground confronted deteriorating working conditions and new work schedules and, in the case of the postal workers, even teamworking itself. Indeed, a TUC survey taken in 1996 recorded the level of industrial actions as "twice as high as that in the first Trends survey for the same period in 1995."[68] In Germany, a series of "warning" strikes confronted major metal-working employers' attempts to cut employment levels and health benefits. In France in December 1996, airline workers struck against privatization, while truck drivers paralysed the nation by striking and blockading major highways and ports. The truckers won retirement at 55, encouraging the other major transport unions in France to embrace the same demand.[69]

Strike activity continued to roll across Europe in 1997. In February truckers struck across half of Spain, closing factories and limiting major urban marketplaces. They were demanding a reduction of the retirement age to 60. The borders with Portugal and France were virtually closed. In Greece, a new round of public-sector 48-hour strikes swept the country in February. Among their major demands were higher pension benefits. In early 1997, workers at Crédit Foncier in Paris seized their bank and held the manager hostage. In Germany, coal miners struck and demonstrated against job cuts, eventually forcing the government to modify its original downsizing plan.[70]

In March, a series of actions took place that indicated that bold action was spreading even to groups who had been seen as vulnerable, owing to massive job loss. When Renault threatened to close a plant in Belgium, the workers there seized the factory. Workers at Renault in France, who had not left the job during the 1995 events, began a series of one-hour strikes in support of the Belgian workers. They then held a mass march on Renault headquarters in Paris.[71]

While this return of militancy across much of the industrial North demonstrated the power workers still had, it also revealed the weaknesses of the unions. Born in different times, under different industrial circumstances, they did not always adjust well to the new contours of work and industry. The crisis of the working class was also a crisis of its organizations: not simply their proportional decline, but the structures and ideologies that still guided their functioning.

"Pure and Simple Trade Unionism" Undermined

The basis of the old unionism in the economic North was being undermined by capitalist crisis, industrial restructuring, the transition to lean production, the rise of market regulation, and the changing role of the state. "Pure and simple unionism," focused as it was on routine collective bargaining enclosed in old industry structures and shrinking constituencies within the working class, could not rise to the occasion in either its American business-unionist or European social-democratic forms.

Through all the crises that hit the working class and the trade-union movement across the developed capitalist world in the 1970s and 1980s, the unions had displayed a complacency and routinism that contributed to their own decline and loss of influence. Looking back from the mid-1990s, ILO economist Guy Standing summarized in this way:

> Trade unions and their political allies became more and more atavistic, and, looking back to the 1970s and 1980s, that must be the biggest "failure" for those who value the promotion of redistributive justice.[72]

A few, like the Canadian and some of the British unions, fought and this appears to have paid off in higher union density – even in some of the worst of political situations (under Mulroney and Thatcher). For the leaders of most of western Europe's trade unions the new roles for their organizations in the various "neocorporatist" schemes of the 1970s and early 1980s gave the feeling, if never really the substance, of influence or at least a role as "social partners" – a concept that still disarms many union leaders in Europe and elsewhere. The major pay-off of this "neocorporatism" in countries like Germany and the Scandinavian countries was a high degree

of institutional protection for the unions. In the US, "excuses" for complacency were harder to find – one reason for the 1995 leadership contest at
the AFL–CIO. There, the problem was not that unions were too defensive,
but that they were not defensive enough. Few resisted these trends until
the 1990s.

As the paralysis that gripped not only the leadership but most of the
membership for years, across the industrial world, began to lift and groups
of workers, and in some countries whole sections of the class, took action
once again, the old structures, bureaucracies, and ideas frequently undermined specific struggles and restrained the movement as a whole. With rare
exceptions such change as did occur left the most basic problems inherent
in industrial restructuring and the shift in class power unaddressed.

The almost universal response of the leaders to labor's crisis was to
merge with, or more typically absorb, other ailing unions in order to
increase financial stability. Between 1980 and 1994, there were 52 absorptions and 5 mergers in the US, while in Britain the figures were 144 and 9
respectively. A handful of these mergers had real industrial or strategic
logic, such as those that produced UNISON in Britain's public sector,
UNITE in America's garment industry, or the announced merger of the
United Auto Workers, United Steelworkers, and Machinists to produce an
IG Metall-style metal-workers' union. Most mergers and absorptions,
however, were simply marriages of convenience.[73] Sometimes, as in the
case of the Canadian Auto Workers, this was tied to a perspective of
creating a progressive counterweight to other more conservative unions.[74]
Mostly, however, it produced a trend toward general unionism combined
with older ideas and practices of "pure and simple trade unionism." Real
change was fomenting farther down in the ranks and among activists, but
in only a few cases, like the US Teamsters' Union, had it effected real
change as yet.

The old unions faced a new situation in which the living and working
conditions of the working class as a whole were deteriorating and only the
pace differed from industry to industry and country to country. The
picture was complicated, however, by changes in the structure of the workforce that overlay the common decline in income and working conditions.
These trends gave the appearance of a fragmentation of the working class
rather than a shared immiseration. The difficult questions of race and
gender intersected with the rise of insecure forms of work and the "vertical
disintegration" of production characteristic of lean production.

Union hierarchies based on the older industrial, usually white, often
male, sections of the class found it difficult to adjust to or to educate their
members on these broader social questions. Indeed, they continued to look
to the state, or in Europe the non-state that was the EU, for help even as

these states were drawn into the neoliberal project and the objective centrifugal forces of the world market. Thus, not only was collective bargaining in crisis, but the old style of political unionism, linked as it was to a surrendering social democracy or worse to rightward-moving liberalism, was no longer adequate even to the old collective-bargaining tasks, let alone the new economic, social, and political tasks.

Debate and Challenge in the Unions

The crisis facing unionism across the industrial world increased the frequency and intensity of internal debates and leadership challenges in unions and labor federations as activists tried to bring their unions in line with the new realities. In many cases the roots of opposition trends within the unions are as old as the crisis itself, but often the currents seeking change in union functioning and greater internal democracy have gained force in recent years.

In France, for example, an opposition current within the CFDT had come to represent 25% of the membership by the mid-1990s. Given the difficulty of debate within French unions, the leaders of this current were expelled. They went on to form the new SUD unions in France Télécom and the post office and, more recently in transportation and banking. At the same time, opposition within the CFDT to Nicole Notat's notorious right-wing direction has grown as a result of her role in the 1995 strike movement. Debate has also grown in the CGT.[75]

Debate and leadership contests also erupted in Spain's most militant labor federation, the Comisiones Obreras (CCOO). CCOO has a history of grassroots workplace organization and internal democracy. Furthermore, while Spain has seen a dramatic decline in the rate of unionization since the late 1970s, the CCOO has grown in recent years – by almost 700,000 in 1995. But in recent years it has entered into a number of pacts with the Socialist Party government that led to retreats and concessions and what some felt was an attempt to make the CCOO into "just another trade union." These accommodationist policies led to the formation of an opposition, the "critical sector" or "críticos," which challenged this direction at the 1996 CCOO Congress. The majority retained control of the confederation, while the "críticos" won positions at lower levels. It seems likely that both the election of a right-wing government in March 1996 and the internal opposition within the CCOO were responsible for calling the public-sector general strike in December 1996.[76]

Germany's massive hierarchical unions do not lend themselves to internal debate and there is little tradition of opposition currents within these unions. Yet, in 1995, dissident IG Metall shop stewards, works-council representatives, and rank-and-file activists from many of Germany's auto plants met to draft a statement in opposition to the union's acceptance of capital's "competitiveness" agenda.[77] While they stopped short of forming a national opposition, they returned to the plants to distribute the statement and organize for a change in direction. About twenty-five of these IG Metall militants traveled to the US in April 1995 to attend *Labor Notes* conference and to meet leaders of the New Directions caucus in the United Auto Workers.[78]

In Sweden, a "Union Opposition" formed in that country's largest auto plant, the Volvo assembly plant at Gothenburg. They ran 4 candidates for the National Metal Workers' Union's executive board and 98 for the city-wide delegates council of local union 41. The "Union Opposition" was challenging not only the official leaders' retreats in collective bargaining, but the unions' continued affiliation to the Social Democratic Party, which was implementing deep cuts in Sweden's welfare state. Allied opposition-ists were also contesting union office in other plants across Sweden.[79]

In the United States, opposition and leadership challenges hit more and more unions in the 1990s. The election of Ron Carey as a reform president of the 1.4-million-member Teamsters in 1991, and his re-election in 1996, ended decades of conservative old-guard and even Mafia rule in the AFL–CIO's largest union. The new general executive boards in 1991 and 1996 were the most racially and gender diverse in the union's history. They also included members of the rank-and-file movement, the Teamsters for a Democratic Union (TDU), which had fought for twenty years for internal democracy and a more militant approach to the employers.

Big steps toward greater democracy and militancy were taken during Carey's first five-year term. In addition, the union adopted a progressive approach toward political and social issues. The Teamsters also joined with other, more progressive, unions in cross-border relations with Mexi-can workers. His 1996 52–48% victory over old-guard stand-in Jimmy Hoffa, Jr, whose only qualification was his name, guaranteed the reform process would continue. The old guard, right-wing in politics, pro-company in bargaining, and corrupt in administration, would be finished as a political force in the Teamsters. As a 1997 strategy meeting of TDU activists framed the future, it was no longer a question of simple reform, but of whether a new kind of unionism beyond business unionism could be created. Their answer was "yes."[80]

While dissidents and reformers in other unions were not as successful as Carey and TDU, opposition groups and candidates were common coin in American unions in the 1990s. By the early 1990s, a dozen top union leaders had been deposed in contested elections, according to the

Association for Union Democracy.[81] Union reform attorney Paul Alan Levy summed up the state of internal union politics by late 1996:

> There is extensive intra-union activity in a larger number of national unions, much more than ever before. In service unions such as the Food and Commercial Workers, the Service Employees, and the Hotel Workers, construction unions such as the Bricklayers, the Carpenters, and the Laborers, government unions like the Letter Carriers, the American Federation of Government Employees, and the Treasury Employees, industrial unions like the Machinists and the Auto Workers. Not all of these are genuine rank and file struggles. In many of these situations different groups of officials are fighting with each other. But just as the revolt within the AFL–CIO legitimizes political challenges in national unions, so these struggles at the national level create openings for rank and file struggles at the base.[82]

Probably the most visible change in the US labor movement, however, was the changing of the guard at the top of the AFL–CIO. In 1995 John Sweeney, president of the SEIU, Rich Trumka, president of the UMWA (United Mine Workers of America), and Linda Chavez-Thompson, vice president of AFSCME (American Federation of State, County, & Municipal Employees) challenged the old leadership of the federation, calling themselves the "New Voice" slate. They forced Lane Kirkland, the lackluster leader since the death of George Meany in 1979, to resign and then challenged his temporary successor, Tom Donahue, in the federation's first contested election ever. Although the election was limited to the officers of national unions and AFL–CIO's state and local bodies which make up the delegates to the AFL–CIO's bi-annual conventions, the "New Voice" candidates campaigned among the membership, arousing a level of interest in AFL–CIO affairs seldom seen before.They won the delegate election, which is weighted by union size, by 56%, with Carey's Teamsters supplying the margin of victory.[83]

Though the challengers had been long-time participants in the leadership of the federation, they had seen the need to make some changes in style and functioning if organized labor was not to disappear altogether. While grassroots activity was a factor, it was really the decline and loss of political influence that motivated the "New Voice" candidates. At the same time, their strength on the new AFL–CIO executive board, which was expanded to increase the representation of women and people of color, depended in part on more radical leaders like Carey and Bob Wages of the Oil, Chemical, and Atomic Workers (OCAW).

Sweeney, Trumka, and Chavez-Thompson became highly visible public figures, pushing a more aggressive agenda than the AFL–CIO had seen since its founding in 1955. They took to the streets, picketlines, and TV cameras to proclaim: "American Needs a Raise." Their emphasis was on organizing the unorganized, particularly those in low-wage jobs. Millions of dollars were to be poured into the AFL–CIO's Organizing Institute, which recruits and trains organizers who are then farmed out to affiliated national unions. Much of the activity of the first year in office was more public relations than achievement, but the new leaders did put unions more in the limelight. In 1996, for example, they organized "Union Summer," which put a thousand young people in the field to help out on organizing drives, voter registration, and political campaigns. It helped kindle interest in unions among young people, plunged some of them into direct action and organizing for three weeks each, and caught the imagination of much of the public.

The new AFL–CIO leaders, however, were bound by an ideology still rooted in the "social partnership" mode. One day they would be telling the world that they would organize the unorganized and take on "corporate America." The next they would be addressing businessmen and pleading for cooperation. Sweeney, for example, told the National Press Club that "we can no longer afford the luxury of pretending that productivity, quality, and competitiveness are not our business."[84] Furthermore, they avoided the tough issues facing workers caught in the transition to lean production: downsizing, lengthened work time, speed-up, job-loading, outsourcing, and subcontracting. Their "new" unionism, was more aggressive, but it was basically well within the tradition of American business unionism, with its emphasis on wages and benefits and its implicit surrender of the workplace to management. What the new leaders had achieved, however, was a rise in the expectations of many in or sympathetic to organized labor. That, in itself, was changing the rules of the game in America's unions.

The idea of a new type of unionism, social-movement unionism, had been given birth first in the late 1970s and 1980s in "late developing" nations like South Africa and Brazil, and then in the late 1980s in South Korea and Taiwan.[85] In the developed North only the Canadian Auto Workers used a similar term, but the idea was taking on substance as unions took to the streets of North America and Europe to fight for goals that broad sections of working-class people could identify with. The possibility of this new direction for unionism across the industrial world took further shape as opposition forces within the unions challenged the old directions and leaders. If combined with the return of militancy, and the expanded consciousness that made possible, this new conception of unionism could offer some answers to the apparent fragmentation of the class and to the political dilemma in which the labor movement around the world found itself.

9

Looking South

The pressures of globalization, lean production, and neoliberalism have produced not only a reawakening in much of the industrial world, but an explosive rebellion within the more industrial nations of the South. With production chains reaching deep into the economic South, labor in the North cannot afford to ignore workers in the South – much less view them as "the competition." The new labor movements of the South are, in fact, indispensable allies in the struggle with global capital. To a greater degree than union leaders in North America or Europe, their leaders understand this. These new unions are, after all, a product of international economic integration, of the spread and deepening of capitalist relations in areas that were primarily rural not too long ago. Today, this no longer means simple growth, but a confrontation with capital's unending desire to reorganize production for maximum profits.

Although the shift in the proportion of the world's output to the South has been relatively small, along with earlier efforts at import substitution industrialization and recent growth in East Asia, industrial enclaves have formed and with them new working classes across certain parts of the South. The restructuring of industry after industry that has accompanied deepening international integration along with the rise of international production systems have created a layer of nations that are partly industrial, increasingly urban, as internally uneven as the world in which they exist, yet situated somewhere above the rest of the Third World by most industrial and many economic measures. Modern factories exist side by side with patriarchal systems of homework; glass and steel high-rise downtowns are surrounded by shanty-town neighborhoods, and yesterday's peasants are today's proletarians.

Unions and other working-class organizations are not new to the economic South. Across Asia, union density ranges from about 10% to as high as 40%. In Latin America, the average union density is 20%, and while the figure for Africa as a whole is only 10% this hides the fact that some countries, like South Africa, Nigeria, and Zimbabwe, have very high densities. In Asia, unions in some countries experienced rapid growth in the late 1980s. From 1987 through 1989, for example, union membership in Bangladesh rose by 27%, in the Philippines by 38%, and in South Korea by 100%. It also overlooks the important role of unions in ending the authoritarian regimes throughout much of the continent in the past several years.[1] The other side of the coin, however, is that some of this union membership percentage includes state-dominated unions and federations like the old Federation of Korean Trade Unions and Mexico's Confederation of Mexican Workers (CTM). In the English-speaking Caribbean, there is a strong tradition of trade unionism, but most of these unions are linked to political parties that move in and out of government and, hence, often restrain the actions and independence of these unions.[2] Thus, the picture is a mixed one, in which the dynamics of a changing situation are important.

The work settings into which millions of new workers pour across the economic South can differ greatly. Some are high-tech production complexes, like the new denim textile-garment complex in Coahuila or Ford's state-of-the-art assembly plant in Hermosillo, others are low-tech and labor-intensive, like the garment workshops of Jakarta and Bangkok or the electronics assembly plants of the Caribbean. Beyond the realm of formal employment is the vast informal sector found in most countries of the South. Throughout the Third World, industrialization is accompanied by rapid urbanization and mass unemployment as the migration from country to city far outstrips actual employment opportunities.

There are vast differences in the experience of workers in different parts of the Third World. For many of those in the more industrial countries that went through import substitution industrialization for decades, such as Brazil and Mexico, the most recent experience is one of downward mobility not unlike that in much of the North. Carlos Vilas describes workforce restructuring in much of Latin America in the following grim terms:

> Workers are expelled from previous formal occupations, then reemployed to work in downgraded, lower-paying jobs with poorer working conditions. In sum, a new labor market is being developed that goes beyond the traditional formal–informal segmentation and combines the ingredients of both. State and international agencies together with capitalist corporations (i.e., the formal sector) now rely on forms of employment that conform to the standards of the informal sector such as no minimum wages, no welfare benefits, no unions, no legal protections, and no job security.[3]

This description applies to the experience of many male workers in Latin America, but for women workers there and in Asia the experience is often different. Women in the South have been leaving rural areas seeking employment in or on the edges of the formal sectors that have arisen in the past decade or two in much of the Third World. These jobs are mostly in the growing cities of the South. Jeremy Seabrook describes the case of women workers in Bangladesh's new garment industry as follows:

> The industry, which scarcely existed twenty years ago, has drawn into the labor market an estimated 1,200,000 mainly young people, 80 percent of them women, of whom more than 600,000 live and work in Dhaka. This has led to significant shifts in social values and traditions. It has contributed to growing freedoms for many young women, and at the same time has called forth a reaction on the part of fundamentalists, who consider the weakening of (external) controls over factory workers a disaster.[4]

For these women, like millions of others across the Third World, employment and urbanization are creating new vistas and hopes, even where reaction, by no means limited to fundamentalism, seeks to keep the genie in the bottle. The industry they work in is completely inserted in the world economy. They work on textiles made in South Korea or Hong Kong to create clothes that will be sold in Europe, Japan, or North America, but almost certainly not in Bangladesh. The pay and conditions in these plants are predictably poor. In Dhaka, many of these women, many no more than teenagers, belong to the National Garment Workers' Federation.

Seabrook, who visited these women garment workers in Dhaka, captured the concentrated energy and potential power of these workers, who are clustered by the hundreds of thousands in one of the newer sites of the world's industry. Looking at a country that has seen more than its share of economic misery, in a situation that many would see as hopeless, he nonetheless writes:

> If anyone will change the living conditions and wretchedness of the people of Bangladesh, it will be these young women and the thousands like them who pour forth from the slums of Dhaka each morning to labour on garments that we unthinkingly buy . . .[5]

If Bangladesh seems on the margin of the industrial world, Indonesia represents one of the latest sites of growing industry – the place where jobs go when they leave South Korea or Taiwan. What was said of Dhaka could be said of Jakarta, Indonesia's capital, and its burgeoning new industries. To an even greater degree than in Bangladesh, Indonesia's government wages a constant war of repression against its people, and specifically against unions. Only the government-sponsored and -controlled All-Indonesian Workers' Union (SPSI) is allowed to operate without harassment.

Yet, an independent union federation, the Union for Workers' Prosperity (SBSI – Seritat Buruh Sejahtera Indonesia) functions in defiance of the government – often at a high price for its leaders. It is forced to use lightning tactics, brief strikes, to avoid police or military repression. Drawing on workers like the women of Dhaka, the SBSI called a one-hour general strike in Jakarta in February 1994, which "brought some 250,000 people from the garment, textiles, plastics and metal industries into the streets."[6] In July 1995, 13,000 workers, mostly women, went on strike at the Grand River Industries Corporation garment plant in Bogor. They were led by another independent organization called the "Centre for Indonesian Working Class Struggle" and supported by students. Their demonstration was attacked by police, and many strikers and students were interrogated. Most were released, and an international campaign was launched to free the three who remained in prison.[7]

Women like those in Dhaka, Jakarta, and Bogor exist in the proliferating factories, large and small, throughout East Asia, where they compose an average of 42% of the total workforce.[8] In Latin America and the Caribbean women make up only 27% of the formal workforce, but their large presence in specific industries like garment and electronics and in the growing and changing informal sector means this figure understates their importance. Furthermore, the combination of urban and industrial concentration among women workers lends itself to many forms of collective action. Even in the export or free-trade zones of Asia, the Caribbean, and Latin America, women organize unions and collective action.[9]

Women, for example, account for about two-thirds of the workers in Mexico's *maquiladoras*, where government-controlled unions try to prevent collective action. But collective action by these women workers occurs anyway. For example, on May 29, 1996, the mostly female workforce at Customtrim Corporation's *maquilas* in Valle Hermoso, Tamaulipas, walked off the job in defiance of both management and the government-controlled CTM union. They were demanding the profit-sharing payments that the law requires, but companies frequently withhold. They won with the help of organizations in both Mexico and the US, coordinated by the Coalition for Justice in the Maquiladoras.[10]

As is clear in the case of Brazil and South Africa, as well as Mexico and much of Asia, working-class women also play an important role in the development of broader working-class movements through the organization of neighborhood-based organizations of many kinds.[11] In much of the literature analysing these organizations they are treated as non-working-class "new" social movements because they are not employment-based or because they organize on the basis of informal-sector work. This is a mistake in the first place because women's movements, including feminism, are not new in either the South or the North. Women in Mexico, for example, petitioned for full citizenship in 1824, shortly after independence, while Mexico's First Feminist Congress was held in the heat of the revolution in 1916.[12]

More important, however, is that this type of non-class interpretation misreads the process of class formation and its intersection with traditional and changing gender roles that has brought about specific kinds of women's organizations among the poorest, least formally educated people. To put it another way, by reading these movements and organizations into the text of postmodernism, it becomes more difficult to understand precisely what really is new about them – namely, their working-class nature and what they bring to social-movement unionism.

This also overlooks the fact that much of the changing role of women in the Third World is a direct part of the process of class formation that goes with industrial change. Cecilia Green points out that the role of women in the economies of the Caribbean, for example, has changed as their former domestic food production is replaced by "supermarket-packaged foods" and they enter the lowest rungs of factory work to help pay the bills, while still bearing responsibility for housework and child-rearing.[13] This, of course, is a classic case of gendered "proletarianization."

It would also be a mistake to write off, as Vilas' gloomy picture seems to, the mostly male workers in the formal industries of the Third World, as the general strikes in Nigeria in 1994 and those across much of Latin America in 1996 and 1997 indicate. In Mexico, strikes occur in male-dominated *maquiladoras* as well as in those where women predominate. Like their sisters in Valle Hermoso, the 1,200 male workers at a Ford *maquila* in Nuevo Laredo walked out on July 17, 1995 to head off a sweetheart deal signed by the government-controlled CTM union. They too received help from US unions and forced the CTM to renegotiate the pact.[14] Indeed, changes are taking place within Mexico's labor movement, which will be examined below.

There are two things to be learned from the newer unions of the Third World: the old lesson that where capital digs deep roots a workers' movement is almost certain to be born, and allies in today's world economy to be found; and the new lesson that successful unionism in today's integrated world must be social-movement unionism. This latter lesson has been best taught by the new unions of Brazil and South Africa.

Social-Movement Unionism in the South

Unions are not new to the Third World, but the new labor movements that have arisen in the past twenty years differ from the older ones in important ways. The older labor movements tended to be affiliated with and dominated by either traditional parties of the left or center (Communist, Socialist, or Christian Democratic), or the parties associated with national independence. In Latin America and much of sub-Saharan Africa and Asia this led to the incorporation of the unions into a state-dominated clientelism or control whereby the party took power and implemented an import-substitution regime or, alternatively, to subordination to party priorities, usually in parliamentary politics. The unions, or their leaders, might have had influence within the party, state, or parliament, but they seldom acted like independent workers' organizations.[15]

The rapid changes that accompanied the epoch of globalization, crisis, and the rise of market forces, however, undermined both the import-substitution strategy and the corporatist arrangements that characterized much of the Third World into the 1970s. The organized working class played a key role in confronting or ending military or authoritarian regimes across the Third World. From El Salvador to Nigeria, from Brazil to South Africa, unions have been central to the struggle for democracy or liberation. Indeed, given the central role of the working class in the political upheavals of the past twenty years, it is all the more remarkable that theories like "postmodernism" should have such a resonance among intellectuals of the left.

In general, the labor movements that have taken shape in the South since the late 1970s have opted for greater independence from political parties, even where they formally support one or another party. This more independent stance arises from the experience of both corporatism itself and the complex cross-class process of democratization that has ended military or authoritarian rule. This doesn't signify a retreat from politics, but rather the recognition that workers need independent organizations that can function in both the workplace and the political arena in a period of flux. These new labor movements have tended to look to other organizations of working-class people, whether neighborhood groups, women's organizations, or other social movements, for allies in the political process.

Sometimes, as in Brazil, this has led to the formation of a new working-class party; in other cases it has meant a realignment of left forces, as with the Frente Amplio in Uruguay or the rise of CausaR in Venezuela, or, as in South Africa, an alliance of social movements and parties in the struggle against apartheid. In other, newer labor movements, such as those in South Korea and Taiwan, the question of an independent working-class party has become part of the strategic disucssion as well.[16]

The rise of new labor movements is, of course, part of a broader process of class formation that has accompanied the growth of various industries in select parts of the Third World in the past two decades or so. Class formation in these countries, however, does not and cannot follow the pattern set by the developed industrial nations in the past hundred or more years. The new working classes of the Third World find themselves situated in a sea of poverty and mass unemployment that has no prospect of fading away in a decade or two, given the current organization of the world economy. Much of the new working class, even a majority of it, exists as a growing "reserve army of labor," unemployed, working in the informal sector, and moving between formal and informal types of employment.

Social-movement unionism arises from the recognition that while the new industrial working class has a great deal of power within the economy, unions of industrial workers can only compose a minority of this new class. Alliances with other organizations of the class, including unions in other sectors of the economy, public-sector unions, and neighborhood-based, and often women-led, organizations, are a necessary step toward the "organization of the proletarians into a class," as Marx put it a hundred and fifty years ago. This concept of a unionism that reaches beyond the workplace to other sectors of the class arises from the changes in Third World societies that have been particularly marked in the past twenty years. The peasantry, once isolated in the countryside has been increasingly dissolved as a class as agriculture has been revolutionized and turned into big business. The former peasantry has moved in massive numbers into the cities, where it has become part of a new working class that is still only partially shaped as a class.[17] Social movement-unionism in the South addresses this reality and the many problems that flow from it.

The process of class formation is by no means simple and it has changed direction as economic integration and crisis have deepened. An important change is the relationship of the formal and informal sectors. As Vilas notes, the lines between the two have tended to fade as male workers in older import-substitution industries fall down the employment ladder. But there is more to it than this. In East Asia, the informal sector is shrinking as industry grows. In Latin America, where it is still growing, as well as in Asia, its relationship to the formal sector changes as transnationals and larger local firms outsource phases of production to smaller informal outfits.[18] On the one hand, this clearly undermines unions in the formal sector; on the other, however, it links more informal-sector employment to industry. Social-movement unionism, by reaching beyond stable industrial employment, can address this changing reality.

Social-movement unionism and the sense of class independence insisted on by these new labor movements also arise from another essentially new feature of many Third World societies. Alongside the rise of this working class, half employed, half semi-employed, comes the growth of a modern middle class based in the TNCs and allied financial, communications, and business services. This middle class is not only numerically larger than the older middle classes of the Third World, but is, by virtue of its education and relative wealth, a major factor in politics, including the transition to more democratic political regimes in the past two decades. Much of it is part of a globalized middle class and has a cosmopolitan, rather than narrowly nationalist, outlook.[19] It is also much less dependent on public employment than the traditional Third World middle classes, and tends to have a neoliberal view of the world. Without a strong sense of class independence it would be all too easy for the new unions to get as lost in middle-class-dominated politics as the older "political" unions got lost in clientelism or corporatism.

"New Unionism" in South Africa and Brazil

In the highly visible cases of Brazil and South Africa the new unions that began to take shape in the late 1970s were clearly a result of the very rapid class formation that took place during the 1960s and 1970s on the basis of relatively capital-intensive industries. But as Gay Seidman notes in her study of these two labor movements:

> When the "new unionism" emerged in the late 1970s, activists in both South Africa and Brazil emphasized shop-floor organization and developing workers' capacities to negotiate with employers. By the mid 1980s, however, labor activists in both cases had shifted: rather than concentrating solely on factory-related issues, both labor movements targeted the state as well as employers, seeking to increase the share of the broadly defined working class in the benefits of economic growth.[20]

The struggles against military rule in Brazil and apartheid in South Africa, as well as the crushing poverty of the working-class majority in each country, drew these new unions and their activists into political struggle, but the development of a clear emphasis on class by both COSATU (Congress of South African Trade Unions) and CUT (Central Unica dos Trabalhadores) was due in part to the minority position of industrial workers in those two societies. The early waves of mass strikes brought collective bargaining and rapid union growth. The dynamics of these struggles; the realities of life in the sprawling working-class slums, townships, or *favelas* of the two countries; and the broader fight for political inclusion pulled the union activists toward other sectors of the class even as they continued to fight within the workplace.

Seidman points out that the nature of the new slums into which once-agrarian peoples poured and where they became working-class called forth its own demands. She writes:

> Responding to what Lucio Kowarick calls the "urban spoilation" that accompanied rapid industrial growth – sprawling, impoverished communities denied basic infrastructure and services – urban groups in both Brazil and South Africa struggled for the "collective consumer goods and services that are vital to subsistence: transportation, health, sanitation, housing . . . not to mention other components such as electricity, paving, cultural activities."[21]

These were collective, class demands as they took shape in the residential living space left to a working class in formation. The same description applies to scores of newer urban, industrial-based communities across much of Latin America and Asia. The new union activists lived in or had relatives in these slum neighborhoods. Indeed, the contradiction of working in modern factories owned by global corporations and living in such slums was a factor in promoting a broader social outlook. CUT leader Luís Ignácio da Silva, known as "Lula," said:

> Who lives in favelas today is the worker of the most sophisticated industries of the country, the worker at Volkswagen, of Philips, of Villares, Mercedes, etc.[22]

Their unions brought support to the myriad of neighborhood groups that arose to demand basic infrastructure or even the right to occupy the land. The new neighborhood-based organizations, frequently organized and led by women not working in industry, in turn brought a broader base and new strength to the political movements fighting authoritarian rule and, in Brazil, the formation of the Workers' Party.[23]

The links that were made were probably facilitated by the fact that women played a large role in the new unions from the start by virtue of their heavy labor-force participation in the sectors on which these two federations based themselves. Not only were they the majority in industries such as textiles, garment, food processing, and various services, they were present in significant numbers even in the key capital-intensive metal-working industries where they formed about 10% of the workforce in Brazil and over 12% in South Africa.[24]

In South Africa COSATU, which became the federation of the new industrial unions in 1985, built direct alliances with the neighborhood-based Civics (Black, community-based organizations). In Brazil, the CUT, formed in 1983 and led above all by the metal workers in the plants of the ABC districts around São Paulo, sought alliances with the over 8,000 residents' associations in Brazil's cities that had formed at the same time. The workers, both as residents and as factory workers, came to understand that the underfunded slums were a wage-saving measure for the giant multi-national corporations that employed them, because they kept the costs of living of this new working class so low – allowing for lower wages.[25]

What Seidman's unique comparative study of the these two labor movements shows is that both developed a solid class outlook. Far from seeing the new neighborhood or women's organizations that arose in their countries as non-class "new" social movements, the leaders and activists of CUT, COSATU, and the neighborhood-based organizations themselves saw them as part of a broader, class-based movement. For, indeed, contrary to much postmodernist theorizing, these new movements of factory and neighborhood, men and women, were all rooted in the process of industrialization, urbanization, and class formation particular to much of the Third World in the past two or three decades.

Carlos Vilas makes this point very sharply in terms of the CUT, arguing that is precisely their class outlook that allows them to be the center of attraction for the diverse social movements found in Brazil. He writes:

> Furthermore, autonomy and class perspectives have endowed the unions with a vast social and political representation going far beyond urban or industrial workers to include social movements, the urban poor, the peasantry, and broad segments of the middle sectors.[26]

The political situations in the two countries were very different. Guerrilla warfare had failed in both some time in the 1970s, partly as a consequence of industrialization and rapid urbanization, partly because of the relative strength of the national ruling classes and their military; but the political trajectories that followed were very different. In Brazil, most of the opposition was either business-based, discredited, or repressed. There was no "hegemonic" group on the left to turn to, so the new unions formed a party of their own, the Workers' Party (Partido dos Trabalhadores – PT). The PT was aggressively socialist and sought to represent and include all the working-class-based organizations.

In South Africa, on the other hand, the African National Congress (ANC), a cross-class party, survived repression and remained the most prestigious opposition organization or party in the country. Although there was, and still is, a debate within COSATU about setting up an independent workers' party like that in Brazil, the new unions opted instead to accept the leadership of the ANC in the anti-apartheid movement, while maintaining the independence of the unions. In the 1990s this became a formal alliance between COSATU, the ANC, and the South African Communist Party (SACP), which accepted the ANC strategy of a two-stage development in which South Africa would first go through a period of further capitalist development and democratization.

The opening of serious economic restructuring in the context of international recession in 1992 and 1993, along with the neoliberal direction of policy under the new ANC government headed by Nelson Mandela, has created serious problems for COSATU and the other unions in South Africa. There has been a drain of human resources as leaders have taken political positions at both national and local levels. "Codetermination" has placed enormous demands on remaining leaders and led to some erosion in day-to-day union democracy, or "workers' control" as it is called in COSATU unions. Industrial restructuring wiped out about 15% of COSATU's industrial membership through 1995.[27]

Yet, South Africa's unions, and COSATU in particular, are far from facing the sort of decline many unions in the North have experienced. In fact, in terms of both numbers and union density, unions have made gains. Union membership increased from 1,391,423 in 1985 to a peak of 3,272,768 in 1993; it stood at 3,065,860 in 1995. As a proportion of the workforce, excluding agricultural and domestic workers, union members rose from 22.8% in 1985 to a peak of 53.5% in 1993, and then fell to 50.5% in 1995 – a very high density for any nation.[28]

COSATU has shown steady growth since 1991, despite all the industrial restructuring. It has grown from 1.2 million in 1991 to 1.9 million in 1996, accounting for almost two-thirds of union members in South Africa. Seventy-eight percent of this growth has come from new recruitment, the rest from mergers. Much of this new recruitment has come in the public sector, but manufacturing workers actually grew from 35% to 36% of all COSATU members from 1994 through 1996. COSATU provides living proof that unions with an aggressive organizing policy, a militant bargaining record, and strong ties to working-class communities can grow in a period of relative instability.[29]

Even more important is the fact that, although some leaders have adopted a more conservative "corporatist" outlook since the ANC took government, the unions have not lost their capacity to act independently in the workers' interests. In the spring of 1994, shortly after the ANC became the government, a wave of strikes broke out across the country.[30] On April 30, 1996, COSATU called a one-day general strike in opposition to any restrictions on union rights contemplated by the government. Participation was 75% in major industrial areas, bringing several million workers into the streets – far more than are members of COSATU unions. Furthermore, in 1996 a guest editorial in the *South African Labour Bulletin* reported that "tensions have emerged within the ANC/SACP/COSATU alliance" with strong union opposition to certain privatization plans. In 1997, the confrontation accelerated when COSATU called a successful general strike on June 2 in opposition to the government's version of the new employment standards bill. Further confrontations were likely during the summer.[31] There is debate within COSATU and other unions as well concerning the future of the working-class movement, including the possibility of an independent workers' party. The elections and formation of a new government in 1999, after Nelson Mandela retires, may be a watershed in these debates.[32]

Even the existence of an independent working-class party, as the example of Brazil shows, however, does not put an end to the problems created by today's economically integrated world and the neoliberal policies of most governments. Both the CUT and the PT have been under pressure for some time to moderate their radical class outlook. Furthermore, the impact of restructuring, downsizing, and lean production has taken its toll on the self-confidence of unionists, while the requirements of electoralism and holding municipal or state office have had a moderating influence on the PT. The PT has developed a social-democratic right wing, while the majority Articulação tendency led by Lula has moved toward the center. A strong left wing exists as well, and the PT is far from being anything like a European social-democratic party. But the experience of both South Africa and Brazil reminds us that political direction is not something that can be taken for granted even where strong social-movement unionism has taken root.

There is another irony here. Both COSATU and CUT, as well as the PT, have established extensive international contacts with other new Third World unions, like those in South Korea, many existing unions in North America and Europe, and the European-based international trade secretariats (of which more later).[33] This is an admirable and necessary step toward internationalism. At the same time, however, it brings the debates within North American and European labor into the CUT and COSATU – including the mainstream and right-wing sides of the debate. Pressures to "live with" or even embrace aspects of lean production, not to mention European-style "social partnership," quite naturally become part of the internal debate in the new social-movement unions as a result. Internationalization of the labor movement will increase this problem, not reduce it – a point that will be taken up later.

The Newest "New Unionism"

COSATU and CUT were born in the struggles of the late 1970s and formed in the mid-1980s. The new unionism in South Korea and other parts of Asia, on the other hand, took off in the late 1980s and is still taking shape. As in South Africa and Brazil, the new unions in Korea, as opposed to the old state-dominated Federation of Korean Trade Unions (FKTU), were also part of the resistance to and partial break-up of authoritarian rule. As the mass strikes of 1996–97 showed, this task is far from over. The context in which they arose, however, was very different from either Brazil or South Africa, because Korea's development as an industrial nation followed a somewhat different path.

In a number of important respects Korea's state-driven period of import substitution industrialization from the 1950s through most of the 1980s produced a different society from that of South Africa, Brazil, or Mexico. Korean industry was owned by huge Korean-owned corporations – the *chaebol*. It was very highly concentrated, with the top 100 corporations accounting for 47% of production in the 1980s, compared with about 28% for Japan's top 100 companies. Korea is the only Third World nation whose economy is dominated by large domestically owned TNCs.[34]

South Korea's development reduced the country's rural population over the years so that, by 1993, an incredible 78% of the population lived in urban areas, a proportion equivalent to that of the OECD nations.[35] This reflected an extremely rapid process of class formation in which the rural labor force nose-dived from 65% in the early 1960s to 18% by 1990. The industrial workforce, on the other hand, grew from about 10% of the total workforce to 35% in that period, equivalent to that of a developed industrialized country.[36]

Before the explosion of worker militancy in the late 1980s, South Korean workers bore the brunt of this rapid development. Wages were below those in Hong Kong, Taiwan, or Mexico. In 1985, the average worker earned less than the government's stated minimum living costs for a family of four. In the 1980s, South Korean workers worked an average of 54 hours a week and the rate of injuries and deaths on the job was the world's highest, at 5 deaths and 390 injuries a day. Although Korean industry frequently imitated Japanese production methods (including teams, *kaizen*, etc.) and its capital-intensive industries were early lean producers, its management style is usually described as militaristic, rather than cooperative or paternalistic.[37]

Women played a very large role in both industrial development and the emerging labor movement. They are about 40% of the workforce, which is higher than in most Third World countries, including South Africa and Brazil.[38] In the 1970s, as one Korean labor scholar put it, "women workers have really been the driving force not only to bestow on the nascent labor movement a dynamic character but also to actually lead it at the grassroots level." This dynamism is explained not only by the high labor-force participation rate of Korean women, but by strict employment segregation that leaves women earning 50% of what men earn, 45% in manufacturing. Women, mostly young, fill the jobs in labor-intensive industries like garment, footwear, and other light manufacturing. Unlike in South Africa and Brazil, however, they have virtually no presence in heavy industry. Furthermore, young women workers are often housed in separate company-owned living quarters, which, at least for these workers, has precluded the kind of community role women have played in other Third World countries. When women get married, they are frequently fired.[39]

This high degree of gender segregation has meant that Korea's new social-movement unionism has taken a different form than those of South Africa and Brazil. Growing unity between male and female workers could not be workplace-based. Furthermore, while Korean urbanization went through its shanty-town phase in the 1970s and its industrial slums and neighborhoods are poor enough, there is no large informal sector to provide women who lack formal employment with incomes and some degree of independence, as in much of Latin America. Unity began in the streets during the mass strike movements of the late 1980s and moved on to the eventual merger of two union federations, one based in the predominantly male, heavier industries, the other among medium and smaller employers, where women were the majority.

The huge strike movements of the late 1980s tended to sweep the working class of whole towns into joint actions. Martin Hart-Landsberg described how this happened in two industrial cities, Masan and Chang-won. In the wake of successful strikes by women workers in Masan in 1987, the companies organized thugs (*kusadae*) to beat up the women unionists. Hart-Landsberg writes:

> In response, the workers of Changwon mobilized to oppose these attacks. They joined the workers of Masan in street battles to help the women defend their victories. The end result of this common struggle was that thirty newly formed democratic unions from both cities joined together in December 1987 to form the General Federation of Trade Unions in the Masan–Changwon Area.[40]

This spirit went on to ignite the even larger strikes of 1988, which made Masan–Changwon seem like a "liberated zone," as one worker described it. During these mass strikes, one author wrote:

Files of workers from different factories march, with arms strongly linked, together visiting different sites of strike actions. Workers encouraged each other in a strong sense of solidarity and determination.[41]

The new Korean unionism was born in a period of three years, during which actions and organizations of this sort, often based in one city or region, played a central role both because the deep gender gap needed to be bridged and because, by law, almost all bargaining is done at the enterprise level. Strike activity leapt from 276 disputes in 1986 to 3,749 in 1987, and stayed high at 1,873 in 1988 and 1,616 in 1989. Union membership soared from about one million in 1986 to over two million in 1990. About 500,000 workers are in the new unions and 1.5 million in unions, some controlled by democratic forces, affiliated with the FKTU.

Another indication of growth is that the number of local, firm-level unions grew from 2,618 in 1986 to 7,676 in 1992, while the number of federations grew from 16 to 21 in that period. While the national union density figure is about 25%, in many of the industrial cities it is much higher. For example, a survey of garment and footwear plants in Pusan, which employ mainly women, showed that two-thirds of the companies were unionized. Industrial unions are virtually banned, so local and eventually national federations play an important part in creating a sense of solidarity and social movement.[42]

These new Korean unions and federations went through a series of mergers and unifications. In July 1988, while the strike movements were still strong, eight regional federations like that in Masan–Changwon, representing mainly unions in medium and smaller firms, came together to form the National Council of Labor Movement Organizations, which became the Korean Trade Union Congress (KTUC) in January 1990. Its founding statement summarized its goals as part of the broader movement for democracy:

> On the basis of the mass union movement we will struggle towards achieving economic rights and unite with all democratic peoples' movements which fight for economic and social reform, achieve fundamental changes of the current situation of workers, and pursue our struggle for democracy, self-reliance and peaceful national reunification.[43]

In December 1990, unions from the large companies like Hyundai, Daewoo, and Pohang Iron and Steel, formed the Conference of Large Factory Trade Unions. They pledged to work for the unity of all democratic unions and support the "joint activities on popular interests including prices, housing, taxes, and Uruguay Round negotiations" of the GATT. At this point the KTUC had about 200,000 members, while the Conference had about 100,000, but many of the new unions in the larger *chaebol* corporations remained independent at that time. A third federation, based on white-collar workers, the Korean Congress of Independent Industrial Federations (KCIIF), was also part of the democratic labor movement. Repression continued and in November 1991 all the new unions held a rally of 70,000 workers in Seoul.[44]

In 1994, the various independent federations and those enterprise unions outside of them launched a process to produce unification of the democratic labor movement. In November 1995, the new Korean Confederation of Trade Unions (KCTU), representing about half a million workers, was formed. Still illegal under Korean labor law, the new federation continued to support strikes by member unions in 1996. At the same time, in the context of a limited move toward political openness, more debate and, in 1993, even a contested race for president took place within the FKTU, which began distancing itself from the government.[45] While Korea's new unions represent only a minority of workers, they tend to be well placed in the companies most inserted in the global economy. Further, they have set off a broader process of increased militancy and political awareness in the working class that is likely to affect even the older unions.

The explosive mass strikes from December 26, 1996 on into 1997 affected the entire labor movement to different degrees, according to the state of their organization. The conservative and bureaucratic FKTU was drawn into the struggle for a time, but was unable to mobilize more than a small percentage of its members. A leader of the KCTU described the inability of the older labor federation to mobilize its members effectively in the following terms:

> The FKTU has systematic problems relating to a conservative leadership that has no expereince of struggle. Now the pressure for struggle is coming from the grassroots, but their industrial leadership is very weak.[46]

The grassroots democracy of the newer KCTU unions, combined with a strong sense of class solidarity, provided the means by which hundreds of thousands of workers could be mobilized in a short period of time and by which this mobilization could be sustained and revived. The KCTU leader described the process this way:

> Even though the KCTU was not formed formed until 1995, the individual democratic unions have displayed a strong bond of solidarity since the birth of the democratic labor movement in 1987. The blue-collar manual workers from Chunnohyp, together with Upjoeng Hoey's white-collar and public

sector, and the large democratic union federations inside the Hyundai and Daewoo chaebols, always combined in a solidarity struggle around the issue of the labor laws.[47]

As in other countries where new labor movements have appeared in recent years, the question of an independent workers' party has become part of the internal discussion of the KCTU. The mass strikes naturally make this question more pressing. Speaking in the midst of the strikes, the same KCTU leader said:

> The KCTU does not have any specific proposal to organize a political party at this time. But the situation is such that workers are rapidly developing consciousness. Consequently the demand for a political movement organized by workers grows from the grassroots level as a result of this general strike. The union leaderships are also considering strategy and tactics for this kind of direction.[48]

A new unionism has also come to Taiwan as part of the relaxation of the authoritarian rule of the Kuomintang (KMT), or Nationalist Party, since the late 1980s. Like South Korea, Taiwan was a rapid state-led industrializer through the 1980s, with as many as two million people flooding into the cities between 1952 and 1985, depleting the peasantry and filling the ranks of the working class. In 1994, agricultural employment was less than 10% of the workforce, while industry accounted for almost 40%. Women composed almost 40% of the new workforce created by this rapid development. Taiwan's industry, however, is based more on small firms than South Korea's and includes a larger presence of foreign TNCs. Its firms are also heavy investors in China's developing industrial regions, so that restructuring affects its domestic production. Nevertheless, a high level of strike activity has become common since the mid-1980s.[49]

The new social-movement unionism in Taiwan is a combination of new unions and federations like the Federation of Independent Unions formed in 1988, many independent enterprise-level democratic unions, and of rank-and-file rebellions within older established unions, including some affiliated to the KMT-dominated Chinese Federation of Labor (CFL). It has been characterized by more or less constantly high levels of strike activity by historic standards, growing from 485 in 1975 to 1,600 in 1985 and over 2,000 in 1994.[50] As in South Korea, unions bargain only at the enterprise level in the private sector so that these strikes are mostly at one workplace or company and are frequently illegal in any case. Yet, they keep happening and, as in South Korea, have succeeded in pushing up the wages of Taiwan's workers well above those in most of the South.

Taiwanese workers have engaged in a number of political actions as well as many economic or workplace-based strikes. Dozens of local unions held mass rallies in 1993 and again in 1994 to protest against changes in the labor law. In November 1994, for the first time, a nation-wide political strike was called to protest against an attempt by the government to raise the workers' payments on national health insurance. Some 238 unions and 30,000 workers participated. Mass demonstrations were held in 1995 against privatization of fourteen state-owned enterprises, including the telecommunications company. As in South Korea, the question of forming an independent labor party has become part of the internal discussion of the new unions in Taiwan.[51]

Unlike in South Korea, South Africa, and Brazil, no central federation has emerged as the clear leader of the new unionism in Taiwan. Indeed, much of the action has taken place inside older unions that have been taken over by democratic unionists or forced to become more militant. It is estimated that the new independent unions have about 100,000 members, while the CFL claims about one million. Union density is high, at 33%.[52]

Taiwan stands somewhere between the examples of South Korea, South Africa, and Brazil, and the many countries in which the old corporatist unions are breaking away from the political constraints of state or party domination. This pattern is typical throughout sub-Saharan Africa, where existing unions often played a leading role in bringing down the authoritarian corporatist governments in place since the days of national independence. It can be seen in Argentina, where the unions have staked out independence from the Peronist party, and in Venezuela, where the unions have distanced themselves from the old social-democratic Democratic Action party. Probably the most complex case of this move toward independence by some old corporatist unions is found in Mexico.

Mexico: Transition to a New Labor Movement?

Looking for allies in the labor movements of the South is seldom as simple as making contact with a COSATU or CUT or KCTU. In many nations of the Third World unions are only now in the process of breaking from state or party domination. Mexico presents a particular problem because the roots of the domination of the unions representing the vast majority of organized Mexican workers by the ruling PRI go all the way back to Mexico's revolution of 1910–20. Most unions in Mexico are affiliated to the PRI's Congress of Labor (CT – Congreso de Trabajo) of which the industrially based CTM is the largest of several federations.[53]

The picture of change in Mexico's labor movement is complex. On the one hand, the base of the CTM has been seriously eroded as many of Mexico's older industries are downsized, privatized, or dismantled.[54] This has increased the ability of the government to hold down wages and to sideline or even unseat CTM leaders who seem to stand in the way of the neoliberal project, such as "La Quina," the powerful leaders of the Petroleum Workers' Union. On the other hand, the desperate state of Mexican workers and the many threats to unionism implied in the PRI's neoliberal plans are pushing independent and dissident forces within the working class to act more independently.

There are a few independent unions, including the independent Authentic Labor Front (Frente Auténtico del Trabajo – FAT), the September 19 Garment Workers' Union, organized after the 1985 earthquake in Mexico City, the unions of university employees, and the semi-independent, though formally CT-affiliated, teachers' union (SNTE – Sindicato Nacional de Trabajadores de la Educación). Though they represent only a fraction of the workforce, these independent unions act as a pole of attraction in Mexico's gradually accelerating transition from the 66-year-old corporatist regime of the PRI. Perhaps even more important in the long run, however, is the also gradual process of the break-up of PRI domination of some important unions within the CT and the rank-and-file rebellions within even CTM unions.

Union militancy and rank-and-file rebellion are by no means new to Mexico. They broke out in the 1970s and again in the late 1980s. That story, characterized by heavy repression, is a long one, well told in Dan La Botz's *Mask of Democracy: Labor Suppression in Mexico*, and won't be repeated here. What is important for now is that the structure of repression in Mexico has become increasingly undermined by a series of events discussed earlier. These include the continuing crisis of the economy and the failure of PRI economic policy, the Zapatista rebellion and the broad human-rights movement within Mexico it helped mobilize, the increased economic pressures on all sections of the working class, and the growth of support and solidarity activities in the United States and Canada both for the broad movement for democracy and for dissident sections of the labor movement. While repression remains a reality all too often, these forces have helped to create an opening within labor as well as throughout Mexican society.

There are three aspects to the changes taking place in Mexico's unions. The first is the increased activity of independent unions, particularly the FAT. The second involves a growing independence on the part of some PRI-associated unions. The third is the persistence of rank-and-file rebellions or oppositions within a number of important unions. Naturally, all of these act on each other.[55]

Perhaps the clearest symbol of these changes is that in 1995 and again in 1996 on May 1, celebrated as labor day in Mexico, all the dissident trends within labor marched together by the tens of thousands in Mexico City. They did so in defiance of Mexico's aging CTM patriarch, Fidel Velázquez, who "canceled" the official labor-day march, and, by implication, in defiance of the government. Included in the march were the FAT, dissident locals or rank-and-file groups within several CTM unions calling themselves the "Coordinadora", and the unions of FESEBES – Federación de Sindicatos de Empresas de Bienes y Services, the federation headed by the telephone workers union (STRM – Sindicato de Telefonistas de la República de México) leader Francisco Hernández Juárez.

The significance of these events went beyond the May Day ceremony. Hernández Juárez is leader of a group of union leaders, based mainly on the FESEBES unions, known as the "Forum" which operates openly as a more or less dissident faction within the PRI milieu. Affiliation to the Forum had grown from three unions to twenty-six by 1997. This in itself was unprecedented, but the willingness of these unions to march with supporters of Mexico's political opposition and its anti-government, human-rights movement was testimony to the growing frustration of many unionists with the PRI's failed neoliberal policy. Many of these unions also displayed their anger at the PRI and their willingness to take more independent positions when leaders of twenty-nine of the thirty-nine official unions in the Congress of Labor refused to attend the August 13, 1996 signing of an agreement between the government, business, and the official unions which called for conciliation and restraint rather than confrontation. The final break came when some two dozen unions of the "Forum" group announced they would support candidates of the opposition party in the 1997 mid-term elections. Symbolically, the announcement came only days after the death of Fidel Velázquez in June.[56]

Rebellion also continued within some CTM unions. A long-standing rank-and-file opposition within the CTM local union at Ford's Cuautitlán assembly plant outside of Mexico City, known first as the Ford Workers' Democratic Movement and now as the Cleto Nigmo Committee (CNC) after a Ford worker killed by CTM thugs in 1990. CNC leads a coalition of dissident local unions based in the industrial Valley of Mexico around Mexico City, which acts as part of the human-rights movement as well as providing solidarity among union oppositionists in what is called the "democratic" current. Further to the North, at Ford's Hermosillo assembly plant, a similar dissident movement attempted to take over its CTM local union. Like the Cuautitlán movement, however, it was denied a fair election for union office.

Signs that trade-union independence is in Mexico's political future can also be seen in the willingness of some CT-affiliated unions to act more independently. The Revolutionary Confederation of Workers (COR), a small CT affiliate, backed the FWDM in its 1993 attempt to break from the CTM. In 1996, Alberto Juárez Blancas, president of the CROC, another CT-affiliated federation, threatened to pulled that federation out of the PRI if the party didn't "take up the banner of social justice."[57] The shift of these and the FESEBES union leaders to a more independent stance is not the signal of a new social-movement unionism, although there are officials and activists within these unions who favor such a direction, sometimes as internal oppositionists. But it is a sign that even what might be the Third World's most stable authoritarian corporatist regime is coming apart.

The context in which this is taking shape is one not only of economic crisis, but of a more general political transformation in Mexico that involves the awakening and activation of what is in Mexico frequently called "civil society;" that is, organization and action outside the state or party structures of the past. The birth date of Mexico's new "civil society" is September 19, 1985, when a devastating earthquake shook Mexico City, burying some 10,000 people. The government and the PRI stood helpless in the face of this catastrophe, which came three years after the official opening of the debt crisis – "La Crisis." With the government paralysed and broke, the people of Mexico City set to digging survivors and victims out of the rubble and rebuilding what they could.

La Botz gives the following description of this important beginning:

The people of Mexico City defied their government's plea to remain at home and set about helping each other. By the thousands, and then by the tens of thousands, Mexicans poured into the streets. "They're organizing brigades of 25 to 100 people, little armies of volunteers," wrote (social critic Carlos) Monsivais on the first day. Many of the organizers of the brigades were leftists, leaders of community organizations or women's groups, who, cut off from their organizations, were acting on their own initiative.[58]

One of the better-known organizations to form in the wake of the earthquake was the September 19th Garment Workers' Union, organized by the women who had worked the small garment shops of the city – the kind of workers who are thought to be "unorganizable." They forced the owners to reopen with a union workforce and, almost incredibly, forced the government to grant them official recognition as an independent union. There is no doubt that their example inspired many of today's dissidents.

With most of the unions still locked into the PRI death grip at that time, unions played only a small role in the formation of the many organizations that would shape today's political opposition. The party of this opposition, which formed first as the National Democratic Front for the 1988 presidential campaign of Cuauhtémoc Cárdenas and then became the Party of the Democratic Revolution (PRD – Partido de la Revolución Democrática), for example, received little labor support, although it won heavily in working-class districts in 1988. On the other hand, as many analysts have noted, this was the first time that Mexico's largely women-led urban popular movements (MUPs – Movimiento Urbano Popular) and feminist organizations entered into alliance with a political party – a fact that will continue to shape future politics and the rise of social-movement unionism.

The second "earthquake" to rock Mexican society was the Zapatista rebellion of 1994. This both reactivated much of the "civil society" born in 1985 and gave encouragement to dissident unionists and those trying to organize independent unions. It also sparked similar armed movements in other rural areas. Few, however, believed, as they had in the 1960s and 1970s, that guerrilla warfare could win the day in this now 75% urban country. Rather, these small armies became one more force in the broad movement for democracy.[59]

At the time of writing, Mexican politics appears paralysed in a number of ways. The PRI is discredited and internally divided between the neoliberal technocrats and the older corporatist "dinosaurs." The major mainstream opposition party is the equally neoliberal National Action Party (PAN – Partido Acción Nacional), whose program is no different from that of the PRI technocrats. The alliance of scattered peasant armies and MUPs has been weakened by the ability of the PRI to buy off some of the MUPs, particularly those among the poor working class, with money from the government's National Solidarity Program (PRONASOL – Programa Nacional de Solidaridad). Indeed, one of the problems inherent in many of the organizations of "civil society," is their susceptibility to the temptation of such government largesse.

Judith Adler Hellman, in her analysis of the inability of the "new" social movements to make a breakthrough in Mexico, for example, concludes:

> the characteristic of the Mexican movements that I would identify as most significant in explaining their inability to play a more dynamic role in the push for democracy is their tendency to fall squarely into the logic of client-elism that has guided the political strategies and tactics not only of the official party organizations but of the Mexican opposition movements as well.[60]

This is not to say that all of Mexico's MUPs or social movement organizations have been bought off; many, perhaps, but most have not. Furthermore, clientelism is not inevitable. It was, after all, a major phenomenon in Brazil before the rise of the CUT and PT.[61] What is missing in the Mexican equation, however, is precisely the presence of a radical workers' movement with strong independent unions such as characterizes Brazil and South Africa and acts as a counterbalance to clientelism. The social realities of Mexican life are pushing toward the emergence of just such a movement. In this type of context, it becomes clear that international solidarity by other workers in North America and Latin America consists not only of support for strikes or other collective bargaining activities by Mexican workers, but support for movements like the Ford Workers' Democratic Movement and independent unions like the FAT or even those PRI-affiliated unions willing to take an independent position.

One indication that there is hope for Mexico is the success of the new unionism and its associated political movement, CausaR, in Venezuela. Venezuela had a corporatist system of government very similar to that of Mexico. Acción Democrática ruled from 1945, following a clientelist pattern like that of the PRI, with its allied union federation, the Confederation of Venezuelan Workers (Confederación de Trabajadores Venezolanos – CTV), keeping the lid on class struggle. As in most of Latin America, the guerrilla movements had exhausted themselves by the mid-1970s. In any case the peasantry was too small a social base. By 1980, Venezuela was already 83% urban, while today it is 92% urban.[62]

In the late 1970s, however, a series of strike movements in textiles and steel led to the formation of a new style of unionism called "Matancero" after the industrial district of Matanzas. This was a rank-and-file, direct-action type of unionism. It was led by leftists, most of whom were associated with CausaR, a splinter from the radical-left MAS (Movimiento al Socialismo) in the early 1970s and who challenged the CTV union in the steel industry. Although Matancero unionism didn't develop a national center like the CUT (Central Única dos Trabalhadores) in Brazil, the Venezuelan movement had some of the same characteristics as the CUT–PT alliance. Although, as in Brazil, it began in one industrial district; through CausaR, the movement became national. In 1992, CausaR surprised most observers when it went beyond offices it had held in Ciudad Guyana and other industrial towns to win control of Caracas. Part of both CausaR and its associated unions' success was based in a combination of workplace and neighborhood organizing somewhat like that of the CUT and PT in Brazil.[63] Causa R's main support had been in private-sector unions. In November 1996, 1.8 million public-sector workers in Venezuela struck when the government refused to pay $212 million in promised bonuses.[64]

In general, the working class across Latin America is better organized today than it was twenty years ago during the final hours of the "dark days" of military rule. As the 1990s opened, new independent labor movements existed in Brazil and Venezuela, new unified federations were formed in Colombia (CUT – Central Unitaria de Trabajadores) and Uruguay (PIT–CNT – Plenario Intersindical de Trabajadores – Convención Nacional de Trabajadores), or revived as in Chile (CUT – Central Única de Trabajadores), and a general trend toward independence from the old ruling or social-democratic parties was evident in Peru, Argentina, and elsewhere among older unions or federations.

Added to the growth and increased independence of unions in Latin America is the rise of the urban popular movements, particularly those among slum-dwellers and those led by women. James Cockcroft summarized what was new about the "new politics" that took shape on the basis of these developments in the 1980s:

> They defy the conventional wisdom that the poor are too busy struggling to survive to rebel; that better-paid industrial workers shun joint actions with unemployed shantytown dwellers; or that the complete elimination of democracy by state-terrorist regimes (or modest concessions by moderate ones) permanently deter popular mobilization for change.[65]

Conclusion

A quick scan of the world reveals that, while there is union decline in several major nations of the North, on a world scale independent workers' organizations are more widespread than ever. Denis MacShane, a former official of the International Metal Workers' Federation, provided some perspective on the relative strength of unionism across the globe as of 1992 when he wrote:

> When I first took out a union card 23 years ago there were no trade unions in Spain, Greece, or Portugal, no independent trade unions in Eastern Europe, weak and divided unions in the ex-colonial lands and unions unable to operate under military pressure in Latin America. Now, trade unions of different ideologies exist in many countries, operating at various levels of effectiveness and seeking to function on behalf of their members.[66]

The greatest unknown is the future of workers' organizations in the former Eastern Bloc countries of eastern Europe and the former Soviet Union. For workers in the EU, these eastern countries form the major part of the South, along with Turkey and north Africa. It is here that the TNCs are setting up shop, building parts and assembly plants producing many products and frequently linked to production in the EU. So far, the amount of investment is small, only about $6.5 billion in 1994, according to the World Bank, while trade is beginning to reorient toward the EU – for example, whereas Hungary sent 14% of its exports to EU countries in 1985, it sent 49% in 1994.[67]

What is clear, however, is that the entry of this huge area into capitalism's world market will bring about another difficult shift over time that will have a potentially greater impact on the EU than NAFTA's linking of the US and Canada with Mexico has had on those countries. One writer has described the significance of the transition in eastern Europe as follows:

> the place of East European capitalism in the international economy would not permit in Eastern Europe the levels of real wages or welfare provision that existed in Western Europe. Moreover, the opening up of Eastern Europe's economies and human resources to the West would have the knock-on effect of putting pressure on wages and welfare provision in Western Europe.[68]

The development of working-class organization in eastern Europe is for now a very cloudy phenomenon in which both new independent unions are arising, though with great difficulty, and many of the old state-controlled unions appear to have broken from their state and party ties. Much of what these former state-controlled unions do involves political negotiations with the new governments, often in alliance with enterprise-level management, rather than collective bargaining. The situations in which these unions must function are desperate, with poverty, inequality, and, outside of the Czech Republic and some of the former Soviet republics, soaring unemployment.[69]

Many of the old unions have lost members and resources. Union density in Hungary, for example, was thought to have fallen from the nearly 100% level of the old state-run unions to about 50% in 1997. Furthermore, the AFL–CIO has spent millions in eastern Europe and the former Soviet republics educating union leaders in its brand of business unionism. Nevertheless, MacShane's observation that no real independent unions existed before the overthrow of the old regimes is the right context in which to view today's developments. Though the birthing is difficult, a new labor movement is being born across a huge portion of the world.[70]

Unions across the economic South are growing, but they are under attack just like those in the North. They face the same predatory TNCs, the same competitive forces, sometimes brutal repression, and even more extreme versions of the same neoliberal policies faced by workers and unions in the North. Often both are linked in cross-border production systems. The workforces on which these unions in the South are based are changing, much like those in the North. That is, even as they grow, the nature and distribution of work is becoming more casualized, there are more women in the workforce, sweating is more common, the proportion of service jobs greater, and lean methods in the heart of industry are more widespread. Wages and conditions on the job in the South are almost always worse – even though those in the North are degenerating.

In this globalizing if not globalized world, competition is necessarily creating a downward spiral of working-class living and working conditions. Nothing in any economic policy now seriously under discussion by any major government or group of governments in the world holds out the hope of relief. If it is to come, relief will come at the hands of the working class pulling itself together both "at home" and abroad. The first line of resistance in the South is taking shape in new or changing labor movements. The challenge for workers in the North is to reach out to these workers and their organizations – unions, parties, social-movement organizations – and forge alliances.

International contact between unions is, of course, nothing new. It goes back as far as the late nineteenth century and has existed all along in one form or another. Judging by actions and results, however, it is apparent that the old forms and practices of labor internationalism are not adequate to the task. Change is occurring even at the level of the international labor organizations, but is it deep enough or fast enough or even the right kind of change?

10

Official Labor Internationalism in Transition

Official labor internationalism is expressed through world-wide federations of national union centers, their regional organizations, associated international trade secretariats, regional organizations or federations, and the various international programs of some of the larger national labor federations – each of which will be discussed below. For most of the period since World War Two, the outstanding characteristic of international trade unionism has been the political split between the International Confederation of Free Trade Unions (ICFTU), led for most of this period by Europeans of social-democratic orientation, and the World Federation of Trade Unions (WFTU), led primarily by the state-dominated unions of the Communist Bloc. While the small Christian-based World Confederation of Labor held some ground, the major contenders for leadership of the world's organized workers appeared poised in mutual political hostility along the fault lines of the Cold War.

Labor's participation in the Cold War had many debilitating and even corrupting influences, quite apart from the surface ideological contest between the leaders of the major national and international federations. While unions in the Eastern Bloc never had any independence from their states, those in the West sometimes compromised their independence from their own states in order to join the global fray on the side of capitalism. Nowhere did this practice become more corrupting than in the United States. There, for years, the CIA flooded several US unions and the AFL–CIO with money to fight Communism and spread their conservative "business unionism" around the world. More recently, government money for these same corrupting programs came more regularly from the USAID and the National Endowment for Democracy. This now well-known and sordid story has been told in detail by Victor Reuther and others and won't be repeated here – although the new AFL–CIO leadership's relationship to these programs will be discussed below.[1]

While certainly the most shameful of its kind, the AFL–CIO was not the only Western labor federation to run a government-linked Cold War program. The British Trades Union Congress (TUC), for example, operated a program in cooperation with Britain's Foreign Office. It is alleged that TUC leaders met with the major employers' organization, the Confederation of British Industry (CBI), to discuss foreign affairs under the auspices of the Foreign Office. The government gave the TUC £75,000 a year to do overseas work – chicken feed compared with the millions supplied to the AFL–CIO, but corrupting enough.

Another debilitating Cold War impact on labor is far from unique to the United States: fifty years of the wrong debate. International labor spent almost half a century debating whether Stalinist Communism or Western capitalism (politely modified by social democracy and Keynesian regulation) was the right path for the working class. For millions of workers caught on one side or other of this "debate" it served only to obscure the shortcomings of their own leaders and political representatives. To keep workers in the West loyal to the system, it was easy enough to portray life in the Stalinist East as a form of grey internment and their leaders as dictators. To win workers and many intellectuals in the Third World to the Communist side, you could, at least until the 1980s, point to the rapid rate of industrialization achieved in the Eastern Bloc and the aid they provided for national liberation movements in much of the South. Perhaps most disastrously, the fifty-year diatribe convinced millions of workers in the Communist countries that capitalism and the "free market" were the only real alternative to Stalinist tyranny – the only way to achieve any kind of democracy. The "debate" within the Cold War context did not allow for a third, democratic-socialist, way. Now we must all live with the dire consequences of this deceit.

The official focus of international labor bodies on the Cold War did not help them come to grips with the changing realities of capitalism either. Of course, plenty of labor leaders the world around have talked of the rise of TNCs, globalization, new technology, international competition, and so forth, since the 1950s. Some new organizations even came into being, such as the International Federation of Metal Workers' world auto councils, suggested by Walter Reuther of the UAW, which linked (non-Communist) unions in all the major auto companies across the globe as early as the late 1960s.[2] But overall, official international labor's thinking process was well behind the learning curve, owing in part to its misplaced political focus and its abiding loyalty to "its" camp.

Despite, "North–South" dialogues, official international labor has also not dealt with the problems faced by unionists in the South. For example, political expediency during the Cold War led the ICFTU, despite its oft-stated opposition to state-controlled unions in the Eastern Bloc, to grant affiliation to right-wing state-controlled federations in the Third World like the FKTU in South Korea, the Chinese Federation of Labor in Taiwan, the Trade Union Congress of the Philippines, the Singapore National Trade Union Congress, and the CTM in Mexico.[3] While the ICFTU provided some financial help to the new unions in South Korea and elsewhere, its continued support for the conservative state-dominated unions is no help to the development of a labor movement adequate to today's new challenges.

With the collapse, or "liberalization," of the Communist regimes, the WFTU lost its governmental support and ceased to be a contender for world leadership. The ICFTU became, in effect, the exclusive center of official labor internationalism with 144 affiliated national federations in over 134 countries, representing some 124 million workers as of 1997, and still growing. For example, Italy's giant former-Communist CGIL federation joined the ICFTU in the early 1990s, while Spain's Comisiones Obreras has applied to join.[4] But the organization that became the uncontested world heavyweight champion of the workers was ill cast for the part.

Dan Gallin, general-secretary of the International Union of Food and Allied Workers (IUF) and one of the most perceptive leaders of official international labor, summarized the state of the ICFTU in the post-Cold War world. Here are a few of the things he had to say:

> For practical purposes, the ICFTU today is the representative labor international, the only one that matters. Yet, on the other hand, it is a directionless giant. Those who regarded its primary function as fighting the Cold War are now disoriented . . .
>
> The ICFTU Executive Board is composed of officials of national trade union centers who are preoccupied with national issues and think in national terms. They have a vested interest in believing that there are national solutions for their members' problems and are caught in structural constraints which obstruct a global vision . . .
>
> The institution lives far too much in a bureaucratic world where form takes precedence over substance and preoccupations with turf, jurisdiction and status overshadow the original purpose of the exercise.[5]

The ICFTU is labor bureaucracy three times removed. That is, as a federation of federations, which themselves are organizations of top-level officials, it is far removed from the realities of today's workplace and the thoughts and concerns of labor's rank and file world-wide. Most of its non-Cold War activities have been focused on international agencies like the ILO or the Uruguay Round of GATT negotiations, where ICFTU officials hobnob with corporate, governmental, and multilateral officials. Its major campaign for years consisted of (unsuccessfully) lobbying the multilateral organizations for a "social clause" or corporate code of conduct, a serious case of form over substance. Although the ICFTU supported some of the international boycott campaigns, like that against the apartheid regime in South Africa, the more basic task of supporting new or changing unions in the Third World or former Communist countries was, as Gallin points out, "underfunded and undervalued."[6]

Obsession with the Cold War, national myopia, and distance from workplace realities and new struggles at the rank-and-file level around the world have left the world's major labor center unable to comprehend, let alone develop or even discuss a strategy toward internationalized lean production, the global job crisis, or the world-wide corporate competitiveness agenda that has confused and paralysed labor leaders and activists everywhere.

The tragic irony here is that official international labor, above all the ICFTU, has changed drastically in the last decade or so. Not only have the Communist regimes and the WFTU collapsed, but yesterday's Communist politicians and labor leaders, East and West, North and South, have, with a handful of exceptions, long since become social democrats themselves. At the same time, the authentic social democrats, with few exceptions, have been moving closer to the political center as they are infected with neoliberal ideas. And to make matters worse, international labor's authentic right wing, the American and Japanese labor federations, has increased its influence in labor's world-wide center.

The Changing Political Reality of Official International Labor

The end of the Cold War might be seen as an opportunity for official international labor to adopt a more aggressive stance toward international business. This, however, has not been the case. So far, at least, it has seen a shift to the right in the politics of the ICFTU leadership, particularly as they relate to the issues raised by lean production and other aspects of international economic integration. The AFL and after 1955 the AFL–CIO helped shape the ICFTU's anti-Communist paranoia in the early years of the Cold War – including the split of the European labor movement. But, as Denis MacShane argues, for the Europeans the fight between Communists and social democrats was nothing new: it had been raging in one form or another since the split in the international socialist movement following the Russian Revolution. It was, as MacShane puts it, a matter of "intra-left hostility."[7] AFL–CIO leaders like George Meany and Lane Kirkland were not only anti-Communists; they were genuinely anti-left – despite the parade of ex-socialists and Communists who advised them on Cold War matters long past the end of the Cold War.

Between 1969 and 1984, the AFL–CIO withdrew from the ICFTU precisely because they felt the Europeans were soft on Communists, if not on Communism. This meant that for most of the Cold War, the ICFTU was basically dominated by the German Trade Union Confederation (DGB – Deutscher Gewerkschaftsbund), the Swedish Labor Federation (LO – Landsorganisationen i Sverige), and the British Trades Union Congress (TUC). For many European labor leaders cooperation with Communists at home and dialogue with their counterparts in the Eastern Bloc were an accepted reality even before the collapse of the Communist regimes. While they certainly participated in the Cold War and accepted the national interests of their own states as primary, in general, European union leaders did not like the AFL–CIO's independent international escapades, like the "institutes" that operated with CIA and other government money in the Third World, or the AFL–CIO's hard line on foreign policy in general.

During the 1980s, however, two changes took place which made the ICFTU even more incapable of facing today's realities. First, the AFL–CIO rejoined in 1984, bringing its unreconstructed version of business union-ism, a whopping record of concessions to management at home, and a growing appreciation of labor–management cooperation schemes with it. Second, reflecting the changes in the industrial distribution of the world, the Japanese unions became a major force within the ICFTU. This latter change cannot be underestimated. As an organization of organizations the ICFTU is naturally dominated by the largest and richest national labor federations. These are the AFL–CIO, Germany's DGB, and Rengo, Japan's major and most conservative labor federation. The British TUC and Swedish LO, formerly in the first line, now followed behind.[8] Technically, these large federations can be outvoted at world congresses, but like most organizations of organizations, the ICFTU tends to operate by consensus and those who finance it set the tone of that consensus.

In terms of membership, Rengo, which was formed in 1989 out of a merger of federations, is the third largest union in the world, representing about 8 million members. Its affiliation fees to the ICFTU are, thus, also the third largest at $1.4 million in 1993, after the Americans ($2.3 million), and the Germans ($1.6 million). As in membership, Rengo is trailed by the TUC, which contributed $1.35 million in 1993. In both numbers and financial contributions, the AFL–CIO and Rengo outweigh the Germans,

British, and Swedes combined. In addition, Rengo completely dominates the ICFTU's Asian & Pacific Regional Organization (APRO), where it is allied with the other ICFTU right-wing affiliates mentioned above.[9]

The creation of Rengo in 1989 actually magnified the power of its most right-wing unions, which were formerly affiliated to Domei and which dominate the new federation. Ironically, the more leftist-led unions formerly with the other federation, Sohyo, simply delivered more votes and fees for Rengo in the ICFTU, but have little say in formulating its international policies. Hugh Williamson described Domei and Rengo as follows:

> Domei stood for moderation in relations between workers and management, emphasizing factors such as consensus-based employee–employer relations and industrial democracy. Rengo follows a similar approach today. Industrial militancy and analyses based on social class are almost completely rejected.
>
> Similarly, Domei sought dialogue and accommodation with business interests, and supported corporatist relations with industry and government. Rengo has adopted similar policy positions in the period since 1989.[10]

To put it more bluntly, Rengo embraces lean production, accepts management-by-stress, and advocates a brand of enterprise unionism that is no model for today's world: it is the embodiment of "global business unionism."[11] Of course, its founding principles sound much better than that and more like those of other moderate labor federations. But it is the federation of enterprise-based unions that practice a degree of labor–management cooperation not known even in the United States. Not all workers or unions in Japan or even in Rengo accept this view, while others are at least questioning aspects of it, as in the case of the Federation of Autoworkers' Unions (JAW), but so far as the official international movement and the ICFTU in particular go, Rengo speaks with one voice which seeks "dialogue and accommodation with business interests."

Matters don't end there, because, like the AFL–CIO, the DGB, and other large national labor federations, Rengo runs its own, well-financed international program, particularly in Asia. In 1993, Rengo spent almost $5 million on its overseas programs, about half of it on various affiliation fees. This is actually larger than the AFL–CIO's in-house budget for international activities and fees at that time. While Rengo runs many international programs, some perfectly constructive, the heart of its educational approach to international labor is its Japan International Labor Foundation (JILF).[12]

The JILF was founded by Rengo in 1989 with an initial capital fund of

$12.8 million to serve as an educational center for trade unionists, particularly in Asia. It was set up as a supposedly autonomous non-governmental organization (NGO) so it could receive "official development assistance" (ODA) money from the government. JILF's annual budget was about $3 million in 1993, of which the Ministry of Labor contributed $1.9 million in ODA money. The heart of the JILF's activities is its "invitation program," in which trade union leaders are invited to Japan for an educational program. By 1994, over 500 such leaders, almost half from Asia, overwhelmingly men, had been through this program.[13]

What emerges from interviews with participants in the JILF "invitation program" conducted by Hugh Williamson and the Asia Monitor Resource Center is that the contents of this program center on "Japanese-style" labor relations and unionism. This is hardly surprising, but it does mean that Rengo is actively promoting the cooperative/nonadversarial approach it supports at home throughout the Third World, which is where 80% of the invitees come from. The reactions of the participants vary. Not all are convinced and some are even hostile.[14] Nevertheless, it is clear that Rengo not only seeks greater influence for itself in Asia, but serves as a strong voice in official international labor circles for nonconfrontational unionism.

Indeed, versions of labor–management cooperation, American business unionism, or European "social partnership" dominate the major international educational programs of official international labor. The amount of money flowing into the programs of the ICFTU, the international trade secretariats, and various bilateral trade union educational and development programs is staggering. Government ODA funds for labor-education and development programs were thought to run at about $88.5 million in 1991, while "independent" funds from the AFL–CIO and the Friedrich Ebert Foundation, closely associated with the Social Democratic Party of Germany and the DGB, provided another equal amount. Denis MacShane estimated the total at "over $150 million."[15] Of course, not all of these programs are about labor–management cooperation or "Japanese-style" labor relations, but the ideological bent of many of these programs is clearly toward a unionism that accepts much of business' competitiveness agenda, because that is the ideological outlook that has come to dominate official international labor at its pinnacle.

Are ITSs an Alternative?

One step below the ICFTU are the fourteen current international trade secretariats (ITSs). These are world-wide federations of affiliated national unions in specific industries such as the International Metalworkers'

Federation (IMF), the Postal, Telegraph and Telephone International (PTTI), the International Union of Food and Allied Workers (IUF), the Public Service International (PSI), and the recently merged International Federation of Chemical, Energy, Mine and General Workers' Unions (ICEM). Their function is to provide information, leadership training, support, and at times coordination to national unions operating in internationalized industries and dealing with international companies. While they also deal with various multilateral or inter-governmental organizations, such as the ILO or other departments of the UN, they are more focused on collective bargaining than the ICFTU and, hence, one level closer to day-to-day reality. Most have industrial departments to deal with specific industries like auto or electrical, and some have world corporate councils dealing with single TNCs.[16]

While some of the ITSs are over a hundred years old, their functioning was disrupted by two world wars and the rise of fascism and Stalinism in between. It has really only been since the end of World War Two that they have functioned properly and that their sense of purpose has grown. They are loosely affiliated with the ICFTU and many of them participated actively in the Cold War. Perhaps because of their focus on collective-bargaining matters or the fact that the rival WFTU's international trade unions never amounted to much, the ITSs, for the most part, paid more attention to the development of TNCs and the practical process of international economic integration than did the ICFTU.

In terms of the pressures on the ITSs, Victor Reuther, who helped set up the IMF's world auto councils in the 1960s, put it in these pithy words:

> In the early days of trade unionism discussion about the need for international solidarity generated more hot air than action. Ironically, it was the capitalistic private industries that in the end unified world labor.[17]

Of course, that unification is far from complete, much less effective, but it was certainly the pressures of business internationalization that gave the ITSs a renewed and greater importance in the post-war period and led to some of the activities that characterize the best of them.

One of the more interesting attempts to deal with the rise of the TNCs was the development of world company councils. The idea came first from Walter Reuther of the UAW in the 1960s. The IMF set up a world auto council and then world auto-company councils and similar organizations in the electrical-goods industry. Other ITSs that have adopted this form of coordination are the IUF and the ICEM. In many cases these world council or international company networks reach down to include plant-level representatives, bringing them closer to the rank and file.[18] These exchange information and hold meetings of representatives from all of the countries in which the TNC in question has operations. Sometimes the more powerful unions in the "home" country of the TNC will put pressure on management to relieve a situation abroad. Less frequently, the council or the ITS will launch coordinated world-wide pressure or boycott campaigns, the most famous of which were the IUF's campaigns in support of the Guatemalan Coca-Cola workers during the 1980s.[19]

There is no question that the ITSs perform a valuable function in terms of any perspective for international labor solidarity. At the same time, there are problems, some unique to the ITSs, some similar to those of the ICFTU. Dan Gallin of the IUF, for example, points out that ITSs lack resources to take on TNCs effectively on a regular basis. Indeed, most ITSs have a staff of ten to thirty people to take care of the whole world. Gallin's recommendation is that the current fourteen ITSs merge down to about half that number and concentrate their resources.[20] This might be a good idea, but simply having a bigger staff and budget is not likely to modify the behavior of TNCs much without a clear strategy and the will to act.

The ITSs are, of course, federations of national unions and while the politics and personalities of some ITS full-time leaders shape the more aggressive posture of ones like the IUF or the IMF, they cannot venture far beyond where their major affiliates are willing to go. In this respect, the ability of many ITSs to play an aggressive role in aiding new unionism in the Third World, or in conducting actions that go beyond or interfere with legal and contractual obligations in the North, is limited by their affiliates' attitudes.

In terms of votes at world conferences, almost all the ITSs are dominated by their European affiliates. But, in reality, it is usually the same coalition of major players from the US, Japan, Germany, Britain, and perhaps the Scandinavian countries who set the direction and limits of many ITSs. Thus, the attitudes and politics of the leaders of the major national affiliated unions makes a lot of difference. As in the case of the ICFTU, Japan's enterprise unions have become a stronger force in many ITSs. One study summarizes this increase in ITS activity:

The Japanese, in particular, hold a growing power, adjusting traditional European–American domination. In recent years there has been a noticeable trend of Japanese affiliates becoming far more involved in ITSs. Some ITSs are now effectively handing their Japanese affiliates major responsibility for Asian union development, basing their regional offices in Tokyo and holding international conferences in Japan. Japanese union presidents are also beginning to find high office on ITS executive committees.[21]

It is, of course, natural for Japanese union leaders to take their place in international labor circles and for their large unions to exert influence. Nevertheless, the rise of the Japanese unions in ITSs like the IMF and PTTI also means increased influence for their enterprise-union outlook. To this changing framework of trade-union philosophy must be added the ideological acceptance of HRM, "jointness," or cooperation by important unions like the Amalgamated Engineering and Electrical Union and Transport and General Workers' Union in Britain, the United Auto Workers, United Steelworkers, and Machinists in the US, and the metal-working unions of the French CFDT and even the CGT. In the telecommunications industry and, hence, the PTTI, a similar shift to "jointness," accompanied by an acceptance of drastic re-engineering, is found in the leadership and official positions of the Communications Workers of America (CWA), the Communications and Energy Workers in Canada, and, of course, Japan's huge telecommunications union, Zendentsu.

In other words, within the past several years the ideological focus of many of the largest unions, particularly in the metal and telecommunications industries, has shifted toward the official Japanese position, while Japan's unions have grown more influential. If union leaders who accept more and more of the TNCs' "competitiveness" agenda and are locked into various "joint" schemes with top management play a major and even growing role in an ITS, it is hard to imagine the performance of that international federation improving as the challenges of globalization continue or grow more difficult.

This is not to say that all ITS leaders have embraced lean production or all the new programs associated with it. In its 1995 statement entitled "Union Power and 'Total Quality' in the Workplace of the Future," the IUF argued that "management is seeking a new production model, but the final outcome depends on the union response," and issued this warning:

> Down one path lies a new form of Taylorism embedded in computers which further deskill work and shift information and control to management. New forms of work organizations like TQM can be an integral component of this emerging "neo-Taylorism." "Quality circles" and similar techniques can be used to increase stress, speed up work and "involve" workers in eliminating their own jobs and making their conditions intolerable. "Human Resources Management" is promoted as a substitute for unions, offering an intimate authoritarianism and the illusion of a voice in the workplace as alternatives to trade union representation and struggle.[22]

While even the IUF statement has ambiguities, it concludes with a call for the union to:

remain true to the principal goals of trade unionism which our predecessors battled for in the craft and Taylorist systems before us. We seek to take wages out of competition, share in the gains we produce and negotiate labor standards that reflect human values.

The ITSs have developed over the post-war period, with many refining their analysis of international economic integration and the functioning of TNCs. Some have become much more activist, waging effective solidarity campaigns like that of the IUF for the Guatemalan Coca-Cola workers or the more recent campaign by the Miners' International Federation, now part of ICEM, in support of Colombian coal miners employed by Exxon. These are basically pressure campaigns.[23] None has yet attempted to coordinate strike action across borders, nor is that likely to happen until bigger changes in the national leadership and the membership's consciousness occur.

Ultimately, the real limitation of the ITSs, however, is that, while they are more focused on day-to-day reality and more prone to action that the ICFTU, they are also federations that must act on consensus. They cannot, for example, by-pass their national affiliates, which means they are necessarily captives of the national labor bureaucracies. The ITSs cannot directly reach the rank and file to implement their actions. So, while they must play an important role in developing international solidarity, there remains a need for a more direct rank-and-file approach, on the one hand, and changes at the national level, on the other.

Will American Labor Change?

Since the majority of TNCs are located in the United States, the effectiveness of the ITSs or almost any kind of international approach to confronting TNCs will depend disproportionately on US unions. For most of the post-war period, however, the AFL–CIO and many of its affiliates saw the interests of their unions and members as allied to those of US-owned corporations. The record of "labor imperialism" by US unions goes all the way back to the AFL in the late nineteenth century. But, arguably, it is the past four decades that have seen the most outrageous distortion of the idea of labor internationalism by the AFL–CIO through its overseas institutes: the American Institute for Free Labor Development (AIFLD), which functions in Latin America, the African American Labor Center (AALC), the Asian American Free Labor Institute (AAFLI), and the Free Trade Union Institute (FTUI), which oversees the others. Their activities range from the export of American "business unionism" to aiding the US government in overthrowing or destabilizing elected governments.[24]

While there were always some dissenters from the AFL–CIO's foreign-policy consensus, the grip of the most fierce Cold Warriors began to be challenged in the 1980s over AFL–CIO complicity in US intervention and "low-intensity warfare" in El Salvador and Nicaragua. The National Labor Committee in support of Democracy and Human Rights in El Salvador, composed of twenty national unions, publicly opposed AFL–CIO policy and sent solidarity missions to El Salvador.[25] But the AFL–CIO Department of International Affairs, which oversaw all the institutes, remained an impregnable fortress protected by the top leaders of the federation, while the institutes themselves were funded by the US Congress.

Also, during the 1980s, many US unions found ways to conduct more genuine international solidarity as it became increasingly clear that any imagined link in terms of the world economy between the interests of US-based TNCs and their US workers had been broken as production began to move abroad and restructuring at home wiped out millions of union-organized jobs. The Industrial Union Department (IUD) of the AFL–CIO, which was dominated by unions more likely to oppose AFL–CIO official policy, became the "operational center" for the ICEF (now the ICEM) and conducted a number of international solidarity campaigns through this channel.

In the 1980s and 1990s, "going global" became a frequent part of strike outreach campaigns. The Oil, Chemical and Atomic Workers' Union's campaign against German-owned BASF was an early example. As in many others since, the US union sent representatives to seek support from German unions and other groups in Germany. A more recent example is the annual treks of strikers at A. E. Staley's Decatur, Illinois, plant, which is owned by the British TNC Tate & Lyle, to that company's stockholder meetings. While much of this activity is more symbolic than anything else, unless the union in the "home" country actually intervenes, these sorts of action have helped create a more international outlook among American labor activists.

The growing practice of taking solidarity efforts to the international level helped build toward a more fundamental shift in the AFL–CIO's approach to foreign policy. The new leadership of the AFL–CIO elected in 1995 pledged to dismantle the government-funded "institutes" and bring to an end this shameful practice. John Sweeney, the new president of the AFL–CIO, however, has a long record of participation in the federation Cold War apparatus. Sweeney sat on the boards of all four institutes for years as well as that of the League for Industrial Democracy, a Fabian-style operation that had been taken over by the right-wing, obsessively anti-Communist Social Democrats-USA (SD-USA) some time in the 1960s. All of these received funds from the National Endowment for Democracy, a Congressional agency set up by SD-USA operatives with the active support of the Reagan administration to fund the AFL–CIO's overseas adventures.[26]

Whether Sweeney was converted on the road to the presidency or simply wants to focus on domestic matters, like organizing the unorganized, he has, as of the time of writing, taken some steps toward fulfilling his pledge to get out of the foreign-policy business. Shortly after taking office, for example, he fired William Doherty, longtime head of AIFLD and a known CIA operative. Barbara Shailor from the Machinists' Union, which was associated with the anti-war forces in the AFL–CIO, was appointed head of the International Affairs Department in 1996. The four institutes are to be collapsed into a single American Center for International Labor Solidarity (ACILS). ACILS, it was pledged, would operate "without government supervision." Shailor promises an emphasis on active international solidarity and on educating American workers in the importance of international issues.[27] Whatever ACILS does, this certainly represents a significant change in American labor's role in the international arena.

All Along the Border: Official Alliances in the NAFTA Region

The coming of the North American Free Trade Agreement (NAFTA) brought increased official cross-border efforts by many US unions and even the AFL–CIO. One important project actually began under the old-guard leadership of Lane Kirkland with the formation of the Coalition for Justice in the Maquiladoras (CJM) in the early 1990s. While CJM was not a project of the AFL–CIO, it clearly had its blessing and at least some funding. Furthermore, it was kept clear of AIFLD and the federation's foreign-policy establishment at first. Later, an AIFLD agent began offering money to projects affiliated with CJM, but the offers were rejected and the agent exposed by CJM activists.

The economic rationale for setting up a project to improve conditions in the *maquiladora* plants along the US–Mexico border was obvious enough, given a more than ten-to-one gap in wages and the flow of investment into northern Mexico expected under NAFTA. What was unique, even out of character for the AFL–CIO of that time, was that the CJM would include a broad spectrum of organizations from all three NAFTA countries. It included not only the AFL–CIO and many affiliated unions, but dozens of religious and community-based organizations, the Canadian Auto

Workers, and even the leftist-led non-AFL–CIO United Electrical Workers, long a pariah in top AFL–CIO circles.[28] Furthermore, the CJM would make its own decisions – something the old AFL–CIO leadership seldom encouraged.

The initial idea behind CJM was to campaign for a corporate code of conduct, pressuring individual companies to sign on. This, of course, did not happen, but the CJM conducts meetings of activists along the US–Mexico border meant to increase the effectiveness of local efforts, to assist unionization of *maquila* plants, and educate workers about their rights in both countries. The strike-support work of the CJM, mentioned above, has been particularly effective. The new director of CJM in 1996, Martha Ojeda, was fired and victimized from a Sony plant in northern Mexico for trying to unionize her workplace.[29]

In 1992, the Communications Workers of America made cross-border activity an official part of their strategy. The idea of an on-going international alliance came out of a joint solidarity campaign in 1989 waged by the CWA, Canadian Auto Workers, and Communications, Energy, and Power workers of Canada (CEP) in support of a strike by CWA members at a Northern Telecom facility in New Jersey. Northern Telecom, a Canadian-based producer of telecommunications equipment, was moving plants out of Canada into the US and decertifying the union at these plants. The coalition eventually expanded to include eleven unions in eight countries.[30]

On the heels of that experience, the CWA established a permanent relationship between itself, the Telecommunications Union of Mexico (STRM), and the CEP in 1992. In addition to a cross-border organizing school, this alliance demonstrated that solidarity works in more than one direction. When a group of workers employed by the long distance company Sprint in its Spanish-language service, "La Conexión Familiar", tried to organize into the CWA in 1994, the company shut the service down. Through the PTTI, the telecom ITS, CWA launched a world-wide pressure campaign with demonstrations against Sprint facilities in such diverse places as Brazil and Nicaragua, where Sprint was trying to buy the national phone company. But the heart of the campaign was a formal complaint filed by the STRM in Mexico's National Administrative Office (NAO) under the terms of the NAFTA side agreements on labor. Sprint has a joint venture with Telmex and has resisted representation of its workers by the STRM. On May 31, 1995, the NAO called for consultation by officials from the US and Mexican governments, the only "enforcement" measure under the side agreement. STRM will pressure the government to bar Sprint from Mexico.[31]

Probably the most active and ambitious cross-border alliance is the "strategic organizing alliance" between the United Electrical Workers (UE) and the Authentic Labor Front (FAT) set up in 1992. This alliance, later followed by a similar one between the Teamsters and the FAT, was formed to organize plants of companies that operated in both countries. The UE and Teamsters provided funds for FAT organizers. The initial focus was on General Electric and Honeywell plants in northern Mexico. These efforts were not successful in the short run and the UE–FAT alliance changed its focus from the border area to central Mexico, where unions are more part of the culture. The UE agreed to help support FAT organizers in the metal and electrical industries, which produced a number of successful recruitment drives there.[32]

The two-way nature of the alliance was demonstrated when the FAT helped to win an organizing drive by the UE in Milwaukee, Wisconsin. There, the UE began organizing the workers at the Aluminum Casting & Engineering Company, called AceCo for short, and "SlaveCo" by some of its workers. The plant's Mexican immigrant workers, many of them undocumented, were afraid to join the union for fear they would be deported. So the FAT sent a fired Mexican GE worker who was now an organizer for the FAT metal-workers' union to Milwaukee to help organize the Mexican workers there. The union won the representation election in 1995.[33] Clearly, in today's increasingly integrated economic regions cross-border solidarity is a two-way street.

Plans were being laid in 1997 to carry two-way solidarity a step farther by bringing workplace representatives from unions in the same companies in the US, Canada, and Mexico together on a regular basis. The UE–FAT alliance was one of the few cross-border efforts that attempted to combine the economic logic of the international production chains with consistent grassroots involvement.

One of the first official alliances was that between the Farm Labor Organizing Committee (FLOC), whose US organizing experience is discussed above, and the official Mexican farm laborers' union, SNTOAC (Sindicato Nacional de Trabajadores y Obreros Asalariados del Campo). The idea for the alliance arose when, in the midst of the 1986 negotiations that led to FLOC's three-way contract, Campbell's management threatened to shift their tomato contracts to the state of Sinaloa, Mexico. FLOC's president went to Mexico to meet with the leaders of SNTOAC. They agreed to work together toward coordinating bargaining. While this goal is still distant, the two unions have signed an agreement on a wage-parity formula that will close the gap over time and that FLOC will serve as a "sponsor" for SNTOAC members wanting to work in the US under the terms of the immigration law. SNTOAC is also an example of a CTM union that has been willing to act on its own in recent years.[34]

One of the most notable cross-border alliances involves a work-sharing agreement between the unions at Air Canada in three different countries: the Canadian Auto Workers (CAW) in Canada, the Teamsters in the US, and the Transport and General Workers' Union (TGWU) in Britain. The agreement came about during collective bargaining in the early 1990s, first with the CAW, when Air Canada threatened to move ticket-reservations phone calls to the US; then with the Teamsters when management threatened to move US reservations work to Canada. Given that telecommunications technology makes the location of such work irrelevant, the threat seemed real. Instead of falling for such whipsawing, however, the CAW and Teamsters, joined by the T&G and facilitated by the transport workers' ITS, forged this unique cross-border pact. They agreed that the reservations made in each country were the work of the union workers in that country. Additionally, and most significantly, the three unions agreed that they would refuse to take reservations calls from each other's countries, should the company try to reroute them.[35] This is a precedent that telecommunications workers' unions and others dealing with communications technology would do well to look at.

The growth of cross-border organizing and alliances within the NAFTA framework presents a positive alternative both to the old labor imperialism of the AFL–CIO and to the dead-end "Buy American" nationalism of many unions. Much of this work remains largely symbolic, limited to complaints to the NAFTA-NAOs, pressure campaigns, and demonstrations. Industrial action against TNCs in support of workers in another country remains the rare exception. The IUF-initiated strike by Swedish Coca-Cola workers in support of their Guatemalan colleagues, that by South African Caterpillar workers in support of US CAT strikers called by the IMF and NUMSA, and a wildcat strike at 3M in support of American workers fighting a 3M plant closing in the mid-1980s remain among the few examples of such action. Nevertheless, these cross-border efforts are a step in the right direction and are most effective and significant when they actually affect the workplace, as in the cases of the UE–FAT, FLOC–SNTOAC, and CAW–Teamster–TGWU alliances.

European Works Councils: A Model?

Regionalized production systems, international business reorganizations, and economic integration create strong incentives for cross-border alliances and trade-union structures within each of the major regions. While there are ICFTU and ITS-related regional structures around the world, only in Europe does an official regional structure exist specifically to address the process of economic integration in the form of the European Trade Union Confederation (ETUC), a federation of national trade-union centers in all the countries of western Europe. The ETUC also has European Industry Committees, which include representatives from the national-level unions in the major industries. These are independent of the ITSs and focus solely on EU affairs. There are also Interregional Trade Union Councils, which focus on the problems of workers at the various international borders and exchange information among unions in the major frontier regions within the EU, such as the Saar–Lorraine–Luxembourg and the Barcelona–Toulouse–Montpellier areas.[36]

Originally founded in 1973 by the ICFTU affiliates in western Europe, the ETUC has come to represent the national labor federations of all ideological currents, including Communist and Christian. Only the French CGT remains outside the ETUC, largely because it is the last national federation to oppose the entire Maastricht project. The ETUC occupies a unique political space not really filled by either the ICFTU or the ITSs: a focus on the institutions of the EU and dialogue with the major European employer organizations. That is, the ETUC does not engage in the remaining ideological struggles within European labor, nor does it focus on collective bargaining. It negotiates with and attempts to influence legislation coming from the various structures of the EU (the Commission, Council, European Parliament, etc.) and to carry out the mandated "social dialogue" as well as political negotiations with UNICE and other employer groups. Its Industry Committees talk with specific employer groups toward the same ends. In 1991, on the heels of the Social Charter, it reorganized its own structures to increase its ability to carry out this task.[37]

Arguably, the central project of the ETUC from its birth has been the long fight for European Works Councils. Originally, these were seen as extensions of the German model of codetermination. The most thorough version of these was inscribed in the draft "Vredeling Directive" of 1980, which was superseded by successively more modest versions in 1989, 1991, and the draft that finally passed in 1994. The focus of the ETUC on EU legislation and institutions and the European Works Council Directive in particular makes the ETUC an unusual labor federation, in that its activities and legitimacy derive from a supra-national political structure whose contradictory function is to introduce market regulation across national boundaries, on the one hand, while maintaining a "social partnership" between capital and labor, on the other.

Not only does its existence rest on its stature as "a designated social partner," but much of the funding for its activities comes from the European Commission itself. In other words, it is highly dependent on the very structures that are attempting to implement a regime of deregulation, privatization, and the competitiveness agendas of the region's huge "Euro-companies."[38] Furthermore, the ETUC itself is a consensus organization, whose functional leadership (secretariat), according to one analysis, spend two-thirds of their time trying to get its national affiliates to agree to common positions.[39]

What all of this means is that the ETUC is an unlikely candidate to lead in the development of European-wide struggles, even though the economy is increasingly dominated by TNCs operating throughout the region and beyond in a manner often characterized as "social dumping." That is, the increased imposition in national bargaining of the region's worst conditions along with a general downward pressure on wages and conditions.[40] By virtue of both its function as a lobbying outfit in an increasingly hostile legislative process and its own partnership ideology, it has become a captive in a losing game.

The outcome of the ETUC's major goal for the past twenty years, the European Works Council Directive, demonstrates this all too well. The original aim of the ETUC was the creation of European-wide works councils in TNCs that could both function as codetermination organs and eventually allow for European-level collective bargaining and, hence, upward harmonization of wages and conditions across the region. The actual directive that finally passed in September 1994 provides for neither of these.

The EU directive requires companies operating in two or more countries of the EU with 1,000 or more employees, just over 1,200 companies in all, to negotiate a mechanism to provide employee representatives with information and consultation. Central management itself was to "be responsible for creating the conditions and means neccessary for the setting up of a European Works Council or an information and consultation procedure." It was not even required that this mechanism be a works council, if the parties agreed to an alternative before September 22, 1996. After that there is a "default" position (subsidiary requirements) if the parties cannot agree on some structure within three years. This fall-back position provides for a European Works Council (EWC), with representatives from each EU country (not each facility) in which the company operates, which meets with central management once a year. There can be additional meetings in the event of "exceptional circumstances" such as plant closures or mass lay-offs. But such consultations "shall not affect the prerogatives of the central management." Employee representatives may meet separately prior to meetings with central management.[41]

Of course, there is the question of whether this glass of weak beer is half full or half empty. Some experts, though probably few union officials as yet, see this as a foot in the door for European-level collective bargaining.

After all, much informal bargaining goes on where works councils exist at the national level. The difference, however, is that at the national level there is a trade union to push that agenda. At the European level, there is as yet no such agency focused on collective bargaining, and there is no legal framework for bargaining since the EWC directive fails to provide this.

To its credit, the ETUC's research arm has set up a database on all the companies covered by the directive to keep track of EWC activity. It has also organized hundreds of company-specific meetings of representatives from unions from across the EU to prepare for the coming of the EWCs, but the ETUC, as currently structured, is in no position to push a common European position within the EWCs. Europe remains a contradictory patchwork of nationally minded unions facing very different industrial-relations systems in which the employers alone possess viable cross-border command and action structures in order to implement increasingly similar forms of work organization and lean-production methods.

The more realistic position taken by many labor activists is that at minimum these new EWCs will provide a place for workplace-level representatives to meet and exchange information. This depends on what is legislated by the various EU governments and what is negotiated by the "social partners." The directive itself does not provide for workplace-level representation in its default requirements – only a representative from each country in which the company operates. Judging by the record of the eighty or so voluntary EWC-type set-ups that exist, there is no guarantee that workplace-level representatives will be the basis of most future EWCs. This leads to another problem with the EWCs as currently mandated.

Lacking coherent, independent cross-border organization focused on bargaining and the workplace, union representatives are at a significant disadvantage compared to the companies, which do have such organization – indeed, a chain of command and specialized staff in most cases. With national union representatives looking out for their union's particular interests, the EWCs can become the channel for whipsawing the unions rather than a safeguard against it.

This is not far-fetched at all. The initial rush by many TNCs to negotiate consultative arrangements or EWCs prior to September 1996 was largely an effort to impose weak or even company-dominated structures. In its unity declaration, the ICEM cites the case of GM's initiative on setting up an EWC. It quotes GM's director for European industrial relations as saying in 1995 that the purpose of GM's EWC was "to contain the influence of the German unions." The ICEM concluded:

Unless the European Works Councils, or any transnational councils that may be constructed, serve a *trade union* purpose and are part of a conscious *trade union* strategy from the outset, they will be more of a hindrance than a help to the workers they aim to represent.[42]

Pepsi-Cola went even further and tried to by-pass the unions in its voluntarily negotiated agreement. This American-owned TNC took the initiative in setting up its EWC by calling "snap elections" and putting forward its own candidates. Thus, fifteen of the twenty-one employee representatives attending the first meeting, at which its structure would be determined, were pro-company, nonunion people. Even these were put in hotel rooms with no phone and a personnel manager as room mate. The IUF representative was barred from the meeting. The structure that was negotiated gives the company the initiative and the right to set the agenda of all future meetings and explicitly excludes the IUF. It is being challenged by the IUF.[43]

Under the minimum standards in force since September 1996, companies can not by-pass the unions if the unions are organized nationally to demand a consultative structure. Just how national employee representatives will be selected will by determined by the national enabling legislation that implements this EU directive, so there can be some variation in the methods. In general, it is expected that on the union side, the largest union in the country where central management has its EU headquarters will take the initiative in calling the employee meetings and proposing union positions. There are, however, as yet no proposals for permanent EU-wide union structures to plan strategy or take unified positions.

The ITSs might help fill this void, as the IUF did at Danone, where "European collective framework agreements" provided some minimum standards on some issues, and as the ICEM seems to suggest. In a report on a meeting of its hotel and restaurant trade group in December 1995, the IUF was even more specific about a role for the ITSs. It reported:

> The setting up of European Works Councils, or similar structures, it was emphasized, must not be seen as a goal in itself but as a vehicle for deepening cooperation between unions at local and national level with the regional and international secretariats to advance union organization within the companies.[44]

The IUF and other ITSs have held European-wide seminars and even established company coordinating committees that meet annually. But the ITSs are world-wide organizations with many places to operate in and scores of brush fires to put out, and scarce resources to do the job. Furthermore, as even the statement above indicates, their cross-border or EU-wide work is based on relations of unions to unions, which means top leaders or appointed officials not workplace representatives. At the level of official labor there is also a possible "turf" problem in that the ETUC and its Industry Committees have also provided cross-border discussion in company meetings. So far, however, there really is no structure to coordinate on-going union work in the EWCs based on workplace representatives.

The irony is that most of the employers fought the formation of mandated EWCs for decades but are now in a stronger position to exploit them than ever, since they are now more European-wide organizations than they were twenty years ago. The evidence is also strong that, like GM and Pepsi, Euro-companies are rapidly formulating strategies to take advantage of the new EWCs. They, more than the unions, are likely to have a clear position on what forms and limitations they want the new EWCs to have. As one writer put it:

> In the end one might have the paradoxical situation that management, which in the past strongly opposed the establishment of a legally binding EWC, will discover in it a useful instrument for transnational HRM.[45]

Where the EWCs are accessible to workplace representatives and where these representatives from the different countries can regularly meet independently of the company, it may be possible to use the EWC as a forum for increasing cross-border contact, developing common policies, and actively opposing whipsawing. For this to work, however, some form of cross-border organization or network is necessary outside of official EWC meetings. So far, this type of organization is missing. There is a need for European official labor to rethink its current structures, just as there is a need for North American and Asian labor to develop such structures. For now, unfortunately, the old saying that "Capital acts, labor reacts" seems all too accurate.

Conclusion

Official international labor at almost all levels appears inadequate to the changes taking place in the internationalizing economy and workplaces across the world. Of the existing official organizations, only the ITSs appear to have a clear focus and at least some structure with which to act. Even the ITSs, however, are limited by the fact that they are federations of national unions bound by the policies of the national-level leadership. As yet, they have no direct way to reach down to the workplace without going through the national union. In practice, this frequently means that rank-and-file union members know little or nothing about the international solidarity campaigns they are waging. It also means that without a significant change in most national unions, so many of which are committed to "jointness" or "partnership," these international campaigns will not go beyond the pressure tactics and symbolic actions that limit their effectiveness.

Without dismissing the entire official structure of international organized labor, it is clear that another level of international activity is needed that involves the ranks and the workplace activists from the start. Such activities and efforts exist, but are largely outside the framework of official international labor as defined here, although many of these efforts involve "official" unions at the local, national, and/or cross-border level.

11

Rank-and-File Internationalism: The TIE Experience

Beginning in the late 1970s an accelerating number of efforts to link workers or workplace union activists across borders began to take shape. The organizers of most of these efforts felt the official channels of labor internationalism were too removed from the workplace and frequently too ceremonial in nature. As one such organizer described it, "the official trade union internationalism was one of buffets and banquets."[1] Operating on shoe-string budgets, these new unofficial efforts attempted to go right to the base of organized labor, by-passing the traditional diplomacy associated with the old official approach. The variety of such rank-and-file-based efforts has become too massive to cover them all. What they have in common, however, is that while they will usually have some union involvement, they are mostly organized outside the structure or supervision of the national unions or federations as well as those of the ICFTU or the ITSs, but they can also affect those organizations.

As 1997 opened, the world was treated to what the US trade paper the *Journal of Commerce* called "the first coordinated, global work stoppage by dockworkers."[2] While it was not quite a global walkout, it was indeed, an unprecedented world-wide action. One of the most direct international solidarity campaigns of the decade, it was organized by the shop stewards' organization of the Merseyside dockers in Liverpool, England. Locked out and replaced by scabs for resisting privatization, casualization, and drastic workforce reductions, the Merseyside dockers exemplified the struggle against lean work methods in an industry where the employers were trying to turn the clock back one hundred years to the days of the "shape-up." Although nominally supported by their union, the Transport &

General Workers' Union (TGWU), the dockers conducted their own campaign for reinstatement, at first within Britain.

They soon resolved to make the campaign international. Shipping is, after all, the backbone of global trade. Their employer could isolate them, but action by dockers and longshore workers around the world could turn the tables. In the summer of 1996, the Merseyside dockers held an international rank-and-file conference to call for world-wide actions in their support. Representatives from twelve ports in eight countries attended and agreed to put pressure on their own unions and the International Transport Workers' Federation (ITF), the ITS for all transportation unions, to call a day of action. The first such day, September 28, was only a partial success. But by 1997 the ITF had called on its members to join in a week of actions, beginning on January 20, in whatever way they could. An impressive list of unions around the world signed on.[3]

Longshore and transport workers in over one hundred ports participated in the actions. While many of the actions were more symbolic than direct, in the US, Japan, Greece, and elsewhere actual work stoppage took place. In many more countries, workers refused to handle cargo from ships originating in Liverpool. In the US, the International Longshore and Warehousemen's Union (ILWU) closed down the entire West Coast for eight hours on January 20, with ports in Oregon staying on strike for twenty-four hours, in spite of the fact that the strike had been declared illegal days before.[4]

The power of such an action can be seen in the reaction of the mainstream press. The *Journal of Commerce* wrote:

> The action showed how powerless shipowners are to prevent work stoppages, particularly on the West Coast, where dozens of walkouts and slowdowns in recent months have drawn promises of harsher response.[5]

Even more chilling is the description of the West Coast strike in the *Los Angeles Times*:

> Pacific rim trade sputtered to a halt and dozens of mammoth cargo ships sat idle in their ports Monday as union dockworkers from Los Angeles to Seattle stayed off the job in a one-day show of support for striking longshoremen in Liverpool, England.[6]

The vision of an international action at the heart of world trade pointed to one more vulnerability in the new, more integrated, world of international production. Strikes at a few key ports around the world could cripple trade and the "just-in-time" deliveries of containers destined to overseas facilities. The Merseyside dockers had given world labor a lesson in how to counter the power not only of dock, shipping, and other transportation firms, but of all the TNCs whose vast investments rest on this fragile transportation system. While it was the Liverpool dockers themselves who initiated and organized this action, the support given by the ITF was a sign that rank-and-file initiatives can at times move official labor to bolder action.

In the past two decades there have been countless campaigns in solidarity with specific struggles that have drawn on both official and unofficial labor networks, as well as on other social-movement organizations. While seldom as dramatic or strategically suggestive as the campaign of the Merseyside dockworkers, campaigns like those in support of unionizing *maquila* workers in Guatemala and Mexico, organized respectively by the US–Guatemala Labor Education Project (US–GLEP) in Chicago and the San Diego-based Support Committee for Maquiladora Workers provide visibility and material support to keep this process going. International campaigns on behalf of individual strikes, from the British miners in the mid-1980s to the A. E. Staley workers in the 1990s, are another part of cross-border solidarity. Similarly, on-going organizations or networks like Asian Pacific Workers Solidarity Links based in Japan and Australia play an important role in mobilizing solidarity campaigns and providing information. So too do research organizations like the Asia Monitor Resource Center in Hong Kong, BASE in Rio de Janeiro, CILAS (Centro de Información Laboral y Asesoría Sindical) in Mexico City, the Resource Center of the Americas in Minneapolis, and many more.

Another related independent approach to organized labor's problems in the international economy is what might be termed the international labor rights approach. This approach is pursued both by official international labor and by independent, though union-supported, organizations like the International Labor Rights Education and Research Fund (ILRERF) in Washington, DC, and the London-based International Centre for Trade Union Rights (ICTUR). ICTUR publishes the useful and informative *International Union Rights* several times a year. ILRERF has published reports and books with a focus on the NAFTA area.

ILRERF's focus is on the political/legal rights side of internationalization. In particular, both official international labor and the trade-union-rights organizations campaigned for the inclusion of labor-rights standards and/or a social clause in the Uruguay Round of GATT negotiations that produced the WTO. This campaign was not successful. Indeed, even the proposal for a working party to examine the idea was rejected.[7] But in the final days of 1996, under pressure from the US government, the WTO's

Council of Ministers agreed, in a rather perfunctory statement, to "renew our commitment to the observance of internationally recognized core labour standards." The ILO was recognized as the "competent body to set and deal with these standards," evading any WTO responsibility for such standards.[8]

The only detailed world-wide labor-rights standards are the Labor Conventions of the International Labour Organisation (ILO) of the United Nations. There is no international mechanism to enforce the ILO Conventions. Nations endorse, or as in the case of the US, fail to endorse, the various Conventions, but they are not compelled to enforce them and frequently don't. This is precisely why the idea of writing such standards into trade agreements gained support in labor and human-rights circles.

Insofar as there is an existing model to look to it is the Social Chapter of the Maastricht Treaty and, indeed, this is often put forth as a hopeful beginning for some kind of social, if not precisely trade-union, standards. As argued earlier, however, this was watered down in successive negotiations. In any event, in its final form it contains only very general references to trade-union or representational rights, going no farther than the European Social Charter (ESC). And, as one expert wrote, "the ESC lacks teeth – there is no mechanism for enforcement other than political pressure."[9] The European Works Council (EWC) Directive does not itself add any trade-union rights or provisions. As another guide to the subject put it, "There is no European labor law offering employees comparable rights at European level."[10] Ironically, one of the few international mechanisms concerning trade union rights are the side agreements of NAFTA, which, while they provide the forum for publicizing union-rights violations, offer no real enforcement.

The actual focus of the international labor-rights approach, however, is usually on labor-rights violations in the Third World. The idea of using trade agreements to pressure Third World nations to grant unions the right to organize and bargain by applying some kind of retaliatory trade measures has been labeled "protectionist" by many Third World governments and government-dominated labor federations. In particular, the US government proposal to link labor rights to the Uruguay Round of GATT/WTO negotiations was rejected by most developing countries. They can point to the record of the nationally based labor and human-rights sections of the US General System of Preferences (GSP) and other US trade laws under which "most favored nation" status can be denied to nations not thought to be in compliance. This can lead to trade restrictions. In general, the US trade mechanisms have been used politically or to advance US trade goals more than in the service of trade unions abroad.[11] At the same time, many of the objecting Third World governments are authoritarian and/or neoliberal, and would certainly not favor trade-union rights in any case.

The basic problem with the international labor-rights approach is that there is no world-wide enforcement or appeal mechanism around which to act. Pressure and publicity campaigns in support of trade unionists facing repression abroad are, of course, necessary and can make a difference. In that sense, the work of organizations like those mentioned above is an important part of the broader movement for international labor solidarity. But enforcement of trade-union rights at home and abroad ultimately falls back on the efforts of both official and unofficial labor and its allies.

The idea of linking human and labor rights to international trade agreements is an old one that received a leg-up in 1980 with the publication of the Brandt Commission Report, which proposed linking labor rights to increased trade opportunities.[12] But, ultimately, there is a certain irony about wanting to tie labor rights to the WTO. The new world-wide trade agreement that established the WTO will deepen the problems of trade unions everywhere in at least two specific ways. First, by unleashing a more "liberal" trade regime across the entire spectrum of products, it will intensify competition and restructuring in some industries, notably in deregulating and privatizing services, while compounding the difficulties already faced in goods production. Second, because most of the rules of the WTO are designed to limit the ability of nation-states to exercise an independent, much less pro-working-class, economic policy, it will tend to weaken national-level trade-union rights and standards. Philosophically, of course, the WTO is the neoliberal institution *par excellence*, where labor standards are viewed not only as "externalities," but as barriers to free trade. The strategy of placing the enforcement of labor rights in the hands of such a body seems highly questionable.

None of this is to say that defending the rights of workers to organize and bargain collectively isn't important. A good example of a more direct form of upholding labor rights is the alliance between the Ford Workers' Democratic Movement at the Cuautitlán, Mexico, Ford plant, mentioned earlier, and Local 879 of the United Auto Workers at the Twin Cities Ford assembly plant in St Paul, Minnesota. Members of Local 879 had come into contact with the Mexican Ford workers when one of their leaders, Marco Antonio Jiménez, toured the US in April only months after the shooting of Cleto Nigmo and the beating of several other workers in the Cuautitlán plant by CTM thugs. This began a long direct relationship between the Mexican unionists and Local 879.

Local 879 set up a MEXUSCAN Solidarity Task Force as an official committee of the union. The Task Force helped to organize Ford Workers'

Justice Day on January 8, 1991, a year after the shooting. Workers in Ford plants in the US, Canada, and Mexico wore black ribbons, donated by the Canadian Auto Workers, with Cleto Nigmo's name on them on that day. Local 879 worked with North American-TIE (see below) and *Labor Notes* to organize tours of Ford Workers' Democratic Movement leaders. But the culmination of the solidarity relationship was a signed agreement between the two organizations pledging mutual solidarity. Under this agreement, Local 879 also agree to help fund the Ford Workers' Democratic Movement with contributions from the membership. Political disputes within Local 879 sometimes threatened the alliance, but it has held up and in 1996 was renewed.

The alliance between UAW Local 879 and the Ford Workers' Democratic Movement is unique. Over the years it has built up trust between the two groups and helped to educate the American workers about the conditions, culture, and union views of the Mexican workers. It helped make the 1996 21-city tour of two Mexican Ford activists organized by TIE-North America a success. Furthermore, a delegation of about twenty US and Canadian unionists that went to observe the election, from which the Ford Workers' Democratic Movement was ultimately excluded, made a highly visible splash in the Mexican media and brought the Cuautitlán workers' plight into public view. It has also allowed for a regular flow of information about Ford management tactics in the two countries. It would certainly strengthen the fight for international labor rights if more such on-going alliances existed.

The focus here will be on the organization of on-going contact, exchange, and joint action among groups of rank-and-file workers in different countries. These are what Thalia Kidder and Mary McGinn have called "transnational workers' networks" (TWNs). They are of many kinds. Mujer a Mujer (Woman to Woman), for example, focuses on building networks of women workers in Mexico, Canada, and the US and uniting these with networks of other social-movement organizations. They did much of the solidarity work with the Mexico City September 19th Garment Workers' Union.[13] Unfortunately, it is impossible to focus on all the TWNs.

By far the most ambitious and long-lasting of these TWN efforts is the Transnationals Information Exchange (TIE). Though this organization has existed for almost two decades, its functioning, structure, and perspectives have changed over the years. The TIE experience offers lessons that are key to building rank-and-file internationalism.

TIE: The First Two Phases, 1978–90

The TIE was born at the 1977 conference on TNCs and the Third World in Nairobi, Kenya, sponsored by the World Council of Churches. While this might seem an unlikely place for a rank-and-file trade-union network to see the light of day, Jens Huhn, a long-time staffer at TIE-Bildungswerk in Frankfurt, explains the context:

> The real story starts with the conservative wave in Europe in the late 1970s. The high tide of resistance in the plants in Europe was just going down. The strike at FIAT [had been] broken. In the universities and research institutes there was decreasing interest in the issues of the 1960s and 1970s, such as the multinational corporations. The churches were the hold-outs as centers of left discussion and research.[14]

The meeting in Nairobi was attended by researchers and activists, but also various national research centers like the Institute for Policy Studies in the US, and its off-shoot the Transnational Institute in Amsterdam, the Coventry Workshop in the UK, and the International Documentation and Communications Centre in Rome. In addition, there were local union activists from various countries. Informal meetings at the Nairobi conference led to the idea of setting up an on-going network of research groups, including those from some unions such as the CFDT and the Italian metalworkers' union.[15]

In June 1978 TIE was founded as a network of the organizations mentioned above. In 1980, TIE hired its first employee. For its first few years, TIE focused almost entirely on research and publications. It was research "with the people;" that is, interactive research based on 1960s ideas about workers' democracy. Task forces of researchers and workplace activists, particularly from Italy and Britain at first, were formed to produce reports. The involvement of these workers, mainly from the auto industry in Europe, led to TIE's first transformation.[16]

During the first half of the 1980s, TIE moved from being the center of a network of research groups to a more direct role in facilitating international exchanges among workers, particularly in the auto industry. Still in line with certain 1960s-style ideas, the notion was not to come in with an analysis or a "line" of any sort, but simply to let the workers exchange information and ideas and figure out what to do. "The shop floor knows best," is how Jens Huhn characterizes their view at that time.[17]

TIE did, however, project a grassroots, internationalist unionism. Jan Cartier of the TIE-Amsterdam office describes this as an attempt to counter the "protectionist" approach taken by many unions in which the union works with management to keep the plant open and regards the other plants as competitors. By the mid-1980s, this sort of plant-level or company-level "protectionism" was becoming widespread in the US and to a lesser extent in Europe.[18]

By 1984, TIE was attempting to "globalize" these networks and set them up on a company basis: Ford, GM, VW, etc. Workers from the US, Canada, South Africa, and Brazil were involved as well as the European network. Their 1984 world-wide GM conference was a "watershed." As Huhn describes it:

> We wanted to match, to a certain extent, the power of the multinationals – a bit naive, eh? – but nevertheless match it, through information and democracy.[19]

This shift toward active intervention in international labor affairs naturally brought opposition from some official labor organizations. Although TIE always tried to work with official unions, its grassroots approach created some problems. Among other things, some of the church-oriented people left TIE – although TIE would continue to receive financial support from church groups.

TIE activity among auto workers during the second half of the 1980s consisted of an energetic schedule of world-wide meetings by company, an attempt to produce a world-wide GM workers' newspaper, numerous informational publications about the industry, and a regular *TIE-Bulletin*. According to Jan Cartier, the world-wide perspective of this "networking" approach was based on an analysis that saw the auto industry globalizing its production methods. In line with both the "World Car" and New International Division of Labor theories of that time, TIE expected more and more component production to move to different parts of the Third World, while only assembly remained in the North. As Cartier points out, it didn't happen quite this way.[20]

During this period, TIE also developed a clear way of dealing with the fact that many of the activists from car plants around the world were also political activists, even members of socialist groups hostile to one another. TIE avoided any form of political discrimination, but it also made clear that sectarian wrangling in TIE meetings or propagandizing at TIE events was out. For people to create a functional international network they had to keep what divided them to themselves and share what they had in common – the global analysis and the activist approach to the workplace. Everyone seems to agree that this approach worked well over the years.

One of TIE's most innovative and difficult projects during this period was the Cocoa-Chocolate Network. This was based on "the production chain idea," according to Huhn, which TIE was among the first to develop. It was an opportunity to link industrial workers in Europe with plantation workers and peasants in Latin America and Asia by extending the production chain back from the chocolate factories to where the cacao beans were grown. Like the auto network, this one was characterized by many meetings, an "internationalism of events." It also produced a great deal of analytical material and still publishes the *Cocoa Newsletter*.

To a greater extent than the auto project, the Cocoa Platform, as it came to be called, involved official labor directly. The Dutch and Austrian food-workers' unions (FVN and ANG respectively) and the IUF played a direct role from the start. The involvement of the unions and the IUF certainly extended the reach of the Cocoa Platform, but it also created problems. On the one hand, TIE staff acknowledge, "We need the IUF for expansion of our activities to other regions." On the other hand, TIE staff feel frustrated by the limitations this cooperation implies. Tensions between TIE and the IUF continued to be a problem requiring negotiations and compromise.[21]

TIE's global approach in the second half of the 1980s brought it into new areas of the world. On vacation in Brazil, staffer Jeron Peinenberg interviewed some trade-union activists and was completely taken by the vibrant style of their social-movement unionism. He recommended that TIE open an office there. They did, and the Brazilian program became one of the most ambitious of all the developing regional TIE offices and programs. It also meant that the Brazilians brought their critical social-movement approach to the various world-wide meetings. As Huhn puts it, "They were both the most critical and most enthusiastic people at the meetings."

TIE also opened an office in Asia, where it worked with unions in South Korea, Thailand, Indonesia, and Bangladesh. TIE also works with the Asian Pacific Workers' Solidarity Links (APWSL), mentioned above. Asia has been a particularly difficult area for TIE because of its size, repressive governments, the variety of languages and cultures, and the very different levels of industrialization and even types of industry. TIE has tried to overcome this by focusing on the garment and textile industries, which cut across the region and have some level of unionization. For example, TIE works with the Bangladesh National Federation of Garment Workers.

One recent TIE report briefly described the situation as follows:

In Asia, capitalism has created sharp divisions. There is a lot of distrust among nations and therefore it is difficult to coordinate work in Asia as a whole. The garment/textile project has the potential of bringing together those who are traditionally separated (they have common problems), it makes sense and can be developed.[22]

By the early 1990s, TIE had offices in Amsterdam, Frankfurt, São Paulo, Bangkok, Detroit, and would soon open one in Moscow. It was led by an International Board chosen at Annual General Meetings, and held annual international staff meetings. But the Annual General Meetings had been European-based, and now TIE was world-wide in structure as well as perspective. In 1992, TIE restructured itself to be more in line with its own new reality, but also with a changing perspective. The largely European Board disbanded itself and was replaced by an International Advisory Committee with inputs from all the regional projects, which were themselves given a greater degree of autonomy.[23]

TIE's Third Phase: Regionalization, Analysis, and Education

The growth of TIE and the development of regional offices might have pushed TIE in a more decentralized direction by itself, but there was the problem of simply repeating "exchanges" or of developing activists into "professional internationalists," some of whom did not really take the information and ideas into the workplace. Additionally, it was difficult to sustain the world-wide networks or the publications meant to hold them together. But there was also the recognition by some TIE staffers of changes in the direction of the very production chains on which the auto perspective in particular had been based.

Cartier says the old "globalization" thesis came into question as it became clear that the industry had, instead, regionalized. There was now a European industry in which outsourcing went not to the Third World, but to eastern Europe; a North American industry with most cross-border outsourcing or contracting mainly in Mexico and Canada; and an Asian industry in which Japan dominated, with South Korea a distant second, and both of them outsourcing mainly in East Asia. The Japanese had also moved into North America and Europe to become, in effect, part of those industries.[24] In short, the trend in auto and elsewhere, though not really in Cocoa-Chocolate, which continued as an almost separate project, was taking on the regional character discussed in chapter 4.

Furthermore, in the old global analysis much of the cost-cutting would be done by shifting more production to the Third World, while, in fact, it was now being done within the plants of Europe and North America by introducing management-by-stress. Lean production was hitting these industries, disrupting old patterns of union behavior, weakening unions generally in many countries, and creating a whole new series of problems not envisioned in the old global analysis. This meant not only a focus on the regions, but, as Cartier points out, a need to understand the workplace changes taking place everywhere.[25]

The auto networks were not abandoned, but put on a regional basis and charged with organizing their own events and means of communication. While some national pieces of the network decayed or had ups and downs, by and large the European network continued to provide useful information for the plant-level activists involved. Jens Huhn describes one of many such incidents:

> The people in GM in Spain were told that the workers at the Bochum (Germany) Opel plant did overtime, so they, too, would have to do overtime. The Spaniards called the TIE people at Bochum and learned that they had been told that the Spanish workers already did overtime so they would have to do it at Bochum. Together they stopped the overtime.[26]

Interviews with workers in Spain, Germany, and Britain who were part of this network revealed many such stories. The European auto network also continued to organize educational meetings. There were conferences at Liverpool and Barcelona.

In 1990, TIE opened an office in Detroit to facilitate a North American auto network. The office was placed in the offices of *Labor Notes*, discussed in more detail later, because of that project's large network of union activists in the US and to a lesser extent in Canada and Mexico as well. TIE-North America decided to focus initially on the NAFTA countries. It held its first Trinational Auto Workers' Conference outside Mexico City in 1991. In 1993 it held a Trinational Auto Parts Workers' Conference in Ciudad Juárez, a major center of auto parts *maquiladoras* on the Mexico–US border.

Unlike in Europe, TIE-North America decided also to build a trinational network of union activists in the telecommunications industry of the three NAFTA countries. The first trinational meeting of this network was held outside Mexico City in 1994, and the second in Tijuana in 1996. The first conference and much subsequent "e-mail" dialogue focused on the enormous problems of re-engineering and downsizing. The 1996 conference focused more on the rapid restructuring and merger process sweeping the industries in all three countries. While TIE did not attempt to organize such a network in Europe, the independent union SUD (Solidarité, Unité, Democratie) at France Télécom was working to pull one together and established contact with the North American network.[27]

Largely, but not exclusively, through the auto network, TIE-North America also participated in a number of cross-border solidarity campaigns, particularly those focused on the attempt by the Ford Workers'

Democratic Movement at Ford's Cuautitlán, Mexico, plant first to reaffiliate and then to democratize their CTM union, mentioned above.

Alongside the regionalization perspective, TIE in Europe, North America, and Brazil focused on education at the national and even plant level, particularly lean production and new working methods. Much of this analysis was developed in cooperation with Mike Parker and Jane Slaughter, whose *Labor Notes* books on the topic were among the first to challenge the pretentions and expose the dangers of this extension of mass production. In the US, much of TIE's educational work was done with or through *Labor Notes*. TIE-Moscow faced much more rudimentary educational tasks, arguing that, in seeking a new viable unionism, there were more options than the American or German models being heavily and generously promoted there by the AFL–CIO, DGB, and others.

Such education in a changing industrial and political environment necessarily meant more than lectures, or even exchanges of information. The changing situation described in TIE's new analysis also meant taking a more critical look at the work of TIE activists and groups within the plants. According to Jens Huhn,

> The policy of TIE now is to bring people together, not just to exchange information, but for political debate about their work and where it will go.[28]

At the same time, TIE in Europe was borrowing from the social-movement unionism of the Brazilians by bringing together not only the industrial workers but unemployed workers, who tend to be organized in many European countries. They also put more emphasis than in the past on questions of racism and the rights of immigrant workers, particularly as they arise in the wake of downsizing and outsourcing.

In effect, TIE had become the major world-wide center for the discussion of the new phase of mass production and internationalization, and the concept of social-movement unionism. Beginning in 1993, it decided to hold a world-wide conference every eighteen months to two years, modeled to some extent on the bi-annual *Labor Notes'* conferences in the US.[29] In effect, these are mainly European-based conferences with participants from the other TIE centers. Three have been held, in 1993, 1995, and 1997. These have helped to internationalize some of the analysis and style of unionism TIE now projects.

Over time, it became increasingly clear that despite TIE's policy of working with and avoiding conflicts with official unions, the actual networks that had developed since the mid-1980s were often heavily composed of union activists critical of or even opposed to the current leadership of their own unions. TIE was not in the business of organizing oppositions, but its networks rested to a significant degree on such oppositional elements in many countries. There were exceptions. In Spain, TIE worked with the Catalonia section of the Comisiones Obreras. In Britain, TIE had long worked with the leadership of the TGWU District 6, until that group was politically fractured in 1994. But the developing national-level networks in Germany, Britain, and France were based mainly on oppositionists who shared TIE's critical outlook on the new working practices and the reorganization of production.

In North America the situation is similar in many ways. There are many local union officials who participate in TIE activities who are not oppositionists in terms of the national union leaderships. The International Solidarity Committee of UAW Region 1A has helped on some TIE projects. But some of the TIE-North America auto activists are associated with the oppositional UAW New Directions Movement. So, in many plants across Europe and North America, it is the oppositional militants who bring TIE ideas into the plant and who generally share the TIE analysis of lean production.

In Brazil, TIE worked officially with the CUT and its metal workers' union to develop educational programs. But with time and the massive pressures of restructuring and neoliberal policy, the CUT has become more bureaucratic. Although TIE has not lost its status, CUT structures have become less responsive over time. Also, a trend of "modernizers" has arisen with CUT who want to follow the model of the I.G. Metall and leave behind some of the aspects of social-movement unionism. So, TIE finds itself working with those who want to maintain the democracy, militancy, and social outlook of the CUT.[30]

What happened was not so much a change in TIE policy toward official union structures as a change in the political realities within the unions themselves. The enormous transformation wrought by lean production and management-by-stress created both disorientation and new political fissures within more and more unions about how to deal with this changing phenomenon. Alongside this is the pressing reality of neoliberal policies and market regulation that has paralysed or driven to the right the old social-democratic and labor parties. The Keynesian regime has been dying for years. In its wake, the European corporatism that sheltered union structures is crumbling, American liberalism has conceded much of the neoliberal agenda, Canadian social democracy has collapsed, and even the Japanese miracle and its lean-export model are unraveling. All the political and industrial paradigms that guided the labor bureaucracy in the advanced industrial world are coming unglued, and a debate over the future is necessarily taking shape within both the bureaucracy and the activist layer on which workplace unionism rests.

TIE finds itself in this context with a clear and sharp analysis of the new situation and a style of social-movement unionism that is not shared by most of the officialdom of national or international trade unionism, who cling to variations of neocorporatism. TIE proposes, at the same time, to bring this analysis and debate closer to the shopfloor through national and even plant-level seminars and meetings. Huhn is very insistent that, particularly with the plant-level seminars, the purpose is to reach beyond the oppositionists and older activists to extend the networks. What seems clear, however, is that TIE has become a major international center for the dissemination of the concept of social-movement unionism.

Lessons of the TIE Experience

Perhaps the most obvious lesson of the TIE experience is that it is not really possible for a world-wide network of workplace activists to "match the power of the multinationals." The world-wide auto networks were stretched too thin and were too uneven across the structures of the auto TNCs to come even near. This is a task more appropriate to the ITSs or their world-company councils, should they adopt a more activist agenda. In any case, much of the actual fight with the TNCs must be conducted at the national level even if international cooperation and coordination exist. TIE never tried to become an alternative, rank-and-file ITS. Instead, its emphasis during its first two phases (1978–85, 1985–90) was on revealing the global strategy of the major TNCs in the industries it was working in and relying on the activists in the workplace to act appropriately. In the third phase of development (1990 onward), TIE organizers took a more active leadership role in promoting the new regional/lean-production analysis through local-level educationals and, beginning in 1993, bi-annual "world-wide" meetings. But action was still up to the activists "back home," who were strong in some places, but weak in others.

To have tried to reach beyond this, to attempt to create a sort of rank-and-file ITS, would have meant building an alternative bureaucracy much like that of the ITSs. TIE's decentralized, minimalist organization and structure give it a flexibility that has allowed it to survive. In the disputes within the Sugar Platform, the IUF said that TIE was not "accountable," because it did not have the sort of articulated, hierarchical representative structure that the ITSs have.[31] But TIE is not a hierarchy at all. In fact, its staff is accountable to the activists in the networks as well as to the International Advisory Committee. But this misses the point that TIE is a democracy of activists, a movement-type organization reflecting one current within organized labor internationally.

While TIE remains a world-wide network, its decision to emphasize regional organization and activities is not only in line with production-chain patterns and economic regionalization, but allows TIE to remain close to the workplace. This focus on linking workplace activists, which was part of the second phase of its development, remains key to the whole project. Clearly, this is more viable at the regional level. It has also come to mean more variety in what TIE does in the different regions. In Asia, for example, it has attempted to link together activists and leaders from new unions who have been largely ignored by the ITSs. In Moscow, TIE does very basic education on social-movement unionism, although they don't necessarily use that term. In both these cases they have to build the networks almost from scratch.

In Europe and North America, TIE depended on pre-existing networks within various countries. These weren't even nation-wide networks in many cases. In auto in North America, TIE built primarily on networks pulled together over the years by *Labor Notes*, UAW New Directions (although it went beyond New Directions members), and the Canadian Auto Workers. In telecommunications, it began primarily with *Labor Notes* readers, who were not even a network before the first Trinational Telecommunications Meeting in 1994. TIE-Europe's auto network is a patchwork that includes the Catalonian Comisiones Obreras (CCOO) and individual CCOO members in other plants; a network of German auto workers loosely grouped around the newspaper *Express*; in Italy it has generally been the official metal workers (FLM); most recently in Britain, it has been an informal grouping around the magazine *Trade Union News*; while in most other countries it is simply a collection of individuals.

It is clear that the success of TIE in any given country is dependent on the quality of the network there. In North America, for example, it was possible for TIE to get off the ground rapidly because of the extensive network *Labor Notes* brought to it, not only in the US, but in Canada and Mexico as well. More recently, the New Directions Workers' Education Center run by Jerry Tucker in St Louis and Black Workers for Justice in North Carolina, both of which have worked with *Labor Notes* for years, have come more directly into the TIE-North American network. So have a number of new Latino organizations and local unions, as a result of the Cuautitlán Ford Workers US–Canada solidarity tour in 1996 organized by TIE-North America staffer Julio Cesar Guerrero. Similarly, in Brazil, TIE experienced a fast take-off because it could rely on the CUT's leaders and activists. In Asia and Russia, on the other hand, creating both national and regional networks has proved more difficult.

Building national rank-and-file networks, not only in specific industries but across industrial lines, is a necessary part of international and cross-border work. Naturally, it is not a job that can be done solely by the TIE staff. There need to be national-level projects to pull together such networks that have their basic purpose in intervening in the national labor movements of each country and dealing with everyday issues that face workers on the job. Publications like *Labor Notes, Express,* and *Trade Union News,* education centers like that provided by *Labor Notes* through its lean-production schools and bi-annual conferences, the New Directions Workers' Education Center's solidarity schools, the London-based group around *Trade Union News* that puts on weekend workers' schools, and TIE's own national-level seminars, as well as the many solidarity organizations, are all crucial to building the type of network on which effective international communications can be based.

This is not to suggest that TIE is or should be a sort of coordinator of networks. Rather, TIE should and does operate through these networks with its own program and goals. What is argued here is simply that creating a viable grassroots workers' internationalism requires a grassroots workers' movement at each point of the chain. Workers' internationalism cannot operate like financial markets, with their "product" flying through global cyberspace. It is not enough to "stay in touch" through the Internet. There must be something of substance on the ground at each point. This appears to be the lesson TIE itself drew.

TIE's role in relation to these networks has also changed over time. It has gone from being the facilitator of international networks to influencing the analysis and outlook of the network participants through more intense education, discussion, and debate. While the TIE staff does not push a "line," it does present an analysis and a style of social-movement unionism that mark it as part of a broader international current within the working class. It has developed this analysis and concept of unionism precisely by its on-going contact with the workplace activists who have provided much of the information along with their own overviews and analyses. But it has synthesized all of this and now is presenting an alternative perspective.

From a Network to a Current: *Labor Notes*

By the mid-1990s, national worker-activist networks of the sort TIE depended on had more or less simultaneously developed in a growing number of countries. Networks around publications such as *Labor Notes* in the US, *Trade Union News* in Britain, *Solidaritiet* in the Netherlands, *Express* in Germany, *Labour Notes* in New Zealand, *Rodo Joho* in Japan, *Labor* in Taiwan, *Trade Union Forum* in Sweden, and *Collectif* in France had grown during the 1980s as efforts to pull together a national current of militants within different unions. Although these network-based publications had arisen separately without much contact in their early years, they shared many ideas and a certain outlook on how unions needed to change and function under the new circumstances.

What was unique about these publications and the networks they developed was that they addressed the entire labor movement of their country. They were based on networks or currents within individual unions, but they presented an alternative idea of what trade unions could become to activists across the movement or class as a whole. They were the "other side of the coin" to the retreat and decline seen by unions in many of these countries. Some were "sponsored" by left political tendencies, but all tried to build a broad current among activists, promoting the idea of a more democratic, militant, and socially progressive style of unionism, i.e. versions of social-movement unionism relevant to the national traditions of organized labor.

One of the most developed of these national rank-and-file network publication centers was *Labor Notes* in the US. Formed in 1978 as the Labor Education & Research Project, it began publication of the monthly magazine *Labor Notes*, the name by which the project is best known, in 1979. At first, it was meant simply to provide information and analysis to rank-and-file activists, union reformers or oppositionists, and workplace militants across the labor movement of the US. Soon, however, *Labor Notes* began organizing national conferences, sending out speakers, and aiding rank-and-file opposition movements in various unions.[32]

Labor Notes became well known in the early 1980s for its consistent opposition to the concessionary bargaining sweeping the US at that time. It produced the only book on the topic, *Concessions and How To Beat Them*, by staffer Jane Slaughter.[33] The book argued that concessions were not limited to "troubled" industries or recessionary times, as much of the labor bureaucracy argued. Rather, concessions needed to be defeated by confrontation. The book provided ammunition for workers fighting their union's concessionary posture. National *Labor Notes* conferences on this topic attracted several hundred union activists and located *Labor Notes* squarely in the center of the debate over concessions within the labor movement.

The project went on to get involved in the solidarity movement around the strike against concessions by United Food and Commercial Workers Local P-9 at Hormel's Austin, Minnesota, plant. Though this strike was eventually defeated by the combined forces of the company, the national union leadership, and the government of Minnesota, it spawned an elaborate and wide-spread network of militants, many already *Labor Notes* readers, that contributed to the growth of an oppositional current across the labor movement. *Labor Notes* both contributed to and grew from this current.

In the mid-1980s, *Labor Notes* once again broke new ground with the publication of *Inside the Circle: A Union Guide to QWL*, by Mike Parker. This book took apart the labor–management cooperation programs then evolving in the US. This was followed by two more books by Mike Parker and Jane Slaughter, *Choosing Sides: Unions and the Team Concept*, in 1988, and *Working Smart: A Union Guide to Participation Programs and Reengineering*, in 1994. These books were among the first to reveal the real intentions of the various employee-participation schemes proliferating throughout the 1980s and 1990s. National conferences were organized around these themes and a new series of four-day schools on lean-production methods and how to fight them were launched in 1989. By 1997, hundreds of workplace activists had gone through these schools.

By the mid-1990s, the biannual national *Labor Notes* conferences had become the gathering ground of the rank-and-file oppositional and reform forces in the American labor movement. Over 1,200 activists attended in 1993, 1994, and again in 1997. Although *Labor Notes* never attempted to form an organization, it had helped to create a national network of activists from across the entire labor movement. It provided educational and sometimes organizational support and publicity to oppositional movements within many unions, and more generally helped to build a common identity across union lines. In effect, it had been one of a number of organizations, such as the Teamsters for a Democratic Union or New Directions in the Auto Workers Union, which were contributing to a sense of change and direction for thousands of rank-and-file activists and local union officials.

In the late 1980s, *Labor Notes* took one more step into new territory by agreeing to house and support TIE-North America. While *Labor Notes'* staff had been in touch with TIE for most of the 1980s, it had limited its own work primarily to the US. Its main international engagement in the 1980s was around solidarity work with unions in Central America and in opposition to US intervention there. The move toward taking on permanent international work was a big one for the project. It was, however, a mutually productive one. TIE got an extensive, already developed network of activists in the US as well as good contacts in Canada and Mexico; *Labor Notes* got the benefit of TIE's experience and direction in organizing cross-border exchanges and on-going networks among workplace activists. *Labor Notes* also brought TIE into contact with many other organizations in North America that were key to developing a regional international perspective. Furthermore, much of this network already shared the basic analysis and orientation that TIE was projecting by the mid-1990s.

The success of the TIE perspective of grassroots international networks and nationally based educational efforts to strengthen the militant, democratic forces in the unions depends heavily on the existence and/or development of networks within each country. While *Labor Notes* was not founded on such an international outlook, it brought to that work forces that would have taken years to develop from scratch. This points to the importance of such national networks in any grassroots international perspective or effort.

The bold campaign by the Merseyside dock workers to field world-wide actions against a major user of the scab-run Liverpool docks gives us a glimpse of what is possible when the ranks are organized, persistent, and daring. The ability of the Merseyside dockers to get a warm reception first from rank-and-file activists and then from their unions rested on a common feeling of frustration and anger in ports around the world about the changing conditions being imposed of them. This feeling exists in industry after industry, nation after nation. By now, it is as global as capital itself. Frustration and anger, however, need analysis and perspective. The embryonic social movement union current that is embodied in the national networks that have emerged in many countries (and need to emerge in others) can provide that perspective, while efforts like TIE (and there need to be more of them) can carry this outlook across the world and provide the grassroots movement for change without which official labor, national and international, is not likely to rise to the challenge.

Conclusion

By the mid-1990s, cross-border activities had become more common among the activist layer of the unions in many of the countries of the North and South. Links across the North–South line were being forged by activist organizations like TIE, APWSL, Mujer a Mujer, US-GLEP, CJM, and many others. Of these efforts, however, TIE stood out for its world-wide reach, its practical use of the production-chain concept, and its clear analysis and developing conception of social-movement unionism.

In practice, TIE was addressing the rank-and-file activist layer of the unions in many countries with a unified perspective. It was not a perspective which solved all political or social problems, but it was one that could give rise to a common approach to the workplace and broader social problems created by lean production. More or less unintentionally, TIE found itself based in significant part either on the new unionism in Brazil and Asia or on the dissident or oppositional elements within the older trade unions of the North. Increasingly added to this evolving alliance were newer types of organizations, such as workers' centers, unemployed workers' organizations, and newer independent unions in some places. All of these were increasingly tied together by national networks presenting an alternative view of unionism. What had begun in a period of retreating unionism as a network of researchers had evolved into one of the more organized parts of an international social-movement unionist current that was emerging as the working class once again took center stage across much of the world.

Conclusion

Toward an International Social-Movement Unionism

By the late 1990s, the structure of world capitalism had become clear. Capitalism was now global, but the world economy it produced was fragmented and highly uneven. The old North–South divide had widened in terms of the incomes of the majority. The South was locked into the role of low-wage provider for corporations based in the North. Corporate-dominated systems of production crossed this North–South boundary, producing primarily for the markets of the North. The North itself was now divided into a Triad of major economic regions, which in turn crossed the North–South divide. Astride this divided world were the TNCs operating in each Triad region and beyond. The multilateral agreements and institutions that were said to regulate this process had been rigged to discipline governments and encourage centrifugal market forces. Together, these structures and forces sponsored a virtual race to the economic and social bottom for the workers of the world.

As the twenty-first century approached, however, a rebellion against capitalist globalization, its structures, and its effects had begun. The rebellion took shape on both sides of the North–South economic divide and, in varying degrees, within all three of the major Triad regions. It confronted the most basic effects of the process of globalization at the workplace level as conditions became intolerable. It confronted the conservative neoliberal agenda at the national level and, no matter how indirectly, the plans of capital's rickety multilateral regime at the international level. Its explosive force in some places surprised friends and foes alike. At the center of the rebellion were the working class and its most basic organization, the trade union.

This very class was in the midst of change: its composition was becoming more diverse in most places, as women and immigrants composed a larger proportion of the workforce, and its organizations were in flux – somewhere still declining, somewhere growing, everywhere changing. The rebellion was international in scope, but it was taking place mostly on national terrain. The need to create unity in action across racial, ethnic, and gender lines within the nation and across borders and seas was more apparent than ever. The difficulty of doing so was still daunting.

The rebellion had seemed unlikely because so many of its official leaders were reluctant warriors. The Brazilians, South Africans, Argentines, Venezuelans, Colombians, Ecuadoreans, and South Koreans might want to pick a fight with global capital or its local neoliberal representatives, but what about the "social partners" in Europe, the enterprise unionists in Japan, and the business unionists in North America? The change from paralysis to resistance could be explained by the specifics of each nation, but something lay beneath these specifics that drove labor in so many places toward confrontation.

The turn taken in so many countries in so short a period of time is all the harder to explain in the developed industrial nations because, with notable exceptions, many top trade union leaders had embraced a new "realism" that said competitive business considerations must be adhered to, cooperation with management was the means to that end, and partnership with national or regional capital was the road to employment stabilization. *Business Week* identified a new generation of European labor leaders willing to "deliver on needed cuts in pay and benefits." Among these were Nicole Notat of France's CFDT, John Monks of Britain's TUC, Humbertus Schmoldt of Germany's IG Chemie (chemical workers' union), Sergio Cofferati of Italy's formerly Communist CGIL, and Antonio Gutiérrez of Spain's similarly ex-Communist Comisiones Obreras. What they had in common was a commitment to "flexibility" in the workplace and the labor market.[1] Many more high-ranking names could be added to this roll of dishonor.

It is not so different in North America. The United Auto Workers' new president, Steve Yokich, could approve a dozen or so local strikes against GM, but still permit even more flexibility in the national contracts negotiated in 1996. The new president of the AFL–CIO could call for more militancy in organizing, but call on business leaders to engage in partnership. In Canada, reluctant leaders from the Canadian divisions of the American-dominated international unions resisted the Days of Action behind the scenes, but were forced to go along in the end. Even within some of the newer labor movements of the Third World, voices of moderation and "partnership" could be heard. Yet, the strikes continued.

The reason for this lay partly in the very nature of trade unions. They are ambiguous organizations. On the one hand, they are poised to fight capital in defense of labor. On the other hand, at the top level, they attempt to hold the lines of defense through long-term stable bargaining relations, a rudimentary type of social partnership. The step to a more ideological or even institutional "partnership" between the labor bureaucracy and capital's bureaucracy is not always a big one. But then the winds of economic change and competition come along and the house of cards collapses.

The lines of defense can no longer be held through the routine exercise of the bargaining relationship. A fight is called for and sometimes waged by these same leaders. Typically, it is waged in the name of the old stable relationship. For the top leaders there is no contradiction. There is, however, an underlying contradiction between the new demands of capital and the union's old line of defense. Stability is gone, but the paradise lost of stability and normal bargaining continues to inform the actions of the leaders even when they are confrontational. Their actions sometimes push forward even though their eyes are focused clearly on the past. That this contradiction is likely to limit the effectiveness of the unions is obvious, but it does not preclude such action.

This new generation of top labor leaders took office in a moment of transition across much of the developed industrial world. Most of them built their upward-bound careers during the long period of paralysis and restructuring of the 1980s. They tended to embrace the cooperation agenda of those years as something appropriate to the new global era. Expedience often took on a more ideological shape as the new leaders saw themselves as exponents of a "new realism" or "industrial democracy." They did so without strong opposition from a membership still in shock from the enormous changes. The activists in the workplace might be more suspicious of the new ambience of cooperation that inevitably pushed for more work and longer hours, on the one hand, and destroyed good jobs, on the other. But for most of this period they could not move their rank-and-file to action. The activists were themselves divided over what to do.

But the pressures of lean production, neoliberal austerity, and international competition bore down on more and more sectors of the working classes of more and more nations. The mass strikes of 1994–97 did not come out of nowhere. In most countries where these occurred there was already a pre-history of resistance in specific workplaces. Strikes in France's public-sector industries, such as Air France, France Télécom, the national railroad, and Paris transit began in 1992 or 1993. In fact, they began even earlier among rail workers and nurses in 1987, led by the rank-and-file "coordinations." Spain saw a long string of strikes in important industries as well as earlier mass strikes in 1993 and 1994. Italy had seen strikes called by unofficial "Cobas" among public-sector workers. In the US strikes returned in both the public and private sectors in the early 1990s.[2]

By the time the new leaders took office in the 1990s the mood of the ranks and of the activists was already beginning to change – or become more torn between fear and action. While fear of job loss remained a powerful force among the ranks and activists, it had become impossible to believe the promises of human resources management (HRM), team concept, total quality, or whatever name the new ways of working were known by. The new workplace, whether in the private or public sector, was worse, not better, in most cases. Job loss continued through downsizing and re-engineering. And national social safety nets were being cut back or even dismantled – threatening public employment, on the one hand, and the quality of life for more and more workers, on the other.

The return to action in the 1990s differed from the industrial upheaval of 1967–75 in a number of ways. While it was not on the scale of the 1960s, not yet an upheaval, it was more general – affecting not only more developed nations, but also many of the industrializing nations of the Third World. Like the processes that pushed more groups of workers into action, the rebellion itself was more truly global than any in the past. It pointed to one of the more suggestive strategic ideas of the period: the potential for joint action between the old unions in the North, which were beginning to change, and the new social movement unions in the most industrial nations of the South, which provided a model suited to the new era.

To a greater extent than the 1967–75 upheaval or that of the 1930s or 1940s, this was a rebellion led by public-sector workers.[3] While it was often the more "blue-collar" workers who initiated these events, this wave of mass strikes saw health-care workers, teachers, and others play an important role almost everywhere. Indeed, the more heavily female public-sector occupations swelled the ranks of these mass strikes from the beginning in many countries, reflecting the new role of women in both the workforce and the unions.

Looked at both nationally and internationally, the strikes and struggles that emerged in the mid-1990s reflected many of the changes in the workforce that were supposed to represent fragmentation. In the heat of mass action, however, international differences, ethnic and gender diversity, and old sectoral divisions, for example between public- and private-sector unions, appeared as strengths among both the strikers and the working-class public that expressed almost universal support for these movements. The 1996 strike by Oregon state workers might seem less spectacular than France's 1995 public-sector general strike, but it mobilized the same diversity of manual, service, and professional men and women workers of many races. Similarly, Ontario's one-day general strikes might appear almost tame compared with the struggles in South Korea or France, but this same mixture, in which women play a much larger role and racial and occupational diversity are taken as the norm, was apparent.

The new leaders who came to head many unions and federations in this changing context reflected the past in both ideology and, with some notable exceptions, ethnic or gender composition. Whether or not they were popular, they would certainly linger on for some time as the hesitant generals in a fight they never chose. While debate was growing and in some places oppositional movements forming, the ability of top leaders to hold on is one of the great problems of most trade-union structures. The lack of democracy and leadership accountability was a basic flaw and, under the new circumstances, a serious weakness for unions pushed into a fight. So, the fight for union democracy would have to become part of the agenda for change, if unions were to play an effective role.

Nowhere was the need for political change more apparent than in the area of internationalism. The top leaders who assumed office in the 1990s were certainly more aware of the international dimensions of collective bargaining than those they replaced. Indeed, global competitiveness routinely provided the argument for making concessions and taking retreats in stride. As globally minded as they might be in this sense, however, they still saw the unions and federations they governed in national and nationalist terms, as Dan Gallin pointed out.[4] Writing in *Labor Notes* after reading AFL–CIO president John Sweeney's book, *America Needs a Raise*, one German shop steward said, "I was shocked about the extreme nationalist viewpoint of Brother Sweeney."[5] But, in truth, much the same could be said of the leaders of most national labor federations in the industrial countries. Indeed, that is precisely what acceptance of the corporate competitiveness agenda means – a commitment to a specious "job security" at the national level by supporting the globally active employers of that country.

So, while the contours and vulnerabilities of international production chains may be well enough known in labor circles, very few unions actually acted on this basis. There were important exceptions, such as the UE's new plan to build cross-border networks on an industrial or corporate basis, FLOC's alliance with SNTOAC, Comisiones Obreras' attempts to build alliances with related unions in North Africa, or the CAW–Teamster–TGWU alliance at Air Canada, or the Canadian Auto Workers' work with unions in Mexico. Yet, while most union leaders across the industrial world were quick to send messages or even delegations of solidarity to South Korea or South Africa, or to attend the consensus or ceremonial meetings that pass for official labor internationalism, the more difficult work of building cross-border industrial alliances and networks remained a low priority. The International Trade Secretariats could have played a bigger role in this, but were limited by the nationalism of the affiliates that tend to dominate them.

The problem is not simply that today's leaders for the most part don't do enough on the international level. Most of the struggle against the structures and effects of globalization necessarily occurs on a national plane. That, after all, is where workers live, work, and fight. That also is the lesson of the first round of mass strikes and even the more localized struggles against the global regime of capital. The most basic feature of an effective internationalism for this period is the ability of the working class to mount opposition to the entire agenda of transnational capital and its politicians in their own "back yard." For this agenda, too, is ultimately carried out at the national level. It is the caution in the occasional battle and the open embrace of the enemy in the daily relationship of labor bureaucracy to corporate bureaucracy that is the fundamental problem. It is the ideology of partnership held by so many union leaders and institutionalized in the publications, educational programs, and official positions of the unions and federations that is a barrier to a clear course of action.

The often reluctant leadership is, nevertheless, engaging in battles with capital and the state at the national level. This new level of struggle, in turn, has a transformative power. It is in these kinds of struggle that people and their consciousness change. The inactive or fearful rank and file become the heroes of the street, whether it is in a mass demonstration or a more limited fight around workplace issues. Perceptions of what is possible change as new forces come into the struggle and the power of the class, long denied and hidden, becomes visible. Yesterday's competing ethnic or gender group is today's ally. The activists who have agitated for this fight now have a base; the conservatives in the union are, for the moment, isolated.

It is not possible to predict whether we are entering a period of intensified class struggle or whether the actions of recent years will fade as rapidly as they appeared. The political and economic pressures that produced these strikes and movements, however, will not go away. Neither lean production nor the rule of the market has alleviated the crisis of profitability. Indeed, the storms of international competition are, if anything, more destructive today. If history is any guide, the current period of renewed class conflict is likely to continue for at least a few years, perhaps a decade. These are the kinds of period in which bigger changes in the organization of the class become possible. This, in turn, alters what is possible in the realm of politics.

It is in such periods that the working class can glimpse the possibilities of social change or even revolution. It is in this kind of milieu of struggle and mass motion that answers to Margaret Thatcher's question about free market capitalism, "What is the alternative?", become more apparent. It is also in such periods that certain demands and changes in working-class organization come to the fore: the demand for the eight-hour day in the 1880s; workplace organization and shop stewards in 1914–21; industrial unionism in the 1930s; the forty-hour work week in the 1930s. These ideas motivated millions across the world in earlier times and gave focus to the strike movements, political fights, and new organizations that arose in those times.

The vision appropriate to the era of globalization is social-movement unionism. It has already been born in South Africa, Brazil, South Korea, and elsewhere in the more industrialized parts of the Third World. Within the industrial North it is implied in many of the ideas put forth by oppositional groups within unions, national cross-union networks of union activists, international solidarity networks and committees, official and unofficial cross-border networks, and the only global grassroots industrially based network, TIE. These forces are small, even marginal in some cases, but they speak with a clear voice and offer ideas pertinent to the epoch of capitalist globalization.

Social-Movement Unionism and Union Democracy

Social-movement unionism isn't about jurisdiction or structure, as is craft or industrial unionism. As Sam Gindin writes in his history of the Canadian Auto Workers, it is about "orientation." He writes:

> It means making the union into a vehicle through which its members can not only address their bargaining demands but actively lead the fight for everything that affects working people in their communities and the country. Movement unionism includes the shape of bargaining demands, the scope of union activities, the approach to issues of change, and above all, that sense of commitment to a larger movement that might suffer defeats, but can't be destroyed.[6]

This isn't just a warmed-over version of "political unionism," once common in Latin America and Europe, in which unions support one or another party of the left. Nor is it the same as the liberal or social-democratic "coalitionism" that sees unions and social movements as elements in an electoral coalition. In both of these versions of organized labor's role, the unions and their members are essentially passive troops in an orderly parade to the polls.

In social-movement unionism neither the unions nor their members are passive in any sense. Unions take an active lead in the streets, as well as in politics. They ally with other social movements, but provide a class vision and content that make for a stronger glue than that which usually holds electoral or temporary coalitions together. That content is not simply the demands of the movements, but the activation of the mass of union members as the leaders of the charge – those who in most cases have the greatest social and economic leverage in capitalist society. Social-movement unionism implies an active strategic orientation that uses the strongest of society's oppressed and exploited, generally organized workers, to mobilize those who are less able to sustain self-mobilization: the poor, the unemployed, the casualized workers, the neighborhood organizations.

The current debate in the US labor movement is often organized around the counterposition of the old business-union "service model" versus the newer "mobilizing" or "organizing" models. While the organizing or mobilizing concepts are obviously an improvement on the passive-service model, most versions of this counterposition narrow the debate in at least two ways. First, they leave the question of union hierarchy, the lack of membership control or leadership accountability, out of the debate. This is usually intentional, since much of this debate goes on among labor professionals and staff organizers who are employed by the hierarchy.[7]

As union organizer Michael Eisenscher argues, however, democracy is closely related to a union's ability effectively to mobilize and act. In a vein similar to what was said by the KCTU leader who linked democracy, solidarity, and mobilization, he writes:

> In confronting more powerful economic and social forces, democracy is an instrument for building solidarity, for establishing accountability, and for determining appropriate strategies – all of which are critical for sustaining and advancing worker and union interests. Union democracy is not synonymous with either union activism or militancy. Members can be mobilized for activities over which they have little or no control, for objectives determined for them rather than by them. Given that unions are institutions for the exercise of workers' power, their responsiveness to membership aspirations and needs is determined, in part, by the extent to which members can and do assert effective control over their political objectives, bargaining strategies, disposition of resources, accountability of staff and officers, and innumerable other aspects of organizational performance.[8]

Second, casting the debate as simply one between the "organizing" and "service" models also narrows the discussion by focusing exclusively on the union as an institution – its growth through organizing or its effectiveness in bargaining through occasional membership mobilization from above. But the idea of social-movement unionism is a labor movement "whose constituencies spread far beyond the factory gates and whose demands include broad social and economic change," as one study of the South African and Brazilian labor movements put it.[9] It is a movement in which unions provide much of the economic leverage and organizational resources, while social-movement organizations, like the popular urban movements in Latin America, provide greater numbers and a connection to the less well organized or positioned sections of the working class.

The activation of union members in order to reach and mobilize these broader constituencies is interwoven with the question of union democracy and leadership accountability. The members must have a hand in shaping the union's agenda at both the bargaining and the broad social level if they are going to invest the time and energy demanded by this kind of unionism. To look at it from another angle, as a leader of the opposition in the Transport Workers' Union in New York City put it, "democracy is power."[10]

It is typical of social-movement unions like those in Brazil, South Africa, and Canada that open debates on tough issues take place regularly. To be sure, these unions, too, face a tendency toward bureaucratization. But the members have enough experience in union affairs to resist this trend. In America's bureaucratic business unions or Europe's top-down political unions, the opening of debate is something new and very incomplete. It often has to be forced by grassroots-based opposition movement from within.

Members' involvement in union affairs and power over their leaders are also key to new organizing and recruitment if unions are to become powerful once again. Experience shows that active union members are better recruiters than paid organizers. A recent study done in the United States showed that unions won 73% of representation elections when members did the organizing, compared with 27% when it was done by professional organizers.[11] A passive membership is not likely to devote the time it takes to organize other workers, and passivity is largely a product of bureaucracy.

The fight for union democracy does not come out of nowhere. It is usually a function of conflict within the unions – differences over direction. It is typically the "dissidents" fighting from the ranks or the activist layer for some sort of alternative program of action who demand greater democracy. This process is visible not only in the US, where challenges and "reform" movements have become widespread, but across many of the older unions in the developed industrial nations.

Harmonizing Collective Bargaining and Class Interests

The demands put forth by unions are another key to social-movement unionism. In many countries unions are seen as, or cast by the experts as, the organizations of a privileged minority, a sort of "labor aristocracy." Overcoming this is not simply a matter of the union raising some broad political demands. Most unions, even very conservative ones, do that already. It is, rather, a matter of shaping even the union's bargaining demands in a way that has a positive impact on other working-class people, harmonizing the demands of the union with the broader needs of the class.

A good example of shaping bargaining demands in a broader social direction was the Canadian Auto Workers' (CAW) 1996 collective-bargaining program at the major auto companies. Unlike the United Auto Workers in the US that year, the CAW put forth an aggressive bargaining program that would increase employment in the industry and the country. Shorter work time, restrictions on outsourcing, and guaranteed job levels for the communities in which each plant was located was the heart of the bargaining program. With a bargaining program aimed at protecting and even increasing employment opportunities in the affected communities, it was easy to rally support from the working class of the region.

The CAW reached agreement with Ford and Chrysler, but General Motors (GM) was intent on increasing its level of outsourced production and balked. The CAW struck at GM for twenty-one days, but the turning point came when union members seized a plant from which GM was attempting to remove dies in order to resume production elsewhere. Far from alienating the public, the CAW's dramatic action and subsequent victory were widely supported. As the CAW's Dave Robertson told an audience of US auto workers:

> We also saw solidarity in how the community responded. We were not seen as an isolated aristocracy of labor, but as a social movement that was fighting to preserve communities. And that has to do with how we defined the union.[12]

It is not only the mass political strikes that have been perceived as having broader social implications. Struggles at the workplace or employer level that create jobs or preserve important public services are increasingly seen in this light as well. The various strikes at GM plants in the US, the 1996 CAW contract fight at GM, the French truckers' strike of 1996, the week-long strike by Oregon public workers, and many others were seen by much of the working-class public as a defense of jobs and/or public services that affected much of the working class of the area. In some cases social goals can be both political and bargaining demands. After a California ballot initiative for patient rights failed in 1996, the militant socially minded California Nurses' Association incorporated these rights into their 1997 collective-bargaining program.[13]

In countries where mass political strikes are unlikely in the foreseeable future, this harmonization of the interests of the workers covered in collective bargaining and the broader working-class public can begin to move unions toward a broader social agenda. Harmonization can touch on many of the issues of the crisis of working-class life. For example, when local unions win additional jobs, they also alleviate the health-and-safety or stress epidemic within the plants, taking some pressure off family life as well as improving workplace conditions. Contract demands for child care, pay equity (equal pay for comparable work), immigrant rights on the job, and affirmative action (positive discrimination in the UK) in hiring and promotions to reduce racial and gender inequalities at work can provide bridges across racial, national, and gender lines. White and/or male workers are much less likely to see such demands as threatening if the unions are fighting for and winning more jobs, relief from workplace stress, and growing incomes.

Most of the rebellion against capitalist globalization and its impact occurs on national terrain or even at the level of the workplace. Mass political strikes are, after all, directed at national or local states, which are still the mediators of the international regime. But even these strikes cannot be sustained or repeated regularly. Furthermore, the power and durability of the movement will depend on the strength of organization at the industry and workplace levels. Among other things this means there can not be a trade-off between organizing and recruitment, on the one hand, and strong democratic workplace organization, on the other.

The Teamsters Union in the US is a positive example of deepening democracy and extending recruitment by involving the rank and file. The holding of more democratic elections in 1991, the deepening reform process, which included eliminating one level of bureaucracy and opening more local unions to democratic control, and the successful effort to mobilize members as organizers at Overnite Transportation and elsewhere, have served as a model of how democracy and mobilization go hand in hand.

Internationalizing Union Practice

To say that most struggle is ultimately national or even local is not to say that international links, coordination, organization, and action are not critical to the success of social-movement unionism in today's globalizing international economy. Internationalism must be part of the perspective and practice of union leaders, activists, and members if global capital is to be contained at all.

The analysis presented earlier points toward the centrality of international production chains in developing a multi-layered strategy for dealing with TNCs. While only a minority of workers are employed directly by TNCs, their potential impact at the heart of the world economy gives these workers a uniquely strategic position. Clearly, the TNCs dominate many nominally independent employers, set the world-wide trends in working conditions, and preserve the unequal wage levels that perpetuate competition among workers even in the same TNC. These giant corporations have deep pockets to resist strikes or other forms of action, but they are also vulnerable at many points of their cross-border production chains.

The strong tendency of cross-border production systems to be located within one or another of the Triad regions gives unions in that region the more manageable task of making the links, exchanging information on company tactics or conditions, and eventually coordinating actions with specific goals and demands on a regional basis. The similar tendency of many industries to be geographically concentrated within each nation also lessens some of the difficulties in organizing and coordinating actions that one would find in a truly global production system. Mapping the course of production and ownership and its weak points is by now a fairly well known science.

Simply drawing up abstract plans for crippling internationalized production will be an exercise in futility, however, if the unions involved are too bureaucratic to mobilize their members for the fight and the leaders are committed to partnership and the nationalist thinking it implies. The International Trade Secretariats, which would be a logical forum for international coordination, tend to be dominated by partnership-minded union leaders from the US, Japan, Germany, and Britain. It should be obvious that the real difficulties and conflicts of interest between groups of workers in different countries are daunting enough. Union leaders who are ideologically and institutionally committed to the "competitiveness" of TNCs based in their own country through some kind of partnership program are unlikely to have the vision to overcome these very real stumbling blocks.

Much the same can be said of regionally based cross-border alliances. Simple alliances between leaders, like that between the leaders of the CWA, STRM, and CEP in the NAFTA region, will not be sufficient. At best, they will conduct worthwhile pressure campaigns such as the Sprint

'Conexión Familiar' campaign. At worst, such an alliance will only reflect the existing caution of the union bureaucracy. This could be the fate of the cross-border contacts provided by the European Works Councils as well, if they are not based on workplace representation. Just as national leaders often need to be pushed into bolder actions from below, so cross-border alliances of these same leaders will need to be pressured from the ranks, and local unions to turn these top-down connections into action and grapple with the workplace crisis facing most workers.

The importance of official efforts like the UE–FAT alliance has been their willingness to involve workplace-level activists and leaders. The UE proposal to bring together local unions within the same company across borders will be one of the first official experiments in North America to attempt such grassroots linkages. So far, however, it is the exception.

The unofficial transnational worker networks, like those organized through TIE or the UAW Local 879-Ford Workers' Democratic Movement pact, have an important transformative role to play as more unions experiment with different types of cross-border activities. By themselves, they lack the power and resources of the unions, but they have roots in the workplaces of the industries where they exist. Their role in the overall process of union transformation, of creating an international social-movement unionism, is not primarily as a pressure group. Rather it is to set examples and to act as ginger groups that set people in motion. Right now it is difficult for them to do more than provide information and an overview, but in doing so they contribute to the growth of a current working to change their unions and to a deepening of the international outlook of workplace activists.

All this occurs in a context where enormous economic and social pressures are pushing workers and their unions to act, where action is transforming more and more people and widening their perspectives, and where the old unions have increasingly become the sites of internal challenges and debates over direction. In this situation, the transnational worker networks should serve not as internal opposition groups, but as daily educators on the importance of international work, and the cultural and political tools needed to carry it out. The conferences, meetings, and tours conducted by these networks have an important role in broadening the outlook of the activist layer in particular. Such actions as the networks can mount also play a worker-to-worker educational role, just as local and national actions do.

Local strikes in key locations can be part of this strategy where they can close down international production systems in whole or part. Thus, in situations where a workplace union is part of the transnational worker network, they can go beyond education and symbolic actions actually to influence management decisions, whether this is in defense of victimized workers at home or abroad, or in a fight for common demands in the interests of the workers in all the affected countries. Common cross-border actions by local unions in different countries can cripple even the largest TNCs in their major markets. As the perception of this possibility becomes more widely recognized, the rules of the game will change.

Regulating the World Labor Market from Below: No Strings, No Cuts

Economists will tell you that employment levels are determined by the rates of economic growth, productivity, wage levels, investment, etc. Hours of work, oddly enough, are seldom mentioned as a determinant of the number of jobs a nation generates. In fact, some neoclassical economists call the idea that reduced work hours will create jobs the "lump of labor fallacy."[14] For reasons that are ideologically transparent, these economists emphasize that the higher labor costs associated with reduced work time would only increase unemployment. Lower wages and there will be more jobs, they say. More recently, and once again for convenience, capital has discovered that hours are, after all, a factor in job creation. The negative demonstration of this is the role of part-time work in lowering official US unemployment rates – a model of "job creation" now venerated in European capitals.

Labor has long known that the hours of work are an important factor in determining the number of society's jobs. A nation's production level may well rise and fall with the trends in growth, profitability, trade, investment, or productivity; but at any given level of production a shortening of hours worked across a company, industry, or the economy as a whole will force employers to hire more workers. Over the longer run they can chisel away at these gains through automation. At the national level they can destroy jobs by exporting the work. But the lengths of the work day and the work week, even the length of one's working life, are still factors in determining how many jobs there will be.

The length of working time is labor's counterforce to capital's job-destroying tendencies. It is a way in which labor can regulate the world labor market by restricting the supply of labor. The UAW estimated that if all its members at the Big three (GM, Ford, Chrysler) auto plants worked no overtime, it would create 59,000 jobs in the US auto industry.[15] Indeed, so many TNCs have become so dependent on overtime work that the overtime ban has become an effective weapon by itself – a virtual strike reducing production by as much as a third where workers put in sixty-hour weeks. This tactic was used effectively in 1995 by Steelworkers Local 1938 to stop job cuts in the iron-ore mines of Minnesota.[16]

The movement for the shorter work week has already made gains in Europe, particularly in Germany. At the same time, however, capital has discovered ways of undermining its effects on employment levels. In Britain, for example, the attempt in the early 1990s to win the 37-hour week in the metal-working industries was completely derailed when the unions granted major "flexibility" exceptions and broke up national bargaining. By the end of the shorter-hours campaign, the number of workers working over 48 hours had actually increased, while the number of those *actually* working more than the new 37-hour week exceeded those whose contracts specified a 37-hour week. More recently in Britain small reductions in the work week were held out as bait for accepting long and flexible schedules on the London Underground. In Germany, just as the 35-hour week became official in the metal-working industry, the major auto employers began seeking what they called an "Hours Corridor." This would allow them to schedule longer hours in high-production seasons and short hours in slack times. This allows them to get around the costs of the social provisions during lay-offs and to run long hours in peak seasons without paying overtime.[17]

In effect, the European employers were taking advantage of the European Directive on Working Time, which limits the work week to 48 hours, to undermine the shorter 37- and 35-hour weeks the unions have won. In Britain, both private- and public-sector employers have used the shorter work week to win greater flexibility and anti-social schedules; they have turned the shorter work week idea on its head. This was the importance of the "no strings" demand put forth by the postal workers in their 1996 dispute. If there is to be a genuinely shorter work week, it must be free of flexibility schemes that undermine its intent.

The TNCs have other ways around the job-creating, cost-increasing effects of shorter work time. For example, German firms are moving some phases of production into former Eastern Bloc countries. Even within Germany, the former East Germany still provides a lower-wage, longer-hour alternative. Hence GM/Opel's decision to build its newest assembly plant in Eisenach, where the work week is thirty-nine hours. As if that weren't enough, the Eisenach plant sources its body parts from a GM plant in Spain, where the standard work week is still forty hours.[18]

What all this means is that an effective campaign for genuine shorter work time must be world-wide and must resist de facto wage cuts or debilitating "strings." If the 73 million or more workers directly employed by the TNCs, or the 110 million members of unions affiliated to the

ICFTU and the tens of millions more still outside that organization, began to pull together in a world-wide struggle for the shorter work week, they could have a major impact on the jobs crisis. Progressively reducing work time, while resisting de facto wage cuts and strings, this powerful force at the center of globalizing capitalism could create tens of millions of jobs a year. Insofar as such a movement succeeds in establishing a trend toward shorter work time internationally, it will have taken the first step toward taking labor out of competition in the crucial area of work time.

What is called for is not some centrally coordinated campaign, but a world-wide movement for shorter work time led by the unions with the greatest leverage, those in the TNCs and the public sector, while drawing in and supporting weaker elements in the national economies. At both official and grassroots level, international workplace-based networks can support one another across the regional and even global systems of TNC production. In the first instance, the goal might be to establish standard hours in the regional/Triad systems of the major TNCs.

Obviously, the barriers to such a movement are massive. Not simply global market forces that push the TNCs and other employers to lengthen the work week, but the partnership ideology and practice of so many top union leaders, and the continuing fear among the ranks. What is more, longer hours, overtime, and multiple job holding have become the means for millions of workers to compensate for declining real wages. It is remarkable that well over half of multiple job holders in the US work a regular full-time job.[19] Clearly, the material incentive to continue this pattern of overwork is strong, which is another reason why hourly wages must be increased at least proportionately as hours are reduced – something capital will resist mightily.

This movement for shorter work time only becomes possible as people are transformed by struggle and, in turn, change their organizations. To put this another way, a world-wide movement for shorter work time should be a goal of social-movement unionism from the start – one of its central demands. This fight has, of course, already started in many countries, even under the guidance of old-guard union leaders. It has had successes not only in continental Europe, but even in Japan. In North America, the Canadian Auto Workers have at least opened this front in the collective-bargaining arena. The next step is for the oppositional elements in unions not yet fighting for shorter work time and the transnational worker networks to take up this idea.

Against Neoliberalism: A Labor Politics for the Moment

"Trade unions may be characterized as oppositions that never become governments," writes Dutch sociologist Jelle Visser.[20] Today, labor movements in a growing number of countries have embraced this role with surprising enthusiasm. They have risen to this task in the realization that their power depends to a significant extent not only on their place in production, but on the social safety net they have won over the years. Capital and its neoliberal allies seek to dismantle this state-sponsored safety net from much the same understanding – that the welfare state supports the ability of workers and their unions to hold on through tough times.

As "oppositions that never become governments," unions must fight from the outside. Indeed, in today's world, workers and their unions are more and more cast as outsiders when they refuse or resist the corporate competitiveness agenda and the race to the bottom it implies. The alternative on offer is the paralysis of partnership. Many union leaders hope to have it both ways, but capital's contemporary agenda and the very goals the unions are fighting for, when they fight, are too much at odds. In taking to the streets in opposition to government austerity plans and cut-backs, the unions have found different allies across the working class. Top leaders will continue to waver between these alternatives, at times undermining the struggle, but the direction of this struggle seems clear.

In the realm of politics, it is largely a defensive direction for the moment. The defense of welfare measures, pensions, health-care provision, unemployment benefits, and existing public services has been the motivation for most of the mass and general strikes of the past few of years. It has also become necessary to defend social gains of specific groups, such as affirmative action or immigrant rights, where they exist. Occasionally, in the area of collective bargaining, unions make some advances, as with the French truckers or the fight for the shorter work week in Germany, but mostly it is inherent in the period that most struggles will be defensive until labor builds and expands its power nationally and internationally.

There is a tendency on the political left and among supporters of organized labor to see defensive struggles as somehow bad or inadequate. Yet, almost all labor upheavals and advances in history have originated in defensive struggles – when employers and/or governments attempt to take back something previously won or simply make matters worse. In this process, the defensive struggles provide the time and context in which labor recruits and builds or rebuilds its organizations. The siren voices of "partnership," however, advise that defensive struggles are: (a) hopeless in this global economy, or (b) conservative and backward-looking. They propose instead various forms of broader social partnership that are supposed to mend the economy, providing, of course, that unions abandon their hopeless fight for material improvements on the job, in incomes, or in broader social provisions. These various forms of social partnership or social contract are meant as alternatives to struggle – an easy road to renewed prosperity.

A version of this is the liberal-populist view expressed by writers such as Jeremy Rifkin in the US and Will Hutton in the UK that advocates a sort of "stakeholder" capitalism, in which the various organizations of "civil society" act as a counterweight to, or attempt to take on some institutional role within, major corporations, banks, and other financial institutions that can influence the direction of major business decisions.[21] They emphasize the idea of a "social contract" between capital and "civil society" or "Third Sector" of non-governmental organizations and volunteers that would create a more kind and gentle capitalism. Others call for the use of pension funds as a means of influencing the direction of investments.[22]

All of these schemes share an unspoken view of today's TNCs as passive institutions making bad decisions on the basis of short-sighted views of profitability. There is also an assumption in most cases that these global actors can be controlled at the national level through increased representation by "stakeholders" (like unions or various community organizations) or actual stockholders working through pension funds. In this version, big figures are thrown around to show the potential power of pension funds, should they ever come under democratic control. For example, in the US, pension funds control 25% of all stocks. What is not mentioned is that the other 75% of stocks are safely in the hands of the nation's wealthiest 10% of families (25% of all stocks) and the financial institutions (50%) that these same families disproportionately influence or own.[23]

The usual argument for pension-fund capitalism is that this is a way democratically to affect society's investment priorities. In fact, in the US, one of the few countries, along with the UK, where pension funds have any importance, stocks have not been a source of investment funds for decades. Capital expenditures come almost entirely from internally generated profits. From the early 1950s, internal funds covered 95% of capital expenditures, and since 1990, 109%. Since the early 1980s, more stock has "disappeared" than been issued. The reason is that stocks have become one of capital's more recent competitive weapons in the war for market share, the merger and acquisition boom of the 1980s and 1990s – $1.5 trillion in mergers and acquisitions and $500 billion in buybacks.[24] This is a game pension funds cannot play.

These various stakeholder and stockholder proposals always rest on an analysis that dissolves real power relations. The capitalist corporation becomes just one more porous institution with neutral goals and various "stakeholders" whose interests can be harmonized with one another and with society as a whole. As one group of British researchers said in reference to Will Hutton's rendition, "the vision rests on a political fantasy about general benefits for all stakeholders and their economic analysis does not confront the structural reality of redistributive conflict between stakeholders."[25] The most obvious conflict is that between the workers and the real owners, but there are others as well, such as that between business customers and households in setting prices or rates.

In other versions, ownership becomes "social" simply because the capitalist class shares ownership through stocks, bonds, mutual funds, and other claims on wealth. As the Austrian Marxist Rudolph Hilferding pointed out in 1910, however, stock ownership was actually a way of centralizing capital. It allowed the biggest capitalists to expand their business by using the capital of many small stockholders; it didn't decrease their control or power, but enhanced it.[26] The modern mergers and acquisitions are just the contemporary form of this reality. Indeed, the biggest buyers of stocks in recent years have been corporations engaged in mergers and acquisitions. Since the early 1980s, fully $1.4 trillion in stock has been gobbled up in mergers and acquisitions, while another $500 billion has gone to corporate buybacks of stock – all enhancing the power of those at the center of control.[27]

Even more remarkable than the attempt to turn stock ownership into some form of social democracy is the assessment of the capitalist state on which Rifkin's vision of a "Third Sector" rests heavily. Knowing that the NGOs and volunteer organizations that compose this "Third Sector" are themselves financially strapped, he proposed a number of government funding programs. In order to make this sound realistic, he argues that government is becoming "less tied to the interests of the commercial economy and more aligned with the interests of the social economy."[28] It is hard to imagine just which contemporary government he could possibly be talking about.

The problems with all these alternatives to struggle is that today's corporations, led by the TNCs, are clearly predators waging class war to expand their world-wide empires and restore the legendary profit rates of decades ago. Governments are following their lead, coming more and more under the influence of "the commercial economy," not less. Under these circumstances something more than an amorphous "civil society" is needed as a counterweight, and that is the organized working class and its allies. Finally, of course, there is nothing in these proposals that guarantees real job creation, since the basic mechanisms of investment and internal profitability are left untouched.

The current emphasis on social safety-net issues and increased equality within the class, material issues from which working-class people can gain and strengthen their position, offers the best way to gather in broader forces and increase the power of the working class. All the various schemes for representation in the institutions of capital end up as versions of partnership in which unions or other members of "civil society" are dragged into the war that is real capitalist competition, which is more likely to destroy jobs than create them. Labor cannot advance through such competition. Its historic role is to limit and eventually suppress this destructive force. Social safety-net demands are one more way in which unions and their working-class allies can "take labor out of competition."

The fight for shorter work time, labor's major offensive issue, can and should also become a political fight as it did in the nineteenth century and the 1930s. The struggle to preserve publicly funded pensions, Social Security in the US, is a part of this fight to reduce total work time. But a national standard of thirty-five hours a week or less (with no pay reductions and no strings) implemented through legislation would contribute immediately to employment growth, strengthening the position of the working class. It is obvious that in most countries the old political parties of the left and the working class are unwilling, perhaps unable, to wage such a fight. It falls once again to the "oppositions that never become governments."

In the realm of international policy, renegotiating trade agreements would be part of a long-range program. But in terms of the politics of the moment, there is one goal that would do more to bring about "upward leveling" across the world than any other – cancellation of the Third World debt. For the Third World, debt to the banks of the North has been like a mortgage that never ends. As of 1994, according to the World Bank, this debt stood at 2.5 trillion, compared with $906 billion in 1980, about the time the Third World debt crisis surfaced.[29] This is an increase of over 250% in spite of the fact that almost all new Third World borrowing has been to pay off the initial debt, which in effect has been paid off many times over.

The cancellation of this debt or even its progressive reduction would free billions of dollars in interest paid annually to banks or bond-holders in the North by governments of the South. Where unions and other organizations were able to fight for the proper distribution of the new resources this would free up, social programs that provide the necessary safety net for so many in the Third World could be restored or even expanded. The parameters of struggle would be altered across the Third

World. Obviously, a constructive redistribution of this potential wealth would require strong labor movements in both North and South. But it is a common goal that could do much to bind the movements in these two parts of the world that capital has sought to play against one another.

Toward a World-Wide Social-Movement Union Current

The pressures of globalization and lean production, the transforming powers of renewed struggle, and the fresh forces that have come to the working class in recent decades are all pushing the working class and its organizations in a more aggressive and confrontational direction. Because so many top leaders still think and act in terms of the corporate competitiveness/partnership agenda, this process often begins with or includes internal union conflict. Debate and challenges are more common within unions and there are new social–movement unions in parts of the economic South to provide "role models" for activists in the North. Yet, there is nothing inevitable about the outcomes of these debates or challenges.

As noted earlier, the newest generation of top leaders in much of the North are the products of the 1980s, deeply committed to one or another form of partnership with capital. In fact, the end of the Cold War and the gathering in of more federations and unions in the ICFTU and the ITSs, on the one hand, and the rise in influence of the US, German, Japanese, and British leaders in these bodies, on the other, mean that the partnership advocates have a wider audience than in the past. They have behind them a seductive chorus of social-democratic politicians, and threats and promises from many of the TNCs themselves.

The context for a debate over the direction of world labor may be more favorable, but a fight is required. An international current is needed to promote the ideas and practices of social-movement unionism. The material for such a current is already at hand in unions such as those in South Korea, South Africa, Brazil, and other newer unions in Asia; in major tendencies within changing Latin American unions; in a few unions in the North, like the Canadian Auto Workers, the United Electrical Workers in the US, and SUD in France, among others; in oppositional or reform groups within unions; in the national networks of activists around publications such as *Labor Notes*; those in the international solidarity networks such as APWSL, CJM, US–GLEP, and the Maquiladora Workers' Support Committee; and the industrial networks of TIE.

Obviously, this is a diverse current and not an ideologically defined, left political tendency. It includes people from a variety of tendencies and even more of those with no left background. It contains organizations as different as unions and oppositional networks. It is world-wide, cutting across the North–South divide and spanning the three Triad regions.

What this current shares is not a single organization or a central leadership, but a view of what unionism can be in today's globalizing world. Central to this view of social-movement unionism are union democracy and leadership accountability, membership activation and involvement, a commitment to union growth and recruitment, a vision and practice that reach beyond even an expanding union membership to other sectors and organizations of the working class. This view sees unions as taking an active, leading role in the struggles against international and domestic capital and their neoliberal political allies.

Social-movement unionism is an orientation guided by these ideas and visions. It is not an attempt to reshape national labor-relations systems or make all unions have the same structure. While an industrial strategic approach is important, social-movement unionism can guide the actions of today's typical, merged general unions, as the case of the CAW indicates. It can be the practice and outlook of a single occupational union such as the California Nurses' Association, or of a government department or agency-based union such as SUD in France's telecom and postal systems. It can be a region of a national labor federation, such as the Catalan CCOO. What matters most is that its practice is a rank-and-file practice and not simply a matter of the progressive politics of a small group of leaders.

Above all, social-movement unionism is a perspective to be fought for on an international scale. The recognition of a common perspective by activists in different countries will both facilitate an internationalist practice and reinforce the struggle for this orientation at every level of existing working-class organization. It is a perspective that can maximize working-class power by drawing together the different sectors within the class around those organizations with the greatest existing and potential power at this juncture, the unions. It is a perspective that embraces the diversity of the working class in order to overcome its fragmentation. While it is not about "reforming" the old mass parties of the left, it is far more likely to move them off center than any amount of lobbying or conventional "boring within." It is, above all, a means, a rehearsal, for self-emancipation from below.

Conclusion

The reorganization of the world economy through the process of capitalist globalization paralysed much of the working class of the North for almost two decades. In many industrial nations, unions have declined as a proportion of the workforce, while the changing organization of work has appeared to fragment the class and its organizations permanently. The same process produced new labor movements in some parts of the South, while reviving older unions in other Third World areas. International labor appeared to be marching out of step.

By the mid-1990s, rebellion and militancy were sweeping through large parts of both the North and the South. The pressures associated with capitalist globalization pushed more working people into action. Furthermore, the shape and consequences of unregulated international economic integration became more apparent. The impersonal forces of the world market took on the faces of the neoliberal politicians charged with removing the final barriers to market control. Yesterday's invisible hand became highly visible, the process, in effect, politicized. The state had not disappeared so much as changed direction. States make good targets for mass discontent and the unions in many countries finally stepped into the vacuum left by the retreating parties that they had once supported – or even still did. Not surprisingly, public-sector unions led this rebellion. For the first time in decades, international labor was once again marching in step.

Beneath the surface, workplace rebellion also returned, particularly where the new ways of working had been in place for a while. The pressures on the workforce that Stephen Roach had spoken of had begun to produce the "worker backlash" he had warned of. Most of it was workplace guerrilla warfare, jostling over just how lean and mean conditions would be. But now and then it broke out as a militant action by the whole workforce. Increasingly, it took the form of new groups of workers organizing or joining unions. They spaned all countries and sectors: public and private, industry and service. While unions in some industrial countries had seriously declined, there was more hope of a reversal in fortunes. Globally, independent unionism now embraced more of working humanity than at any time in history.

The merging of workplace struggles with bigger political fights by labor across international lines offers a unique opportunity to revitalize unions and draw on the strengths and numbers of other working-class organizations and communities. The biggest as well as the most basic fights still occur at the national level, but the opportunity and necessity to reach across borders are greater than ever. The contours of globalizing capitalism are now apparent, as are its weak points. If a small group of English dock workers can reach across the planet and pull off a world-wide action, imagine what unions and international labor bodies with a clear purpose and the democratic organization to activate their members could do.

For this to happen, a new leadership more in tune with the times will have to arise from an angry and activated rank and file – not above them, but with them. Social-movement unionism, by whatever name, can be the democratic vision and the practice around which such a new leadership can rally and reach out across the many lines capitalism draws between people. If the struggles against the effects of globalization continue, as they most likely will, and more people are drawn into action, the leaders among them will be better able to look around and see that, as one African-American labor educator likes to say: "We are the leaders we've been looking for."[30]

Epilogue

A Socialist Direction

The current revival of working-class activity opens new possibilities. If the force of this revival grows, which is not guaranteed, it will alter our view of the alternatives. Alternatives, after all, are not usually waiting passively for those of good heart; they must be carved out of the situation. David Robertson of the CAW said of the lessons they had learned in their 1996 confrontation with GM, "how necessary it is to keep alive a view of alternatives, to state that things can be different and by fighting you make a difference."[1] The greater the struggle, the greater the alternatives.

Can socialism become one of those alternatives, or must we simply settle for the welfare state, some version of "stakeholder" capitalism, or, worse yet, surrender to the neoliberal/conservative agenda? What seems clear is that without some deeper changes, the driving forces that have led to the global race to the bottom in the first place will still be operating. So will the political currents that ride the crest of intensified market forces. Indeed, the imposition of some welfare provisions as a result of increased struggle and/or some growth and strengthening of unionism would no doubt confound capital's crisis of accumulation. These kinds of social provisions can only be a launching platform for a strengthened labor movement, not a secure place with an indefinite future.

Yet, few things seem more remote today than socialism. Its decades of putative association with the totalitarian Communist regimes tarnished it for many. The collapse of those same regimes seems to have rendered it a failed idea to others. The abandonment of any socialist goals by parties still bearing the name has only added more confusion and futility for many more who once thought socialism a goal worth fighting for. Indeed, as socialist activist and theoretician Hal Draper wrote almost forty

293

years ago, "Socialism's crisis today is a crisis in the *meaning* of socialism."[2] So, its possibility is at least in part a question of what we are talking about.

Modern socialism as anything more than an idea or theory is a creature of the labor movement. Its ideas would have moldered in old books or died with Karl Marx and a handful of other radical intellectuals around a hundred years ago, if millions of workers, hundreds of trade unions and labor federations, and scores of working-class political parties had not embraced the ideas and perspectives they called socialism. Its appeal to these workers and their organizations as the movement gained momentum over a hundred years ago was simple: socialism was the rule of the working class.

This rule by the working class was seen as the culmination of a historical development of that class, in conflict with the capitalist class as well as in conflict internally, "from its origin in the industrial revolution of the eighteenth and nineteenth centuries to the present period of capitalist crisis, as a class *preparing for power*," as British trade union and socialist leader J. T. Murphy put it in 1934.[3] This history is not predetermined or orderly. It has ups, downs, and major setbacks. Yet, as the rule of monarchs, aristocrats, and slaveholders has given way to that of the capitalist class, so the crisis-ridden rule of capital could give way to that of the working class, though not without a fight. This transition to democratic rule by the working-class majority was the essence of socialist revolution.

As the majority class in many countries and the inheritor of the revolutionary democratic tradition of the previous hundred or more years, the working class would necessarily express its rule through far deeper and broader forms of democracy than those of the capitalist state. While it was assumed that most capitalist enterprises would be expropriated and most forms of economic organization would be collective and democratic, the "details" were left to the new working-class rulers and their leaders to figure out once they achieved power.

The twentieth century has dealt ruthlessly with this original vision of socialism as democratic working-class rule. Brutal wars, failed revolutions, bloody counter-revolutions, the rise of bureaucratic and totalitarian states, defeated working-class organizations, and the transformation of the old socialist and Communist parties into timid parties of reform and, now, conformity, have buried the very meaning of socialism in the wreckage of eight decades. The theories that have been developed to explain or apologize for all of this have frequently done more harm than good, carrying the idea of socialism farther and farther from its roots in the labor movement. The ghastly rewriting of Marxism by the Stalinist bureaucracies of the Communist bloc is only the most extreme example. In this theory, the working class was reduced to a function of economic trends, on the one hand, and orders from "the party" leaders, on the other.

Other theories that attempted to deal with the failures of the twentieth century have simply substituted other forces (the Communist bloc, the party) or classes (the peasantry) for the working class or reduced socialist politics to the pursuit of coalitions big enough to win elections. The final dissolving of the concept of class as an active agency of change at the hands of postmodernists and others is only the last intellectual nail in the ideological crucifixion of socialism. If the concept of class has proved too persistent a reality to bury theoretically, some of the intellectuals of the second half of the twentieth century who still claimed the mantle of socialism have seemed bent on burying the whole project in language. Ever more obscure terminology became the trade of structuralist, post-structuralist, neo-Gramscian, Western Marxist, and discourse theorists. Plain discussion of socialist ideas, perspectives and politics, accessible to the merely educated, became impossible in these rarifeed circles. What is more, the "Marxism" of some of these theorists has been ripped from its historical outlook and reduced to a conversation, a mere discourse of ideas.[4] In all of this, the working class figured little, if at all, scarcely even as an analytical concept, and not at all as a participant.

While a theoretical and, perhaps, linguistic reckoning with the events, trends, and theories of the twentieth century is badly needed, the purpose of this epilogue is more limited. It is to suggest two things: (1) despite all the layers of new technology, the current period of capitalism is in certain important ways more akin to the conditions of one hundred years ago than of other periods in the twentieth century, only on a far greater world-wide scale; and (2) that the original vision of socialism as a deeply democratic product of working-class struggle and self-organization has a deep resonance with the rise and reshaping of trade unionism and other forms of working-class struggle occurring today.

Capitalism Pure and Simple

Capitalism is not the same today as it was one hundred years ago. Quite aside from the technological wonders and dangers produced during the twentieth century, it would be unimaginable for any social system to go through several decades of turmoil and emerge the same. The modern state is bigger and more universal than in the 1890s; the transnational corporation is a norm of capitalist organization, not an exception; and the sheer scale of production of goods and services is far greater than anyone at the turn of the last century could have imagined. So, parallels with the past need to be approached with caution.

Nevertheless, there are three aspects of today's economic, social, and political world that bear an uncanny resemblance to that of a hundred or so years ago. The first is that no existing social system competes with capitalism for the future. Indeed, to a greater extent than a century ago there are no pre-capitalist societies of any economic significance. Even the last few bastions of "post-capitalist" Communist bureaucratic collectivism vie with one another to imitate the dominant system. There is no other social system to blame, no other systemic target for working-class politics than capitalism.

Second, the system itself operates more nearly in its pure and simple market-driven form than it has for most of the twentieth century. Indeed, with the elimination of colonialism, it is more and more the forces of the market that recreate uneven development on a world scale. The recent decline of American economic domination parallels Britain's crumbling hegemony a century ago – reducing the role of any regulating power. Within the nation, deregulated domestic and international markets create the sort of ruinous competition that ruled a hundred years ago. These trends create a desperate need for working-class organization, above all unions, in more and more parts of the world to defend living and working standards from the market-driven race to the bottom. At the same time, they render older forms of unionism ineffective.

Third, with few exceptions the state and the institutions of capitalist politics have been captured by neoliberal/conservative movements and politicians, meaning that, for now, that state offers no "comfort zone" other than what can be captured or preserved through intense struggle. Furthermore, the objective power of international markets imposes limits on reform projects for those unwilling to break the rules and take risks, which is certainly the vast majority of contemporary professional politicians, left, right, or center. In much of the world, the situation virtually begs for a political alternative.

Similar conditions led to the growth of socialism as a specifically working-class movement throughout what was then called the "advanced," meaning more industrial, capitalist world. Today, these conditions bring forth new labor movements where class formation is new in much of the Third World and force changes in older labor movements long victimized by the very same economic forces. Like the labor movements that arose or changed (as in the transition from craft to general and then industrial unionism) in the past, those fighting for survival or growth today must do so without the protective cloak of the "Keynesian" state. If much of the twentieth century saw the declining independence, or increased state-

dependence, of trade unionism and other forms of working-class organization, today we see the collapse of liberal and social-democratic protections
in the North and the demise of political clientalism in the South. Whatever
organizational gains are made or defended today by the working class are
increasingly torn from a hostile political and economic terrain.

Unions and The Return to "Classic" Capitalism

For most people, trade unions, regardless of their professed politics or
ideology, seem as removed from the idea of socialist revolution, the rule
of the working class, as any institution in society. At best they are, as
Dutch sociologist Jelle Visser put it, "oppositions that never become
governments," at worst they are conservative (racist and sexist) bastions
of some "aristocracy of labor." In either case, they are bureaucratic
organizations with a narrow economic core agenda focused primarily on
their members. They may start out radical, like those in South Korea,
Brazil, and South Africa, but inevitably, one common view tells us, they
become bureaucratic and narrow in focus.

This "common sense" view of unions is widely held on the left as well
as in the academic mainstream. It is rooted in a quintessentially twentieth-
century view resting heavily on the theoretical works of anti-socialist
sociologists such as Robert Michels and Max Weber, elitists like Sidney
and Beatrice Webb, and others who saw rising bureaucracy as the central
and inevitable feature of "modern" society. In one form or another,
Michels' theory of the "Iron Law of Oligarchy" has informed most
twentieth-century analysis of trade unionism. The Webbs, who observed
the phenomenon of bureaucratization even earlier, took this type of
thinking further by endorsing the growth of trade-union bureaucracy as
desirable.[5]

Reinforcing this viewpoint are more recent industrial relations and
sociological studies, theories, and analyses developed during the decades
of state-dependence, party domination, and stable bargaining under conditions of vigorous economic growth. Virtually all this body of description,
analysis, and theory had in common the view that both the increased
bureaucratization of large organizations and the growing state domination
of economic life were inevitable, irreversible, and probably desirable.[6] The
rapid withdrawal of the state from direct economic management in the
past decade argues against the state-domination thesis, while the rise of
democratic unions in the more industrial countries of the South and the
partial reversal of bureaucratization in the US Mine Workers in the 1970s,

the Teamsters in the 1990s, and, to a lesser extent, other unions in the US brings Michels' "Iron Law of Oligarchy" into question.

Much of this literature focuses on the institutional arrangements of collective bargaining or internal union structures. Such arrangements and structures typically outlast and, therefore, conceal deeper changes in consciousness, militancy, and political conflict among the different layers of union membership and hierarchy. They also conceal changes in relations between capital and labor, unions and the state. Even mass strike movements or successful oppositional movements do not necessarily undo such arrangements and structures in the short run. Much of the debate over such changes that are recognized in current studies is often cast in formalistic terms, such as the European industrial-relations debate over whether unions are experiencing institutional "convergence" or "divergence" under conditions of European economic integration.[7]

The mainstream sociological and industrial-relations institutional interpretations of unions are basically static. Unions are complex organisms with different social layers affected by a myriad of changing conditions – including, often, intra-union conflict. Equally important, capital and the state have clearly abandoned the era in which unions were not only tolerated, but accorded some measure of institutional legitimacy – a fact that reinforced bureaucratic internal life. They have opted for "classic" capitalism, in which the workers and their organizations must increasingly fend for themselves against hostile employers and governments.

Along with the continued formal existence of yesterday's institutional arrangements, the language of "social partnership" and labor–management cooperation has tended to obscure the real alterations in daily practice – the sometimes piecemeal, sometimes wholesale attacks on all the conditions of working-class life. Beneath the "talk," however, the reality of the social relations of production is progressing to a state similar to that of one hundred years ago. Indeed, it is worse than a hundred years ago in some respects, because at that time working-class living standards were rising across much of the industrial world, while they are now declining. State regulation of economic activity was advancing; now it is receding. Despite desperate attempts by labor leaders to hold on to or regain an anchorage in the state or in partnership with a single employer, the reality has been irreversibly altered to one of increasingly open hostility and conflict.

The False Dichotomy of the "Economic" and the "Political"

For Marx and most other socialist theorists and leaders in the late nineteenth century, the working class was seen as the agent of social transformation because of its critical place in production and the fact that it composed a majority, at least in the developed capitalist countries. None of them imagined that the working class was suited to this historic task because of its "political correctness" at any given time or because workers were, as a class, morally superior to other people. There were, however, two presumptions about this social class: (1) its conditions gave it a more collective/democratic outlook than society's other classes; and (2) the struggles that it was drawn into by virtue of its conditions had a transforming effect on the people who composed this class.

The latter proposition has been brought into question in the twentieth century. A good deal of socialist thought over the last ninety years has drawn an indelible line between economic and political struggle. The undeniable proposition that not all basic struggles lead to political class conflict or socialist consciousness has become fetishized into a dismissal of the more fundamental forms of working-class struggle as "economic" dead ends. Instead, it has been argued again and again, workers should be drawn into "political" struggles, which, it is claimed, will create the kind of broader consciousness on which the fight for fundamental social change can be built. Political action is placed above and counterposed to the basic fight to preserve or improve living and working conditions through direct conflict with the employers. The choice of just what is sufficiently "political" to properly transform consciousness is invariably pre-empted by some self-appointed group.

This view is probably based on the fact that in capitalist society there is a real separation of the "economic" and the "political" in one sense. The capitalist class derives its power from its ownership and control of the means of production – from the economic realm, not from the state. As was argued earlier, the state – the political realm – arises from the needs of capital to mediate conflict and regulate property rules. The state protects the property from which capital's power emanates, but it is not the ultimate source of that power. For this reason working-class parties, say the British Labour Party, can form a government, but as long as they don't fundamentally challenge capital's ownership and control of production, they don't affect its power. In this sense, capitalism is different from most of the societies that preceded it, such as feudalism, where economic and political power were fused.

When speaking of the dynamics of class struggle and the development of class consciousness or socialist politics, however, there are at least three problems with the dualistic counterposition of the "economic" and the "political." The first is that the "political" side of working-class struggle and organization or that of the left has not in any way solved the problem of conservative or non-socialist consciousness. If anything, it has proved even more catastrophic and conservatizing than the "economic." Across the world, the traditional mass parties of the working class and the political left are more conservative than ever – more removed from the ideas of socialism and from their working-class base. They are, if anything, more bureaucratized and "professionalized" than the unions. Their political-ness has not saved them from this fate; much less has it improved the consciousness of the working class.

The organizations of the revolutionary socialist left, which might more rightfully lay claim to the kinds of political ideas that embody full-fledged socialist consciousness, are smaller and more fragmented than ever. The intensely (and frequently narrow) theoretical political-ness of many such groups tends to isolate them from the vast majority of working-class people. Ironically, their members do their best work and gain the greatest following when they engage in the merely "economic" struggles of the day, even if their theory often disparages such activity. Clearly, politics has not proved a remedy to uneven or conservative consciousness any more than wage or workplace struggles.

The second objection to the dualization of working-class experience and activity into the "economic" and the "political" is that it leaves out a vast and crucial area of life and activity, namely the "social." All the matters of social reproduction, the family, gender, race, nationality, language, and culture fall between the cracks of the economic–political duality. If any-thing should have been learned in the twentieth century it is that these aspects of working class social life, organization, and self-activity are as critical to the consciousness of the class as either the "economic," in the narrow sense in which that is usually used, or the "political" as that is typically expressed. As this book has argued, the working class is necess-arily a changing social mosaic, not an undifferentiated "economic" mass. Both economic and political trends and events impact different sectors of the working class in different ways and to different degrees. A working-class politics or a trade unionism that ignores or downplays these aspects of life will not go much farther than one that attempts to leap over the merely "economic" to engage in "politics."

The third problem with the method of counterposing economic and political struggle, as the second implies, is that there is no such dichotomy in real life. To be sure, in "normal" times trade unions conduct limited struggles for limited goals, while political parties present a broader agenda, including social issues. Union "politics" in such times are typically narrow pressure politics exercised through allied parties. But we have left the norms of the mid-twentieth century well behind and find ourselves confronted with all the grinding problems described in this book and many more, such as the endangered ecology of earth.

In today's world, political parties retreat from broad social agendas, while unions are cast in the role of political actors. In many places there are other working-class organizations that fall between or overlap such categories – workers' centers in North America, unemployed workers' organizations in Europe, urban popular movements in Latin America, the Civics in South Africa, and social movements of women and other oppressed groups almost everywhere. Real working-class people are compelled to move from simple defensive struggles over working conditions, jobs, incomes, or social issues to political confrontations great and small from Decatur, Illinois, to Seoul, South Korea. Indeed, the whole concept of social-movement unionism defies any simple split of working-class life into the "economic" and the "political."

Some of the best studies of social upheaval and political unrest in the "from-below" tradition reveal a constant interaction between fights for basic needs and those for loftier goals. George Rude's classic *The Crowd in the French Revolution* showed how bread marches and riots by the Parisian *sans-culotte* masses flowed into the fights for democratic rights, insurrection against the monarchy, and even massive upheaval against the new democratic regime of the bourgeoisie.[8] Rosa Luxemburg in *The Mass Strike, the Political Party, and the Trade Unions* traced the mass revolutionary strikes of 1905 in Russia to a string of mostly wages and hours strikes going back to 1896.[9]

The interaction can run in more than one direction and feed a variety of social struggles. In *Workers' Control in America* David Montgomery shows how trade unionists in the United States in the years before World War One made use of the Socialist Party to further their union goals in opposition to the employers' open-shop drive.[10] More recently, Robin D. G. Kelley has written in *Hammer and Hoe* and *Race Rebels* of how African-American workers made use of the Communist Party in the 1930s to organize around trade-union, social, and race issues.[11] In both these cases, workers were drawn to socialist ideas and organizations by economic or social struggle and then used the political organization to advance these more basic struggles. These workers saw no contradiction in moving between building socialist organization and social struggle. Indeed, their radical consciousness could only be explained by the interaction of both.

Today, once again, this old story of basic "economic" struggle leading to bigger social and political confrontations is being retold from France to Canada to South Korea. As in the case of the 1905 mass political strikes in Russia described over ninety years ago by Luxemburg, those of the last couple of years are rooted in scores of basic struggles over jobs, hours, conditions, social programs, and wages in the last several years. Trade-union issues are transformed into political issues not because of any formula devised by the left, but by events initiated largely by capital or its governments. Indeed, such mass strike movements as those in 1905 Russia or in 1968 France only take on their "political" character at the very last minute.

The mass strikes of 1994–97 were not revolutionary in character. This isn't simply because the workers involved didn't see them that way, although that is important. Among other reasons it is because the events involved were far from demanding a decisive solution. Compromise, on the one hand, and intransigence, on the other, are still options for the state or the employers involved, as well as for the workers. Where labor is more forceful, compromise is more likely, as was the case in South Korea and France. Where union action is limited to a day or two or largely symbolic, as in Canada or much of Latin America, intransigence by the state still works. While strikes against large individual firms occur in a more limited economic atmosphere, they seldom challenge the viability of the company, despite protests to that effect from the employer. Showdowns are not yet in the offing in most cases, but the interacting dynamics between struggles over living and working conditions, on the one hand, and political confrontations, on the other, are once again in operation.

In part, this interaction of basic "economic" issues and "politics" is inherent in the re-emergence of the more classic forms of capitalist market regulation. The link between international competitive forces and neo-liberal state policy has tightened as market forces gain strength. While there are aspects of both economic compulsion and ideological choice involved in the current politics of social austerity, it is clear that the forces of capitalist competition play an independent role in the direction of state policy to the degree they are "liberated" from state regulation. The "Berlin Wall" between the "economic" and the "political" that was thought to exist during the era of Keynesian state regulation, when, paradoxically, the relationship of state to economy was more direct, has been brought down by the return of the "classic" capitalist emphasis on market regulation.

It might seem ironic that the state should become a more obvious target of trade-union action precisely as it attempts to remove itself from positive economic intervention except for the fact that it now takes on the task of negative economic and social regulation. Redistributing income upward, crowding labor markets to depress wages (called "welfare reform" in the US), limiting the legal parameters of "normal" trade union activity, and victimizing immigrant and minority populations are, after all, simply other forms of state regulation. That these bring forth opposition from working-class organizations is hardly remarkable.

Preparing for Power

There is another side to the relationship between day-to-day struggle or trade-union organization and broader political or socialist consciousness. The ups and downs of trade-union organization and conflict, along with other kinds of social struggle, are an important part of the history and development of any working class. In times and places where there is no mass socialist movement, these rudimentary forms of struggle are among those that shape the thought of the most active and organized elements of the working class. There is no guarantee that the experience of trade-union struggle will produce socialist ideas, much less organizations. Routine collective bargaining by bureaucratic unions in "normal" times is not likely to lead to more than routine politics. Furthermore, as US history shows over and over, spectacular gains in trade-union organization can be derailed or stultified by the racial and gender divisions within the class as well as by epochal economic or industrial changes. But in times of capitalist crisis and aggression against the conditions of working-class life, when routine collective bargaining cannot be sustained without intensified struggle, if at all, trade-union struggle can open the door to socialist ideas.

Friedrich Engels, along with Marx a pioneer of modern socialism, noted how trade union struggle helps prepare workers for greater political goals. He wrote of the early unions in Britain:

> The active resistance of the English workingmen has its effect in holding the money-greed of the bourgeoisie (capitalist class) within certain limits, and keeping alive the opposition of the workers to the social and political omnipotence of the bourgeois, while it compels the admission that something more is needed than Trade Unions and strikes to break the power of the ruling class. But what gives these Unions and the strikes arising from them their real importance is this, that they are the first attempt of the workers to abolish competition.[12]

Capitalism thrives on competition; unions exist to limit one aspect of this competition, that among workers. Even so conservative an economist as the American John R. Commons recognized a half-century after Engels that unions must "take wages out of competition" in order to advance or even maintain a certain standard of living.[13] While Commons saw this as the basis of a particularly conservative type of craft unionism, Engels saw it as a step toward the creation of a socialist movement or even a piece of socialism imposed on an unwilling capitalist class by democratic workers' organizations. Engels was clear that, by themselves, unions cannot "break the power of the ruling class" and bring about socialism, but he was optimistic that through trade-union struggle workers could "prepare themselves for the great struggle which cannot be avoided."[14]

A century of hindsight warns us to be skeptical about a final conflict that "cannot be avoided," for it has been avoided again and again. Indeed, the fact that Commons and Engels, the social conservative and the social revolutionary, could see the opposite significance in the same phenomenon indicates that we are talking about possibilities, not inevitabilities. With this understanding, however, it is worth pursuing the view of unions and basic class struggle in the formation of socialist consciousness and organization developed by Marx, Engels, and others since.

Marx and Engels were among the first socialists in the nineteenth century to see trade unions as an important and positive development in working-class organization. They saw trade-union struggles as a "military school" for the workers and, more prosaically, a training ground in which they made themselves "fit for administrative and political work." They spoke again and again of unions and basic forms of struggle as a means for "preparation" for greater struggles in the course of which "'subjects' come of age." That is, in these struggles an understanding of the social conflict taking place deepens and the role of organized workers in shaping social and political events becomes clearer to the workers themselves. The sense of what is possible expands and the belief that "ordinary" working people can direct production and even rule politically grows.[15]

In our time, the example of Brazil provides an almost classic scenario of class formation begetting a mass trade-union movement, which through struggle becomes the center of a broader class movement, and then the basis for a socialist party, the Workers' Party (Partido dos Trabalhadores – PT). All this development, training, and learning took place in a compressed period of time, from the late 1970s up to the near electoral victory of 1989, by which time the PT had become large enough nearly to win the national election. Since that time, to be sure, other equally "classic" trends have set in as the PT has developed a self-conscious social-democratic wing and moderated some of its early radicalism. Yet, as a party of the working class it remains unparalleled in its attempt to extend workers' power and its attachment to a democratic vision of socialism. So far, of course, it is one of the few such examples.

In general, the left in the twentieth century has tended to blame the failure of the potential of basic social and economic struggle to produce socialist consciousness or organization on either the economic–political dichotomy, leadership betrayals, or the "incorrectness" of one or another party's positions or type of organization. Without denying the validity of some of these criticisms or the shallowness of others, there is another side to this failure of socialist organization and consciousness to develop out of basic struggle in the late twentieth century that is of more immediate importance.

The Fight for Social-Movement Unionism

While the level of trade-union and basic social struggle appears on the rise across most of the world, in the more developed nations it is forced to express itself through trade-union structures and ideologies inherited from the epoch of relative stability and economic growth. There are, as this book has tried to show, many other forms of working-class social struggle and organization. Yet, in their size and critical location in production, the unions remain the central organized expression of day-to-day class conflict. In small defensive fights the unions often fall back on "community" support, but in the great confrontations it is typically the unions that pull the other organizations into the struggle. Attempts to leap over them to the "political" or to by-pass them through the "community" are recipes for marginalization. Even where the unions only have a small membership, as in France or Spain, their ability to mobilize broader sections of the class is greater than that of any other type of working-class or social-movement organization.

As relics of another era, however, today's unions are in most cases poorly suited to be military, administrative, or political "schools" for workers, as Engels proposed. With some exceptions, they remain the bureaucratic institutions formerly shaped for routine collective bargaining and corporatist politics. Furthermore, they are retreating from the little patch of socialism they once imposed on capital as they allow bargaining to fragment and even enter into competitive "partnerships" with the enemy. Confrontation one day turns to partnership the next. Strikes are waged to hold the line, but "competitiveness" is sought to save jobs. Thus, both organizationally and ideologically, most unions in most industrial nations are poorly suited to advance class consciousness or even pursue decisive struggles.

The process that Marx, Engels, Murphy, and others have pointed to, however, does occur. In Canada, for example, where the labor movement is a mixture of conventional business unions and more democratic "movement unions," as the Canadian Auto Workers sometimes call themselves, the Ontario Days of Action, one-day strikes followed by mass demonstrations, had just such an affect. Sam Gindin of the CAW explains how:

The Days of Action were about building an opposition and changing the mood, and therefore the range of options, in Ontario. They revived the flagging hopes of some, deepened the commitment of others, and brought new people into politics. They led to new links across union-coalition lines, developed new organizational skills, and exposed weaknesses we'd later have to address. They increased economic and political literacy and developed a conscious need to continually educate ourselves about capitalism. They made serious inroads into the hegemony of right-wing ideas. They created that intangible space and collective self-confidence that set the stage for future struggles, big and small, over jobs, collective bargaining, municipal democracy, and rights of citizenship.[16]

Even where there has been no central mass actions like the Ontario Days of Action, increasingly bitter strikes, lock-outs, and other forms of conflict provide more partial opportunities for such advancement of the movement. Class resentment, if not full-blown consciousness, is increasing and with it a greater awareness. Certainly, the awareness that capital is acting like a class and attacking labor across the board is wide-spread. Rudimentary class consciousness is on the rise in many places, driven by the struggles, even where these are curbed by the organizational and ideological limits of the unions. Sometimes the struggle pushes against the limits of the formal union boundaries, as with the rank-and-file "assemblies" that conducted the French strikes of 1995 on a daily basis. Sometimes, a local union or a union section takes the lead in initiating a strike that the national union wished hadn't happened, as in the US. Sometimes, it involves the formation of new unions, as in France, South Korea, and many other parts of the economic South. At other times, it means new types of organization that exist on the edges of the trade-union movement, like workers' centers in North America. All represent advances in organization and consciousness.

It also means the intensification of debate and political conflict within the unions in order to expand their ability to mobilize and struggle. The rise of internal, rank-and-file-based opposition movements and organizations in unions in North America and Europe was noted in chapter 7 and elsewhere in this book. Such debate and conflict are necessary to make the unions more fit for conflict and are themselves a political training ground. Such struggles within the unions play a role in the formation of a new leadership for a new period, particularly where the issues raised by opposition forces point toward a more militant, democratic, and socially minded unionism. This is by no means always a simple process of replacing old leaders with new: it is most effective where union politics flow from or interact with struggles against the employer; it is weakest where it is a mere electoral challenge by new leaders or some coalition of the old and the new.

Insofar as this kind of conflict focuses on real issues and a democratic, class-based conception of unionism, it helps to broaden consciousness. Rank-and-file-based organization, with its own discussions and strategic debates, is the key to maximizing the potential of internal union conflict. Where the union itself is highly bureaucratic and the membership excluded from participation in its actual internal affairs, the rank-and-file organization becomes the "school" Engels spoke of. When these sorts of rank-and-file-based movements connect across union lines, as in the networks described earlier around various publications like *Labor Notes* or organizations like TIE, a new and broader consciousness can spread more rapidly.

In general, periods of dramatic social and political change, whether revolutionary or limited to major reforms, are characterized by the spread of popular organizations: the clubs and societies of revolutionary Paris from 1789 through 1794; the workers' councils of 1905 and 1917 in Russia; similar worker-based councils of 1956 in Hungary; trade unions in the US of the 1930s, and civil-rights, students', and women's organizations of the 1960s; and countless other examples. Periods of conservative reaction, on the other hand, are typified by the decline, exhaustion, or suppression of organization among the working classes and oppressed peoples. Clearly, we have been through an intensely conservative period, in which the old organizations of the working class and those of the social movements of the 1960s suffered setbacks or long-term decline across much of the industrial world.

At the same time, unionism and other forms of working-class organization have arisen in resistance to the austerity of the period in places where unions were weak or non-existent before, particularly in the economic South. By now, the level of active working-class organization on a world scale is greater than when the conservative ascendancy set in a quarter of a century ago. Now the weakened labor movements of the North have joined the newer unions of the South in resistance. At least, the possibility and certainly the idea of growth have returned to many unions across the North, in part as a result of internal conflict. There is the potential for the balance of forces to shift once again, this time in favor of the working class.

If intensified struggle opens minds and organization provides a "school" for honing skills, understanding society, and even "preparing for power," then the potential for going beyond what is currently on offer politically is inherent in the new global situation. There is, of course, nothing inevitable about the return of socialist ideas, much less organizations. Yet, the alternatives currently put forth by progressives and social democrats of all kinds, stakeholder capitalism, civil society/Third Sector counterforce, etc., do not offer much material solace to the world's majority. This majority cries out for something with more meat on its bones, something that capitalism has been increasingly less willing or able to deliver on a world scale for some time.

This means, as Gindin argues in the context of the debate in Canada's labor movement, real alternatives lie in the confrontation of capital by an increasingly mobilized and organized working class. Writing in early 1997, Gindin says:

> The real issue of "alternatives" isn't about alternative policies or alternative governments, but about an alternative *politics*. Neither well-meaning policies nor sympathetic governments can fundamentally alter our lives unless they are part of a fundamental challenge to capital. That is, making alternatives possible requires a movement that is changing political culture (the assumptions we bring to how society should work), bringing more people into every-day struggles (collective engagement in shaping our lives), and deepening the understanding and organizational skills of activists along with their commitment to radical change (developing socialists).[17]

If the analysis of this book, that lean production and market regulation are far from being the antidote to and are, indeed, the cause of increasing uneven development and the race to the bottom for the world's working-class majority, is right, then the active forces seeking change will look for alternatives. If a convincing, democratic version of socialism as the rule of the working class can be put forth in the context of the real struggles and organizations of the working class, it has a chance to take on a material force it has lacked for decades.

Perhaps to a greater extent than in most of the twentieth century, the opportunity for this idea and movement to spread globally is also more inherent in today's capitalist world than at any time in the past seventy years. It is not simply that the process of capitalist globalization has pushed more and more people into resistance; it has also knit them together in new ways – through dense webs of capitalist ownership (TNCs), extended cross-border production chains, multinational free-trade or single-market regions, new and wide-spread forms of accessible communications, etc. These new transnational ties point not only to new international trade-union strategies, but to the old notion of an international working class, which was also a foundation of the original socialist project.

If capitalism is now more global than ever, so too is the working class it begets. Indeed, class formation is now in many ways an international, if not really global, process. The division of labor in the production of the world's wealth is more truly international than at any time. To put it one way, it is not simply that the makers of a single automobile are found in many countries, but that the making of this car requires the increased input of workers in telecommunications, transportation, and countless "services" in many countries. All these workers are drawn more intimately into the production process than in the past. The resulting division of labor is more geographically encompassing than in the rest of this century or probably at any time.

Even within most nations, the world-wide class that is still forming also crosses borders with greater regularity, is more ethnically diverse, and international in nature. If all these trends have thrown old working-class organizations and modes of thought off balance, as with the rise of racism in so many countries, it also lays the basis for far-reaching lines of communication that did not exist to the same extent for much of this century. Both in the international division of labor and in the geographic movements of working people, a transnational working class has arisen and spread.

The material substance of working-class internationalism is at hand. Like the idea of socialism to which it is linked, however, it needs to be consciously organized. National chauvinism, racism, and sexism do not go away automatically, any more than the hope that the ruling class will bend to pressure and do the right thing. Indeed, to one degree or another, these are the "default" positions of most people at most times – often unspoken views that have gone unchallenged in more "normal" times or been reinforced in conservatives times. Intense social struggle can shake such ideas loose and open minds to new ones. The greater the forces that are drawn into the struggle, the more alternatives begin to appear as possibilities.

One significant aspect of social-movement unionism is that it builds or allies with broader forces and challenges old ideas – opening doors to new possibilities. It can help to undermine an existing conservative balance of power, as it has begun to in South Africa, Brazil, South Korea, and elsewhere. It can make the very concept of class more real, as it is in more and more countries. In extending working-class power and increasing class consciousness social-movement unionism prefigures a deeper socialist politics. Another aspect is that this conception of unionism has grown out of the new material circumstances imposed by capitalist globalization: it is the child of this process. It is not an idea or strategy that originated in some circle of intellectuals, but one that arose from real working-class experience.

The direction of this brand of unionism confronts many of the "default" ways of interpreting the world. Crafted by experience in the whirlwinds of international economic integration and intensified capitalist competition, social-movement unionism can serve as today's national platforms from which to launch the international labor movement of tomorrow. The embryos of this international movement exist in the networks increasingly criss-crossing borders in search of practical solidarity. Such activity strongly challenges old ideas about who are our friends and who are our enemies. The clearer vision of the realities of world-wide class conflict is often carried by the newer leaders and arising oppositions within the various labor movements that are still rooted in the old balance of forces and the fiction of "partnership."

The socialist movement of the future, if it is to be, will be shaped in these fights for a more effective way to challenge capital at home and abroad, as well as in the major confrontations between labor and capital. Those who are simply looking for a better life would do well to look to a renewed socialist movement for hope. Those who already seek a socialist future need, in turn, to look to those fighting for a better life, no matter how basic that fight might seem.

Notes

Introduction

1. Gerard Greenfield, "Global Business Unionism," *Asian Labour Update* 22, August–October 1996, p. 3.
2. Jeremy Brecher and Tim Costello, *Global Village or Global Pillage: Economic Reconstruction From the Bottom Up*, Boston, South End Press, 1994, pp. 173–184.
3. United Nations Conference on Trade and Development (UNCTAD), *World Investment Report 1996*, New York, United Nations, 1996, p. xiv; World Bank, *World Development Report 1996*, Washington, World Bank, 1996, pp. 210–213.
4. UNCTAD, 1996, pp. 3, 6, 10.
5. James Petras, "Alternatives to Neoliberalism in Latin America," *Latin American Perspectives* 24(1), January 1997, p. 81.

1 World-Class Working Class

1. E-mail transmissions from "Arm The Spirit" through January 1997; and LabourNet (UK), January 24, 1997.
2. United Auto Workers, *Solidarity*, December 1996, p. 5.
3. Former United Auto Workers' President Doug Fraser, "Statement Upon Resignation from the Labor–Management Group, July 19, 1978," in Kim Moody, *Political Directions for Labor*, Detroit, Labor Education & Research Project, 1979, p. 29.
4. This account is taken from *Labor Notes* 215, January 1997; and from e-mail transmissions from "Arm The Spirit" through January 1997.
5. *Business Week*, January 27, 1997, pp. 44–48; e-mail from "Arm The Spirit" through January 1997.
6. "Arm the Spirit," January 1997.
7. *Washington Post*, January 25, 1997; Institute for Global Communications, "labornews," February 8, 1997.
8. *New York Times*, February 6, 1997; Institute for Global Communications, "labornews," February 8, 1997.
9. Steve Jeffreys, "France 1995: The Backward March of Labour Halted?" *Capital & Class* 59, Summer 1996, pp. 7–8.
10. Jeffreys, pp. 15–16.
11. Daniel Bensaïd, "Neo-Liberal Reform and Popular Rebellion," *New Left Review* 215, January/February 1996, p. 112.
12. Bensaïd, pp. 109–110.
13. Dominique Mezzi, "Trade Union Recomposition," *International Viewpoint* 277, May 1996, pp. 23–26.

14. Interview with SUD officials, Paris, August 1996; Mezzi, 1996, pp. 23–26.

15. Christian Picquet, "Communist Shell Breaks," *International Viewpoint* 277, May 1996, pp. 27–28.

16. Kevin P. Q. Phelan, "Out of Africa: Immigrants Spark French Movement," *Third Force*: 4(6), January/February 1997, p. 26; interview with officials of SUD, Paris, August, 1996.

17. *Guardian*, November 30, 1996.

18. Interviews with SUD union officials and other union activists in Paris, August 1996; *Guardian*, November 26, 1996, November 28, 1996, November 30, 1996; Dominique Mezzi, "A Private Sector Strike for Dignity," *International Viewpoint* 284, January 1997, pp. 21–22; *Business Week*, June 16, 1997, p. 49.

19. *Guardian*, December 14, 1996, p. 8; *Business Week*, June 16, 1997, pp. 49–50.

20. Interviews and discussions with members of the Canadian Auto Workers, November 1996–January 1997.

21. *Labor Notes* 202, January 1996; speech by David Robertson of the Canadian Auto Workers to the New Directions Conference, Detroit, November 1996.

22. Interviews with members of the Canadian Auto Workers, November 1996, January 1997.

23. Jeffreys, pp. 9–11; Canadian Auto Workers, *Contact* 26(40), December 8, 1996.

24. For strikes not already documented see: James Petras, "Alternatives to Neoliberalism in Latin America," *Latin American Perspectives* 24(1), January 1997, p. 81; *Foreign Labor Trends* 96–4, p. 3; Comissio Nacional de Catalunya, *Lluita Obrera* 130, December 1996, pp. 8–9; Jeremy Seabrook, *In the Cities of the South: Scenes from a Developing World*, London, Verso, 1996, p. 94; *Justice Speaks* 13(10), June 1996; AFL–CIO, *Work in Progress*, Washington, June 18, 1996, p. 3; SoliNet, December 3, 1996; Institute for Global Communications, "labornews," February 3, 1997, February 6, 1997, February 8, 1997, February 23, 1997; *New Life*, January/February 1997; communications from TIE-Brazil and CGT Argentina.

25. Patrick Bond, "Neoliberalism Comes to South Africa," *Multinational Monitor*, May 1996, pp. 8–14.

26. Presentations at the July 1996 Conference of Social Economists, Newcastle, UK; interviews with trade unionists in December 1996, London, UK.

27. Kim Moody, *An Injury to All: The Decline of American Unionism*, London, Verso, 1988, pp. 165–182; Seth Rosen, "A Union Perspective," in Jean T. McKelvey, ed., *Cleared for Takeoff: Airline Labor Relations Since Deregulation*, Ithaca, NY, ILR Press, 1988, pp. 15–16.

28. *Business Week*, July 11, 1994, pp. 116–117.

29. Marc Cooper, "The Heartland's Raw Deal: How Meatpacking is Creating a New Immigrant Underclass," *The Nation* 264(4), February 3, 1997, pp. 11–17.

30. Moody, pp. 179–182.

31. This account is taken from interviews with and presentations by Jerry Tucker, Staley, and Caterpillar workers from 1993 through 1996; *Labor Notes*, 1993–1996; *Impact: The Rank & File Newsletter* 4(10), January 1997.

32. *Labor Notes* 187, October 1994; 203, February 1996.

33. This account is based on discussions with and presentations by Jerry Tucker and several Staley activists over the duration of the struggle, 1993–1996.

34. *Labor Notes* 214, January 1997.

35. *Labor Notes* 199, October 1996.

36. *Labor Notes* 214, January 1997.

37. National Public Radio, "Morning Edition," February 12, 1997; interviews with strikers, Detroit, February 1996; AFL–CIO letter announcing June march on Detroit, February 1997.

38. Interview with Leonard Grbinik, Recording Secretary, USWA Local 1375, February 1996; USWA Local 1375, *Warren Steelworker* 2(4), December 1995.

39. *Labor Notes* 202, January 1996.

40. Kim Moody and Simone Sagovac, *Time Out: The Case for a Shorter Work Week*, Detroit, Labor Notes, 1995, pp. 5–6.

41. *Labor Notes* 206, May 1996.

42. *Labor Notes* 206, May 1996.

43. *Labor Notes* 206, May 1996; Institute for Global Communications, "labornews," January–February 1997.

44. *Journal of Commerce*, February 12, 1997.

45. Verbal and video presentation by SEIU organizer at New Directions Solidarity School, Sequoia Seminar Center, California, February 1997.

46. This account is based on my own experience in Labor Party Advocates and attendance at the June 1996 Labor Party Convention, as well as many discussions with LPA and LP leaders and activists.

47. *New Party News* issues for 1995 through January 1997.

48. *Newsweek*, June 19, 1995, p. 14.

49. Marc Cooper, "Harley-Riding, Picket-Walking Socialism Haunts Decatur," *The Nation*, April 8, 1996, p. 23.

50. Brian Deer, "Still Struggling after all these Days," *New Statesman*, August 23, 1996, pp. 12–14.

51. Dan Gallin, "Inside the New World Order: Drawing the Battle Lines," *New Politics* 5(1), summer 1994, p. 123.

52. Quote from Tom Laney, UAW Local 879, UAW New Directions, 1992.

2 A Certain Kind of Globalization

1. *Economic Notes* 65(1), January 1997; International Labour Office (ILO), *World Employment Report 1995*, Geneva, ILO, 1995, p. 1.

2. Richard Barnet and John Cavanaugh, *Global Dreams: Imperial Corporations and the New World Order*, Simon & Schuster, New York, 1994, p. 296; ILO, 1995, p. 1.

3. Gordon Clark and Won Bae Kim, *Asian NIEs and the Global Economy*, Baltimore, Johns Hopkins University Press, 1995, *passim; Financial Times*, November 14, 1996.

4. United Nations Development Programme (UNDP), *Human Development Report 1996*, United Nations, New York, 1996, p. 13.

5. World Bank, *World Development Report 1996*, Washington, Oxford University Press, 1996, pp. 2, 188–189, 210–211.

6. UNCTAD, *World Investment Report 1995*, New York, United Nations, 1995, p. xx.

7. UNCTAD, *World Investment Report 1994*, New York, United Nations, 1994, pp. 24, 34.

8. Peter Dicken, *Global Shift: The Internationalization of Economic Activity*, second edition, London, Paul Chapman Publishing, 1992, pp. 1, 45.

9. World Bank, *World Development Report 1996*, New York, Oxford University Press, 1996, p. 1.

10. Karl Marx, *Manifesto of the Communist Party*, London, Lawrence & Wishart, 1943, p. 13.

11. Anwar Shaikh, "Political Economy and Capitalism: Notes on Dobb's Theory of Crisis," *Cambridge Journal of Economics* 1978: 2, p. 234.

12. Howard Botwinick, *Persistent Inequalities: Wage Disparity Under Capitalist Competition*, Princeton, Princeton University Press, 1993, p. 129.

13. For a more detailed and technical account of this contradiction in capitalist accumulation see Botwinick, pp. 77–80.

14. Angus Maddison, *Monitoring the World Economy 1820–1992*, Paris, Organization for Economic Cooperation and Development (OECD), 1995, p. 61.

15. V. I. Lenin, *Imperialism: The Highest Stage of Capitalism*, New York, International

Publishers, 1939, pp. 62–67; Anthony Brewer, *Marxist Theories of Imperialism: A Critical Survey*, 2nd edn, London, Routledge, pp. 73–87, 109–135.

16. Maddison, pp. 37–38.

17. World Bank, 1996, pp. 210–211, 216–217.

18. United Nations Conference on Trade and Development, *TNCs and World Development*, London, International Thomson Business Press, 1996, p. 4; United Nations, 1994, p. 20; Maddison, p. 227.

19. Eric Hobsbawm, *The Age of Extremes: A History of the World, 1914–1991*, New York, Vintage Books, 1994, pp. 55–141; A. G. Kenwood and A. L. Lougheed, *The Growth of the International Economy 1820–1990*, London, Routledge, 1992, pp. 163–231.

20. Maddison, pp. 227, 239.

21. Dicken, p. 53; UNCTAD, *World Investment Report 1995: TNCs and Competitiveness*, Geneva, United Nations, 1995, p. 4.

22. Dicken, p. 18

23. Dicken, pp. 18, 58.

24. UNCTAD, 1994, pp. 3–5; UNCTAD, 1995, pp. 3–4.

25. UNCTAD, 1995, p. 192–197; Dicken, p. 49.

26. UNCTAD, 1995, p. 39.

27. UNCTAD, 1993, p. 1; UNCTAD, 1995, p. xx.

28. UNCTAD, *World Investment Report 1996*, New York, United Nations, 1996, pp. 450–454.

29. Speaker at University of Iowa Conference on Globalization, Ames, Iowa, March, 1993.

30. Maddison, p. 74.

31. Dicken, pp. 51–54; DeAnne Julius, *Global Companies and Public Policy: The Growing Challenge of Foreign Direct Investment*, London, Pinter Publishers, 1990, p. 14.

32. UNCTAD, 1996, p. 3.

3 North–South Divide: Uneven Development

1. Dicken, p. 53.

2. World Bank, 1995, p. 4.

3. UNDP, 1996, p. 48.

4. Maddison, p. 22; World Bank, *World Development Report 1995*, Washington, World Bank, 1995, p. 54.

5. United Nations Development Programme, *Human Development Report 1994*, New York, United Nations, 1994, p. 143; Maddison, p. 22.

6. UNDP, 1996, p. 13.

7. World Bank, *World Development Report 1989*, Washington, World Bank, 1989, pp. 174–175. This was the last year the *WDR* (*World Development Report*) included total figures on world manufacturing value added. United Nations Industrial Development Organization (UNIDO), 1993–94, pp. 4, 22.

8. UNIDO, 1993–94, pp. 4, 22.

9. Julius, p. 22; Council of Economic Advisors, *Economic Report of the President 1991*, US Government Printing Office, Washington, 1991, p. 96; UNCTAD, 1995, p. 14.

10. UNCTAD, 1994, p. 27; UNCTAD, 1995, p. 391; UNCTAD, 1996, p. 4.

11. See, for example, Maddison's list of top global investor nations in 1914, or Lenin's in 1910, compared with that of the United Nations through 1994. Lenin, 1939, pp. 60–61; Madison, p. 63; UNCTAD, 1995, pp. 407–410.

12. UNCTAD, 1994, p. 16; UNCTAD, 1995, pp. 391–396; World Bank, 1995, pp. 166–167, 178–179.

13. Roberto Korzeniewicz and William Martin, "The Global Distribution of

Commodity Chains," in Gary Gereffi and Miguel Korzeniewicz, eds, *Commodity Chains and Global Capitalism*, Westport, CT, Praeger, 1994, p. 73.

14. Maddison, p. 36.

15. Maddison, p. 36.

16. UNIDO, *Industry and Development: Global Report 1993–94*, Vienna, United Nations, 1993, p. 277, 285.

17. UNCTAD, 1994, p. 16; World Bank, 1996, pp. 210–213.

18 *Business Week*, June 9, 1997, p. 70.

19. Saskia Sassen, *The Global City: New York, London, and Tokyo*, Princeton, Princeton University Press, 1991, pp. 20–34.

20. Sassen, p. 19.

21. UNCTAD, 1993, pp. 82–83

22. UNCTAD, 1996, p. 25.

23. Sassen, pp. 62–63.

24. Joseph Grunwald, "Opportunity Missed: Mexico and Maquiladoras," *Brookings Review* 9(1), Winter, 1990–91, pp. 44–48.

25. Stephen Thomsen and Stephen Woolcock, *Direct Investment and European Integration: Competition among Firms and Governments*, Pinter Publishers, London, 1993, pp. 102–103.

26. Eileen Rabach and Eun Mee Kim, "Where is the Chain in Commodity Chains? The Service Sector Nexus," in Gereffi and Korzeniewicz, p. 127.

27. One discussion of this is David Barkin, *Distorted Development: Mexico in the World Economy*, San Francisco, Westview Press, 1990, pp. 57–97; Doug Henwood, "The Free Flow of Money," *NACLA Report on the Americas* 29(4), January/February 1996, pp. 11–17.

28. World Bank, 1996, p. 221; Henwood, pp. 11–17.

29. *Financial Times*, December 16, 1993; *Guardian*, December 16, 1993; *Wall Street Journal*, December 16, 1993.

30. Karl Marx, *Capital*, Vol. I, New York, International Publishers, 1967, p. 754.

31. World Bank, *World Development Report 1993*, New York, Oxford University Press, 1993, p. 269.

32. Eliana Cardoso and Ann Helwege, *Latin America's Economy: Diversity, Trends, and Conflicts*, Cambridge, MA, 1992, pp. 87–88; Belinda Coote, *The Trade Trap: Poverty and the Global Commodity Markets*, Oxford, Oxfam, 1992, pp. 3–11.

33. Anwar Shaikh, "Free Trade, Unemployment, and Economic Policy," in John Eatwell, ed., *Global Unemployment: Loss of Jobs in the '90s*, Armonk, NY, M. E. Sharpe, 1996, p. 76.

34. Gary Gereffi and Donald L. Wyman, *Manufacturing Miracles: Paths of Industrialization in Latin America and East Asia*, Princeton, Princeton University Press, 1990, pp. 17–23, *passim*.

35. Gary Gereffi, "Capitalism, Development and Global Commodity Chains, " in Leslie Sklair, ed., *Capitalism and Development*, London, Routledge, 1994, p. 226.

36. For example, see Jeremy Seabrook, 1996, *passim*.

37. Sandor Halebsky and Richard Harris, *Capital, Power, and Inequality in Latin America*, San Francisco, Westview Press, 1995, p. 6.

38. ILO, 1995, p. 12.

39. See Clark and Kim, 1995, *passim*.

40. Coote, p. 10.

41. A. Shaikh and E. A. Tonac, *Measuring the Wealth of Nations: The Political Economy of National Accounts*, Cambridge, Cambridge University Press, 1994, p. 222.

42. OECD, *Historical Statistics 1960–1993*, Paris, OECD, 1995, pp. 50, 73.

43. Dicken, p. 5.

44. *Business Week*, June 9, 1997, p. 70.

4 Corporate Power and International Production

1. Dicken, pp. 122–124.
2. Neil Smith, *Uneven Development: Nature, Capital, and the Production of Space*, London, Basil Blackwell, 1990, pp. 88–89. This is not to say that all capital is immobile, as in neoclassical trade theory. Clearly capital is mobile in the sense that production sites can be moved. But even this process involves the devaluation of an old site and investment in a new one – the "whizzing" of money from somewhere to somewhere else and the building of production facilities. What composes "relatively long periods" these days, of course, depends on what type of physical capital is involved – computers have shorter lives than machine tools or buildings. The real point Smith is making is that whether one is producing a good or a service, some amount of physical capital in some place is required.
3. William J. Abernathy, *The Productivity Dilemma: Roadblock to Innovation in the Automobile Industry*, Baltimore, Johns Hopkins University Press, 1978, pp. 36–38, 114–145.
4. Rabach and Kim, in Gereffi and Korzeniewicz, pp. 124–125.
5. Quoted in Smith, p. 93.
6. World Bank, 1995, p. 51.
7. Tom Barry, *Mexico: A Country Guide*, Albuquerque, Interhemispheric Education Resource Center, 1992, pp. 79–81; Harley Shaiken, *Mexico in the Global Economy*, San Diego, University of California at San Diego, 1990, *passim*.
8. *Working Together: Labor Report on the Americas* 20, September–October 1996.
9. US Bureau of Labor Statistics, "Hourly Compensation Costs for Production Workers in Manufacturing, 31 Countries or Areas, 40 Manufacturing Industries, 1975 and 1984–95", pp. 2, 92.
10. Richard Child Hill and Yong Joo Lee, " Japanese Multinationals and East Asian Development: The Case of the Automobile Industry," in Sklair, pp. 289–310.
11. *Business Week*, February 3, 1997, pp. 50–52; interviews with TIE staff, Germany, July 1996.
12. Helen Shapiro, "The Mechanics of Brazil's Auto Industry," *NACLA Report on the Americas* 29(4), January/February 1997, pp. 28–33.
13. Cornelius Graak, "Telecom Operators in the European Union: Internationalization Strategies and Network Alliances," *Telecommunications Policy* 20(5), 1996, pp. 341–355.
14. Interview with official of the Communications Workers' Union, British Telecom, August 1996; Graak, pp. 341–355; Peter Drahos and Richard A. Joseph, "Telecommunications and Investment in the Great Supranational Regulatory Game," *Telecommunications Policy* 19(8), pp. 619–635.
15. World Bank, 1996, pp. 211, 213.
16. UNIDO, 1993–94, pp. 15–18.
17. Council of Economic Advisors, *Economic Report of the President 1996*, Washington, US Government Printing Office, 1996, p. 280.
18. Barnet and Cavanaugh, p. 16.
19. UNCTAD, 1993, pp. 166–173.
20. UNCTAD, 1993, p. 173.
21. Michael J. Piore and Charles Sabel, *The Second Industrial Divide: Possibilities for Prosperity*, New York, Basic Books, 1984.
22. ILO, 1995, p. 45.
23. UNCTAD, 1996, p. 10.
24. UNCTAD, 1995, p. 45.
25. Thomsen and Woolcock, p. 22.
26. Bennett Harrison, *Lean and Mean: The Changing Landscape of Corporate Power in the Age of Flexibility*, New York, Basic Books, 1994, pp. 151–171.
27. UNCTAD, 1993, p. 19; UNCTAD, 1995, p. xx.

28. Communications Workers of America (CWA), *Changing Information Services*, Washington, DC, CWA, 1994, pp. 8, 26; Graak, pp. 341–355; *Business Week*, November 18, 1996, pp. 54–55.

29. Harrison, p. 47.

30. Harrison, pp. 150–171.

31. See Dicken, pp. 122–124.

32. Paul Hirst and Grahame Thompson, *Globalization in Question*, Cambridge, Polity Press, 1996, p. 37.

33. Roberto Korzeniewicz and William Martin, "The Global Distribution of Commodity Chains," and Hyung Kook Kim and Su-Hoon Lee, "Commodity Chains and the Korean Automobile Industry," in Gereffi and Korzeniewicz, pp. 74–78, 282.

34. Botwinick, pp. 150–155.

35. Dicken, pp. 307–308.

36. Richard Child Hill and Yong Joo Lee, "Japanese Multinationals and East Asian Development: The Case of the Automobile Industry", in Sklair, pp. 297–310.

5 The Rise and Limits of Lean Production

1. John Price, "Lean Production at Suzuki and Toyota: A Historical Perspective," in Steve Babson, ed., *Lean Work: Empowerment and Exploitation in the Global Auto Industry*, Detroit, Wayne State University Press, 1995, pp. 84–85, 96–97.

2. Maryann Keller, *Collision: GM, Toyota, Volkswagen and the Race to Own the 21st Century*, New York, Doubleday, 1993, pp. 155–156, 194.

3. Adam Opel AG, *The Opel Production System*, Russelheim, Opel, 1993, p. 3; James P. Womack, Daniel T. Jones, and Daniel Roos, *The Machine that Changed the World*, New York, Rawson Associates, 1990.

4. Antonio Gramsci, *Prison Notebooks*, New York, International Publishers, 1978, pp. 310–313.

5. Christian Berggren, "Are Assembly Lines just More Efficient? Reflections on Volvo's 'Humanistic' Manufacturing," in Babson, pp. 278–279.

6. Abernathy, p. 24.

7. Karel Williams, Colin Haslam, Sukdev Johal, John Williams, and Andy Adcroft, "Beyond Management: Problems of the Average Car Company," in Babson, p. 136.

8. Canadian Auto Workers (CAW), *Work Reorganization: Responding to Lean Production*, Toronto, CAW, 1993, p. 3.

9. Williams *et al., passim.*

10. Interview and plant tour, Toyota, Tahara, Japan, April 1994.

11. Mike Parker and Jane Slaughter, *Working Smart: A Union Guide to Participation Programs and Reengineering*, Detroit, Labor Notes, 1994, pp. 67–90.

12. Parker and Slaughter, 1994, p. 74.

13. CAW, p. 4.

14. Hideo Totsuka, "The Transformation of Japanese Industrial Relations: A Case Study of the Automobile Industry," in Babson, p. 117

15. . Mike Parker and Jane Slaughter, "Unions and Management by Stress," in Babson, p. 45.

16. Parker and Slaughter, in Babson, p. 49.

17. Price, pp. 81–104

18. Parker and Slaughter, 1994, pp. 134–144

19. Miguel Martinez Lucio, "Interpreting Change: Debates in Spanish Industrial Relations," *European Journal of Industrial Relations* 1(3), November 1995, pp. 378–379.

20. Tom Keenoy, "Review Article: European Industrial Relations in Global Perspective," *European Journal of Industrial Relations* 1(1), March 1995, p. 161.

21. John O'Grady, *Job Control Unionism vs the New HRM Model*, Kingston, Ontario, IRC Press, 1995, pp. 1–3.

22. O'Grady, p. 2.

23. Interview at Toyota, Tahara, Japan, April 1994.

24. Adrienne E. Eaton, "New Production Techniques, Employee Involvement and Unions," *Labor Studies Journal* 20(3), fall 1995 p. 19.

25. Interviews with workers from the Mercedes-Benz Bus Assembly Plant, Mannheim, Germany, September 1994, July 1996.

26. James Rinehart, Chris Huxley, and David Robertson, "Team Concept at CAMI," in Babson, p. 224.

27. David Robertson, unpublished transcript of a speech given to the TIE Lean Production Conference, Germany, November 1994.

28. Robertson, TIE Conference.

29. Botwinick, pp. 150–155.

30. Anwar Shaikh, "Free Trade, Unemployment, and Economic Policy," in John Eatwell, ed., *Global Unemployment: Loss of Jobs in the 1990s*, Armonk, New York, M. E. Sharpe, pp. 59–78.

31. Interviews at Toyota's Tahara, Japan, Plant 4, April 1994.

32. UNCTAD, 1994, p. 271.

33. Anthony Ferner and Paul Edwards, "Power and Diffusion of Organizational Change Within Multinational Enterprises, " *European Journal of Industrial Relations* 1(2), July 1995, p. 246.

34. Interviews with workers from: Mercedes-Benz Bus Assembly Plant, Mannheim, Germany, September 1994, July 1996; Nissan Assembly Plant, Barcelona, Spain, September 1994, July 1996; Nissan Assembly Plant, Tokyo, Japan, April 1994; Opel Assembly Plant, Bochum, Germany, September 1994, July 1996; Opel Assembly Plant, Eisenach, Germany, July 1996; Peugeot Assembly Plant, Ryton, UK, August 1996; Peugeot Assembly Plant, Socheaux, France, August 1996; Renault Assembly Plant, Cléon, France, and Technical Center, Paris, August 1996; Rover-BMW Assembly Plant, Oxford in Horsham, UK, August 1994; SEAT–Volkswagen Assembly Plant, Matorell, Spain, August 1994, July 1996; Toyota City, April 1994; Vauxhall, Ellesmere Port, UK, August 1994; TIE Trinational Auto Workers' Conference, Oaxtepec, Mexico, 1992; TIE Trinational Auto Parts Workers' Conference, Ciudad Juárez, Mexico, 1993.

35. Interview with union officials from Communication Workers' Union, Royal Mail, London, UK, August 1996.

36. Elly Leary and Marybeth Menaker, *Jointness at GM: Company Unionism in the 21st Century*, Woonsocket, RI, UAW New Directions Region 9A, 1994, pp. 31–44.

37. AT&T, "A Report on the Workplace of the Future Conference," March 8, 1993, pp. 1–2.

38. *New York Times*, May 12, 1996; CWA, Letter from Morton Bahr, President of the CWA, to Robert Allen, CEO of AT&T, February 22, 1996.

39. CAW, 1993, p. 3.

40. Interviews with Ben Watanabe, Osaka and Tokyo, Japan, April 1994.

41. Yoshihiko Kamii, "An Overview of Japan's Foreign Direct Investment," in Hideo Totsuka, Michael Ehrke, Yoshihiko Kamii, and Helmut Demes, eds, *International Trade Unionism at the Current Stage of Economic Globalization and Regionalization*, Tokyo, Saitama University and Friedrich Ebert Foundation, 1994, p. 18.

42. Kim Moody, "NAFTA and the Corporate Redesign of North America," *Latin American Perspectives* 22(1), winter, 1995, pp. 95–112; interviews with: officials of the Comisiones Obreras (CCOO), International Department, Barcelona, Spain, September 1994, July 1996; Heiner Kohnen, TIE, Frankfurt, Germany, September 1994, July 1996.

43. *Ward's Automotive World*, April 1996, pp. 3–5.

44. Womack, Jones, and Roos, p. 155.

45. *The Voice*, UAW New Directions, July 1996.

46. *The Voice*, UAW New Directions, July 1996.

47. Womack, Jones, and Roos, p. 157.

48. Naeyoung Lee and Jeffrey Cason, "Automobile Commodity Chains in the NICs: A Comparison of South Korea, Mexico, and Brazil," in Gereffi and Korzeniewicz, pp. 228–230.

49. Parker and Slaughter, 1994, p. 32.

50. O'Grady, *passim*; OECD, *Flexible Working Time, Collective Bargaining, and Government Intervention*, Paris, OECD, 1995, pp. 86–87.

51. Moody and Sagovac, pp. 10–23.

52. CAW, 1993, p. 8.

53. Interviews: Watanabe, 1994; Cohen, 1996; Opel, Eisenach, Germany, 1996; Mercedes, 1996.

54. Moody and Sagovac, p. 14.

55. Gerhard Bosch, "Synthesis Report," in OECD, 1995, p. 19.

56. OECD, 1995, p. 19.

57. Moody and Sagovac, pp. 15–17.

58. *Monthly Labor Review*, July 1996, p. 75.

59. Chris Tilly, *Half a Job: Bad and Good Part-Time Jobs in a Changing Labor Market*, Philadelphia, Temple University Press, 1996, pp. 17, 89.

60. Sheila Rowbotham, *Homework Worldwide*, London, Merlin Press, 1993, p. 50.

61. Rowbotham, *passim*.

62. *Labor Notes* 172, July 1993, pp. 1, 10.

63. Tilly, pp. 14–15.

64. Interview with union officials at Peugeot, Ryton, UK, August 1996.

65. Moody and Sagovac, p. 22.

66. OECD, *Employment Outlook*, Paris, OECD, July 1996, p. 194.

67. Interviews at: Nissan, CCOO, Barcelona, Spain, July 1996; Telefónica, CCOO, Barcelona, Spain, July 1996.

68. Interview with Comisiones' representatives at Telefónica, Barcelona, Spain, July 1996.

69. OECD, 1996, p. 8; Ferner and Hyman, 1992, p. 534.

70. OECD, 1996, p. 194.

71. OECD, 1995, pp. 103–165.

72. Linda Dickens, *Whose Flexibility? Discrimination & Equality Issues in Atypical Work*, London, The Institute of Employment Rights, 1992, pp. 37–38.

73. Interviews with workers from Rover–BMW, Oxford, UK, 1994 and SEAT–VW, Matorell, Spain, 1994, 1996.

74. Interview with worker from GM, Zaragoza, Spain, October 1996.

75. Interview with works-council members at GM/Opel Assembly plant, Eisenach, Germany, July 1996; Bruce Allen, "Stepping beyond Lean to Agile," Ontario, Canada, mimeo, 1996, pp. 10–11.

76. OECD, 1995, pp. 51–52.

77. Patricia Fernandez-Kelly, "Labor Force Recomposition and Industrial Restructuring in Electronics: Implications for Free Trade," unpublished paper for Johns Hopkins University Institute for Policy Studies, Baltimore, 1992.

78. Interviews at SEAT–VW, Matorell, Spain, 1994.

79. Sue Milsome, "The Impact of Japanese Firms on Working and Employment Practices in British Manufacturing Industry," London, Industrial Relations Services, 1993.

80. Paul Osterman, "The Transformation of Work in the United States: What the Evidence Shows," in Bryan Downie and Mary Lou Coates, eds, *Managing Human Resources in the 1990s and Beyond*, Kingston, Ontario, 1995, pp. 78–88.

81. Parker and Slaughter, 1994, p. 2.

82. Adrienne Eaton, "New Production Techniques, Employee Involvement and Unions," *Labor Studies Journal* 20(3), p. 32.

83. Gordon Betcherman, "Workplace Transformation in Canada: Policies and Practices," in Downie and Coates, pp. 111–113.

84. Sam Gindin, *The Canadian Auto Workers: The Birth and Transformation of a Union*, Toronto, James Lorimer & Company, 1995, pp. 210–212, 257–263; CAW, 1993.

85. Testimony at TIE Trinational Auto Workers' Meeting, Oaxtepec, Mexico, 1992, and Ciudad Juárez, Mexico, 1993; and TIE Trinational Telecommunications Workers' Meeting, Oaxtepec, Mexico, 1994.

86. Keller, pp. 36, 148–155; *The Voice*, UAW New Directions, July 1996.

87. Philip Garrahan and Paul Stewart, "Lean and Mean: Work, Locality, and Unions," in Cyrus Bina, Laurie Clements, and Chuck Davis, eds, *Beyond Survival: Wage Labor in the Twentieth Century*, Armonk, NY, M. E. Sharpe, 1996, pp. 161–172.

88. Milsome, p. 42.

89. Michael Terry, "Workplace Unionism: Redefining Structures and Objectives," in Richard Hyman and Anthony Ferner, eds, *New Frontiers in European Industrial Relations*, Oxford, Basil Blackwell Ltd, 1994, p. 240.

90. *Labor Notes* 209, August, 1996; *Guardian* (UK), September 11, 1996.

91. Otto Jacobi, Berndt Keller, and Walther Muller-Jentsch, "Germany: Codetermining the Future," in Anthony Ferner and Richard Hyman, eds, *Industrial Relations in the New Europe*, Oxford, Basil Blackwell Ltd, 1992, p. 245.

92. Interviews at Opel, Bochum, Germany, 1994, 1996, and Mercedes, Mannheim, Germany, 1994, 1996.

93. Ulrich Jurgens, "Lean Production and Co-Determination: The German Experience," in Babson, p. 295.

94. Jurgens, pp. 300–301.

95. Jurgens, pp. 292–293.

96. Interview with shop steward, Opel, Eisenach, Germany, 1996.

97. GM, Flint, 1994, GM-Opel, Bochum, Germany, 1994, 1996.

98. *Trade Union News*, November–December 1994, p. 22.

99. Ida Regalia, "How the Social Partners View Direct Participation: A Comparative Study of 15 European Countries," *European Journal of Industrial Relations* 2(2), 1996 pp. 211–234.

100. Goetschy and Rozenblatt, pp. 404–423.

101. Interviews with workers from Renault, Paris, 1994, 1996.

102. Interviews with workers from Peugeot, Paris, 1996.

103. Ferner and Hyman, 1994, pp. 548–554, 583–591.

104. Price, pp. 81–107.

105. Steve Babson, "Lean Production and Labor: Empowerment and Exploitation," in Babson, ed., pp. 14–19.

106. Babson in Babson, ed., p. 19.

107. Paul Blayton and Peter Turnbull, "Confusing Convergence: Industrial Relations in the European Airline Industry – A Comment on Warhurst," *European Journal of Industrial Relations* 2(1), March 1996, p. 10.

108. Womack, Jones, and Roos, pp. 102–103.

109. *Labor Notes* 206, May 1996.

110. Dan La Botz, *A Troublemakers' Handbook: How To Fight Back Where You Work – and Win*, Detroit, Labor Notes, 1990, pp. 6–8.

111. *Labor Notes* 211, October 1996.

112. David Robertson, speech at UAW New Directions Conference, November 9, 1996.

113. David Harvey, *The Condition of Postmodernity: An Inquiry into the Origins of Cultural Change*, Cambridge, MA, Basil Blackwell, 1989, pp. 240–242; Erica Schoenberger,

"Competition, Time, and Space in Industrial Change," in Gereffi and Korzeniewicz, pp. 51–66.

114. Schoenberger, p. 57.
115. Parker and Slaughter, 1994, pp. 228–229.
116. Interviews at Toyota, Tahara, Japan, 1994; and Tokyo, Japan, 1994.
117. Williams *et al.*, pp. 136, 149.
118. Keller, p. 58.
119. Price, p. 82.
120. Williams *et al.*, p. 145.
121. US Department of Commerce, *1974 Annual Survey of Manufacturers*, Washington, US Department of Commerce, 1976, p. 10; *1994 Annual Survey of Manufacturers*, Washington, US Department of Commerce, 1996, p. 1–24.
122. US Department of Commerce, *1994 Annual Survey of Manufacturers*, Washington, US Department of Commerce, 1995, pp. 1–24, 1–54.
123. *New York Times*, January 30, 1996.
124. Interviews at Toyota, Tahara, Japan 1994.
125. Allen, p. 17.
126. *The Economist*, February 10, 1996.

6 Corporatism, Neoliberalism, Free Trade and the State

1. Simon Gunn, *Revolution on the Right*, London, Pluto Press, 1989, pp. 1–19.
2. Leo Panitch, *Working Class Politics in Crisis: Essays on Labour and the State*, London, Verso, 1986, pp. 193–199.
3. Hal Draper, *Karl Marx's Theory of Revolution, Volume II: The Politics of Social Classes*, New York, Monthly Review Press, 1973, p. 108.
4. Fritz Rath, "The Coordinates of Trade Union Policy for Europe," in Wolfgang Lecher, ed., *Trade Unions in the European Union: A Handbook*, London, Lawrence & Wishart, 1994, pp. 237–273.
5. Panitch, p. 209.
6. Edwards and Hyman, pp. 258–262; Leo Panitch and Donald Swartz, *The Assault on Trade Union Freedoms*, Toronto, Garamond Press, 1988, p. 101.
7. Gunn, pp. 91–94.
8. Gunn, p. 17.
9. Guy Standing, "Globalization, Labour Flexibility and the Era of Market Regulation," Center for Social Theory and Comparative History, University of California at Los Angeles, May 6, 1996, p. 6.
10. Labour Party, "Building Prosperity – Flexibility, Efficiency and Fairness at Work," London, Labour Party, 1996, p. 1.
11. Hal Draper, "The New Social Democratic Reformism," in E. Haberkern, ed., *Socialism From Below*, London, Humanities Press, 1992, pp. 88–105.
12. Draper, pp. 88–105.
13. Attributed to William Winpisinger, President of the International Association of Machinists, *c.* 1983.
14. Labour Party, p. 1.
15. Moody, 1988, pp. 118–135; Panitch, 1988, pp. 14–15; Simon Head, "The New Ruthless Economy," *The New York Review*, February 29, 1996, p. 50.
16. Jelle Visser, "European Trade Unions: The Transition Years," in Hyman and Ferner, pp. 80–103; Christel Lane, "Industrial Order and the Transformation of Industrial Relations: Britain, Germany and France Compared," in Hyman and Ferner, pp. 167–191.
17. Peter Barberis and Timothy May, *Government, Industry, and Political Economy*, Buckingham, UK, Open University Press, 1993, pp. 64–65.

18. Fritz Rath, "The Co-ordinates of Trade Union Policy for Europe," in Lecher, pp. 237–249.

19. Harvie Ramsay, "Euro-Unionism and the Great Auction: An Assessment of the Prospects for Organized Labour Post-Maastricht," unpublished paper, Department of Human Resource Management, University of Strathclyde, Scotland, December 1993.

20. Paul Marginson and Keith Sisson, "The Structure of Transnational Capital in Europe: The Emerging Euro-company and its Implications for Industrial Relations," in Hyman and Ferner, pp. 186–189; Ramsay, *passim*.

21. Lecher, pp. 257–264; Ramsay, *passim*.

22. Marginson and Sisson, pp. 189–1990; Ramsay, *passim*.

23. "Social Policy White Paper – Part One," *European Industrial Relations Review* 248, September 1994, pp. 13–15.

24. Marginson and Sisson, p. 188.

25. Daniel Singer, "The Real Europebattle," *The Nation*, December 23, 1996, p. 21.

26. US Department of Commerce, *Statistical Abstract of the United States 1995*, Washington, US Government Printing Office, 1995, pp. 809, 817.

27. US Bureau of Labor Statistics, "Hourly Compensation Cost for Production Workers in Manufacturing in 31 Countries or Areas: 40 Manufacturing Industries 1975 and 1984–95," Washington, US Department of Labor, 1996, unpublished data, p. 2.

28. World Bank, *World Development Report 1996*, Washington, World Bank, 1996, p. 189.

29. Dennis N. Valdes, "Legal Status and the Struggles of Farmworkers in West Texas and New Mexico, 1942–1993," *Latin American Perspectives* 22(1), pp. 117–137.

30. Walt Vanderbush, "Mexican Labor in the Era of Economic Restructuring and NAFTA: Working to Create a Favorable Investment Climate," *Labor Studies Journal* 20(4), winter 1996, p. 82.

31. US International Trade Commission (USITC), *The Likely Impact on the United States of a Free Trade Agreement with Mexico*, Washington, USITC, Publication 2353.

32. *North American Free Trade Agreement*, Vol. I, Washington, US Government Printing Office, 1992, p. iii.

33. *Business Week*, April 16, 1993, pp. 84–92.

34. Tom Barry, *Mexico: A Country Guide*, Albuquerque, Interhemispheric Education Resource Center, 1992, pp. 79–81; James Cockcroft, *Mexico: Class Formation, Capital Accumulation, and the State*, New York, Monthly Review Press, 1983, pp. 157–165.

35. Kevin J. Middlebrook, *The Paradox of Revolution: Labor, the State, and Authoritarianism in Mexico*, Baltimore, Johns Hopkins University Press, 1995, pp. 271–272.

36. United Nations Commission for Transnational Corporations, *Foreign Direct Investment and Industrial Restructuring in Mexico*, New York, United Nations, Series A, No. 18, 1992, p. 58.

37. Joseph Grunwald and Kenneth Flamm, *The Global Factory: Foreign Assembly in International Trade*, Washington, Brookings Institution, 1985, pp. 137–179; *US–Mexico Free Trade Reporter* 2(7), October 5, 1992, p. 8.

38. Harley Shaiken, *Mexico in the Global Economy*, San Diego, University of California at San Diego, 1990, p. 11.

39. Jorge Carillo, "The Restructuring of the Car Industry in Mexico: Adjustment Policies and Labor Implications," Austin, University of Texas, Paper 90–01, 1991.

40. *La Jornada*, December 26, 1991.

41. *Shaiken*, pp. 9–44; Raul A. Fernandez, *The Mexican–American Border Region: Issues and Trends*, Notre Dame, University of Notre Dame Press, 1989, pp. 103–105.

42. Moody and McGinn, pp. 9–10.

43. Dan La Botz, *Democracy in Mexico: Peasant Rebellion and Political Reform*, Boston, South End Press, 1995, p. 101.

44. David Barkin, *Distorted Development: Mexico in the World Economy*, San Francisco, Westview, 1990, pp. 84–90.

45. Barkin, *passim*; Barry, *passim*; Cockcroft, *passim*.

46. World Bank, "Mexico: Toward Growth, Structural Reform, and Macroeconomic Stability in Mexico," Washington, World Bank, 1988.

47. Barkin, pp. 57–72, 90–97; James Petras and Morris Morely, *US Hegemony under Siege: Politics and Development in Latin America*, London, Verso, 1990, pp. 190–208.

48. World Bank, 1988; Barry, p. 111.

49. US International Trade Commission, "Review of Trade and Investment Liberalization Measures by Mexico and Prospects for Future United States–Mexico Relations," Washington, USITC Publication 2326, 1990.

50. John Warnock, *The Other Mexico: The North American Triangle Completed*, Montreal, Black Rose Books, 1995, p. 85.

51. Barry, p. 125; *Multinational Monitor*, May 1991.

52. Petras and Morely, pp. 190–208; *Multinational Monitor*, May 1991.

53. Barry, pp. 107–108; World Bank, *World Development Report 1991*, Washington, World Bank, 1991, p. 231.

54. Warnock, pp. 261, 269; *Washington Post National Weekly Edition*, October 7–13, 1996.

55. *Working Together: Labor Report on the Americas* 20, September–October 1996.

56. *Boston Globe*, August 25, 1996.

57. US Bureau of Labor Statistics, 1996, p. 2.

58. Carlos Heredia, "Downward Mobility: Mexican Workers after NAFTA," *NACLA Report on the Americas* 30(3), November/December 1996, p. 34; interview with José Santos of the Ford Workers' Democratic Movement and CILAS (Centro de Información Laboral y Asesortia Sindical – Center for Labor Research and Union Support), Mexico City, Detroit, October 1996.

59. Lawrence Mishel and Jared Bernstein, *The State of Working America 1994–95*, Armonk, NY, M. E. Sharpe, 1994, pp. 33–44.

60. Dicken, pp. 151–155.

61. Herman Daly and Robert Goodland, "An Ecological–Economic Assessment of Deregulation of International Commerce Under GATT," Washington, World Bank, Environment Department, 1993.

62. *Financial Times*, July 26, 1994.

63. World Bank, 1995, p. 105; *The Economist*, November 5, 1994; *Financial Times*, June 1, 1995; *Transmitter*, Telecommunication Workers' Union, British Columbia, Canada, 1995.

64. World Bank 1996, pp. 214–215.

65. Giovanni Arrighi, *The Long Twentieth Century: Money, Power, and the Origins of Our Times*, London, Verso, 1994, pp. 27–84, 269–324.

66. Council of Economic Advisors, *Economic Report of the President*, Washington, US Government Printing Office, 1996, pp. 234–243.

7 Pulled Apart, Pushed Together

1. Charles Leadbeater, "Power to the Person," *Marxism Today*, October 1988, pp. 14–19.

2. Joel Rogers, "How Divided Progressives Might Unite," *New Left Review* 210, March/April 1995, p. 9.

3. See, for example, E. J. Hobsbawm, *The Age of Empire, 1875–1914*, London, Abacus, 1987, pp. 112–164.

4. Richard Hyman, "Trade Unions and the Disaggregation of the Working Class," in Marino Regini, ed., *The Future of Labour Movements*, London, Sage, 1992, p. 166.

5. Lewis Feuer, *Marx & Engels: Basic Writings on Politics and Philosophy*, New York, Anchor Press, 1959, p. 16.

6. Karl Marx, *Grundrisse: Introduction to the Critique of Political Economy*, Baltimore, Penguin Books, 1973, p. 651.

7. Hyman, in Regini, p. 166.

8. Panitch, 1986, p. 17.

9. Hyman, in Regini, p. 164.

10. This section draws on Andrew Sayer and Richard Walker, *The New Social Economy: Reworking the Division of Labor*, Cambridge, MA, Basil Blackwell, 1992.

11. Moody, 1988, pp. 100–101.

12. Ronald W. Schatz, *The Electrical Workers: A History of Labor at General Electric and Westinghouse, 1923–60*, Chicago, University of Illinois Press, 1983, pp. 232–236.

13. Sayer and Walker, p. 209.

14. Sayer and Walker, p. 147.

15. Marx, 1973, p. 769.

16. Sayer and Walker, p. 120.

17. Sayer and Walker, p. 157.

18. Parker and Slaughter, 1994, p. 107.

19. Sayer and Walker, p. 121.

20. Sayer and Walker, p. 157.

21. Allen, pp. 21–24.

22. US Department of Commerce, 1994, pp. 558, 752.

23. Harrison, p. 47.

24. US Department of Commerce, *US Census of Manufacturers*, Industry Series, Washington, 1987, pp. 37A-12, 13; 1992, pp. 37A, 13–14.

25. Harrison, p. 51.

26. US Department of Commerce, 1995, p. 748, adjusted for inflation.

27. Sayer and Walker, pp. 148–157.

28. Arrighi, pp. 85–158; John Hope Franklin, *From Slavery to Freedom: A History of Negro Americans*, New York, Vintage, 1969, pp. 42–59, 87.

29. Moody, 1988, pp. 72–76.

30. Bill Fletcher, Jr and Peter Agard, *The Indispensable Ally: Black Workers and the Formation of the Congress of Industrial Organizations, 1934–1941*, Boston, Fletcher and Agard, 1987; August Meier and Elliot Rudwick, *Black Detroit and the Rise of the UAW*, New York, Oxford University Press, 1979.

31. Michael Goldfield, *The Decline of Organized Labor in the United States*, Chicago, University of Chicago Press, 1987, pp. 238–239.

32. Mike Davis, *Prisoners of the American Dream: Politics and Economy in the History of the US Working Class*, London, Verso, 1986, p. 92.

33. Robin D. G. Kelley, *Hammer and Hoe: Alabama Communists During the Great Depression*, Chapel Hill, NC, University of North Carolina Press 1990, p. 151.

34. Meier and Rudwick, pp. 207–222.

35. Kelley, p. 227.

36. Davis, p. 92.

37. Davis, pp. 91–93.

38. US Department of Commerce, 1995, pp. 36, 445.

39. Mishel and Bernstein, pp. 167, 188.

40. US Department of Commerce 1995, pp. 756–757.

41. Black Workers For Justice (BWFJ), "Organizing the South: A Southern Strategy for Labor," Rocky Mount, North Carolina, pamphlet, 1992, *passim*.

42. Rodolfo Acuna, *Occupied America: A History of Chicanos*, New York, Harper & Row, 1988, *passim*; Zaragosa Vargas, "Rank and File: Historical Perspectives on Latina/o Workers in the US," unpublished paper, Ohio State University, 1995, p. 1.

43. Acuna, pp. 220–235.

44. Valdes, pp. 117–132.

45. Alex Stepick, "Miami: Capital of Latin America," in Louise Lamphere, Alex

Stepick, and Guillermo Grenier, eds, *Newcomers in the Workplace: Immigrants and the Restructuring of the US Economy*, Philadelphia, Temple University Press, 1994, p. 133.

46. Vargas, p. 2.

47. Johnathan D. Rosenblum, *Copper Crucible: How the Arizona Miners Strike of 1983 Recast Labor–Management Relations in America*, Ithaca, NY, ILR Press, 1995, *passim*; Eric Mann, *Taking On GM: A Case Study of the UAW Campaign to Keep GM Van Nuys Open*, Los Angeles, University of California, 1987, *passim*.

48. US Department of Commerce, 1995, pp. 444–445.

49. Valdes, pp. 122–128; Philip L. Russell, *Mexico Under Salinas*, Austin, TX, Mexico Resource Center, 1994, pp. 324–330.

50. Russell, p. 328.

51. World Bank, 1995, pp. 64–66.

52. Russell, p. 328.

53. Warnock, p. 186.

54. Lamphere *et al.*, pp. 3–5.

55. Russell, pp. 324–325.

56. Moody, 1988, p. 281.

57. Lamphere *et al.*, pp. 1–19; Fernandez-Kelly, 1992.

58. Valdes, pp. 117–137; Fernandez-Kelly, 1992.

59. Lamphere *et al.*, pp. 25–77.

60. Hector Delgado, *New Immigrants, Old Unions: Organizing Undocumented Workers in Los Angeles*, Philadelphia, Temple University Press, 1993, pp. 14–15.

61. OECD, 1995, p. 39; OECD, 1996, p. 192.

62. Lamphere *et al.*, pp. 25–77;

63. Jill Rubery and Colete Fagan, "Does Feminization Mean a Flexible Labour Force?" in Hyman and Ferner, 1994, p. 152.

64. Helen I. Safa, "Economic Restructuring and Gender Subordination," *Latin American Perspectives* 22(2), spring 1995, pp. 32–50.

65. Diane Elson, "Uneven Development and the Textile and Clothing Industry," in Sklair, pp. 189–209; Dicken, pp. 233–263.

66. Elson, in Sklair, pp. 189–228; Dicken, pp. 239–251, 253–257.

67. Jeffrey Henderson, *The Globalization of High Technology Production*, London, Routledge, 1989, pp. 141–145.

68. Seabrook, 1996, pp. 86–130.

69. Ian M. Taplin, "Strategic Reorientations of US Apparel Firms," in Gereffi and Korzeniewicz, pp. 205–221.

70. Delgado, pp. 13–14.

71. Baldemar Velasquez, speech at 1993 Labor Notes Conference, Detroit, April 1993.

72. This account is taken from my own participation in the Detroit Newspaper strike, discussions with strike activists, and my observations of Sterling Heights and other working-class suburbs around Detroit.

73. Michael Barone and Grant Ujifusa, *The Almanac of American Politics 1992*, Washington, National Journal, 1992, pp. 635–637.

74. Committee for Doug Young, "Douglas Young, Newspaper Striker for State Representative, 32nd District," Shelby Township, Michigan, 1996.

75. Maralyn Edid, *Farm Labor Organizing: Trends and Prospects*, Ithaca, NY, ILR Press, 1994, pp. 58–60; Moody, 1988, pp. 286–287.

76. Baldemar Velasquez, speech at 1995 Labor Notes Conference, Detroit, April 1995.

77. Trip to El Paso, Texas, May 1993.

78. Valdes, p. 128.

79. Valdes, pp. 125–128; Carlos Marentes, speech at 1993 Labor Notes Conference, Detroit, April 1993.

80. *Labor Notes* 211, October 1996.

81. *Labor Notes* 186, September 1994.

82. LAMAP, profile, "Joel Ochoa: Organizing the Future," Los Angeles, 1996.

83. LAMAP, *El Nixtamalero*, "Boletín de los Trabajadores Tortilleros Publicado por LAMAP" 1(2), September 26, 1996.

84. Ken Paff, presentation at a meeting of the *Labor Notes* Policy Committee, Detroit, January 1997.

8 Crisis of the Working Class

1. Moody, 1988, pp. 86–87.

2. Panitch and Swartz, pp. 24, 101.

3. P. K. Edwards and Richard Hyman, "Strikes and Industrial Conflict: Peace in Europe?" in Hyman and Ferner, 1994, pp. 260–261.

4. Moody, 1988, p. 82.

5. Goldfield, pp. 17–21; Visser, p. 82.

6. Bernard Keeling, "Structural Change in the World Steel Industry," in Gijsbert van Liemt, ed., *Industry on the Move: Causes and Consequences of International Relocation in the Manufacturing Industry*, Geneva, ILO, 1992, p. 175.

7. Richard Peet, *International Capitalism and Industrial Restructuring*, London, Allen & Unwin, 1987, pp. 20–22.

8. Hobsbawm, 1994, p. 304.

9. Goldfield, pp. 8–22.

10. Moody, 1988, pp. 165–191; US Department of Labor, "Union Members in 1993," *News* 94–58, February 9, 1994; *News* 97–27, January 31, 1997; Goldfield, p. 16; Gindin, p. 247.

11. Visser, pp. 82, 99; Martínez Lucio, p. 489; Lecher, p. 91.

12. Ferner and Hyman, p. 562; Marginson and Sisson, pp. 15–50.

13. *Labor Notes* 215, February 1997.

14. *Business Week*, December 2, 1996, pp. 58–66; Clark and Kim, *passim*.

15. John H. Dunning, *The Globalization of Business: The Challenge of the 1990s*, London, Routledge, pp. 324–326.

16. Harrison, *passim*.

17. US Department of Commerce, 1995, p. 555; *Wall Street Journal*, January 2, 1996.

18. Dunning, p. 324.

19. Marginson and Sisson, p. 22.

20. Lecher, pp. 237–273; L. Ulman, B. Eichengreen, and W. T. Dickens, *Labor and an Integrated Europe*, Washington, The Brookings Institution, 1993, pp. 61–63, 80–99.

21. Parker and Slaughter, 1994, 4–5; *The Nation*, April 8, 1996, pp. 21–25; interviews with workers from Rover, Britain, 1994; Peugeot, Britain, 1996; SEAT, Spain, 1994, 1996.

22. Hobsbawm, 1994, p. 289.

23. World Bank, 1996, p. 195.

24. For example, Jeremy Rifkin, *The End of Work: The Decline of the Global Labor Force and the Dawn of the Post-Market Era*, New York, G. P. Putnam's Sons, 1995.

25. Peter Drucker, "The Age of Social Transformation," *Atlantic Monthly* 274(5), November 1994, pp. 53–80.

26. US Bureau of the Census, *Annual Survey of Manufacturers 1994*, Washington, US Bureau of the Census, 1996, pp. 1–7.

27. World Bank, 1996, p. 195; OECD, 1996, p. 191.

28. Council of Economic Advisors, *Economic Report of the President 1996*, Washington, Government Printing Office, 1996, p. 334.

29. *Monthly Labor Review*, July 1996, p. 80; Eurostat, *Basic Statistics of the Community*, Luxembourg, Statistical Office of the European Communities, 1994, p. 142.

30. US Department of Labor, *Employment & Earnings*, Washington, US Department of Labor, January 1995.

31. US Department of Commerce, Statistical Abstract of the United States, Washington, US Department of Commerce, 1994, pp. 405, 420.

32. Eurostat, p. 140; *Monthly Labor Review* July, 1996, p. 74.

33. Simon Head, "The New Ruthless Economy," *New York Review*, February 29, 1996, p. 49.

34. Head, p. 47.

35. OECD, 1996, p. 192.

36. Rowbotham, pp. 18–27.

37. Dave Elsila, "Putting the Screws on Workers: Dollar-an-Hour Jobs in Our Own Back Yard," *Solidarity* 39(11), November 1996, pp. 14–17.

38. OECD, 1996, pp. 68, 72.

39 *Business Week*, June 2, 1997, p. 6.

40. OECD, *Historical Statistics 1960–1993*, Paris, OECD, 1995, p. 98.

41. *Labor Notes* 200, November 1995.

42. Parker and Slaughter, 1994, pp. 1–8.

43. *The Economist*, November 25, 1995, pp. 57–58..

44. Osterman, 1995, p. 77.

45. ILO, 1995, pp. 55–56.

46. Moody and Sagovac, p. 24; American Federation of Government Employees Local 2006, *The Communicator*, May 1996.

47. Graak, pp. 341–355.

48. Anthony Ferner, "The State as Employer," in Hyman and Ferner, 1994, pp. 55–56.

49. *Economic Notes* 65(1), January 1997.

50. Bureau of Labor Statistics, *Monthly Labor Review*, March 1994, p. 62.

51. *Wall Street Journal*, June 17, 1996.

52. JAW (Japan Auto Workers), pp. 1–5.

53. Interviews at Toyota, Tahara, Japan, April, 1994.

54. US Department of Labor, unpublished data, 1993.

55. *Monthly Labor Review* 119, July 1996, pp. 105–106.

56. London Hazards Centre, *Hard Labour: Stress Ill-Health and Hazardous Employment Practices*, London, London Hazards Centre, 1994, p. 22.

57. ILO, 1993, pp. 65–68.

58. Interviews and discussions with US auto workers in Detroit and Flint, Michigan, and telecommunications workers in New York and Seattle, 1994–96. Presentations at the 1994 TIE Trinational Telecommunications Conference, Oaxtepec, Mexico.

59. ILO, 1993, p. 65.

60. London Hazards Centre, p. 15.

61. London Hazards Centre, p. 23.

62. London Hazards Centre, p. 3.

63. Parker and Slaughter, 1994, p. 225.

64. ILO, 1993, pp. 70–73.

65. US Department of Labor, "Major Work Stoppages, 1996," *News* 97–44, February 12, 1997.

66. *Labor Notes* 206, May 1996.

67. *Labor Notes* all of 1995 through February 1997; *The Warren Steelworker* 2(4), December 1995; United Steelworkers of America (USWA), *The Strike at Wheeling Pittsburgh*, Pittsburgh, USWA, 1996.

68. Trades Union Congress (TUC), *Trade Union Trends: Bi-annual Survey Results No. 3 September 1996*, London, TUC, 1996, p. 10.

69. Interviews with officers of the Communication Workers' Union, Royal Mail, December, 1996; e-mail transmissions from "SoliNotes," December 3, 1996; report on National Public Radio, "Morning Edition," January 1997.

70. Institute for Global Communications (IGC), InterPress Service, February 17, 1997; IGC, "labornews," January 29, 1997, February 3, 1997; "ICEM Update," March 11, 1997.

71. *Financial Times*, March 4, 1997; Reports at the TIE World-Wide Conference, Frankfurt, Germany, March 7–9, 1997.

72. Standing, p. 5.

73. Gary N. Chaison, *Union Mergers in Hard Times*, Ithaca, NY, ILR Press, 1996, pp. 1–29, 79–94; *Labor Notes* 198, September 1995.

74. Gindin, pp. 256–281.

75. Christophe Aguiton, "French Radicals Create New Trade Unions," *International Viewpoint* 278, June 1996, pp. 7–9; interviews with SUD and CGT activists, Paris, August 1997.

76. Jesús Albarracín and Pedro Montés, "Spain: Fight for the Soul of the Union," *International Viewpoint* 273, January 1996, pp. 19–22; CCOO, *Gaceta Sindical Internacional* 8, April 1996, pp. 5–9; interviews with CCOO officials and activists, Barcelona, Spain, July 1996.

77. "Against the Argument of Competitiveness and its Acceptance Through Unions," TIE-Internationales Bildungswerk, 3 October 1995.

78. Interviews with IG Metall shop stewards, works-council representatives, and activists at Mercedes-Benz and Opel, Germany, July 1996; Detroit, April 1995.

79. Peter Lindgren, "Sweden: Left Challenge in Volvo," *International Viewpoint*, e-mail posting, February 7, 1997.

80. *Labor Notes* 214, January 1997; presentations at Teamsters for a Democratic Union Planning Meeting, Detroit, February 22–23, 1997.

81. Kim Moody, "Labor: The Shake Up from Below," *Cross Roads* 25, October 1992.

82. Paul Alan Levy, transcript of speech to the National Lawyers' Guild, Autumn 1996.

83. *Labor Notes* 201, December 1995.

84. Staughton Lynd, "From the Bottom Up," *Boston Review* XXI (2), April–May 1996 and 3/4, summer 1996, pp. 6–7.

85. Gay W. Seidman, *Manufacturing Militance: Workers' Movements in Brazil and South Africa, 1970–1985*, Berkeley, University of California Press, 1994, pp. 1–12.

9 Looking South

1. ILO, 1993, pp. 44–51.

2. Cecilia Green, "At the Junction of the Global and the Local: Transnational Industry and Women Workers in the Caribbean," in Lance A. Compa and Stephen F. Diamond, eds, *Human Rights, Labor Rights, and International Trade*, Philadelphia, University of Pennsylvania Press, 1996, p. 126.

3. Carlos Vilas, "Economic Restructuring, Neoliberal Reforms, and the Working Class in Latin America," in Sandor Halebsky and Richard L. Harris, eds, *Capital, Power, and Inequality in Latin America*, Boulder, CO, Westview Press, 1995, p. 149.

4. Seabrook, pp. 115–116.

5. Seabrook, p. 130.

6. Seabrook, p. 94.

7. *Asian Women Workers' Newsletter* 14(4), Hong Kong, October 1995.

8. World Bank, 1995, p. 219.

9. Sheila Rowbotham and Swatsi Mitter, *Dignity and Daily Bread: New Forms of Organizing among Poor Women in the Third World and First*, London, Routledge, 1994, pp. 73–94.

10. Coalition for Justice in the Maquiladoras (CJM), *Newsletter* 6(2), summer 1996.

11. See, for example, Rowbotham and Mitter, *passim*; Judith Adler Hellman, "The Riddle of the New Social Movements: Who They Are and What They Do," in Halebsky and Harris, pp. 165–180.

12. Francesca Miller, "Latin American Women and the Search for Social, Political,

and Economic Transformation," in Halebsky and Harris, pp. 185–205; La Botz, 1995, p. 160.

13. Green, p. 129.

14. CJM, *Newsletter* 6(1), "Annual Report 1995," Spring 1996; Vilas, in Halebsky and Harris, p.149.

15. For discussions of this in different contexts see Ruth Berins Collier and David Collier, *Shaping the Political Arena: Critical Junctures, the Labor Movement, and Regime Dynamics in Latin America*, Princeton, Princeton University Press, 1991; Henk Thomas, ed., *Globalization and Third World Trade Unions: The Challenge of Rapid Economic Change*, London, Zed Books, 1995.

16. *NACLA Report on the Americas* 29(1), July/August 1995, pp. 15–32; *Workers' Liberty*, p. 14; interview with Kuo Kuo Wen from the Taiwan Labor Front, Detroit, March 1997.

17. Thomas, pp. 38–53.

18. Thomas, pp. 50–53; Vilas, pp. 146–148.

19. For a description of such people in Asia see Seabrook, pp. 210–216.

20. Seidman, p. 197.

21. Seidman, p. 198.

22. Seidman, p. 170.

23. Maria Helena Moreira Alves, "Something Old, Something New: Brazil's Partido dos Trabalhadores," in Barry Carr and Steve Ellner, eds, *The Latin American Left: From the Fall of Allende to Perestroika*, Boulder, CO, Westview Press, 1993, pp. 230–237.

24. Seidman, pp. 219, 247.

25. Seidman, pp. 167–171, 197–221, 230–231.

26. Vilas, p. 158.

27. Jeremy Baskin, "Unions at the Crossroads: Can They Make the Transition?" *South African Labour Bulletin* 20(1), February 1996, pp. 8–16.

28. Baskin, p. 9.

29. Templeton Filita, "COSATU Marching Forward," *South African Labour Bulletin* 21(1), February 1997, pp. 36–41.

30. Zolie Mtshelwane, "Struggle as Usual in the New South Africa," *South African Labour Bulletin* 18(3), July 1994, pp. 6–10.

31. *Justice Speaks* 13(10), June 1996; Sakhela Buhlungu, "Editorial Notes," *South African Labour Bulletin* 20(1), February 1996, p. 3 "Trade Unions," Co-operative for Research and Education, Johannesburg, South Africa, June 1–13, 1997.

32. A strong example of the argument for the independence of the unions in both industry and politics was the speech by Abraham Agulhas, President of the Chemical Workers' Industrial Union, at the 1995 Labor Notes Conference, Detroit, April 1995.

33. COSATU, "Breaking Boundaries: Building an International Workers' Movement," Cape Town, Umanyano Media Services, 1994.

34. Martin Hart-Landsberg, *The Rush to Development: Economic Change and Political Struggle in South Korea*, New York, Monthly Review Press, 1993, pp. 62–65; Walden Bello and Stephanie Rosenfeld, *Dragons in Distress: Asia's Miracle Economies in Crisis*, San Francisco, Food First Books, 1990, pp 63–75.

35. World Bank, 1995, pp. 222–223.

36. Bello and Rosenfeld, p. 23; World Bank, 1996, p. 195.

37. Bello and Rosenfeld, pp. 24–25.

38. World Bank, 1996, p. 195.

39. Alice Amsden, *Asia's Next Giant: South Korea and Late Industrialization*, New York, Oxford University Press, 1989, pp. 203–204; Bello and Rosenfeld, pp. 25–28.

40. Hart-Landsberg, p. 276.

41. Hart-Landsberg. p. 276.

42. ILO, 1993, p. 50; World Bank, 1995, p. 84; Bello and Rosenfeld, p. 31; US Department of Labor, *Foreign Labor Trends*, "Korea," Washington, US Government

Printing Office: 95–35, 1995; Jung Duk Lim, "Pusan, Korea: Second City Blues," in Clark and Kim, p. 183; Hugh Williamson, "New Labour Movements and International Trade Unionism in Asia," in H. Totsuka, M. Ehrke, Y. Kamii, and H. Demes, eds, *International Trade Unionism at the Current Stage of Economic Globalization and Regionalization*, Saitama, Japan, Saitama University, p. 141; Hugh Williamson, *Coping With the Miracle: Japan's Unions Explore New International Relations*, London, Pluto Press, 1994, p. 310.

43. Hart-Landsberg, pp. 277–279.

44. Hart-Landsberg, pp. 279–280.

45. US Department of Labor, 95–35; *South African Labour Bulletin* 19(1), March 1995, p. 4; Institute for Global Communications, "Labor News," January 20, 1996.

46. Interview with Kwang Ho Lee, editor of the KCTU's weekly newspaper, in *Workers' Liberty* 38, March 1997, p. 13.

47. *Workers' Liberty*, p. 14.

48. *Workers' Liberty*, p. 14.

49. Bello and Rosenfeld, pp. 215–223; US Department of Labor, *Foreign Labor Trends: 96–4*, "Taiwan," Washington, US Government Printing Office, 1996, p. 3.

50. *Foreign Labor Trends* 96–4, p. 1.

51. US Department of Labor, 96–4, p. 3; interview with Kuo Kuo Wen of the Taiwan Labor Front, conducted in Detroit, March 1997.

52. Williamson, in Totsuka *et al.*, p. 141; Williamson, 1994, p. 310.

53. LaBotz, 1992, pp. 39–41.

54. Middlebrook, pp. 319–323.

55. Except where otherwise stated, this account is taken from discussions with Dan La Botz and José Santos of the Cleto Nigmo Committee/Ford Workers' Democratic Movement at the Cuautitlán Ford plant.

56. *CJM Newsletter*, Summer 1996; *Wall Street Journal*, July 2, 1997.

57. *Mexico Labor New*, Mexico City, Internet, November 15, 1996.

58. La Botz 1995, p. 69.

59. La Botz, 1995, pp. 65–82,

60. Hellman, pp. 172–179.

61. Moreira Alves, pp. 230–234.

62. Collier and Collier, pp. 252–268; World Bank, 1996, p. 205.

63. Daniel Hellinger, "The CausaR and the Nuevo Sindicalismo in Venezuela," *Latin American Perspectives* 23(3), summer 1996, pp. 110–128.

64. E-mail transmission: "SoliNotes," December 3, 1997.

65. James Cockcroft, "In Latin America: The New Politics Challenge," *New Politics* 3(1), summer 1990, pp. 16–18.

66. Denis MacShane, "The New International Working Class and its Organizations," *New Politics* 4(1), summer 1992, p. 136.

67. World Bank, 1996, pp. 132–136.

68. Kate Hudson, "Social Democracy and Post-Communism: The Hungarian Example," *Labour Focus on Eastern Europe* 54, summer 1996, p. 64.

69. Hudson, pp. 68–76; World Bank, 1996, pp. 66–76.

70. Laszlo Andor, "Trade Unions in Hungary," *Labour Focus on Eastern Europe* 54, summer 1996, pp. 68–76.

10 Official Labor Internationalism in Transition

1. Victor Reuther, *The Brothers Reuther and the Story of the UAW: A Memoir*, Boston, Houghton Mifflin, 1976, pp. 411–427; Beth Sims, *Workers of the World Undermined: American Labor's Role in US Foreign Policy*, Boston, South End Press, 1992, *passim*.

2. Burton Bendiner, *International Labour Affairs: The World Trade Unions and the Multinational Companies*, Oxford, Clarendon Press, 1987, pp. 62–88.

3. Dave Spooner, *Partners or Predators: International Trade Unionism and Asia*, Hong Kong, Asia Labour Monitor Resource Center, 1989, p. 13.

4. MacShane, p. 143; *Asian Labour Update* 22, August-October 1996, p. 20.

5. Dan Gallin, "Inside the New World Order: Drawing the Battle Lines," *New Politics* 5(1), summer 1994, pp. 127–128.

6. Spooner, p. 14; Gallin, p. 128.

7. Williamson, 1994, p. 4.

8. Spooner, pp. 12–14.

9. Williamson, 1994, pp. 300–311.

10. Williamson, 1994, pp. 59–60.

11. Gerard Greenfield, "Global Business Unionism," *Asian Labour Update* 4, August-October 1996, p. 4.

12. Spooner, p. 49; Williamson, 1994, p. 296.

13. Williamson, 1994, pp. 182–183.

14. Williamson, 1994, pp. 202–222.

15. Williamson, 1994, pp. 224–225.

16. Bendiner, pp. 49–56; John P. Windmuller, "International Trade Secretariats: The Industrial Trade Union Internationals," *Foreign Labor Trends* 95-4, Washington, US Department of Labor, 1995, pp. 3–29.

17. Reuther, p. 400.

18. International Federation of Chemical, Energy, Mine and General Workers' Unions (ICEM), *Power and Counterpower: The Union Response to Global Capital*, London, Pluto Press/ICEM, 1996, p. 56; Joe Uehlein, "Using Labor's Trade Secretariats," *Labor Research Review* 13, spring 1989, pp. 31–41.

19. Bendiner, pp. 62–88.

20. Gallin, pp. 128–129; Spooner, p. 66.

21. Spooner, pp. 20–21.

22. International Union of Food, Agricultural, Hotel, Restaurant, Catering, Tobacco, and Allied Workers' Associations (IUF), *News Bulletin* 65(3–4), 1995, p. 2.

23. Kenneth S. Zinn, "Labor Solidarity in the New World Order: The UMWA Program in Colombia," *Labor Research Review* 23, spring/summer 1995, pp. 35–43.

24. Sims, *passim*; Reuther, pp. 411–427.

25. Daniel Cantor and Juliet Schor, *Tunnel Vision: Labor, the World Economy, and Central America*, Boston, South End Press, 1987, pp. 6–20.

26. Sims, pp. 50, 104–107.

27. *Working Together: Labor Report on the Americas* 20, September–October 1996.

28. *CJM Newsletter/Annual Report 1995* 6(1), San Antonio, Texas, spring 1996.

29. Martha Ojeda, Director of CJM, speech at the UAW New Directions 1996 Conference, Detroit, November 1996.

30. Communications Workers of America (CWA), *Changing Information Services: Strategies for Workers and Consumers*, Washington, CWA, 1994, pp. 29–32.

31. Steve Early and Larry Cohen, "CWA: Defending Workers' Rights in the New Global Economy," Burlington, MA, CWA District 1, mimeo; *The Morning NAFTA: Labour's Voice on Economic Integration* 5, May 1996, Canadian Labour Congress.

32. Discussions with a UE official, February 1997.

33. Terry Davis, "Cross Border Organizing Comes Home: UE & FAT in Mexico & Milwaukee," *Labor Research Review* 23, spring/summer 1995, pp. 23–29.

34. Moody and McGinn, pp. 49–50; Baldemar Velasquez, speech at the 1995 Labor Notes Conference, Detroit, April 1995.

35. "International Jurisdiction Agreement By and Between: The CAW Canada and its Local 2213, the Teamsters' Airline Division, the Transport and General Workers' Union, and the International Transport Workers' Federation (ITF)," CAW Local 2213, 1994.

36. Rath, pp. 249–255.

37. Rath, pp. 247–248, 253–254; Thorsten Schulten, "European Works Councils:

Prospects for a New System of European Industrial Relations," *European Journal of Industrial Relations* 2(3), November 1996, pp. 304–324.

38. Lowell Turner, "The Europeanization of Labour: Structure Before Action," *European Journal of Industrial Relations* 2(3), November 1996, pp. 325–332.

39. Rath, p. 248.

40. Turner, pp. 326–332.

41. Schulten, pp. 309–311; Trade Union Congress/Labour Research Department, *A Trade Unionists' Guide to European Works Councils*, London, TUC/LRD, 1995, pp. 6–11, 51–58.

42. ICEM, p. 57.

43. Transport & General Workers' Union, *T&G Record* October 1996.

44. *News Bulletin* 66(1–2/1996), IUF.

45. Schulten, p. 319.

11 Rank-and-File Internationalism: The TIE Experience

1. Interview with Jens Huhn, staff TIE-Bildungswerk, Frankfurt, Germany, July 1996.

2. *The Journal of Commerce*, January 22, 1997.

3. *International Viewpoint* 282, November 1996, pp. 20–21; e-mail from Chris Bailey, UK, January, 1997.

4. *The Journal of Commerce*, January 22, 1997.

5. *The Journal of Commerce*, January 22, 1997.

6. *Los Angeles Times*, January 21, 1997.

7. Daniel Ehrenberg, "From Intention to Action: An ILO–GATT/WTO Enforcement Regime for International Labor Rights," in Compa and Diamond, p. 164.

8. *International Union Rights* 4(1), 1997, p. 31.

9. Bob Hepple, "A Five-Tier Social Scale for Europe?," *International Union Rights* 1(3), first quarter 1993, p. 3.

10. Rath, p. 238.

11. R. Michael Gadbaw and Michael T. Medwig, "Multinational Enterprises and International Labor Standards," and Terry Collingsworth, "International Workers Rights Enforcement", in Compa and Diamond, pp. 141–162, 227–250.

12. Alston, p. 74.

13. Thalia Kidder and Mary McGinn, "In the Wake of NAFTA: Transnational Workers' Networks," *Social Policy* 25(4), summer 1995, pp. 14–21.

14. Interview with Jens Huhn, Frankfurt, Germany, July 1996.

15. Marsha Niemeijer, "Grassroots Labour Internationalism: The Transnationals Information Exchange," unpublished thesis, Amsterdam, 1996, pp. 10–12.

16. Huhn, 1996; Niemeijer, p. 13.

17. Huhn, 1996.

18. Interview with Jan Cartier, TIE-Amsterdam, July 1994.

19. Huhn, 1996.

20. Cartier, 1994.

21. Huhn, 1996; TIE, "International Staff Meeting," São Paulo, Brazil, June 1995, p. 5.

22. TIE, "International Staff Meeting," p. 3.

23. Niemeijer, p. 13.

24. Cartier, 1994.

25. Cartier, 1994.

26. Huhn, 1996.

27. Interview with SUD representatives, France Télécom, Paris, August 1996; Report on the Trinational Telecommunications Conference, TIE-North America, Oaxtepec,

Mexico, February 1994; Trinational Telecommunications Workers' Conference, TIE-North America, Tijuana, Mexico, October 1996.

28. Huhn, 1996.
29. TIE, "International Staff Meeting," p. 2.
30. Facts from Huhn, 1996, though the interpretation is my own.
31. TIE, "International Staff Meeting," p. 5.
32. This account of is based both on my experience with *Labor Notes* since its origins and on a review of its literature and discussions with other staffers.
33. Jane Slaughter, *Concessions and How to Beat Them*, Detroit, Labor Notes, 1983.

Conclusion: Toward an International Social-Movement Unionism

1. *Business Week*, December 16, 1996, pp. 61–65.
2. Edwards and Hyman, pp. 250–277; Bensaïd, pp. 109–116; interviews with CGT officials, Air France, September 1994; Moody, 1995, pp. 81–91.
3. For a detailed view of the upheaval of 1967–75 in various US industries see, Glenn Perusek and Kent Worcester, *Trade Union Politics: American Unions and Economic Change 1960s-1990s*, Atlantic Highlands, NJ, Humanities Press, 1995, *passim*.
4. Gallin, pp. 127–128.
5. *Labor Notes*: Number 214, January 1997.
6. Gindin, p. 268.
7. See, for example, Stephen Lerner, "Reviving Unions: A Call to Action," and responses in *Boston Review* 21(2), April/May 1996, 21(3/4) summer 1996, pp. 1–5.
8. Michael Eisenscher, "Critical Juncture: Unionism at the Crossroads," Center for Labor Research, University of Massachusetts-Boston, working paper, May 2, 1996, p. 3.
9. Seidman, p. 2.
10. Tim Schermerhorn, New Directions Caucus, Transport Workers' Union Local 100, Labor Notes Discussion, January 1997.
11. *Business Week*, February 17, 1997, p. 57.
12. *The Voice of New Directions* February 1997.
13. Presentation by the California Nurses Association local official at New Directions Solidarity School, California, February 8, 1997.
14. Paul A. Samuelson, *Economics*, 11th edn, New York, McGraw-Hill, 1980, pp. 540–541.
15. UAW New Directions Movement, "Forced Overtime: Killing the American Dream?" St Louis, MO, leaflet, 1993.
16. Interview with United Steelworkers' Local 1938 officials, at New Directions Solidarity School, Madison, Wisconsin, June 1996.
17. Brian Bercusson, *Working Time in Britain: Toward a European Model*, Part II: Collective Bargaining in Europe and the UK, London, Institute of Employment Rights, 1994, pp. 12–16; interviews with IG Metall Stewards, Mercedes-Benz, Mannheim, Germany, July 1996.
18. Interview with works council members, Opel, Eisenach, Germany, July 1996; with Comisiones Obreras General Secretary at SEAT assembly plant, Matorell, Spain, July 1996.
19. Anne E. Polivika, "A Profile of Contingent Workers," *Monthly Labor Review* 119(10), October 1996, p. 16.
20. Visser, in Regini, p. 17.
21. Rifkin, pp. 236–295; Will Hutton, *The State We're In*, London, Jonathan Cape, 1995.
22. Robert Pollin, "Financial Structures and Egalitarian Economic Policy," *New Left*

Review 214, November/December 1995, pp. 26–61; Richard Minns, "The Social Ownership of Capital," *New Left Review* 219, September/October 1996, pp. 42–61.

23. Mishel and Bernstein, p. 242; US Department of Commerce, 1995, p. 532.

24. *Left Business Observer* 76, February 18, 1997.

25. Julie Froud, Colin Haslam, Sukdev Johal, Jean Shaoul, and Karel Williams, "Stakeholder Economy? From Utility Privatization to New Labour," *Capital & Class* 60, winter 1996, pp. 119–134.

26. Anthony Brewer, *Marxist Theories of Imperialism: A Critical Survey*, London, Routledge, 1990, pp. 89–91.

27. *Left Business Observer* 76, February 18, 1997.

28. Rifkin, pp. 236–274.

29. World Bank, 1996, pp. 220–221.

30. Elyse Bryant, closing speech, 1993 Labor Notes Conference, Detroit, April, 1993.

Epilogue: A Socialist Direction?

1. *The Voice of New Directions* February 1997.

2. Hal Draper, "The Two Souls of Socialism," in E. Haberkern ed., *Socialism From Below*, Atlantic Highlands, NJ, Humanities Press, 1992, p. 2.

3. J. T. Murphy, *Preparing for Power: A Critical Study of the History of the British Working-Class Movement*, London, Pluto Press, 1972, p. 23.

4. For an interesting exposition of this see E. P. Thompson, *The Poverty of Theory and Other Essays*, NY, Monthly Review Press, 1978, pp. 1–192.

5. Robert Michels, *Party Politics: A Sociological Study of the Oligarchical Tendencies of Modern Democracy*, New York, Collier Books, 1962, pp. 342–356, *passim*; Draper, 1992, pp. 15–18; Steve Early, "Review of Staughton Lynd, *Living Inside Our Hope: Essays on Rebuilding a Radical Movement*," unpublished, May 1996.

6. Moody, 1988, pp. 51–55.

7. Paul Blyton and Peter Turnbull, "Confusing Convergence: Industrial Relations in the European Airline Industry – A Comment on Warhurst," *European Journal of Industrial Relations* 2(1), pp. 7–20.

8. George Rude, *The Crowd in the French Revolution*, London, Oxford University Press, 1959, *passim*.

9. Rosa Luxemburg, *The Mass Strike, the Political Party, and the Trade Unions*, London, Merlin Press, no date, originally 1906, pp. 21–41.

10. David Montgomery, *Workers' Control in America: Studies in the History of Work, Technology, and Labor Struggles*, New York, Cambridge University Press, 1979, pp. 48–83.

11. Kelley, 1990, *passim*; Robin D. G. Kelley, *Race Rebels: Culture, Politics, and the Black Working Class*, New York, The Free Press, 1994, pp. 103–121.

12. Quoted in Hal Draper, *Karl Marx's Theory of Revolution, Volume II: The Politics of Social Classes*, New York, Monthly Review Press, 1978, pp. 91–92.

13. Quoted in Peter Capelli and Timothy H. Harris, "Airline Union Concessions in the Wake of Deregulation," *Monthly Labor Review*, June 1985, p. 37.

14. Draper, 1978 p. 92.

15. Draper, 1978, pp. 94–99.

16. Sam Gindin, "Rising from the Ashes: Labor in the Age of Global Capitalism," *Monthly Review* 49(3), July–August, 1997

17. Gindin, 1997, pp. 139–156.

Index

Action Coalition of Strikers and
    Supporters 29
America Needs a Raise (Sweeney) 273
American Federation of Labor–Congress
    of Industrial Organizations 29;
    foreign policy 238–9; genuinely anti-
    left 230–1; moving US towards global
    solidarity 237–9; new leadership
    198–200; new strategies 177; tackling
    racism 156–8, 161
Argentina 72
Arrighi, Giovanni: *The Long Twentieth
    Century* 137
auto manufacture *see* production

Babson, Steve 106–7
Bangladesh: rising union membership
    202; women and urban jobs 203
Barnet, Richard: *Global Dreams* (with
    Cavanaugh) 74
Belgium 194–5
Beltran, Pete 160
Bernstein, Eduard 121
Black Workers for Justice 158–9, 161, 176,
    263
Blair, Tony 122
Blayton, Paul 107
Botwinick, Howard 45, 91
Brandt, Willy 121
Brandt Commission Report 253
Brazil 205, 223, 304; new unionism
    208–12; production chains 72; TIE
    activity 261
Brecher, Jeremy: *Global Village or Global
    Pillage* (with Costello) 4
Bridgestone/Firestone 24–7
Britain: changes in socialism 121–2; class
    anger 35–6; decline of manufacturing
    182–3; Engels on British unions
    303–4; industrial militancy of 1960s
    and 70s 181–2; Labour Party and

trade unions 22–3; lean practices 103;
    Liverpool dock privatization 9, 10;
    politics and class 299; post-war
    growth 56; poverty 189; Royal Mail
    actions 10, 194; Thatcher and the
    unions 123
Buchanan, Pat 30, 31
Business Week: defining richness 57

California Nurses' Association 279
Canada *see also* North American Free
    Trade Agreement: days of action 9,
    19–21, 305–6
Canadian Auto Workers 19–21;
    bargaining program 278; NAFTA
    alliances 239–40, 242; non-value
    added labor 88; outsourcing 93; strike
    unbundles lean production 108
Canadian Union of Public Employees
    19–21
capitalism *see also* neoliberalism;
    transnational corporations: basic
    motivations remain constant 12–13;
    capital mobility 79–83; changes in
    this century 295–7; class anger 35;
    downsizing and outsourcing 29–31,
    190; expanding webs of control 75–9;
    fragmentation of business structure
    150–4; industrial relations and classic
    capitalism 297–8; investment and
    infrastructure 57–9; Keynesianism to
    corporatism 117–19; Marx on
    production, society and globalization
    43–5; mergers and acquisitions 151,
    153–4, 184–5; rise of the transnational
    corporation 46–51; stakeholder 286–7,
    293, 307; state and multilateral
    institutions 135–40; uneven
    development 53–63, 73–4, 308; world
    power divisions 51–3
car manufacture *see* production